Data-Driven Intelligent Modeling and Optimization Algorithms for Industrial Processes: 2nd Edition

Data-Driven Intelligent Modeling and Optimization Algorithms for Industrial Processes: 2nd Edition

Guest Editors

Zixin Huang
Sheng Du
Li Jin
Xiongbo Wan

MDPI

Basel • Beijing • Wuhan • Barcelona • Belgrade • Novi Sad • Cluj • Manchester

Guest Editors
Zixin Huang
School of Electrical and Information Engineering
Wuhan Institute of Technology
Wuhan
China

Sheng Du
School of Automation
China University of Geosciences
Wuhan
China

Li Jin
School of Automation
China University of Geosciences
Wuhan
China

Xiongbo Wan
School of Automation
China University of Geosciences
Wuhan
China

Editorial Office
MDPI AG
Grosspeteranlage 5
4052 Basel, Switzerland

This is a reprint of the Special Issue, published open access by the journal *Algorithms* (ISSN 1999-4893), freely accessible at: https://www.mdpi.com/journal/algorithms/special_issues/1U8J01X7RS.

For citation purposes, cite each article independently as indicated on the article page online and as indicated below:

Lastname, A.A.; Lastname, B.B. Article Title. *Journal Name* **Year**, *Volume Number*, Page Range.

ISBN 978-3-7258-4911-6 (Hbk)
ISBN 978-3-7258-4912-3 (PDF)
https://doi.org/10.3390/books978-3-7258-4912-3

Contents

About the Editors

Zixin Huang

Zixin Huang received his B.S. and M.S. degrees in Engineering from Wuhan Textile University, Wuhan, China, in 2013 and 2016, respectively. He received his Ph.D. from the School of Automation, China University of Geosciences, Wuhan, China, in 2020, and received his postdoctoral fellowship from Nankai University, Tianjin, China, in 2023. He is currently a Postdoctoral Fellow with Shanghai Jiao Tong University, Shanghai, China. He is a senior visiting scholar at the University of Science and Technology of China, Anhui, China. He is currently an Associate Professor with the School of Electrical and Information Engineering, Wuhan Institute of Technology. His current research interests include nonlinear system control and intelligent control. Dr. Huang is a senior member of the Chinese Association of Automation.

Sheng Du

Zixin Huang received his B.S. and M.S. degrees in Engineering from Wuhan Textile University, Wuhan, China, in 2013 and 2016, respectively. He received his Ph.D. from the School of Automation, China University of Geosciences, Wuhan, China, in 2020, and received his postdoctoral fellowship from Nankai University, Tianjin, China, in 2023. He is currently a Postdoctoral Fellow with Shanghai Jiao Tong University, Shanghai, China. He is a senior visiting scholar at the University of Science and Technology of China, Anhui, China. He is currently an Associate Professor with the School of Electrical and Information Engineering, Wuhan Institute of Technology. His current research interests include nonlinear system control and intelligent control. Dr. Huang is a senior member of the Chinese Association of Automation.

Li Jin

Li Jin received her B.S. degree in Automation and her Ph.D. degree in Control Science and Engineering from China University of Geosciences, Wuhan, China, in 2016 and 2021, respectively. She was a joint Ph.D. student with the Department of Electrical Engineering and Electronics, University of Liverpool, Liverpool, U.K., from 2018 to 2020. She was a Postdoctoral Fellow in Control Science and Engineering, China University of Geosciences, Wuhan, China, from 2022 to 2024. She is currently a Professor in the School of Automation, China University of Geosciences, Wuhan, China. Her current research interests include power system stability analysis and control, time-delay system, and robust theory and application.

Xiongbo Wan

Xiongbo Wan received his B.S. degree in Information and Computing Science from Huazhong Agricultural University, Wuhan, China, in 2006, and his M.S. degree in Probability Theory and Mathematical Statistics and his Ph.D. degree in Control Theory and Engineering from the Huazhong University of Science and Technology, Wuhan, in 2008 and 2011, respectively. From 2012 to 2013, he was a Visiting Scholar with Akita Prefectural University, Akita, Japan. From 2011 to 2014, he was a Lecturer and then an Associate Professor with the College of Engineering, Huazhong Agricultural University. From 2016 to 2017, he was a Visiting Scholar with the Department of Computer Science, Brunel University London, Uxbridge, U.K. Since 2015, he has been with the China University of Geosciences, Wuhan, where he is currently a Professor with the School of Automation. His research interests include fault diagnosis, state estimation, and model predictive control of complex industrial systems.

algorithms

MDPI

Article

Data Assimilated Atmospheric Forecasts for Digital Twin of the Ocean Applications: A Case Study in the South Aegean, Greece

Antonios Parasyris *, Vassiliki Metheniti, George Alexandrakis, Georgios V. Kozyrakis and Nikolaos A. Kampanis

Coastal & Marine Research Laboratory (CMRL), Institute of Applied and Computational Mathematics (IACM), Foundation for Research and Technology-Hellas (FORTH), GR-71110 Heraklion, Greece; vasmeth@iacm.forth.gr (V.M.); alexandrakis@iacm.forth.gr (G.A.); gkoz@iacm.forth.gr (G.V.K.); kampanis@iacm.forth.gr (N.A.K.)

* Correspondence: antonisparasyris@iacm.forth.gr

Abstract: This study investigated advancements in atmospheric forecasting by integrating real-time observational data into the Weather Research and Forecasting (WRF) model through the WRF-Data Assimilation (WRF-DA) framework. By refining atmospheric models, we aimed to improve regional high-resolution wave and hydrodynamic forecasts essential for environmental management. Focused on southern Greece, including Crete, the study applied a 3D-Var assimilation technique within WRF, downscaling forecasting data from the Global Forecast System (GFS) to resolutions of 9 km and 3 km. The results showed a 4.7% improvement in wind speed predictions, with significant gains during forecast hours 26–72, enhancing model accuracy across METAR validation locations. These results underscore the positive impact of the integration of additional observational data on model accuracy. This study also highlights the utility of refined atmospheric models for real-world applications through their use in forcing ocean circulation and wave models and subsequent Digital Twin of the Ocean applications. Two such applications—optimal ship routing to minimize CO_2 emissions and oil spill trajectory forecasting to mitigate marine pollution—demonstrate the practical utility of improved models through what-if scenarios in easily deployable, containerized formats.

Keywords: data assimilation; digital twin; dynamic downscaling; oil spill forecasting; optimal ship routing; WRF-DA; NEMO; Wavewatch III

1. Introduction

The South Aegean is an economically and environmentally significant region [1] with complex topography and physical characteristics [2]. Accurate weather and ocean-wave forecasts are essential to support a range of Digital Twin of the Ocean (DTO) applications [3], i.e., interoperable models that aim in the digital representation of the ocean physical environment, such as harbor/ship-routing safety assessment, marine pollution management, and more [4]. To enhance forecast accuracy, data assimilation (DA) techniques are employed by integrating in situ observations into numerical models [5].

In the South Aegean, the availability of atmospheric (near) real-time in situ datasets significantly surpasses that of oceanic data. This limited availability of oceanographic data, combined with the large dimensionality and non-linearity of ocean-wave models, introduces data uncertainties that can limit the efficiency of DA [6]. Ocean circulation and wave models are particularly sensitive to wind field selection [7–9], as wind fields play a critical role in determining the momentum and heat fluxes that drive these systems. Correcting atmospheric input can potentially improve predictions of ocean circulation and wave models [10,11]. These factors highlight the importance of DA-enhanced atmospheric forecasts.

Numerous DA techniques exist to improve atmospheric numerical models. Among the most widely used are three-dimensional variational DA (3D-Var) [12], four-dimensional variational DA (4D-Var) [13,14] and sequential methods such as the Kalman filter and hybrid methodologies combining them with variational methods [15], ensemble Kalman filter [16], and ensemble optimal interpolation [17]. Variational methods process all observations holistically, providing a more consistent and coherent estimate of the model state [14]. Sequential methods, on the other hand, process observations as they are collected, making them more adaptable to real-time data [18]. Although sequential methods can be preferred in real-time operational forecasting due to their ability to handle fluctuating data availability, they are prone to transmitting observational noise, which can reduce the precision of the estimated state [19].

For this study, the 3D-Var method was selected as it is computationally less expensive—an important factor given the operational daily cycle [12]. It is also less demanding in terms of data requirements, making it suitable for the sparse real-time in situ datasets available in this region, and it performs well for both short-term and longer forecasting horizons [20].

The main aim of this study was to cost-effectively correct the atmospheric forecasting model in the South Aegean for use as input in DTO applications where DA cannot be performed. The paper is organized as follows: Section 2 presents the methodology of the DA applied to the atmospheric model and details the DTO model specifics. The 3D-Var results along with the DTO model results using the corrected atmospheric forecast in comparison to the original one are presented in Section 3. Discussion of the results, along with demonstration of further DTO applications, are showcased in Section 4.

2. Materials and Methods

2.1. Case Study and Data Availability

The area of interest is geographically focused around the island of Crete, in the south of Greece, an area of high economic interest and human activity as the Heraklion port is the third highest passenger traffic port in Greece, with strategic positioning as it interconnects three continents (Europe, Asia, and Africa) [1]. Thus, perspective users of the marine tools created for better marine planning, accident avoidance, decrease in CO_2 emitted by ships, etc., can include but are not limited to the Hellenic Coast Guard, port authorities, coastal municipalities, ship owners and companies, citizens, etc. The users of those tools require a Digital Twin of the Ocean solution that offers validated, high-resolution information and services; accurate short-term forecasts; decision support; early warnings; and alerts. To that end, we describe improvements to the models that are being made in our case study, as well as their integration with such DTO tools for thematic applications.

The initial forcing for the operational Weather Research and Forecasting (WRF) is derived in real time from the Global Forecast System (GFS) forecasting model by the National Oceanic and Atmospheric Administration (NOAA) and National Center for Atmospheric Research (NCAR) (2015) that provides forecasts with a spatial resolution of approximately 27 km × 27 km and a temporal resolution of 6 h, being extremely coarse for observing fine-scale wind phenomena [21]. As seen in Figure 1, the domain of interest is dynamically downscaled two times, firstly to a 9 km × 9 km grid named D01, and then to a 3 km × 3 km finer grid centered around Crete (D02).

Firstly, we introduce the available data sources for the area of interest, for both initializing the models with relevant forcing data and observational data that are used for DA and validation of the models. The area of interest is the South Aegean Sea; the Cretan Sea; part of the border region of the Ionian Sea; and the Levantine Sea surrounding the island of Crete, Greece. The two nested subdomains of the WRF program are shown in Figure 1. The available data are as follows:

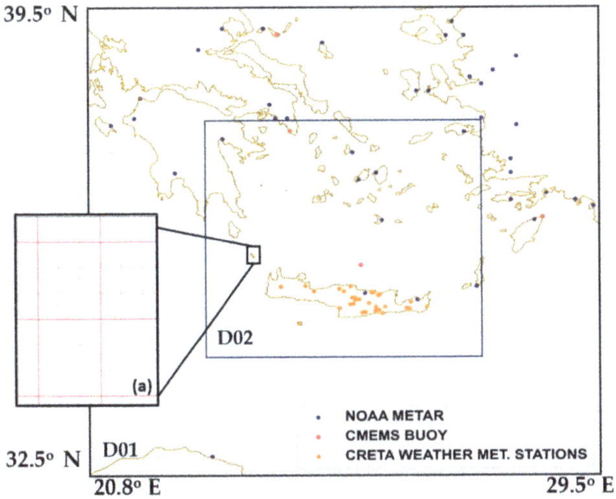

Figure 1. The two downscaled domains of interest for the WRF application in southern Greece. Ground METAR stations are indicated by blue dots. Red dots are buoy locations, and orange signifies additional CretaWeather Meteorological stations used for DA. Coordinates of the bounding box are shown around the domain, with indications on inner and outer domain D01–D02, as well as (**a**) a zoomed map of Antikythera Island with the 3 km grid (grey) and 9 km grid (red) overlay.

Data Source I: Cretaweather.gr offers in situ data information in high temporal resolution (5 min) in available stations. Additional station locations from CretaWeather are marked in Figure 1 as orange dots.
Data Source II: NOAA METAR ISH ground data: NOAA National Centers for Environmental Information (2001): Global Surface Hourly (https://www.ncei.noaa.gov/access/search/index, last accessed online 28 October 2024). These data were accessed through the RNOAA library, which downloads and updates real-time data from the NOAA ISD-ISH database. This dataset is curated by NOAA, so each observation is accompanied with control flags that indicate its quality, and the stations' uptime is monitored to reduce missing value cases.
Data Source III: CMEMS Marine Data store to download the in situ data near real time from the "copernicusmarinetoolbox" API (https://help.marine.copernicus.eu/en/articles/7949409-copernicus-marine-toolbox-introduction, last accessed online 28 October 2024), product: Mediterranean Sea—near real-time (NRT) in situ quality-controlled observations, hourly updated and distributed by INSTAC within 24–48 h from acquisition on average (https://data.marine.copernicus.eu/product/INSITU_MED_PHYBGCWAV_DISCRETE_MYNRT_013_035/description, last accessed online 28 October 2024).
Data Source IV: For the initialization of WRF with external atmospheric forcing, the NCEP operational GFS analysis and forecasts were used as the initial meteorological fields for the simulation. The data are 0.25-degree spatial resolution that correspond to approximately 27 km. More information about the dataset can be found in [22]. The WRF model is initially run without the application of DA and is henceforth referred to as the Control run, with downscaling of the computational grid at D01 (9 km grid) and at D02 (3 km grid) in the domains outlined in Figure 1.

As seen, the data available in the coarser domain D01 that measure oceanic variables (Data Source III, Section 2.1) are limited to 4 locations, which drop down to 2 for the finer resolution subdomain D02, and that can be used for validation. This makes the creation, calibration, and validation of such a system extremely difficult. To overcome this, additional data that have never been used before to the authors' knowledge have been added in the form of atmospheric data (Data Source I, Section 2.1), and the observational network uses meteorological stations similar to [23].

2.2. 3D/4D-Var Techniques

The goal of any variational DA technique is to find the optimal state x, henceforth called "analysis", that minimizes a cost function [24]. For the case of the 3D-Var method, the main differentiation being that it is a time-independent method that is less computationally demanding and requires less data but may suffer from accurately capturing fast evolving weather systems. However, it can provide accurate results for more slowly time-paced variables and is still useful for many practical applications due to the low computational cost. The method can be summarized in minimizing functional J with respect to the Analysis state x in the following cost function [12]:

$$J(x) = \frac{1}{2}\Big[(x - x^b)^T B^{-1}(x - x^b) + (y - H(x))^T R^{-1}(y - H(x))\Big], \tag{1}$$

where superscripts T, -1 are the standard notation for transpose and inverse operators; x^b is the background state or field (previous forecast or initialization); and y is the observation vector. $H(x)$ is the observation operator that maps the model variable to the observation space, introducing additional representation errors. Additionally, this method requires the estimation of the background and observation error covariance matrices (B, R), respectively. The computation of the observation and most importantly the background error covariance matrices is a heavily discussed and researched topic (see, e.g., [13,20,24,25]). The approach for estimating matrix B for the case study considered here is discussed in the next sections.

The extension of 3D-Var is named 4D-Var, which similarly to 3D-Var solves an optimization problem, with the main difference being that it considers data over specific time bins, which allows it to account for the temporal evolution of the atmosphere, in contrast to the 3D-Var that is not time dependent, and it considers a single analysis time by assimilating observations from that specific time into the model. This difference makes the 4D-Var more computationally intensive due to the use of the fully nonlinear model and consideration of the entire assimilation window. Hence, it makes it more suitable for research and high-performance computing environments, whereas the 3D-Var can be easier implemented for operational purposes [12,26], and it can be used to correct the initial and boundary conditions of the outer domain in an operational setting. In equation form, 4D-Var considers the splitting of the time dimension in discretized n time-bins, and the observations $\boldsymbol{y}_i$ that belong to each time bin are used. So, Equation (1) is transformed into

$$J(x) = \frac{1}{2}\left[(x - x^b)^T B^{-1}(x - x^b) + \sum_i^n (y_i - H_i(x_i))^T R^{-1}(y_i - H_i(x_i))\right], \tag{2}$$

where the observational last term on the right hand side is a sum over all time bins [14].

Variational methods offer an advantage over sequential techniques by achieving a state x that effectively assimilates all available observations simultaneously through the minimization of J. However, the use of variational data assimilation comes with certain drawbacks, most notably its reliance on several assumptions, with a main one being that the error statistics do not propagate in time [26]. This leads to a very strong reliance of the assimilation results on the background error calculation, which is often hard to accurately quantify. The precision of prescribed errors becomes pivotal for the accuracy of the resulting analysis, given that imperfect observations and prior information are integral inputs in the assimilation process [25]. The last limitation is shared with sequential DA techniques.

Additionally, while the variational approach allows for the incorporation of linearized dynamical and physical processes, it is crucial to acknowledge that real errors within the Numerical Weather Prediction (NWP) system can exhibit highly nonlinear behavior. This poses a challenge for variational data assimilation, especially in scenarios characterized by strong nonlinearity, such as convective scale or tropical weather systems. Recognizing this limitation has led to the development of hybrid methodologies with varying resolutions to address challenges in specific weather scenarios. For instance, Liu, Ban, Hong, and Kuo [13] introduced a multi-resolution incremental 4D-Var technique for operational purposes. This approach reduces computational requirements since the data assimilation system and the WRF model forecast are not required to have a common resolution. Last but not least, a primary drawback of variational techniques lies in their significant computational cost. This is particularly evident in the computation of the inverse of matrix B, a matrix with dimensions $(n \cdot m) \times (n \cdot m)$, where n and m represent the number of grid points in the X and Y dimensions of the model, respectively. In high-resolution regional models, this computational burden can quickly become impractical. The time required for this process must be carefully managed, especially in operational settings where the improved forecast must be generated within a timeframe typically not exceeding a day, aligning with the re-run schedule of our operational setup. For the above reasons, the method applied in this case study is the 3D-Var.

2.3. Configuration Set-Up

The weather forecasts were conducted using WRF (WRF-4.4), with data assimilation executed by the WRF Data Assimilation model (WRF-DA-4.4). WRF is capable of delivering atmospheric simulations appropriate for a wide array of applications, while WRF-DA generates the analysis—integrating ground-based observations to produce perturbed initial and boundary conditions for WRF. Both models were configured to offer a coupled system of high spatial resolution analysis and forecasts covering southern Greece. The WRF model was initialized at 00 UTC and ran daily with a ramp-up period of 24 h, forecasting the next 72 h. This will henceforth be referred to as the forecasting horizon. More details on similar WRF runs and the parametrizations made for the specific test case are presented in [21], but with different forcing data, so an additional validation is performed here to establish the baseline control case run. The nesting configuration is illustrated schematically in Figure 1.

Concerning the WRF-DA preprocessing, the system requires the observations to be translated into littleR format, which is a specific ASCII-based file format (https://www2.mmm.ucar.edu/wrf/users/wrfda/OnlineTutorial/Help/littler.html, last accessed online 28 October 2024). Then, the littleR files are processed through the WRF preprocessor, and the observational errors are calculated depending on the category of the sensor that is reported in the littleR file (SYNOP, BUOY, etc.), as well as the prescribed height of measurement, elevation, and pressure. It is assumed that the errors of the field measurements are statistically independent of each other, so the observational covariance matrix R is diagonal, and its values represent each sensor's instrumental error [12], suggested by the WRF-DA suite. Quality control of the observations was carried out so that outliers, duplicates, and observations that are not in the analyzed space–time window were removed. A crucial part of the accuracy of any variational DA technique is the approximation of the covariance matrix B, as shown in Equations (1) and (2). There are two methods implemented within WRF-DA to approximate the matrix B: the Ensemble method (ENS) and the climatological approach known as the National Meteorological Center method (NMC), introduced by Parrish and Derber [27]. The Ensemble method uses ensemble perturbations from a given set of forecasts. However, for regional studies, the NMC method is more commonly used. Since our model has been run operationally on a daily basis, forecasting four days in each run, the overlapping forecasted days from different simulations can be utilized to approximate the model error, denoted by ε_b. This procedure assumes that background errors can be effectively represented by statistical data derived from averaged forecast differences, typically from a series of month-long forecasts with 36 h and 12 h validity at the same time. This concept is expressed in the following equation form:

$$\boldsymbol{B} = \overline{(\boldsymbol{x}^b - \boldsymbol{x}^t)(\boldsymbol{x}^b - \boldsymbol{x}^t)^{\boldsymbol{T}}} = \overline{\varepsilon_b \varepsilon_b{}^{\boldsymbol{T}}} \cong \overline{(\boldsymbol{x}^{i+36} - \boldsymbol{x}^{i+12})(\boldsymbol{x}^{i+36} - \boldsymbol{x}^{i+12})^{\boldsymbol{T}}}, \quad (3)$$

where $\boldsymbol{x}^t$ is the unknown true atmospheric state, and the use of an overbar signifies the average over all samples that are collected beforehand for the estimation of the background error. The subtracted states x^{i+36},x^{i+12} are all the forecasted outputs that co-occur and originate from a specific WRF simulation that has been run 1 day apart [28]. This is carried out by the following utility: https://github.com/wrf-model/GENBE_2.0 (last accessed online 28 October 2024). To approximate this matrix, simulations are performed for 2-month periods during winter and summer conditions separately, and they are used to assimilate data in each period accordingly, as it has been shown to affect the accuracy of the DA [20]. One major drawback of this technique is that the background error covariances are estimated offline and have similar characteristics to climatological statistics, which do not evolve with time and hence are not flow-dependent. While the NMC method described is computationally efficient [20], it can occasionally lead to a minimal influence of the 3D-Var on the background field, or potentially exacerbate the results relative to actual observations. To address this issue, the objective is to employ distinct background covariances contingent upon the season, as previously described. Additionally, if the accuracy does not meet satisfactory thresholds, using a similar analysis that we present in Section 3, adjustments can be made to the temporal window that is considered for the creation of covariance matrix B.

2.4. Algorithmic Process of WRF-DA 3D-Var

After calculating the covariance matrix B (be.dat in WRF terms) and first guess (fg for WRF notation) files, one has to update the namelist of WRF to compute the corrected initial state. The complete algorithmic flow chart is shown in Figure 2, where the order of operations one must follow to achieve a corrected WRF forecast is outlined for the 3D-Var technique specifically. To summarize the process of WRF-DA, one begins by creating initial conditions for WRF (wrfinput) through the WRF Preprocessing System (WPS). This step uses the GFS meteorological fields described in Data Sources IV (Section 2.1). The next step involves applying WRF-DA to the generated wrfinput file, assimilating observational data to produce a refined wrfvar_output file, which serves the purpose of an updated data-assimilated wrfinput. Subsequently, to ensure consistency with the new initial conditions, the boundary conditions need to be updated for the entire forecast period.

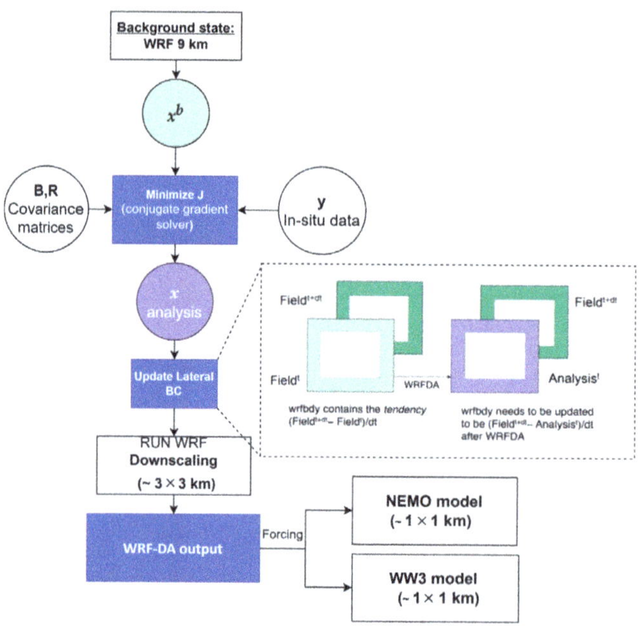

Figure 2. WRF-DA flow chart adapted by [21] with boundary condition (BC) update for all time-steps based on the new analysis computed by WRF-DA. This update was performed on the outer parent

domain D01 with the 9 km resolution. The WRF output was then used to force hydrodynamic and wave forecasting models. B and R are the background and observational error covariance matrices, and x_b, x, and y are the background field, analysis field, and observation vector, respectively, as seen in Equation (1).

Noted by dotted lines in Figure 2, there is an explanation of how boundary conditions are updated using the analysis x at time step t instead of the initial background field x^b as seen in Equation (1), and then how the background field at time step (t + dt) is updated in subsequent time steps using a perturbed time derivative (Field(t + dt) − Analysis(t))/dt. Since the denominator includes dt (the time increment), as the time interval between the analysis time t and each subsequent step increases, the effect of the data assimilation (DA) analysis at step t on the boundary condition diminishes. This is expected, as the influence of observations at the initialization time on the model should naturally decrease over time. In the whole flow chart, the respective steps are color-coded with their explanation for the readers' convenience.

Finally, the process concludes with the execution of WRF to generate a new downscaled forecast in all nested subdomains (D01 and D02 in Figure 1). We note that the process mentioned applies only to the parent WRF domain D01, since the initial and boundary conditions for the child domain D02 are inherited by interpolating the values from the parent domain D01 [29]. Then, this updated forecast can be used as alternative forcing for a range of applications, which in our case are based on wave and hydrodynamic forecasting.

To address the elevated computational demands typically associated with variational methods, the solver chosen for minimizing the functional in Equation (1) is the iterative conjugate gradient. In comparison to alternative optimization methods available within the Weather Research and Forecasting (WRF) framework, such as the quasi-Newton approach, the conjugate gradient method is deemed less computationally demanding. Additionally, preconditioning through WRF-DA options are employed as described in the introduction article of WRF 3D-Var to mitigate the computational complexities associated with inverting the correlation matrix B [12]. The strategic utilization of the conjugate gradient solver and preconditioning techniques contributes to the enhanced computational tractability of the overall variational methodology [30].

2.5. Performance Metrics

The error metrics that are used to validate the atmospheric models using observational data from the closest meteorological stations to the computational grid, employing the nearest neighbor algorithm, are presented. Additionally, the same metrics are used for the comparative analysis of the DA model and its control case counterpart, which is the downscaled model without any data used to correct it.

A strong statistical framework was created to back up the analysis mentioned above. The following error metrics have been summarized in [31] and are the most regularly utilized in a variety of various disciplines (for example, weather prediction and hydrology) where models are validated using observational data.

(a) **The bias and absolute bias metric**

$$BIAS = \frac{1}{N}\sum_{i=1}^{N}(M_i - O_i) = \overline{M} - \overline{O}, \quad (4)$$

where N denotes the number of records, M the model prediction, and O the observation records. This statistical parameter provides information in a standard way about systematic errors, i.e., the tendency of the model to overestimate or underestimate the predicted values. BIAS serves as a measure of differences between observations and model predictions, with ideal values closer to zero. Note that bias can be positive or negative, indicating overprediction or underprediction. Sometimes it is of more use to calculate the absolute value of the difference of measured and observed values, which will henceforth be referred to as absolute bias.

(b) **Root mean squared error (RMSE)**

$$RMSE = \sqrt{\frac{\sum_{i=1}^{N}(M_i - O_i)^2}{N}}, \quad (5)$$

RMSE (root mean squared error) is utilized as a measure of the variability of the error and offers an indication of the efficacy of the model to predict the general behavior of the system. The ideal value is 0, and the lower the better applies [32].

(c) **The correlation coefficient:**

$$r = \frac{\sum_{i=1}^{N}((x_i - \overline{x})(y_i - \overline{y}))}{\left(\sum_{i=1}^{N}(x_i - \overline{x})^2 \sum_{i=1}^{N}(y_i - \overline{y})^2\right)^{1/2}}, \quad (6)$$

which measures the linear correlation between forecasts (y_i) and observations (x_i) and takes values lower or equal to 1, with the higher values being the better ones [31,32].

2.6. Digital Twin of the Ocean Components

Regional high-resolution ocean circulation and wave forecasting models require accurate atmospheric forcing inputs [33]. WRF-DA outputs are used as inputs in a regional configuration based on the Nucleus for European Modeling of the Ocean (NEMO v3.6) framework, which solves the primitive equations [34]. The configuration's domain covers the surrounding area of the Cretan Island (Cretan Sea and part of the Levantine Sea; 22.993–26.925° E and 34.4218–36.0915° N), with a horizontal grid resolution of ~1 km and 72 vertical levels, with a decreasing resolution from the surface to the bottom from 1 m to 191 m (deepest point 4695.7 m). For the open boundary conditions surrounding the domain, forecast data from the CMEMS platform were used (https://data.marine.copernicus.eu/product/MEDSEA_ANALYSISFORECAST_PHY_006_013/description last accessed online 28 October 2024).

WRF-DA outputs were also used as inputs in a regional configuration based on the Wavewatch III (WWIII) wave model [35], surrounding the area of 22.705–27.457° E, 33.95–36.81° N.

3. Results

We here introduce and comment on the results, firstly validating the dynamical downscaling control case study that featured the implementation of the WRF. Results of the application of 3D-Var to the case study are discussed, for a test case consisting of a time period of 92 days with a forecast horizon of 3 days each. The respective dates cover a summer case from 15 July 2024 to 15 October 2024 in order to show the improvement and highlight the challenges associated with this task. For consistency purposes, this time window is also used to compare the impact that the atmospheric DA has on wave and hydrodynamic modelling when used as alternative forcing.

This study presents the implementation of the 3D-Var technique within a WRF-DA model framework, focusing on a case study encompassing the region around the island of Crete. The model is configured to correct daily runs of 3-day forecasts over a 3-month period. A notable challenge highlighted in Section 2 is the substantial computational burden associated with this approach, necessitating intricate parameter optimization. Specifically, the computational demands are exemplified by a customized WRF run, where the initial 27 km input forcing undergoes dynamical downscaling to spatial resolutions of 9 km and 3 km through consecutive one-way nesting procedures. This process, executed on an Intel Xeon cluster with 64 cores, requires approximately 5 h to complete. Subsequently, real-time data acquisition, transformation into "littleR" format files, and functional minimization entail an additional half-hour on the same cluster. The subsequent assimilated run demands another 5 h of computational time, employing MPI parallelization between the CPU cores.

To achieve reliable results, a significant number of daily runs, specifically 92, was considered in this study in order to mitigate statistical errors. Furthermore, there are many tunable parameters in this methodology that are case specific, for example, VAR_SCALING, a multiplier to the background error parameter since it is seen to be often underestimated, was proposed in the work of [20] as equal to 3, but in our case, this showed a deterioration of the results, indicating that the background error was not overestimated in our case. Fine-tuning these parameters was performed solely through trial and error, requiring significant computational resources and time. While only small differences were observed, the best configuration was selected for operational use in our tests. It is important to note that model calibration is an ongoing process, and most forecast data providers continuously perform and update their calibrations to enhance their services. Additionally, the reliable selection of observation points that provided a continuous stream of observations without missing values was of the essence, and the only way to overcome this burden is with continuous testing and validation through observational data.

This validation poses additional challenges, notably the discretization error arising from the fact that observation points and model nodes do not typically coincide. The proximity of meteorological stations to model grid points influences the validation process, with errors persisting unless a more refined model is introduced, which introduces additional points in the finer grid and reduces the distance from the model's grid point to the observational one. This approach increases the computational cost and time, which can become a computational burden when considering operational forecasting systems that run on a continuous schedule.

To ensure that the model approximates the real atmospheric conditions and is able to forecast without the resolution handicapping the forecasting skill, we performed a comparative analysis between the 27 km spatial resolution forcing used to initialize the WRF model and the 3 km dynamically downscaled model, which is then mentioned as the control case in our subsequent step of data integration within the WRF-DA model.

3.1. Downscaled Model Validation

The metrics, which are shown in Table 1, were the BIAS, RMSE, and correlation coefficient, and concluded with a definitive improvement on average of all the stations. The validation ran operationally for the first 6 months of the year 2023, considering daily forecast runs with a 1 day ramping-up period and 3-day forecasting horizon, and we averaged the results in hindcast mode by collecting observations from the nine METAR stations that fell within the bounding box area of the finer and smaller domain of 3 km (D02), as seen in Figure 1, but eventually removing three stations that did not offer a continuous data stream in the same 3 h resolution that the other six had. Although anomalies, such as those observed at the SAMOS station, may arise, they did not negate the overall enhancement that the dynamically downscaled 3 km model shows, as evidenced by metric averaging across all stations. Thus, in the last line, we averaged the error metrics of all available stations, finding all three of the considered metrics to favor the downscaled model.

Table 1. Comparison of error values for the GFS model, which was run with a 27 km spatial resolution and WRF 3 km downscaled model on wind speed data utilizing the BIAS, RMSE, and correlation coefficient metrics for the first six months of 2023 (the better result is denoted with a bold font).

	BIAS		RMSE		Correlation Coefficient	
Station Name	GFS (27 km)	WRF (3 km)	GFS (27 km)	WRF (3 km)	GFS (27 km)	WRF (3 km)
SAMOS	**−1.276**	−1.751	4.415	**3.451**	**0.242**	0.008
SYROS	−1.060	**−0.299**	4.804	**3.844**	0.048	**0.332**
EL VENIZELOS	−2.578	**−1.515**	5.250	**3.915**	0.029	**0.400**
NIKOS KAZANTZAKIS	−2.922	**−0.490**	5.676	**4.063**	0.127	**0.210**
KARPATHOS (AIRPORT)	−0.368	**0.202**	4.132	**4.000**	**0.271**	0.259
PAROS	−3.258	**−0.968**	5.706	**3.510**	0.268	**0.371**

More specifically, the validation of the downscaled atmospheric model, as shown in Table 1, demonstrated a notable improvement of approximately 24% in RMSE, averaged across all stations. The bias improvement cannot be expressed as a percentage, given that bias encompasses both positive and negative values, indicating when the model overpredicts (positive bias) or underpredicts (negative bias). Correlation coefficients were computed at each individual validation station, showing larger values indicating better performance in all but two stations.

This underscores the significance of higher-resolution models in enhancing atmospheric forecasting accuracy in practical applications. However, it is important to note that the efficacy of such models is contingent upon various factors, including downscaling ratio [13], terrain, and orographic resolution [36], which may vary across different test cases.

Following the successful validation of the 3 km WRF hereby mentioned as the Control case study, we proceeded by introducing the operational parametrizations for the 3D-Var case, subsequently comparing the extent of improvement observed, using the Control case as a reference. To be able to express the improvement of the models percentagewise, the remaining comparative results between the control and 3D-Var cases are presented in terms of absolute bias.

3.2. 3D-Var Results

The presentation of DA results underscores the persistent challenge in refining wind speed forecasts, despite advancements in assimilation techniques. Wind speed stands out as a critical variable for subsequent wave and hydrodynamic models. A test case was examined, incorporating all available data sources (I, II, and III, Section 2.1) whenever they were available, augmenting the NOAA METAR and POSEIDON Buoys dataset with approximately 30 meteorological stations situated across the island of Crete. The inclusion of additional observation locations was anticipated to significantly enhance accuracy, demonstrating a path towards improved forecasting precision. Notably, not all stations seen in Figure 1 always have availability of data to be assimilated, and hence we only included in each run the stations that had data availability closer to the analysis time, which is the time of the simulation when the functional J from Equation (1) is minimized (here we used the 00:00 of the hindcast day).

In Figure 3, the plot shows the absolute bias for wind speed for both the case of the control simulation (WRF without any DA) and the corrected one with the 3D-Var, under the dynamically downscaled 3 km spatial resolution. The predicted values at each case were compared to the corresponding observations by the six METAR stations of Dataset II, and these biases were plotted with representative values across 3 months of daily simulations for each forecast hour in 3-hourly temporal resolution that most METAR data showcased, with their mean values shown in stars. Additionally, their 90th percentiles over the 92 simulations are shown with the shaded same color areas. Those simulations fall within mostly summer period in Greece, performed during the months of mid-July to mid-October 2024, and hence the covariance matrix that was calculated for the summer period was used.

As the lower value translates to improved model in absolute bias terms, we observed that between forecast hours 26 and 72, the mean values as well as the percentiles for the 3D-Var case were consistently lower than the control case. Evidently, calculating the average percentagewise improvement from the control simulations to the 3D-Var case, for all simulations in the wind speed variable compared to the observational data, we found a 5.6% improvement, whereas the overall improvement for all forecast hours was calculated at 4.7%.

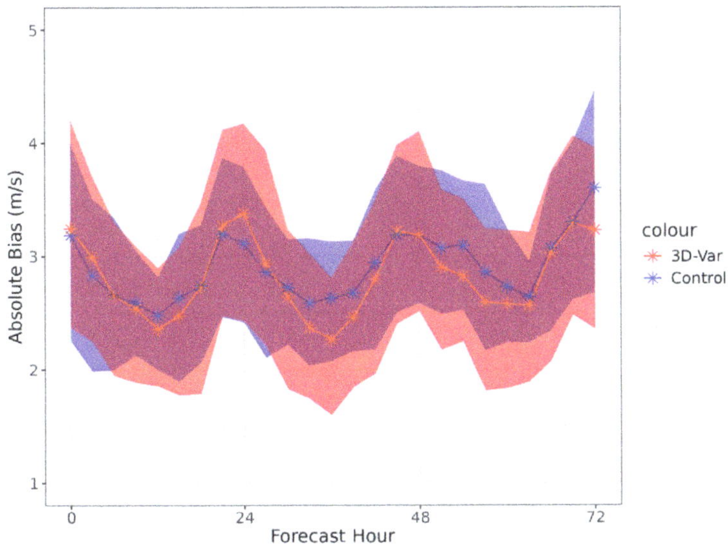

Figure 3. Absolute bias statistics for 3 months from 15/7/2024 to 15/10/2024, comparing Control and 3D-Var for each forecast hour 1–72. Blue and red shading indicate the 90th percentile across all simulations, and stars are the mean value of the errors for 10 m wind speed, compared to the observed value at each station.

This finding is consistent with [20], which features a 3D-Var study with dynamical downscaling in the southern region of China, which also demonstrated bigger contributions of the 3D-Var around the middle of the forecast horizon period. In comparison with their study, our case study showcased comparable improvement percentages, although in our case, we had considerably less observational data coverage. Specifically, in our wider D01 region shown in Figure 1, there were approximately 30 METAR stations provided by the NOAA ISD/ISH dataset, which were mostly consistently available throughout the simulation period, the nearly 40 stations of Data Source IV as well as 4 buoys from Data Source III (Section 2.1), compared to the study of [20] that featured more than 300 METAR stations and resulted in an average improvement in 10 m wind speeds of about 4% throughout their entire forecast horizon.

Additionally, in Figure 4, a bar chart is presented depicting absolute biases for each station utilized in the validation process from the METAR data that were used for validation putposes. Note that some METAR stations that were used for DA were not used for validation, since the specific 3D-Var technique implemented requires data availability only during the analysis time, whereas for validation, we used the entire forecasting horizon. Furthermore, some stations had available data with a coarser 6 h temporal resolution instead of the 3 hourly that we calculated for the errors of Figure 3. Hence, for consistency, the six stations shown in Table 1 and Figure 4 are retained as validation stations.

This analysis reveals that all stations except SAMOS exhibited an improvement in wind speed over the 3 month period selected for validation. It is noteworthy that the errors shown in Figure 4 could include systematic errors in the model originating from the geometrical discretization but could also be due to the spatial validation mechanism that was chosen to be the nearest neighbor from the observation location to the grid points. Since the resolution of the finer model under examination was 3 km, this discrepancy could result in a significant difference of the model value with the METAR measurement. Nevertheless, METAR comparisons are a widely used validation method for such applications [21] and should be taken as an indicative measure averaged across all available stations, as shown in Figure 3, for multiple daily simulations, which introduces a degree of difficulty in the calibration of proposed models, as the computational cost for each simulation is high, as previously discussed.

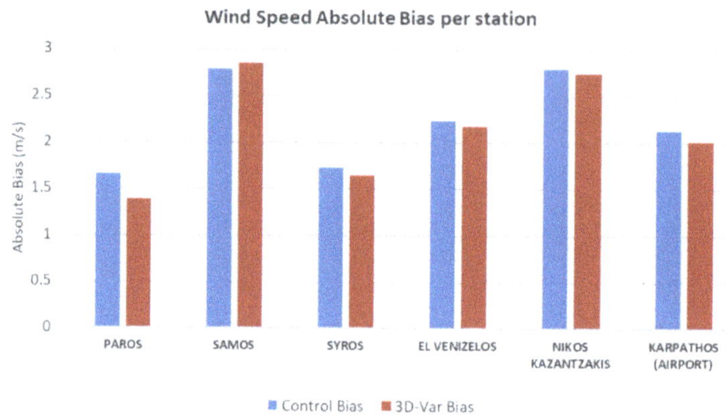

Figure 4. Absolute bias error metric compared to observations per validation meteorological station in D02 averaged for all forecast hours for wind speed magnitude. Blue and orange indicate control and 3D-Var case, respectively.

Figure 5 is similar to Figure 4 for temperature absolute bias values, where most stations did not show significant improvements, except NIKOS KAZANTZAKIS station, which is the Cretan airport in Heraklion, closest to the assimilated stations from Data Source I (Section 2.1). We note that different variables might have higher errors per validation station, which is attributed to geographic differences that might hinder the model's performance depending on distance to shore, elevation, mountaneous regions nearby, etc.

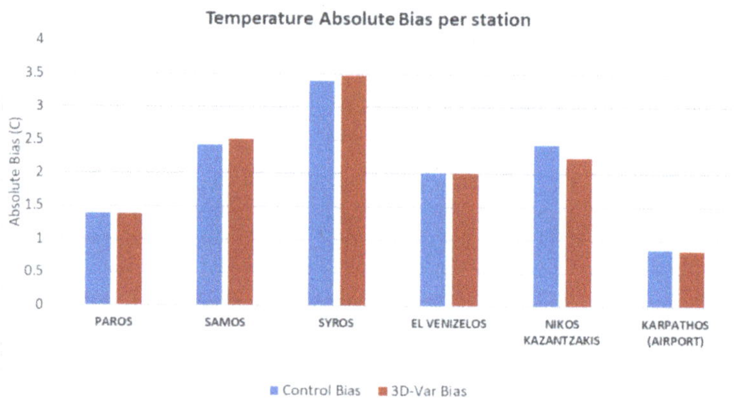

Figure 5. Absolute bias error metric compared to observations per validation meteorological station in D02 averaged for all forecast hours for temperature. Blue and orange indicate control and 3D-Var case, respectively.

3.3. Ocean and Wave Model Validation

We performed a validation of the ocean circulation (NEMO) and wave model (WWIII) in Figure 6 for two model set-ups: one that uses WRF atmospheric forcing (Control run) and one that used WRFDA (DA run), for the same time period that the DA validation was performed. A comparison is shown for the values of sea surface temperature (SST) and significant wave height (SWH) against in situ, satellite, and model reanalysis products. For the in situ dataset, buoy measurements from Data Source III (Section 2.1) falling within the set-up's domain were used. For the satellite comparison, values of the CMEMS SST satellite Level 4 data product (https://doi.org/10.48670/moi-00172, last accessed online 28 October 2024), closest to the buoys' coordinates, were used. In the SWH case (Figure 6b), satellite values were not available. For the reanalysis dataset, the coarser resolution (approximately 4 km) CMEMS analysis-forecast products were used (https://data.marine.copernicus.eu/product/MEDSEA_ANALYSISFORECAST_PHY_006_013/description, https://doi.org/10.25423/cmcc/medsea_analysisforecast_wav_006_017_medwam4, last accessed online 28 October 2024) as a validated model closer to the ground truth. The first day of each daily forecast, for the grid point closest to the buoy coordinates, was considered to reconstruct the time-series shown in Figure 6a of SST (NEMO results) and Figure 6b of SWH (WWIII results) for both model runs that used the WRF and the WRF-DA atmospheric forcing.

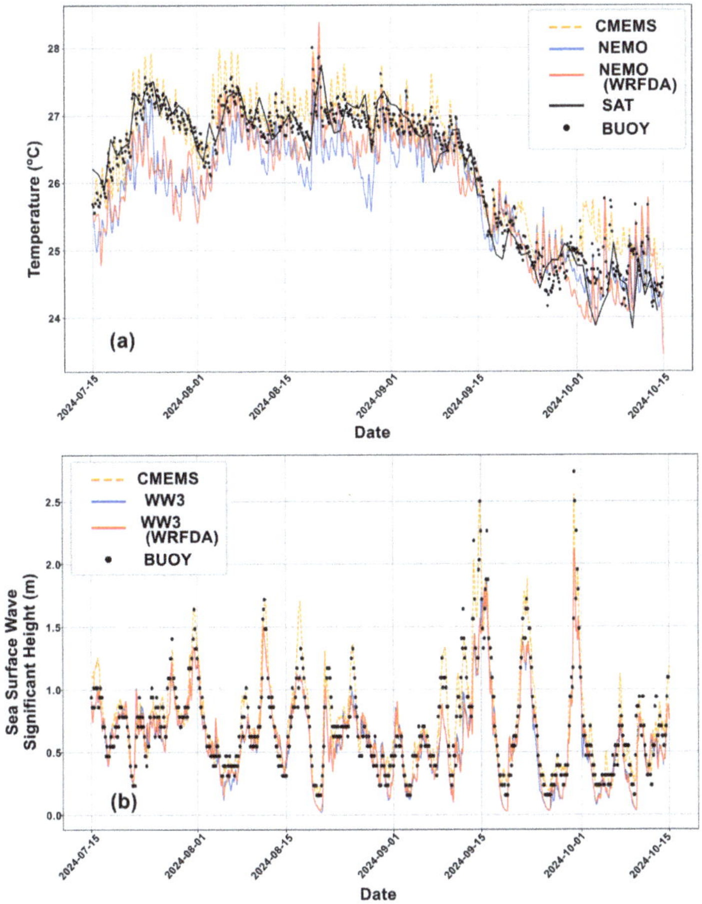

Figure 6. Validation of the (**a**) sea surfac e temperature (SST) variable computed with Nemo 3.6 (first day of each forecast) forced by WRF Control and Nemo forced by WRF-DA and compared to CMEMS SST (analysis), satellite values, and buoy observations with 3-hourly frequency at the location of the Buoy ID 61277 near Santorini (25.1307° E, 35.7263° N) and (**b**) sea surface significant wave height of WWIII forced by WRF Control WWIII forced by WRF-DA (first day of each forecast) compared to CMEMS SWH (analysis) and the same buoy measurements.

The SST results (Figure 6a; Table 2) exhibit strong agreement between NEMO outputs (both configurations) and the observational datasets, with the greater discrepancies observed during the summer periods. The addition of WRF-DA as the model's forcing slightly improved the agreement of NEMO with the observational and reanalysis datasets, as reflected by reduced deviations in temporal patterns. Specifically comparing the model results to the BUOY data, the RMSE dropped from 0.52 °C (number of samples, N = 703) to 0.49 °C when WRF-DA was included (Table 2). Similarly, for the comparison to the SATELLITE observations, the RMSE decreased from 0.62 °C (N = 92) to 0.57 °C when WRF-DA were used (Table 2). Lastly, for the comparison to the CMEMS analysis, the RMSE dropped from 0.62 °C (N = 2208) to 0.59 °C with WRF-DA (Table 2). These improvements, albeit small, highlight the benefits of data assimilation in enhancing predictive accuracy in the regional hydrodynamic configuration.

Table 2. Comparison of RMSE values for the entire validation period shown in Figure 6 for the NEMO model–sea surface temperature (SST) variable in °C, compared to BUOY, SATELLITE, and CMEMS (analysis model) as well as forecast values of the WWIII–significant wave height (SWH) variable. Corresponding control and data assimilated (DA) cases signify if the forcing for those models was the control case or from the WRF-DA. N is the number of samples.

Model	Case	BUOY	SATELLITE	CMEMS (Analysis)
NEMO SST	CONTROL	0.52 °C (N = 703)	0.62 °C (N = 92)	0.62 °C (N = 2208)
	DA	0.49 °C (N = 703)	0.57 °C (N = 92)	0.59 °C (N = 2208)
WWIII SWH	CONTROL	0.20 m (N = 676)	-	0.21 m (N = 2208)
	DA	0.20 m (N = 676)	-	0.21 m (N = 2208)

The WWIII SWH outputs (both configurations) (Figure 6b) showed good agreement with the observational datasets (BUOY and CMEMS), except at the extreme values. The inclusion of WRF-DA did not lead to significant changes in the model output (Figure 6b; Table 2), where the comparison to the buoy values resulted in RMSE at 0.2 m (N = 676), as well as the comparison to the CMEMS product to RMSE = 0.21 m (N = 2208) for both model outputs. These values are considered acceptable, given the high variability of the forecasted SWH, which ranged between 0.16 and 2.73 m. Additionally, the results exhibited overall consistency (Figure 6b), which underscores the forecasting ability of the model in diverse conditions. The above indicates the robustness of the model's performance under both configurations.

4. Discussion

The DA results presented in the previous section show that increasing the number of observation locations and incorporating diverse sources enhanced the realism of the downscaled model, even when using the simplest and most computationally efficient variational data assimilation method (3D-Var). The comparison with real observation data and the evaluation of forecast biases over an ensemble of three months of daily runs provide statistically significant results, with improvements observed at wind speed variable at every validation station except SAMOS that provided a consistent, gap-free data stream. More specifically, the test case examined was performed during a mostly summer period in Greece, leading to an overall reduction in wind speed bias from the control case to the 3D-Var one of 4.7%, using the improvements per validation meteorological station of Figure 4 and averaging on all stations, with a 5.6% increase during forecast hours 26–72 for the wind speed variable. For the temperature, mild improvements were noticed in Figure 5, mostly concentrated at the METAR of the Heraklion airport, which was the closest station to the denser network of assimilated meteorological stations from Data Source I (Section 2.1). A comparable reduction of approximately 4% is reported in [20] for the wind speed variable. The model enhancement using data has inherent uncertainties between studies and can be attributed to both the amount of data assimilated and the differing locations of the validation stations used in each study. As noted in [20], the data employed for DA informs the model upstream by aligning with the direction of the more dominant wind direction, which changes seasonally, considering the average dominant direction. Ideally, it is essential to identify the dominant flow direction and utilize stations positioned to convey information from the point of measurement to the point of validation. This approach enhances model accuracy for various applications. It is important to highlight that this aspect was beyond the scope of our research due to the limited number of observation stations available, even with the addition of stations from Data Source I (Section 2.1). This makes the purpose of this work more evident, as a first step to further improve realism in a regional downscaled model, also maximizing computational efficiency to be able to run it operationally with minimum cost in order to be used as forcing for ocean simulations that enable a more reliable core modelling framework for digital twin applications.

Another potential increase in the accuracy of the enhanced model can be achieved by modifying the data assimilation (DA) methodology, specifically by employing the more computationally demanding and state-of-the-art 4D-Var method (Equation (2)). This method assimilates more data by considering a temporal window for data assimilation. Studies, such as [37], focusing on a similar geographic region, suggest that for wind speed variables, the 3D-Var method might still be superior, despite the 4D-Var analysis focusing on a similar region. While significant enhancements, ranging from a 5 to 10% reduction in mean absolute bias, were observed for temperature fields, the improvement for wind speed remained slightly positive, with reductions ranging from 0.4 to 2% in mean absolute bias, albeit inconsistently across the forecast horizon. Their investigation, conducted during the occurrence of Medicane Ianos in Greece, introduces additional complexity due to the integration of IMERG precipitation data across Europe, which poses further challenges. Nevertheless, these findings highlight the potential benefits of the WRF-DA for operational forecasting systems and contribute to ongoing efforts to optimize and parameterize models for diverse test cases and scenarios.

The validation results of the ocean circulation and wave models (Figure 6) that are based on the data assimilated WRF downscaled model are particularly promising, especially given that the CMEMS model solutions are already corrected with observations through 3D-Var. In contrast, the regional ocean circulation and wave forecasting models operate on an operational cycle, using the aforementioned WRF forcing, which is corrected only with atmospheric data—data that are far more abundant and readily available compared to the limited ocean observations in the area.

Below, two thematic applications are presented that showcase the usefulness of the introduced models on solving real-life problems and offer solutions as containerized applications, with a focus on the ease of use by prospective end-users. The containerization of these tools also aids in the replicability and transferability of the applications, since prospective users can alter input variables and run different what-if scenarios with alternative weather and oceanic conditions, without the need of advanced research knowledge, which contributes to the wider adoption of the tools, which aim at lowering CO_2 emissions and adhering to Green Deal policies, as well as mitigating pollution and enabling safer maritime practices.

4.1. Application to the Optimal Ship Routing Algorithm

Ship weather routing, which involves suggesting low-emission routes, holds significant potential for contributing to the decarbonization of maritime transport [38]. The graph-search VISIR-2 model (discoVerIng Safe and effIcient Routes) (https://zenodo.org/records/10960842, last accessed online 28 October 2024) incorporates several innovations: refined velocity composition with currents and leeway; no restrictions on vessel type provided the performance curve is available; a cartographic projection, rapid coast intersection screening via a K-dimensional tree; and a least-CO_2 emissions algorithm with dynamic graph edge weights demonstrating quasi-linear computational performance [39]. Numerical experiments conducted with VISIR-2 in the Mediterranean Sea throughout 2022 [40] utilized Metocean analysis fields and report that for a 125 m ferry, CO_2 savings were calculated at 2% CO_2 compared to the least-distance route on average and up to 49% savings on about 10 days per year with dire weather conditions. VISIR-2 integrates meteorology, oceanography, ocean engineering, and computer science to evaluate the impact of ship routing on decarbonization efforts within the shipping industry. For our case study, Figure 7a demonstrates an indicative example in the Cretan Sea, connecting port of Heraklion to Chania port, utilizing operational downscaled forecasts of 1 × 1 km grid NEMO and WWIII simulations for 5 July 2024. The three alternate routes minimizing distance, time, and CO_2 emissions are shown, along with the time-averaged significant wave height and direction, as well as the sea surface circulation speed and direction throughout the duration of the trip. As is shown, the minimum CO_2 route is southern, utilizing the anticyclonic pattern of the currents during the trip from Heraklion (HER) to Chania (CHA). The route minimizing CO_2 calculated 0.8% less emissions compared to the least distance route, translating in total saving for the trip of approximately 52 kg of CO_2. The example provided is a proof of concept, and it is noted that these results were obtained during non-extreme weather conditions. Additionally, the routes that the higher-resolution models were implemented in were limited to the region where the models were run and constrained by computational cost, which currently do not include the open sea that would have higher waves and a more significant CO_2 savings [39]. This application is freely available in Iliad Marketplace (https://ocean-twin.eu/marketplace/product/ship-routing, last accessed online 28 October 2024) with relevant details and links for the prospective end-user to both download forecast data and access application packages that can be adapted for replication of the digital twin application.

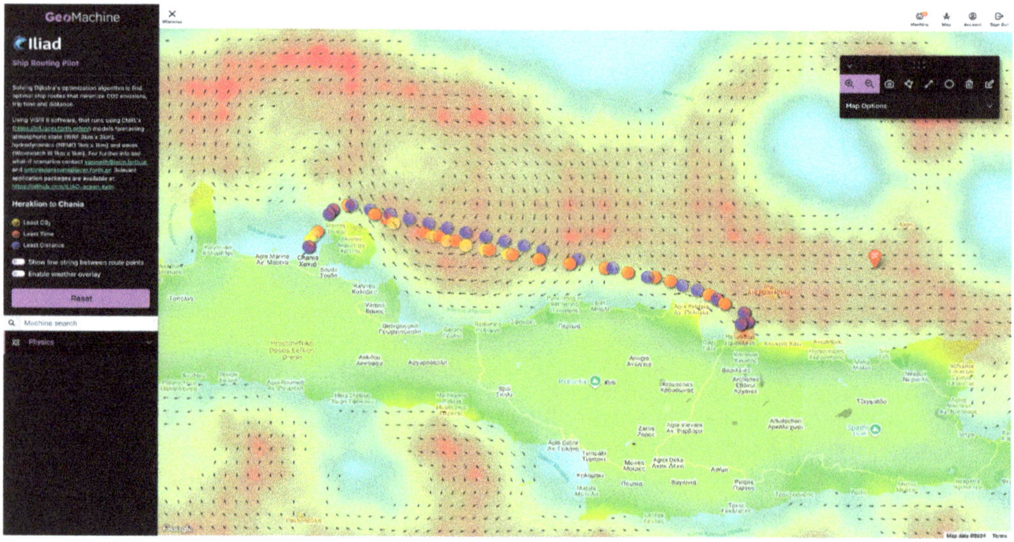

(**a**)

Figure 7. *Cont.*

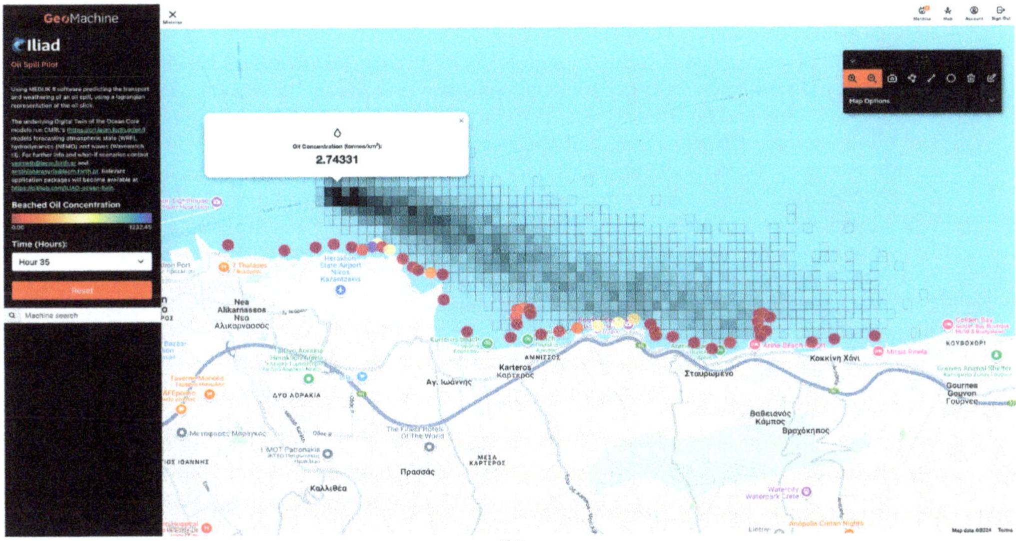

(**b**)

Figure 7. Visualization of the DTO application results of (**a**) a ship routing application simulating the Heraklion to Chania port route and (**b**) surface oil spill concentration (grey color: tonnes/km^2) and beached oil concentration (colored circles) forecasted after 35 h of hypothetical spill release; test case above Heraklion, Greece. Both visuals are available through Geomachine.com (accessed on 28 October 2024).

4.2. Application to Oil Spill Forecasting

Oil spill trajectory forecasting is a complex process that requires both high-resolution forecasting services regarding the ocean and atmospheric states, as well as a model that predicts the transport and weathering of the oil spill. For this application, MEDSLIK II [33,41] (www.medslik-ii.org, last accessed online 28 October 2024) has been utilized, and the whole pipeline description can be easily accessed through Iliad Marketplace (https://ocean-twin.eu/marketplace/product/oil-spills, last accessed online 28 October 2024). This on-demand service tool allows users to simulate what-if predictive scenarios and is coupled with an automatic SAR detection tool that can trigger the oil-spill forecasting service. Figure 7b shows an example of such a hypothetical scenario near Heraklion on the Cretan Island, south of Greece. The functionalities of the DTO application allow the user to choose either an instantaneous spill of prespecified oil mass or a continuous spill case, specifying a spill rate and duration.

The front-end of the thematic applications was carried out through the Geomachine platform (www.geomachine.com, last accessed online 28 October 2024). Since the applications are containerized, the next step is to be able to adapt them for use in cloud services, so the user can trigger simulations within the machines that are integrated in Geomachine. The two applications of optimal ship routing and oil spill forecasting are shown in Figure 7 as example cases for the visual front-end.

5. Conclusions

This study explores the application of data assimilation techniques, focusing on operational atmospheric state forecasting. The use of variational methods, particularly WRF-DA 3D-Var, demonstrates potential in refining the WRF model using real-time data. Despite the small observed improvements over the control case, several factors such as discretization errors and localized accumulation of errors in the covariance matrix may contribute to the limited effectiveness of the 3D-Var correction. Furthermore, the observed improvements with 3D-Var underscore the model's potential for enhancing forecast accuracy.

The small percentage of improvement for WRF-DA can be attributed to several reasons. Firstly, discretization errors may play a role, stemming from the mismatch between model grid points and observation locations, where the nearest neighbor algorithm has been used for direct comparison, and this discrepancy can lead to inaccuracies in the comparison of gridded model data with localized meteorological station data. Secondly, localized accumulation of errors in the covariance matrix B, calculated over a finite time period, may influence the effectiveness of the 3D-Var correction. This suggests a need for further refinement in the estimation of covariance matrices, potentially through prolonged observation periods or enhanced data preprocessing techniques. Lastly, the location of the observation points for assimilation into the model and the validation stations plays a significant role, as implied by [20].

This improved atmospheric model can serve as a foundation for correcting the wave and currents models, illustrating the interconnectedness between atmospheric and sea state modeling. A thorough comparative analysis of the results obtained by the corrected wave model with real-time buoy and in situ meteorological station data will guide the choice of the most suitable approach for operational wave forecasting and atmospheric state data assimilation. This test case, explored in the wider region of the island of Crete, showcases the potential of these refined models in practical applications, thereby contributing to the development of a high-resolution digital twin for ocean applications, demonstrating an on-demand service of optimal ship routing that aids in minimizing CO_2 emissions.

Author Contributions: Conceptualization, A.P.; methodology, A.P., V.M. and G.V.K.; software A.P. and V.M.; validation, A.P. and V.M.; formal analysis, A.P.; investigation, A.P. and V.M.; resources, A.P., V.M. and G.V.K.; data curation, A.P.; writing—original draft preparation, A.P., V.M. and G.A.; writing—review and editing, A.P., V.M., G.V.K., N.A.K. and G.A.; visualization, A.P. and V.M.; supervision, A.P. and N.A.K.; project administration, A.P., N.A.K. and G.A.; funding acquisition, N.A.K. All authors have read and agreed to the published version of the manuscript.

Funding: This project has received funding from the European Commission's Horizon 2020 Research and Innovation programme under grant agreements no. 101037643.

Data Availability Statement: Data are available from the corresponding author upon request.

Acknowledgments: Data acquisition was from Cretaweather.gr, and computational time was granted by Meluxina under ID u100862 and AWS EC2 server under the GRNET-EDYTE Amazon grant. We acknowledge the help of Iliad Partner Blue Lobster for access and setting up the visualizations through Geomachine.

Conflicts of Interest: The authors declare no conflicts of interest.

References

1. Chatzinikolaou, E.; Arvanitidis, C. Status, values and present threats in Heraklion harbour (Crete, Greece). *Reg. Stud. Mar. Sci.* **2016**, *8*, 252–258. [CrossRef]
2. Theocharis, A.; Georgopoulos, D.; Lascaratos, A.; Nittis, K. Water masses and circulation in the central region of the Eastern Mediterranean: Eastern Ionian, South Aegean and Northwest Levantine, 1986–1987. *Deep. Sea Res. Part II Top. Stud. Oceanogr.* **1993**, *40*, 1121–1142. [CrossRef]
3. Spanoudaki, K.; Kozyrakis, G.; Metheniti, V.; Parasyris, A.; Kampanis, N. The Cretan Sea oil spill Digital Twin pilot for the ILIAD Digital Twin of the Ocean. In Proceedings of the EGU General Assembly Conference Abstracts, Vienna, Austria & Online, 23–28 April 2023; p. EGU–11561.
4. Kallos, G.; Galanis, G.; Emmanouil, G. Assimilation of ENVISAT altimeter and scatterometer data in real time wave predictions. In Proceedings of the Advances in SAR Oceanography from Envisat and ERS Missions, Frascati, Italy, 23–26 January 2006; p. 4.
5. Navon, I.M. Data Assimilation for Numerical Weather Prediction: A Review. In *Data Assimilation for Atmospheric, Oceanic and Hydrologic Applications*; Park, S.K., Xu, L., Eds.; Springer: Berlin/Heidelberg, Germany, 2009; pp. 21–65.
6. Hoteit, I.; Luo, X.; Bocquet, M.; Kohl, A.; Ait-El-Fquih, B. Data Assimilation in Oceanography: Current Status and New Directions. In *New Frontiers in Operational Oceanography*; CreateSpace Independent Publishing Platform: Scotts Valley, CA, USA, 2018; pp. 465–512.

7. Artale, V.; Iudicone, D.; Santoleri, R.; Rupolo, V.; Marullo, S.; D'Ortenzio, F. Role of surface fluxes in ocean general circulation models using satellite sea surface temperature: Validation of and sensitivity to the forcing frequency of the Mediterranean thermohaline circulation. *J. Geophys. Res. Ocean.* **2002**, *107*, 29-1–29-24. [CrossRef]
8. Ruti, P.M.; Marullo, S.; D'Ortenzio, F.; Tremant, M. Comparison of analyzed and measured wind speeds in the perspective of oceanic simulations over the Mediterranean basin: Analyses, QuikSCAT and buoy data. *J. Mar. Syst.* **2008**, *70*, 33–48. [CrossRef]
9. Durrant, T.H.; Greenslade, D.J.M.; Simmonds, I. The effect of statistical wind corrections on global wave forecasts. *Ocean. Model.* **2013**, *70*, 116–131. [CrossRef]
10. Son, D.; Jun, K.; Kwon, J.-I.; Yoo, J.; Park, S.-H. Improvement of wave predictions in marginal seas around Korea through correction of simulated sea winds. *Appl. Ocean. Res.* **2023**, *130*, 103433. [CrossRef]
11. Hisaki, Y. Sea Surface Wind Correction Using HF Ocean Radar and Its Impact on Coastal Wave Prediction. *J. Atmos. Ocean. Technol.* **2017**, *34*, 2001–2020. [CrossRef]
12. Barker, D.M.; Huang, W.; Guo, Y.R.; Bourgeois, A.J.; Xiao, Q.N. A Three-Dimensional Variational Data Assimilation System for MM5: Implementation and Initial Results. *Mon. Weather. Rev.* **2004**, *132*, 897–914. [CrossRef]
13. Liu, Z.; Ban, J.; Hong, J.-S.; Kuo, Y.-H. Multi-resolution incremental 4D-Var for WRF: Implementation and application at convective scale. *Q. J. R. Meteorol. Soc.* **2020**, *146*, 3661–3674. [CrossRef]
14. Huang, X.-Y.; Xiao, Q.; Barker, D.M.; Zhang, X.; Michalakes, J.; Huang, W.; Henderson, T.; Bray, J.; Chen, Y.; Ma, Z.; et al. Four-Dimensional Variational Data Assimilation for WRF: Formulation and Preliminary Results. *Mon. Weather. Rev.* **2009**, *137*, 299–314. [CrossRef]
15. Wang, X.; Barker, D.M.; Snyder, C.; Hamill, T.M. A Hybrid ETKF–3DVAR Data Assimilation Scheme for the WRF Model. Part I: Observing System Simulation Experiment. *Mon. Weather. Rev.* **2008**, *136*, 5116–5131. [CrossRef]
16. Schwartz, C.S.; Romine, G.S.; Weisman, M.L.; Sobash, R.A.; Fossell, K.R.; Manning, K.W.; Trier, S.B. A Real-Time Convection-Allowing Ensemble Prediction System Initialized by Mesoscale Ensemble Kalman Filter Analyses. *Weather. Forecast.* **2015**, *30*, 1158–1181. [CrossRef]
17. Li, S.; Wang, P.; Wang, H.; Peng, Y.; Liu, Z.; Zhang, W.; Liu, H.; Wang, Y.; Che, H.; Zhang, X. Implementation and application of ensemble optimal interpolation on an operational chemistry weather model for improving PM2.5 and visibility predictions. *Geosci. Model Dev.* **2023**, *16*, 4171–4191. [CrossRef]
18. Lorenc, A.C. The potential of the ensemble Kalman filter for NWP—A comparison with 4D-Var. *Q. J. R. Meteorol. Soc.* **2003**, *129*, 3183–3203. [CrossRef]
19. Talagrand, O. Assimilation of Observations, an Introduction (Data Assimilation in Meteology and Oceanography: Theory and Practice). *J. Meteorol. Soc. Jpn. Ser. II* **1997**, *75*, 191–209. [CrossRef]
20. Lam, M.; Fung, J.C. Model Sensitivity Evaluation for 3DVAR Data Assimilation Applied on WRF with a Nested Domain Configuration. *Atmosphere* **2021**, *12*, 682. [CrossRef]
21. Kozyrakis, G.V.; Spanoudaki, K.; Varouchakis, E.A. Long-term wave energy potential estimation in the Aegean and Ionian seas using dynamic downscaling and wave modelling techniques. *Appl. Ocean. Res.* **2023**, *131*, 103446. [CrossRef]
22. National Centers for Environmental Prediction/National Weather Service/NOAA/US Department of Commerce Research Data Archive at the National Center for Atmospheric Research, Computational and Information Systems Laboratory, NCEP GFS 0.25 Degree Global Forecast Grids Historical Archive. 2015. Available online: https://rda.ucar.edu/datasets/d084001/citation/# (accessed on 28 October 2024).
23. Torres-Quezada, J.; Coch, H.; Isalgué, A. Data set of climatic factors measured in a low latitude region with warm and humid climate: Solar radiation, cloud cover and sky temperature. *Data Brief* **2021**, *38*, 107404. [CrossRef]
24. Ide, K.; Courtier, P.; Ghil, M.; Lorenc, A.C. Unified Notation for Data Assimilation: Operational, Sequential and Variational (Data Assimilation in Meteology and Oceanography: Theory and Practice). *J. Meteorol. Soc. Jpn. Ser. II* **1997**, *75*, 181–189. [CrossRef]
25. Samos, I.; Louka, P.; Flocas, H. Assessing the Accuracy of 3D-VAR in Supercell Thunderstorm Forecasting: A Regional Background Error Covariance Study. *Atmosphere* **2023**, *14*, 1611. [CrossRef]
26. Samos, I.; Flocas, H.; Louka, P. A Background Error Statistics Analysis over the Mediterranean: The Impact on 3DVAR Data Assimilation. *Environ. Sci. Proc.* **2023**, *26*, 158. [CrossRef]
27. Parrish, D.F.; Derber, J.C. The National Meteorological Center's Spectral Statistical-Interpolation Analysis System. *Mon. Weather. Rev.* **1992**, *120*, 1747–1763. [CrossRef]
28. Stanesic, A.; Horvath, K.; Keresturi, E. Comparison of NMC and Ensemble-Based Climatological Background-Error Covariances in an Operational Limited-Area Data Assimilation System. *Atmosphere* **2019**, *10*, 570. [CrossRef]
29. Shamarock, W.C.; Klemp, J.B.; Dudhia, J.; Gill, D.O.; Liu, Z.; Berner, J.; Wang, W.; Powers, J.G.; Duda, M.G.; Barker, D.; et al. *A Description of the Advanced Research WRF Model Version 4.3*; OpenSky: Boulder, CO, USA, 2021. [CrossRef]
30. Liu, Y.; Zhang, L.; Lian, Z. Conjugate Gradient Algorithm in the Four-Dimensional Variational Data Assimilation System in GRAPES. *J. Meteorol. Res.* **2018**, *32*, 974–984. [CrossRef]
31. Taylor, K.E. Summarizing multiple aspects of model performance in a single diagram. *J. Geophys. Res. Atmos.* **2001**, *106*, 7183–7192. [CrossRef]
32. Tian, Y.; Nearing, G.; Peters-Lidard, C.; Harrison, K.; Tang, L. Performance Metrics, Error Modeling, and Uncertainty Quantification. *Mon. Weather. Rev.* **2015**, *144*, 607–613. [CrossRef]

33. Zodiatis, G.; Lardner, R.; Spanoudaki, K.; Sofianos, S.; Radhakrishnan, H.; Coppini, G.; Liubartseva, S.; Kampanis, N.; Krokos, G.; Hoteit, I.; et al. Chapter 5—Operational oil spill modelling assessments. In *Marine Hydrocarbon Spill Assessments*; Makarynskyy, O., Ed.; Elsevier: Amsterdam, The Netherlands, 2021; pp. 145–197.
34. Madec, G.; Bourdallé-Badie, R.; Bouttier, P.-A.; Bricaud, C.; Bruciaferri, D.; Calvert, D.; Chanut, J.; Clementi, E.; Coward, A.; Delrosso, D. NEMO Ocean Engine. 2017. Available online: https://zenodo.org/records/1472492 (accessed on 28 October 2024).
35. Tolman, H.L. User manual and system documentation of WAVEWATCH III TM version 3.14. *Tech. Note MMAB Contrib.* **2009**, *276*. Available online: https://polar.ncep.noaa.gov/mmab/papers/tn276/MMAB_276.pdf (accessed on 28 October 2024).
36. Siewert, J.; Kroszczynski, K. Evaluation of High-Resolution Land Cover Geographical Data for the WRF Model Simulations. *Remote Sens.* **2023**, *15*, 2389. [CrossRef]
37. Vourlioti, P.; Mamouka, T.; Agrafiotis, A.; Kotsopoulos, S. Medicane Ianos: 4D-Var Data Assimilation of Surface and Satellite Observations into the Numerical Weather Prediction Model WRF. *Atmosphere* **2022**, *13*, 1683. [CrossRef]
38. Mannarini, G.; Carelli, L. VISIR-I.b: Waves and ocean currents for energy efficient navigation. *Geosci. Model Dev. Discuss.* **2019**, 1–47. [CrossRef]
39. Mannarini, G.; Carelli, L.; Orović, J.; Martinkus, C.; Coppini, G. Towards Least-CO2 Ferry Routes in the Adriatic Sea. *J. Mar. Sci. Eng.* **2021**, *9*, 115. [CrossRef]
40. Mannarini, G.; Salinas, M.; Carelli, L.; Petacco, N.; Orović, J. VISIR-2: Ship weather routing in Python. *Geosci. Model Dev.* **2024**, *17*, 4355–4382. [CrossRef]
41. De Dominicis, M.; Pinardi, N.; Zodiatis, G.; Archetti, R. MEDSLIK-II, a Lagrangian marine surface oil spill model for short-term forecasting—Part 2: Numerical simulations and validations. *Geosci. Model Dev.* **2013**, *6*, 1871–1888. [CrossRef]

algorithms MDPI

Article

Disassembly of Distribution Transformers Based on Multimodal Data Recognition and Collaborative Processing

Li Wang [1], Feng Chen [1], Yujia Hu [2,*], Zhiyao Zheng [2] and Kexin Zhang [3,4,*]

[1] Materials Branch, State Grid Zhejiang Electric Power Co., Ltd., Hangzhou 310015, China
[2] Zhejiang Huadian Equipment Testing and Research Insitute Co., Ltd., Hangzhou 310015, China
[3] Huzhou Institute of Zhejiang University, Huzhou 313000, China
[4] Institute of Cyber-Systems and Control, Zhejiang University, Hangzhou 310027, China
* Correspondence: xjtuhyj@stu.xjtu.edu.cn (Y.H.); zhangkexin@zju.edu.cn (K.Z.)

Abstract: As power system equipment gradually ages, the automated disassembly of transformers has become a critical area of research to enhance both efficiency and safety. This paper presents a transformer disassembly system designed for power systems, leveraging multimodal perception and collaborative processing. By integrating 2D images and 3D point cloud data captured by RGB-D cameras, the system enables the precise recognition and efficient disassembly of transformer covers and internal components through multimodal data fusion, deep learning models, and control technologies. The system employs an enhanced YOLOv8 model for positioning and identifying screw-fastened covers while also utilizing the STDC network for segmentation and cutting path planning of welded covers. In addition, the system captures 3D point cloud data of the transformer's interior using multi-view RGB-D cameras and performs multimodal semantic segmentation and object detection via the ODIN model, facilitating the high-precision identification and cutting of complex components such as windings, studs, and silicon steel sheets. Experimental results show that the system achieves a recognition accuracy of 99% for both cover and internal component disassembly, with a disassembly success rate of 98%, demonstrating its high adaptability and safety in complex industrial environments.

Keywords: power system transformers; multimodal perception; transformer disassembly; RGB-D camera; deep learning

1. Introduction

Transformers play a crucial role in transmission and distribution systems, and their reliable operation is essential for grid stability. However, with aging equipment and increasing maintenance demands, transformer disassembly has become progressively more complex. Traditional manual methods are not only inefficient but also hazardous and environmentally damaging, underscoring the need for safer, automated solutions [1–3]. Current technologies still rely heavily on manual labor, requiring skilled operators and presenting safety risks, such as mishandling bolts or fasteners, which can lead to injury. Furthermore, disassembling welded covers requires precise cutting and handling, and errors in identifying key components can damage critical parts [4]. Enhancing disassembly efficiency while ensuring safety remains a key challenge in transformer recycling and maintenance [5,6].

Significant progress has been made in the automation of transformer disassembly, particularly in the context of electric vehicle battery recycling. With the advancement of deep learning techniques in the industry [7–9], researchers have developed multimodal image fusion and intelligent control technologies to enhance component identification and operational efficiency [10]. Cognitive robotics, which integrates vision systems with intelligent planning, enables robots to adapt dynamically in real-time, improving system flexibility [11]. Robotic arms, combined with deep learning, are increasingly employed for disassembling industrial transformers, allowing for the precise targeting of bolts and welded parts [12]. Additionally, multimodal fusion techniques, which combine 2D images with 3D point cloud data from RGB-D cameras, significantly enhance target recognition in complex environments [13]. Automated and semi-automated wire stripping machines have also been introduced to improve the recycling of waste wires. For example, pneumatic automatic wire strippers can increase efficiency by 25% compared to manual methods [14]. Researchers have also developed a multi-diameter cable-cutting machine for cables with varying diameters. Experiments have shown that adjusting the pusher extension distance improves both cutting speed and quality, enhancing the efficiency and performance of industrial cable processing [15].

Recent advancements have led to the development of automated transformer disassembly methods that leverage machine learning and image recognition technologies. Researchers have designed robot-based disassembly systems, primarily for recycling waste transformers, which integrate multimodal data fusion to identify and process complex structures such as bolts and welds [16]. The incorporation of IoT and big data technologies has also enabled the remote monitoring and dynamic operation of these systems, facilitating real-time analysis and optimization of the disassembly process [17–19]. For electronic waste, intelligent robotic and vision-based solutions use multimodal data to accurately identify hazardous and recyclable materials, efficiently processing them on automated platforms [20]. Moreover, multimodal fusion technology, combining RGB-D cameras with deep learning models, improves disassembly automation by accurately detecting and evaluating critical components like welds and bolts [21]. To address the challenges of recycling small-diameter waste transformer wires—where traditional mechanical knives wear quickly and lack automation, and methods like incineration or chemical stripping lead to environmental pollution—a device utilizing ultrasonic cutting technology has been developed. This approach offers high efficiency and minimal wear, providing an effective solution for stripping waste transformer wires [15].

Despite global advancements in automated transformer disassembly, several challenges remain. In complex industrial environments, ensuring robustness and accuracy is particularly difficult when dealing with worn bolts or deformed weld joints, where current algorithms often struggle with efficiency and precision, especially in real-time applications [22,23]. While multimodal data fusion holds promise for complex scene recognition, improving real-time processing and reducing latency are critical challenges that still need to be addressed. Striking a balance between computational efficiency and accuracy is a key focus of ongoing research. Furthermore, given the diversity of power equipment models and specifications, developing adaptable automated disassembly systems that can accommodate various equipment types is becoming increasingly important [10,11].

To address the limitations of current technologies, this study aims to improve the efficiency and safety of transformer disassembly through the use of multimodal technology, proposing an intelligent system that integrates multimodal data processing, deep learning, and automated control. The system starts by accurately identifying the transformer cover type using 2D images and 3D point cloud data from an RGB-D camera, then selects the most suitable disassembly strategy based on real-time conditions. For screw-fastened covers, the system assesses the screw conditions and performs automated disassembly. For welded covers, it employs precise edge detection and cutting path planning. The system extracts 2D image features of the internal transformer structure using a convolutional neural network (CNN), mapping these features into 3D space. It then utilizes the K-Nearest Neighbor (KNN) algorithm and positional coding for 3D feature fusion, accurately locating cutting components (e.g., screws, copper plates, studs, silicon steel sheets) through target detection and executing the cutting process based on the planned path. This approach enables the efficient disassembly of waste transformers. Additionally, the developed wire extraction line effectively separates wire insulation from metal cores, enhancing both the integrity and efficiency of wire recovery.

2. Transformer Disassembly System Preprogram Design

This paper proposes a transformer disassembly system based on multimodal sensing and intelligent control for the efficient and safe disposal of used transformers. The system integrates RGB-D cameras, multimodal data fusion, and deep learning models to enable fully automated transformer disassembly. The process is divided into two main components: the cover plate and the internal structure.

2.1. General Scheme for Transformer Disassembly System

The disassembly process of the transformer is shown in Figure 1 and consists of five main steps. First, data from the transformer's cover plate are collected through sensors, providing the necessary support for identifying the type and structure of the cover plate. Next, the system uses the collected data to identify and classify the transformer cover plate and selects the appropriate disassembly method, such as unscrewing screws or welding and cutting, to complete the disassembly of the cover plate. After the cover plate is removed, the sensors further collect data on the internal components of the transformer, helping the system understand its internal structure and component characteristics. Then, the system performs precise identification and disassembly of the internal components of the transformer to ensure that important parts are effectively separated. Finally, the system processes the transformer's winding section, stripping the copper wire for recycling. The entire process is efficient and safe, leveraging multimodal perception and intelligent control technologies to achieve the full disassembly of obsolete transformers.

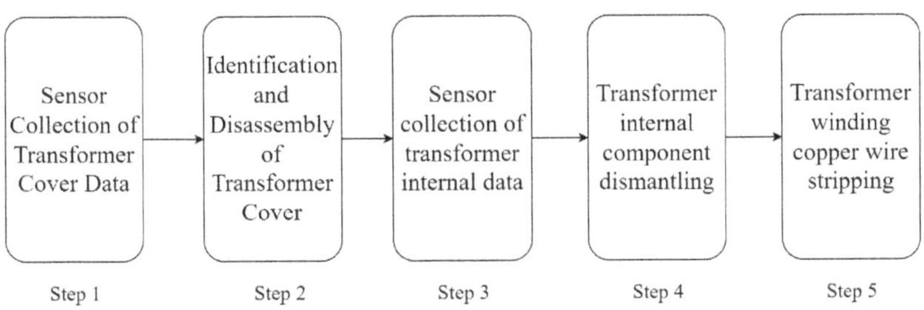

Figure 1. General scheme for transformer disassembly system.

2.2. Transformer Cover Disassembly Program

The cover disassembly process is illustrated in Figure 2. The system captures multi-view 2D images and 3D point cloud data using RGB-D cameras, employing fusion algorithms to improve feature extraction and address recognition challenges in complex environments. Initially, the system identifies the cover connection type using a pre-trained classification model, categorizing it as either screw-fastened or welded.

For screw-fastened covers, the system uses an improved YOLOv8 model integrated with a Mask Attention mechanism to accurately detect screw locations. Once identified, the system assesses the condition of each screw. If any screw is found to be slipping or damaged, the system automatically switches to cutting mode for disassembly, ensuring continuous operation.

For welded covers, the system employs a segmentation model based on an enhanced STDC network to precisely segment the cover and its components, enabling the accurate identification of weld seams and optimal cutting path planning. An improved SegFormer model generates the weld cut line, incorporating multi-scale feature extraction, positional encoding, and geometric feature assistance modules to enhance edge precision. Additionally, dynamic edge distance adjustment mechanisms are applied to different components, avoiding critical areas and ensuring safe cutting operations.

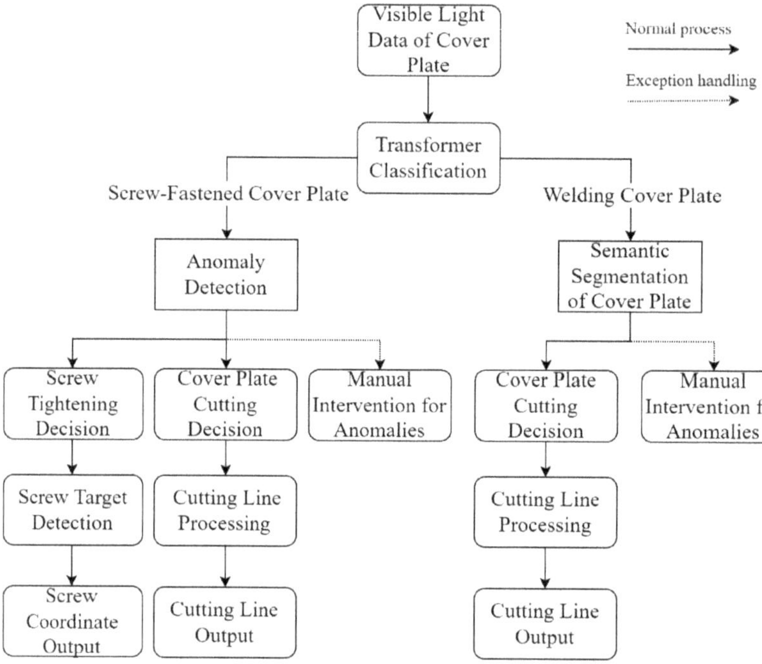

Figure 2. Schematic diagram of the transformer cover disassembly process.

2.3. Transformer Internal Component Disassembly Program

The disassembly process of the internal components of the transformer is illustrated in Figure 3. After the cover is removed, the system begins processing the internal parts, focusing on the identification and disassembly of complex components such as windings, studs, and silicon steel sheets. Using RGB-D cameras positioned at multiple angles, the system collects 3D point cloud data and employs the ODIN model for semantic segmentation and object detection, alternately integrating 2D and 3D information to achieve precise identification.

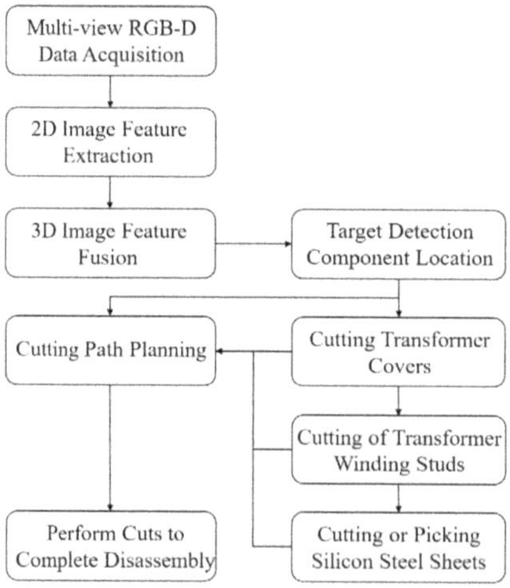

Figure 3. Schematic diagram of the disassembly process of the internal components of the transformer.

The system constructs a 3D point cloud model of the transformer's interior by merging multi-view images with depth data, enabling the effective segmentation and localization of complex structures. The KNN algorithm, combined with positional encoding, ensures accurate identification of intricate geometric structures like windings and studs. Once identified, the system plans the cutting path and executes the disassembly based on the specific characteristics of each component, ensuring a smooth and efficient transformer disassembly process.

2.4. Transformer Copper Winding Stripping Methods

The transformer copper wire winding stripping system comprises two main components, as shown in Figure 4: wire constant tension release technology and intelligent wire removal technology. These two systems work in tandem to achieve continuous and efficient wire extraction, facilitating effective wire recycling.

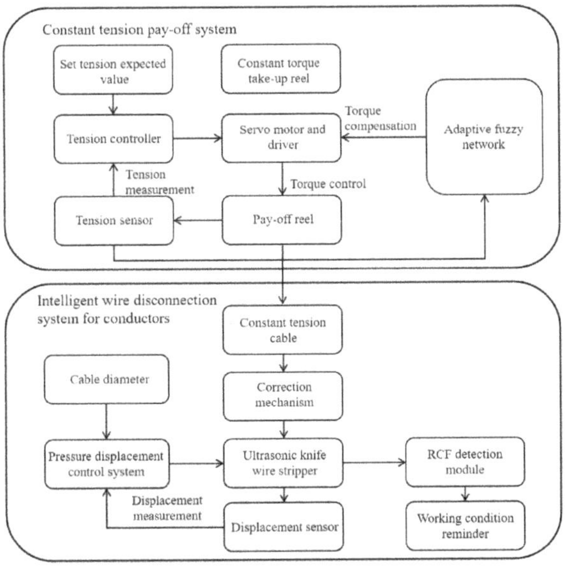

Figure 4. Overall flowchart of transformer copper wire winding stripping method.

The principle of payoff tension control operates as follows: The payoff motor speed regulates the forward speed of the production product at the payoff stage, while the traction speed or take-up speed governs the speed at the traction or take-up locations. These speeds are synchronized through data processing and coordination by the main control unit, creating a speed differential that generates the required payoff tension on the production product. The constant tension intelligent servo unwinding system is a high-precision control system designed to manage the wire unwinding process. By precisely controlling the unwinding tension, it prevents stretching, deformation, or breakage of the wire, ensuring product quality and production efficiency. In this system, a servo motor accurately controls the output torque of the unwinding mechanism to maintain a stable wire feeding speed. Tension sensors continuously monitor tension fluctuations during the feeding process. The controller utilizes a combination of traditional PID control and adaptive fuzzy neural networks to optimize the servo motor's control strategy. The intelligent wire removal system for conductors uses an ultrasonic cutter head to strip the outer insulation layer of the wire within a constant tension payoff system. It integrates a control algorithm that leverages pressure and vision sensors to regulate the cutting depth of the insulation layer, ensuring complete removal while protecting the cutter head. To enhance precision, the system is equipped with a displacement sensor that accurately measures the robotic arm's movement, ensuring operational accuracy. An ARM microcontroller serves as the control system, employing PID algorithms for real-time control of the cutter head's feed depth. Additionally, a camera monitors the wire removal process, while the RCF algorithm, integrated with a neural network, performs real-time detection to confirm whether the wire has been fully stripped.

2.5. Exception Handling and Manual Intervention

To enhance the automation and adaptability of the system in complex situations, various anomaly detection and handling mechanisms have been developed. When issues arise—such as screw slippage, weld recognition failures, or equipment obstructions—the system automatically pauses and triggers an alert for manual intervention. Additionally, an optimization mechanism based on historical data has been integrated to improve anomaly assessment. By dynamically adjusting the judgment threshold through comparisons between current inspection results and historical maintenance data, the system seeks to minimize manual interventions, thereby improving overall disassembly efficiency.

3. Transformer Tank Cover Disassembly Algorithm

3.1. Image Acquisition and Pre-Processing

The RGB-D camera captures both 2D images and 3D point cloud data, enhancing image features through multimodal fusion techniques. This camera not only provides rich texture information but also delivers accurate depth data, which can be integrated through multimodal fusion methods [24,25]. During data processing, the system performs not only 2D and 3D feature fusion within a single view but also cross-view multiscale feature extraction, enriching spatial information and improving target detection across different sizes while enhancing the model's generalization performance [26]. Specifically, the RGB image features and 3D point cloud data are effectively combined using an adaptive attention mechanism, resulting in improved overall detection accuracy [25]. The acquired image data are illustrated in Figure 5.

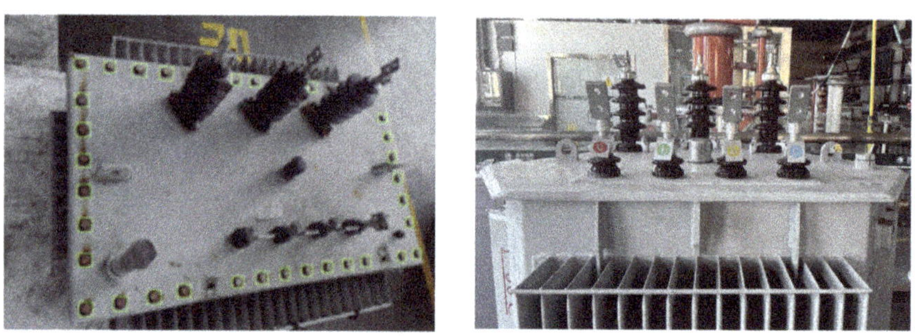

(a) Screw-fastened cover　　(b) Welded cover

Figure 5. Two types of transformer cover. (**a**) Screw-fastened cover. (**b**) Welded cover.

3.2. Detection and Evaluation of Cover Types

In transformer maintenance and recycling, accurately identifying the type and assessing the condition of the cover plate is crucial for automated disassembly. Transformer covers are primarily secured either by screws or welding. For screw-fastened covers, an inspection and evaluation of the screws is necessary, whereas welded covers necessitate specific cutting operations. Traditionally, operators determine disassembly strategies through manual inspection, which can be inefficient and pose safety risks. Therefore, implementing automated systems can enhance both the efficiency and safety of disassembly processes by accurately recognizing cover types and automatically assessing their conditions.

In order to address the above problems, this paper proposes an automated identification scheme utilizing a pre-trained EfficientNetV2 [27] model. This model effectively classifies how the transformer cover is connected to the enclosure.

$$C = \text{EfficientNetV2}(F_{\text{fusion}}). \tag{1}$$

The system processes the fused feature map F_{fusion} to produce classification results, categorizing the connection method of the cover plate into screw-fastened or welded. This approach enables rapid and accurate identification, streamlining subsequent operations such as screw detection or welding and cutting tasks.

For screw-fastened covers, the system necessitates the further detection and evaluation of screws, particularly assessing for deformation or slippage. This paper employs an improved Scan2CAD [28] scheme, which accurately aligns RGB-D data with the transformer's CAD model, enhancing screw detection accuracy. Scan2CAD extracts features from the RGB-D image I_{RGB} and the CAD model M_{CAD} using a 3D CNN, facilitating precise alignment.

$$F_{\text{aligned}} = \text{Align}(F_{\text{RGBD}}, F_{\text{CAD}}; W_{\text{CNN}}) \tag{2}$$

where W_{CNN} is the weights of 3D CNN, and F_{aligned} is the aligned feature map. Based on the feature alignment, this paper utilizes the improved PointNet++ [29] model to detect screw and cover deformation. The system extracts the screw deformation features Z_{screw} and cover deformation features Z_{plate} using the PointNet++ model.

$$Z_{\text{screw}} = f_{\text{PointNet++}}(F^{\text{screw}}_{\text{aligned}}) \tag{3}$$

$$Z_{\text{plate}} = f_{\text{PointNet++}}(F^{\text{plate}}_{\text{aligned}}). \tag{4}$$

The model analyzes the differences between the RGB-D data and the CAD model to assess severe deformation in screws and cover plates. To enhance its capability in complex scenarios, this paper introduces a historical data enhancement scheme. By incorporating historical maintenance data, the model adaptively adjusts the judgment threshold, optimizing detection for common failure modes such as screw slipping, thread wear, and local cover plate deformation. Historical data features are integrated into the PointNet++ model and compared with current inspection results to evaluate the similarity of failure modes.

$$Z_{\text{history}} = f_{\text{history}}(H_{\text{history}}). \tag{5}$$

The detection results of screw deformation are utilized not only to assess disassembly difficulty but also to estimate the torque required for unscrewing. To achieve this, this paper employs a graph neural network (GNN) to estimate the unscrewing moment T_{estimate} [30]. The GNN model leverages the geometric deformations of the screws and cover along with material properties, generating a force simulation based on the discrepancies between the RGB-D data and the CAD model, ultimately calculating the unscrewing moment.

$$T_{\text{estimate}} = f_{\text{GNN}}(Z_{\text{screw}}, Z_{\text{plate}}, M_{\text{CAD}}). \tag{6}$$

When the estimated torque T_{estimate} exceeds the allowable range of the device, the system determines that the screws cannot be removed through conventional screwing methods. In such cases, the system automatically transitions to alternative disassembly methods, such as cutting operations.

$$\text{Anomaly} = \begin{cases} 1, & T_{\text{estimate}} > T_{\text{threshold}} \; or \; Z_{\text{screw}} \\ 0, & \text{otherwise.} \end{cases} \tag{7}$$

Finally, based on the detection results of the screws and cover plate, the system makes a corresponding disassembly decision. If abnormalities such as screw slippage, deformation, or serious cover plate distortion are detected, the system automatically selects a cutting program. Conversely, if the screws and cover plate are in a normal condition, the system opts for the screw-unscrewing disassembly method. This approach, driven by intelligent detection and decision-making, enhances disassembly efficiency while reducing safety risks and improving precision.

3.3. Disassembly of Screw-Fastened Cover Plate

To fully leverage the transformer's feature conditions, this paper employs a target detection method based on YOLOv8 [31] integrated with Mask Attention [32] for the precise localization of each nut. Given the challenges associated with transformer nuts, such as rust, contamination, and breakage, traditional target detection methods may struggle to effectively utilize depth information and subtle features. This approach enhances the target detection network by incorporating Mask Attention to focus on small targets like nuts on the cover plate. Additionally, it introduces embedded nut template matching to initialize the Query against the complex backgrounds of the transformer cover, accounting for possible occlusions, partial wear, or rust. This strategy aims to better utilize the shape and distribution characteristics of the nuts, thereby improving detection accuracy in complex environments. The modified network structure is illustrated in Figure 6.

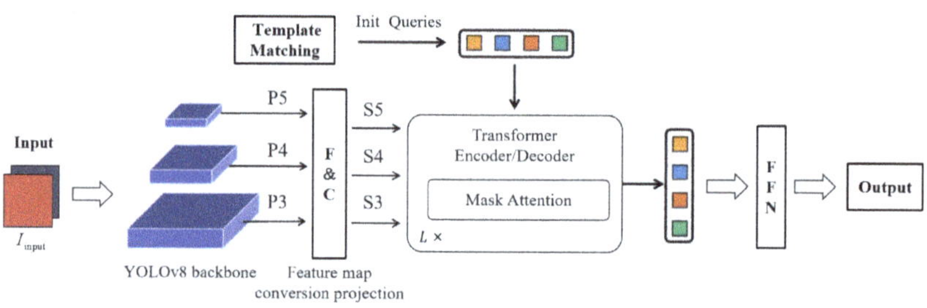

Figure 6. Process of target detection.

3.3.1. Multi-Scale Feature Extraction

To address the challenges posed by the complex backgrounds on the transformer cover and the small size of the nuts, this approach utilizes YOLOv8's backbone for multi-scale feature extraction. By employing feature maps at various scales, the system effectively captures both the intricate details and the broader context of the nuts.

The input image is initially processed by the backbone network of YOLOv8 for feature extraction. This backbone employs a series of convolutional layers and modules to extract multi-scale features from the image, resulting in three key feature maps: the third-level feature map P_3, the fourth-level feature map P_4, and the fifth-level feature map P_5.

3.3.2. Feature Map Conversion and Projection

Each feature map, P_3, P_4, and P_5, is first spread and then converted to a vector in D dimensions using linear projection to fit the subsequent processing steps. The specific process is described as follows:

$$F_i = \text{Flatten}(P_i),\ i \in \{3,4,5\} \tag{8}$$

$$S_i = F_i W_i,\ S_i \in \mathbb{R}^{N_i \times D} \tag{9}$$

where W_i is the projection matrix an $N_i = H_i \times W_i$ is the number of flattened features [33].

3.3.3. Mask Attention for Region Extraction and Optimization

To enhance the accuracy of nut detection, particularly when nuts are contaminated, rusted, or partially obscured, this paper integrates a Mask Attention mechanism into the target detection framework. By generating masks through Mask Attention, the system focuses on critical features within specific regions, thereby improving recognition accuracy. Once the feature extraction is completed, the resulting feature map is further processed by a six-layer transformer that incorporates the Mask Attention module.

At each layer, the global information $\text{GAP}(S_i^{(l)})$ of each feature map is extracted by global average pooling. Next, it is processed using a lightweight convolutional network to generate a preliminary mask $M_i^{(l)}$.

At each layer, the global information $\text{GAP}(S_i^{(l)})$ of each feature map is extracted through global average pooling. This information is then processed by a lightweight convolutional network to produce a preliminary mask $M_i^{(l)}$.

$$M_i^{(l)} = \text{Softmax}(\text{Conv}(\text{GAP}(S_i^{(l)}))) \tag{10}$$

where $S_i^{(l)}$ represents the feature map of the l-th layer, $l = 1, 2, \ldots, 6$, $\text{GAP}(S_i^{(l)})$ denotes the global average pooling of the feature map $S_i^{(l)}$, Conv is the convolutional operation, and $M_i^{(l)}$ is the mask normalized by Softmax operation to adjust the importance of each pixel within the feature map. This Mask Attention mechanism allows the model to focus on target areas while minimizing background interference, effectively ignoring irrelevant information, such as oil contamination on the transformer cover, thereby enhancing nut detection accuracy.

The generated mask $M_i^{(l)}$ is applied to the input feature map $S_i^{(l)}$ using element-wise multiplication to obtain the masked feature map $\widehat{S_i^{(l)}}$:

$$\widehat{S_i^{(l)}} = M_i^{(l)} \odot S_i^{(l)} \tag{11}$$

where $\odot$ is the element-wise multiplication operation, and $\widehat{S_i^{(l)}}$ is the masked feature map. Mask Attention hones in on the region where the nut is located by a masking strategy, effectively filtering out noise from the complex background and greatly improving the detection of nuts in the presence of contamination, occlusion, etc.

The masked feature map $\widehat{S_i^{(l)}}$ is fed into the multi-head self-attention mechanism for further processing.

3.3.4. Initialization of Embedded Square-Nut Template Matching Query

To efficiently detect nuts on transformer covers, particularly when encountering various nut types, the Query is initialized with an embedded square-edge nut template match, which ensures that Query accurately captures the geometric features of the nut and adapts to variations in the size and shape of the nut.

(1) Predefined Orthogonal Nut Templates: Templates for positive N-sides define the geometry and dimensions of the nut, allowing for the flexible adaptation to various nut types. The vertices of the template can be calculated using the following formula:

$$(x_i, y_i) = \left(x_c + l \cdot \cos(\frac{2\pi i}{N}), y_c + l \cdot \sin(\frac{2\pi i}{N})\right), \ i = 1, 2, \ldots, N \tag{12}$$

where (x_i, y_i) is the center coordinates of the nut formwork, l is the side length of the template defining the size of the nut, and N is the number of sides of the square polygon, allowing the model to adapt to various nut designs [34].

(2) Matching Templates and Candidate Boxes: After generating the candidate box, each Query is initialized using the embedded nut template. Given a detected nut region represented by the candidate box $B_i = (x_i, y_i, w_i, h_i)$, the initialization process of the Query is as follows:

Adjust the side length of the template by the size of the candidate box l_{match} that makes the template fit the actual size of the nut:

$$l_{\text{match}} = \frac{w_i + h_i}{2}. \tag{13}$$

Generate matched nut template vertices:

$$T^N_{\text{match}} = \left\{ x_i + l_{\text{match}} \cdot \cos(\frac{2\pi j}{N}), y_i + l_{\text{match}} \cdot \sin(\frac{2\pi j}{N}) \right\}_{j=1}^{N}. \tag{14}$$

This formula matches the center coordinates of the candidate box to the vertices of the positive N-side template, thus providing a geometric basis for the subsequent Query [35,36].

(3) Geometry initialization of Query: The matched positive N-sided nut templates are used as the initial Query for subsequent target detection tasks. The geometry of each Query after initialization is as follows:

$$Q_i^{\text{init}} = T^N_{\text{match}}. \tag{15}$$

This Query contains the geometric information of the nut, serving as an effective input for the subsequent multi-head self-attention mechanism.

3.3.5. Multi-Head Self-Attention Mechanism

(1) Generate Query, Key, and Value vectors: First, the feature map $\widehat{S_i^{(l)}}$ is mapped into the Query vector $Q_i^{(l)}$, key vector $K_i^{(l)}$, and value vector $V_i^{(l)}$ through linear transformations using the learnable weight matrices $W_Q^{(l)}$, $W_K^{(l)}$, and $W_V^{(l)}$, respectively.

$$Q_i^{(l)} = W_Q^{(l)} Q_i^{\text{init}} + W_Q^{(l)} \widehat{S_i^{(l)}},\ K_i^{(l)} = W_K^{(l)} \widehat{S_i^{(l)}},\ V_i^{(l)} = W_V^{(l)} \widehat{S_i^{(l)}}. \tag{16}$$

(2) Compute the Attention Scores: Attention scores are calculated using the Query vector $Q_i^{(l)}$ and key vector $K_i^{(l)}$. These attention scores are applied to the value vector $V_i^{(l)}$ after normalization through the Softmax function.

$$\text{Attention}(Q_i^{(l)}, K_i^{(l)}, V_i^{(l)}) = \text{Softmax}(\frac{Q_i^{(l)} (K_i^{(l)})^T}{\sqrt{d_k}}) V_i^{(l)} \tag{17}$$

where d_k is the dimension of the Query and Key vectors to scale the attention score.

(3) Multi-head Attention Fusion: The multi-head self-attention mechanism concatenates the results and generates the final feature representation $Z_i^{(l)}$ using a linear transformation:

$$Z_i^{(l)} = W_O^{(l)} \text{Concat}(\text{Attention}_1^{(l)}, \text{Attention}_2^{(l)}, \ldots, \text{Attention}_h^{(l)}) \tag{18}$$

where $W_O^{(l)}$ is the linear transformation matrix of the output and h is the number of attention heads.

(4) Residual Concatenation and Normalization: To preserve the information of input features, the input feature maps $S_i^{(l)}$ are summed with the multi-head attention output $Z_i^{(l)}$ using residual concatenation, followed by normalization by the LayerNorm layer.

$$\widetilde{Z_i^{(l)}} = \text{LayerNorm}(Z_i^{(l)} + S_i^{(l)}) \tag{19}$$

where $\widetilde{Z_i^{(l)}}$ is the normalized feature map.

(5) Feed-forward Network (FFN): The output of each layer $\widetilde{Z_i^{(l)}}$ is further processed by FFN, which consists of two linear layers and a ReLU activation function.

$$\mathrm{FFN}(\widetilde{Z_i^{(l)}}) = W_2^{(l)}\mathrm{ReLU}(W_1^{(l)}\widetilde{Z_i^{(l)}}) \tag{20}$$

where $W_1^{(l)}$ and $W_2^{(l)}$ is the linear transformation matrices in FFN.

(6) Calculation of Bounding Box: After processing through the Mask Transformer, the output includes the center coordinates (x, y), width and height (w, h), and category confidence p of each prediction frame. The specific calculations are as follows:

$$\begin{aligned} &\hat{x} = \sigma(\mathrm{output}_x), \quad \hat{y} = \sigma(\mathrm{output}_y), \\ &\hat{w} = \exp(\mathrm{output}_w) \times w_a, \quad \hat{h} = \exp(\mathrm{output}_h) \times h_a, \\ &p = \sigma(\mathrm{output}_p) \end{aligned} \tag{21}$$

where σ is the sigmoid function, output_x, output_y, output_w, output_h, output_p are the outputs of the network and (w_a, h_a) are the width and height of the anchor frame.

(7) Output: The final detection result contains the location and category confidence of the nut.

$$\mathrm{output} = \{(x, y, w, h, p)\} \tag{22}$$

where (x, y) is the center coordinate of the nut. w and h are the width and height of the nut. p is the category confidence.

After the target detection model outputs the 2D detection frame along with the center point, the coordinates are transformed into the world coordinate system using the camera's intrinsic and extrinsic parameters [37]. During the transformer disassembly process, a camera is mounted on top to capture real-time images of the transformer cover. The improved YOLOv8 model is employed to localize the screw positions, outputting their coordinate positions based on the camera's intrinsic and extrinsic references. These coordinates are then provided to the screwing robotic arm for the disassembly operation. The diagram of the target detection effect is shown in Figure 7.

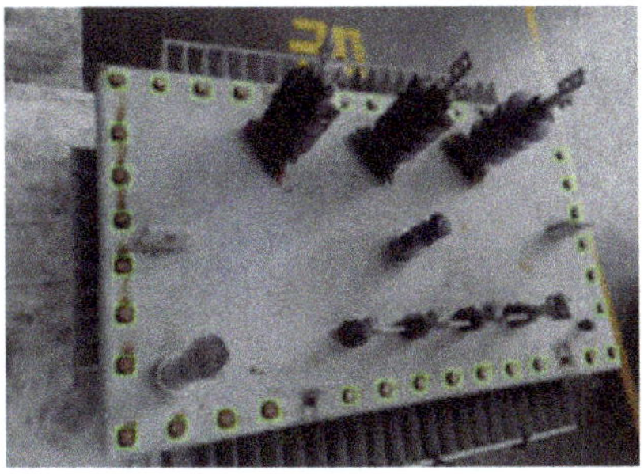

Figure 7. Diagram of the target detection effect.

3.4. Segmentation and Disassembly of Welded Covers

3.4.1. Semantic Segmentation of Welded-Type Cover Plates

The visible light image captured by the camera is input into the cover recognition segmentation network, where the cover and each of its components are finely segmented using the improved Short-Term Dense Concatenation (STDC) network. To better adapt to the structural characteristics of the transformer cover plate and enhance the network's perception of spatial location and geometry, this paper introduces a geometric feature assistant module and position coding, leveraging the spatial distribution characteristics of the transformer cover plate components. This approach optimizes the segmentation performance of the STDC network for various components.

(1) Feature Extraction: The input image I_{input} is fed into the STDC network for feature extraction, which gathers multi-scale features through multiple convolutional layers and STDC modules. Based on the traditional feature extraction, this paper introduces a geometric feature assist module, specifically designed for segmenting complex components on the surface of the transformer cover, such as screws, bushings, and release valves.
The geometric feature assist module first detects geometric structures (e.g., circles, lines, edges) in the image and generates a geometric feature map F_{geo}. These geometric features are fused with the multi-scale features F_{STDC} extracted through the STDC module to produce an enhanced feature map F_{enhanced}.

$$F_{\text{geo}} = \text{Geo\_Feature}(I_{\text{input}}) \tag{23}$$

$$F_{\text{enhanced}} = F_{\text{STDC}} + \alpha \cdot F_{\text{geo}} \tag{24}$$

where α is the coefficient of the geometric feature map [24].

(2) Multi-scale Feature Fusion: To improve the segmentation of various components on the cover, particularly screws and sleeves with spatially fixed locations, the enhanced STDC network employs a multi-scale feature fusion strategy combined with a position coding mechanism to boost its spatial sensing capability.
The position encoding module incorporates the spatial position information of each pixel $\text{Pos}(x, y)$ into the feature map. The feature maps at different scales F_s are combined with the corresponding position encoding for feature fusion, resulting in a higher-resolution fused feature map F_{fusion}.

$$F_{\text{fusion}} = \sum_{s=1}^{S} w_s \cdot (F_s + \text{Pos}(x, y)) \tag{25}$$

where F_s is the input feature map of the s-th scale, w_s is the corresponding weight, S is the number of scales, and $\text{Pos}(x, y)$ is the position encoding of the pixel [25].

(3) Sampling on the Feature Map: The extracted enhanced multi-scale features are up-sampled by a full convolutional network (FCN) to produce the segmentation result image. This up-sampling process employs the inverse convolution operation and integrates both geometric features and position encoding to ensure accurate segmentation results, particularly in edge regions.

$$M = \text{Deconv}(F_{\text{fusion}}) \tag{26}$$

where M is the segmentation result image [25]. The cover segmentation result is shown in Figure 8.

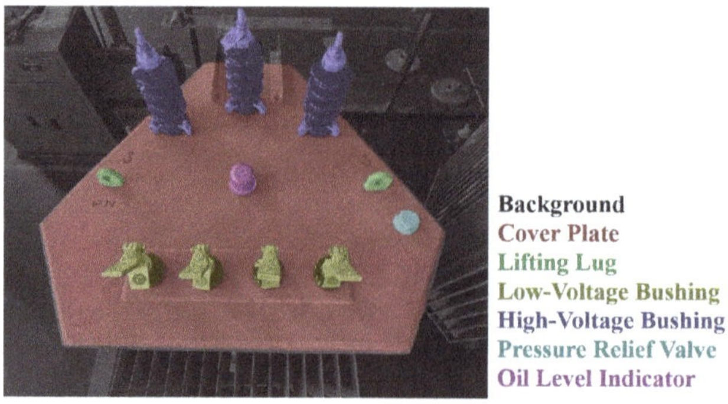

Figure 8. Result of the transformer cover segmentation.

3.4.2. Automated Cutting Line Generation for Welded-Type Cover Plates

To achieve the effective separation of the transformer cover from the housing, a graphic-based processing method is proposed. This approach aims to accurately extract edges and generate safe, reliable cut lines by considering the geometric features of the transformer cover (e.g., bolt holes, piping interfaces) and the contamination present in the industrial environment (e.g., oil stains, light reflections). Additionally, this method incorporates mask expansion for each component to ensure that the cut line remains at a safe distance from the edge of the transformer cover, preventing cuts into other components.

(1) Semantic Segmentation of Images: First, the input image of the transformer cover I_{input} is processed by a semantic segmentation model to generate a mask M_{mask} that identifies the location of key components such as bolt holes and pipe connections.

$$M_{\text{mask}} = \text{SemanticSegmentation}(I_{\text{input}}) \tag{27}$$

where M_{mask} is the binary image containing each component area.

(2) Surface Part Mask Expansion Treatment: To maintain a safe distance for cutting, the mask is expanded using morphological operations, resulting in an inflated mask M_{dilated}.

$$M_{\text{dilated}} = \text{Dilation}(M_{\text{mask}}, k_i) \tag{28}$$

where k_i is the size of the dilation kernel. The expansion treatment ensures that the cut line remains clear of the actual boundaries of the part, avoiding cuts into critical components [28].

(3) Canny Edge Detection: Canny edge detection is performed on the inflated mask M_{dilated} to extract the initial edges of the transformer cover E_{initial}:

$$E_{\text{initial}} = \text{Canny}(M_{\text{dilated}}) \tag{29}$$

where E_{initial} denotes the edge information extracted by the Canny operator, including the edges of each component and the outer contour of the transformer cover plate [28].

(4) Generation of Closed-loop Contours: Discontinuous edges are connected by a shortest path algorithm and a minimum spanning tree algorithm to create a complete closed-loop profile E_{closed}.

$$E_{\text{closed}} = \text{Close}(E_{\text{initial}}) \tag{30}$$

where the closed-loop operation connects disconnected edges, ensuring that the generated edges form complete closed contours, suitable for subsequent cut line generation [30].

(5) Selection of Suitable Contours and Smoothing: A closed-loop profile matching the transformer cover is selected and smoothed to create the optimized profile E_{smooth}:

$$E_{\text{smooth}} = \text{Smooth}(E_{\text{closed}}). \tag{31}$$

Smoothing is accomplished by spline interpolation, which reduces noise and irregularities in the edges, ensuring the continuity and smoothness of the cut line in practical applications [29].

4. Algorithm for Disassembly of Internal Transformer Components

4.1. Semantic Segmentation of Multimodal Transformer Components

In the automated disassembly of transformers, the semantic segmentation of internal components is crucial for ensuring accurate disassembly. The internal structure of a transformer is complex, containing various components such as screws, copper plates, winding studs, and silicon steel sheets, each differing significantly in physical location and geometry. Therefore, achieving efficient multimodal component recognition and segmentation is a key objective for the automated system.

To address this challenge, this paper proposes a semantic segmentation scheme for multimodal components based on the ODIN model. The ODIN model utilizes a design centered on cross-view feature fusion, enabling the effective processing of multi-view data through alternating 2D in-view fusion and 3D cross-view feature fusion [38]. In the transformer disassembly scenario, the system captures internal images of the transformer using a multi-view RGB-D camera, combining these data with depth information to extract and fuse 2D and 3D features at different scales. This model maintains high accuracy in complex component recognition tasks, particularly when multi-view information is incomplete or data are missing, as ODIN's feature fusion technique significantly enhances component recognition accuracy.

The ODIN model is employed for 2D and 3D semantic segmentation, incorporating cross-view feature fusion techniques. Transformer data are captured using RGB-D cameras and IMUs. The model leverages multi-scale feature fusion, which enhances the detection of targets of different sizes and improves generalization performance across multiple scenes. During transformer disassembly, the ODIN model enables accurate 2D and 3D instance segmentation and the identification of components such as screw support columns that need to be cut, ensuring high-precision target localization and segmentation to support subsequent disassembly operations.

The ODIN model structure is shown in Figure 9, and its functionality is achieved through the following key components:

(1) Alternative 2D and 3D Information Fusion: Two-dimensional feature fusion occurs within each image view, which is subsequently projected into 3D space for cross-view feature fusion. Finally, the fused 3D features are reprojected back to the 2D plane. The 2D feature fusion is conducted using pixel coordinates, while 3D feature fusion utilizes spatial coordinates for positional encoding to ensure information consistency.

(2) Multi-scale Feature Fusion: ODIN conducts feature fusion at different scales to enhance the detection of targets of various sizes. This is accomplished by utilizing multi-scale feature maps during both 2D and 3D feature fusion, ensuring that targets of different sizes are effectively detected and segmented.

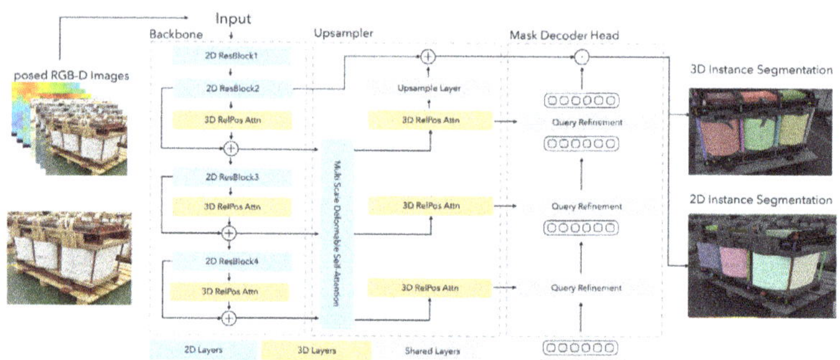

Figure 9. The process of the ODIN modeling transformer.

In the 2D feature extraction process, multi-scale feature maps are extracted using Swin Transformer [39]. These feature maps are fused at multiple scales:

$$F_{\text{fused}} = \sum_{s=1}^{S} w_s \cdot F_s \qquad (32)$$

where F_s represents the feature map of the s-th scale, w_s denotes the corresponding weight, and S is the number of scales.

In the 3D feature fusion process, the KNN algorithm is used to select neighboring points in 3D space, with feature fusion achieved through relative position encoding.

$$\text{Attention}(Q, K, V) = \text{Softmax}(\frac{QK^T}{\sqrt{d_k}} + \text{PE}_{3D})V \tag{33}$$

where Q, K, V are the Query, key, and value vector, respectively. PE_{3D} is the position encoding of the 3D space.

(3) Target Detection and Feature Classification: Target detection using the ODIN model predicts the category and location of the component by the following equation.

$$Y = \sigma(W \cdot F_{\text{fusion}} + b) \tag{34}$$

where W and b are the weight and bias of the model, respectively, and F_{fusion} is the fused feature map.

During the transformer disassembly process, the ODIN model alternately fuses 2D and 3D features from image data acquired by multi-view RGB-D cameras. When the input is a single RGB image, the model skips the 3D fusion layer, while when the input is an RGB-D sequence, the model extracts 2D features within each view before projecting them into 3D space and combining feature information from different views for cross-view fusion, ensuring a comprehensive perception of the transformer's internal structure. This allows ODIN to accurately identify screws, support columns, and other components that need to be cut, reducing the risk of misuse and improving disassembly efficiency and safety. The ODIN model employs multimodal feature fusion and a pre-trained 2D backbone network to maintain high-performance recognition and segmentation capabilities in complex scenarios, fully meeting disassembly requirements. The process of segmentation and identification of internal components of the transformer is shown in Figure 10.

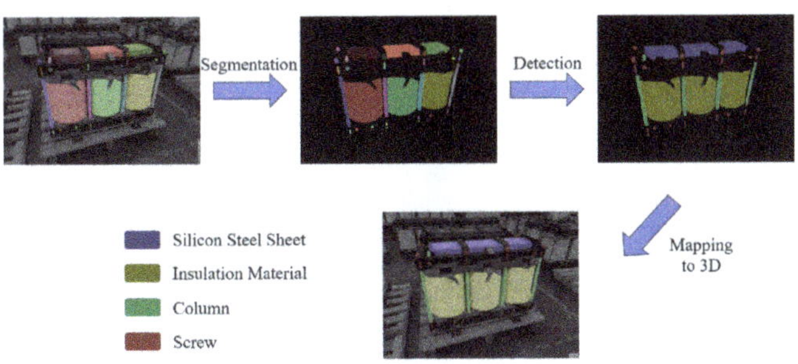

Figure 10. The process of segmentation and identification of internal components of the transformer.

4.2. Technical Route for Disassembly of Internal Components

The overall process of internal component disassembly involves acquiring the 3D model and depth information of the transformer using a multi-view RGB-D camera. This is followed by extracting 2D image features and mapping them to 3D space using a CNN, then combining the KNN algorithm and positional coding to perform 3D feature fusion. The system accurately recognizes the locations of the components to be cut (e.g., screws, copper plates, studs, silicon steel sheets) through target detection techniques, and subsequently executes the cutting operation based on the generated cutting path.

The steps are as follows:

(1) Cutting the cover plate first: Separate the cover plate from the inside of the transformer by recognizing and cutting the screws and copper plates beneath it.

(2) Cutting the studs: Cut the studs around the windings to separate the cleat from the windings.

(3) Final treatment of the silicon steel sheet: Separate the silicon steel sheet from the winding by cutting or lifting it.

In the specific implementation of the program for disassembling the internal components of the transformer, each step follows the same technical approach: first, visual sensors are employed to collect internal data from the transformer. Next, neural network methods are used for feature extraction and fusion. The target detection technique is then applied to identify the components of the transformer that need disassembly at each step. Finally, an optimization method based on the identified components generates the cutting path plan, allowing the cutting machine to follow this path and complete the overall disassembly process of the transformer.

4.3. Multimodal Data Acquisition for Transformer Internal Components

Through the RGB-D cameras installed on the top and four sides of the transformer, multi-view images and depth information are acquired, capturing the 3D data of components such as screws and covers. The top camera, positioned directly above the transformer, captures a top view and obtains depth information for the screws and covers located on the upper surface. Meanwhile, RGB-D cameras installed on each of the four sides provide omni-directional data acquisition from various angles, ensuring comprehensive information about the transformer. This setup lays a solid foundation for subsequent operations, including semantic segmentation and other analyses.

An efficient image acquisition strategy is developed based on the camera mounting method. The RGB-D camera, installed as described, can capture multi-view images from both above and the sides of the transformer. For each image, the acquired RGB image is denoted as $I(x,y)$ and the depth map as $D(x,y)$, where x and y represent the pixel coordinates of the image.

Considering the optical properties of the camera, accurate and usable 3D data of transformer components such as screws and covers can only be obtained if the internal and external parameters of the camera are accurately determined. The internal reference matrix of the camera K defines the relationship between pixel coordinates and the camera coordinate system, while the external reference matrix $[R \mid T]$ describes the transformation from the camera coordinate system to the world coordinate system, where R is the rotation matrix and T is the translation vector. However, the optical characteristics of the camera lens can cause geometric distortion in images, necessitating the use of calibration methods for camera distortion correction to obtain complete internal and external parameters.

The internal reference matrix K and distortion parameters of the camera k_1, k_2, k_3, p_1, p_2 were obtained using the Zhang Zhengyou calibration method [37]:

$$\begin{aligned} K &= \begin{pmatrix} f_x & 0 & c_x \\ 0 & f_y & c_y \\ 0 & 0 & 1 \end{pmatrix} \\ x_{\text{corrected}} &= x(1 + k_1 r^2 + k_2 r^4 + k_3 r^6) + x + 2p_1 xy + p_2(r^2 + 2x^2) \\ y_{\text{corrected}} &= y(1 + k_1 r^2 + k_2 r^4 + k_3 r^6) + y + 2p_2 xy + p_1(r^2 + 2y^2) \end{aligned} \tag{35}$$

For each calibration image, the rotation matrix R and translation vector T of the camera relative to the calibration plate are calculated to determine the camera's relative position and orientation. The coordinate system transformation method is employed to generate the external reference matrix by combining the rotation matrix R and the translation vector T into the transformation relation matrix $[R \mid T]$. This matrix describes the transformation from the camera coordinate system to the world coordinate system.

$$RT = \begin{pmatrix} R & T \\ 0 & 1 \end{pmatrix} \tag{36}$$

After that, the depth map projection method is utilized to project the pixel coordinates into the 3D space using the depth map $D(x, y)$ along with the camera parameters K and $[R \mid T]$, yielding the 3D coordinates P_{3D}:

$$P_{3D} = K^{-1} \cdot [R \mid T] \cdot \begin{bmatrix} x \\ y \\ D(x, y) \\ 1 \end{bmatrix} \tag{37}$$

where $P_{3D} = [X, Y, Z]^T$ is the point in 3D space.

4.4. Feature Extraction and Classification

In the cutting process of transformers, feature extraction, fusion, and target detection techniques are crucial for achieving high-precision automated cutting. Firstly, for each transformer component image, multi-scale feature extraction is performed on the RGB image I_{xy} using a CNN to generate feature maps F_s^{xy} at different scales, represented as

$$F_s^{xy} = \text{CNN}_s(I_{xy}) \tag{38}$$

This multi-scale feature extraction method can effectively capture the surface information of the component, providing a foundation for subsequent 3D feature mapping. After completing the 2D feature extraction, the 2D features are projected into the 3D space using the depth map D_{xy} along with the internal and external parameter matrices K and RT sum of the camera. The coordinate points in the 3D space are obtained as follows:

$$P_{3D} = K^{-1} \cdot (RT)^{-1} \cdot D_{xy} \tag{39}$$

With this step, the features are converted from a 2D plane to a 3D point cloud, ensuring an accurate correspondence with the physical space.

To enhance the spatial consistency of the 3D features, a KNN algorithm is employed to identify the neighboring points of each 3D point. The features are then fused by combining the positional encoding and attention mechanisms.

$$F_{3D}^{\text{fused}}(P_{3D}) = \sum_{P_j \in N(P_{3D})} \text{Attn}(F_{3D}(P_{3D}), F_{3D}(P_j), PE(P_{3D}, P_j)) \tag{40}$$

The method can effectively integrate spatial information and is particularly suitable for fusing features of complex transformer structures, such as the contact surface of windings and silicon steel sheets.

After feature fusion, the ODIN deep learning model is leveraged to perform target detection on the fused 3D features, identifying the key components of the transformer. For the detection of screws, the model predicts them using the following equation:

$$Y_{\text{screw}} = \sigma(W \cdot F_{3D}^{\text{fused}}(P_{3D}) + b) \tag{41}$$

This process outputs the target location and category, providing accurate coordinate information for subsequent cutting path planning.

Although the basic process of feature extraction and target detection is consistent, the characteristics of different transformer parts lead to varying complexities in the detection methods. For simpler parts like screws and copper plates, feature extraction mainly relies on surface information. In contrast, for windings and studs, the structural complexity necessitates higher accuracy to capture intricate details. The contact surface between the silicon steel sheet and the winding requires consideration of its spatial contact characteristics, relying on positional encoding in 3D feature fusion to ensure accurate detection.

Therefore, in the transformer cutting task, the accurate identification of different components is achieved by effectively combining 2D and 3D information along with utilizing feature extraction and target detection techniques. The structural differences among components necessitate the application of varied feature extraction and detection strategies, ultimately enabling efficient automated cutting.

5. Transformer Copper Winding Stripping Methods

5.1. Constant-Tension Intelligent Unwinding System

A constant-tension intelligent unwinding system is a high-precision control system designed to manage the wire-unwinding process, and it is primarily used in the production and processing of cables, fiber optic cables, and similar materials. Its design goal is to prevent wire stretching, deformation, or breakage by accurately controlling the unwinding tension, thereby ensuring product quality and production efficiency. The system mainly comprises servo motors and drives, tension sensors, and intelligent controllers. The system structure is shown in Figure 11.

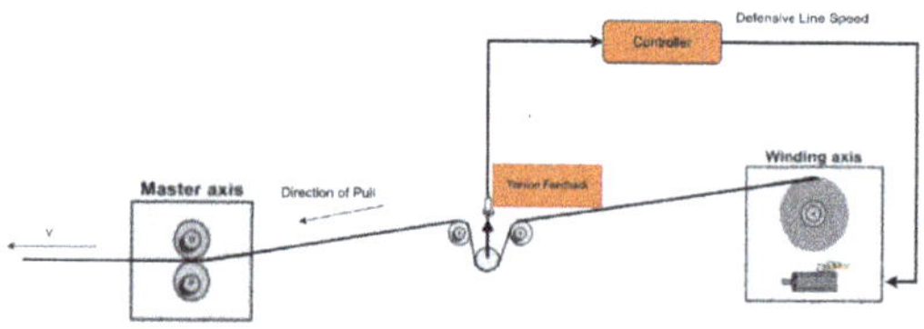

Figure 11. Constant-tension intelligent unwinding system structure.

A constant-tension intelligent unwinding system achieves continuous and constant tension release of the wire from the bobbin through the collaboration of various hardware components, ensuring stability and reliability during the unwinding process. The system primarily consists of the following parts:

(1) Driven payoff reel: The primary function of the follower pulley is to release the wire by making contact with it. The follower pulley rotates with the master pulley, allowing the wire to be released from the bobbin in a slow and even manner.
(2) Active payoff reel: The primary function of the active wheel is to drive the rotation of the driven payoff wheel, thereby controlling the release speed and tension of the wire. It is typically powered by a motor that adjusts its speed based on feedback from the tension signal, ensuring constant tension during the payoff process.
(3) Servo motor: The servomotor enables precise speed control of the active payoff wheel based on instructions from the tension controller. By finely adjusting the rotational speed of the active payoff wheel, it effectively controls the wire's release speed, which is essential for maintaining constant wire tension.
(4) Rollers: The rollers guide the wire's path and ensure a smooth release from the bobbin. Typically arranged between the driven and active payoff pulleys, they help maintain a steady course for the wire.
(5) Tension sensors: The primary function of the tension sensors is to detect the real-time tension of the wire and provide feedback signals to the tension controller. Common types include pressure and load sensors, which accurately measure the wire's tension.
(6) Controllers: The controller is a crucial component of the system, responsible for adjusting the rotational speed of the active payoff wheel based on feedback from the tension sensor to maintain constant wire tension. Tension controllers typically use PID algorithms or other neural network algorithms to quickly and accurately adjust the tension.

The constant tension control algorithm is based on PID tension control, represented by the following equation:

$$u_{\text{PID}}(t) = K_p e(t) + K_i \int_0^t e(t)dt + K_d \frac{de(t)}{dt} \quad (42)$$

where $e(t)$ is the error signal and K_p, K_i, K_d are the proportional, integral, and derivative coefficients, respectively. By using the set tension value, the tension error calculated from the tension sensor feedback enables tension stabilization control through PID. However, since wires of varying thicknesses and specifications require different settings, a single PID configuration may not provide stable control. Therefore, tension compensation is introduced as a feedforward quantity to enhance performance.

5.2. Design of Adaptive Fuzzy Neural Networks

The core idea of adaptive fuzzy neural networks is to map input data into an implicit space through fuzzification, allowing for training and prediction within that space. These networks offer significant advantages over traditional neural networks when handling fuzzy and uncertain data.

The design of the adaptive fuzzy neural network involves three key components: data collection, network construction, and network training. The application of the adaptive neural network in the constant tension control system will be described in detail for each of these parts below.

(1) Collection of Tension Data: High-precision tension sensors collect real-time wire tension data, including the tension magnitude, change trends, and other time series information. These collected data are then normalized for subsequent neural network training. Additionally, environmental state data—such as wire diameter and friction coefficient of the insulation layer—are gathered as auxiliary inputs for the neural network.

(2) Adaptive Neural Networks Construction: The adaptive neural network comprises several layers specifically designed for the constant-tension system. The input layer receives and normalizes various external input signals. The fuzzification layer applies a Gaussian affiliation function to fuzzify these inputs. The rule layer combines the fuzzy input variables using predefined fuzzy rules. The inference layer computes the final fuzzy output variables through fuzzy inference. The defuzzification layer converts these fuzzy outputs into specific numerical values. The final output layer processes these numerical outputs into control commands, which also serve as feedback signals to regulate the active payoff system's operation. The defuzzification layer and the output layer are represented in Equation (43).

$$u_{ij}(t) = \exp\left[-\frac{(a_i(t) - c_{ij}(t))^2}{2\sigma_{ij}^2(t)}\right], \quad j = 1, 2, \ldots, m \tag{43}$$

where u_{ij} is the output of j-th affiliation function corresponding to the i-th input at time t. $c_{ij}(t)$ and $\sigma_{ij}(t)$ are the center and width of the j-th affiliation function, respectively.

$$\phi_{ij}(t) = f_i \prod_{i=1}^{n} u_{ij}(t), \quad j = 1, 2, \ldots, m \tag{44}$$

$$f_i = \frac{1}{1 + \exp(-h_i)} \tag{45}$$

$$h_i = \phi_j(t-1)\lambda_j(t) \tag{46}$$

where $\phi_j(t)$ is the output of the j-th rule layer at time t, and $\phi_j(t-1)$ denotes the output at the previous moment. f_i represents the sigmoid function, h_i is the internal variable, and $\lambda_j(t)$ refers to the feedback weights for recursive links.

$$\bar{\phi}_j(t) = \frac{\phi_j(t)}{\sum_{j=1}^{m} \phi_j(t)} \tag{47}$$

$$y(t) = \sum_{j=1}^{m} \omega_j(t) \cdot \bar{\phi}_j(t) \tag{48}$$

where $y(t)$ is the network output, $\omega_j(t)$ represents the output weights of the network, and $\phi_j(t)$ is the output of the defuzzification layer.

To enhance the convergence of the network, this paper adjusts the parameters of the recursive fuzzy neural network using a gradient descent algorithm with an adaptive learning rate.

$$\eta = \eta_{\max} - d(\eta_{\max} - \eta_{\min})/D \tag{49}$$

where $\eta_{\max}$ and $\eta_{\min}$ are the maximum and minimum learning rates, respectively, d is the current iteration step, and D is the total number of iteration steps. In the initial stage, the parameters are adjusted significantly to enable rapid optimization, saving time. As the number of iteration steps increases, the learning rate is gradually reduced to ensure the network's stability.

5.3. Wire Intelligent Disconnection Technology

The wire removal system employs an ultrasonic cutter head to strip the outer insulation layer of the wire in a constant-tension payoff system. By designing a control algorithm that leverages pressure sensors and vision sensors, the depth of the insulation cut is regulated to ensure complete insulation removal, thereby safeguarding the cutter head. The system is illustrated in Figure 12.

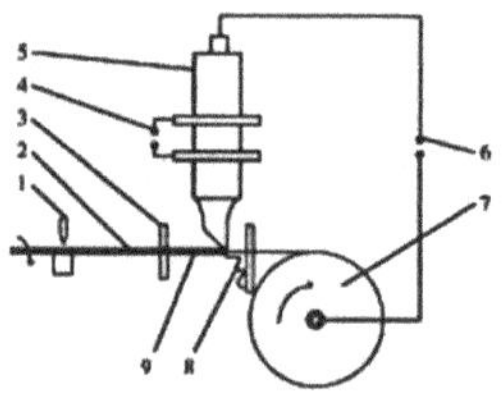

1.Preliminary straightening mechanism 2.Unstripped wire 3.Straightening plate
4.Pressure sensor 5.Ultrasonic transducer and cutting tool 6.Control signal access
7.Wire drawing wheel 8.Cut wire sheath 9.Wire metal core

Figure 12. Intelligent wire removal system.

5.4. RCF-Based Edge Detection Technique

By fusing feature maps from various scales, the RCF model effectively captures different levels of detail, excelling particularly in edge detection tasks. We utilize RCF as a detection network for measuring the thickness of the wire insulation layer, enabling two key functions: first, it detects the cutter head's feed depth (i.e., the insulation thickness to be cut) in real time, ensuring the cutter head's feed exceeds this thickness for effective cutting; second, it verifies the quality of the insulation layer peeling, providing feedback signals to the system in case of subpar quality.

The network is depicted in Figure 13. It comprises a backbone, an RCF module, and an edge thickness regression prediction head, utilizing ResNet-50 as the backbone network. The RCF module includes a series of convolutional layers and activation functions for fusing edge features and generating edge response maps. Meanwhile, the edge thickness regression prediction head predicts both the classification categories of wire-stripping results and the thickness of the wire insulation layer.

The loss function comprises classification loss and thickness regression loss. The classification loss uses cross-entropy loss to minimize the distance between the predicted and actual labels of the wire-cutting results. In contrast, the thickness regression loss employs squared loss to minimize the difference between the predicted and labeled thickness values.

In training the RCF network, rather than classifying samples into positive and negative, the network averages the labeling results from multiple labelers to obtain a final edge probability value between 0 and 1. A value of 0 indicates pixels not labeled by any labeler, while a value of 1 signifies that all labelers marked those pixels.

We define a parameter η; when the averaged result exceeds η, it is classified as a positive sample, while a result of 0 indicates a negative sample. Any other pixel results are ignored. The loss for each pixel is then calculated based on these classifications.

$$l(X_i; W) = \begin{cases} \alpha \cdot \log(1 - P(X_i; W)) & \text{if} \quad Y_i = 1 \\ 0 & \text{if} \quad 0 < Y_i \leq \eta \\ \beta \cdot \log(P(X_i; W)) & \text{if} \quad otherwise \end{cases} \tag{50}$$

where

$$\alpha = \lambda \cdot \frac{|Y^+|}{|Y^+| + |Y^-|} \tag{51}$$

$$\beta = \frac{|Y^-|}{|Y^+| + |Y^-|} \tag{52}$$

The total loss is the sum of the loss of all pixels:

$$L(W) = \sum_{i=1}^{|I|} (\sum_{k=1}^{K} l(X_i^{(k)}; W) + l(X_i^{(\text{fuse})}; W)) \tag{53}$$

By incorporating scale information, the trained RCF network can accurately determine in real time if the cutting depth exceeds the insulation layer thickness. Additionally, by adjusting the threshold value, the network can modify its tolerance for the completeness of the wire insulation cut, enabling the autonomous assessment of whether the insulation has been fully removed.

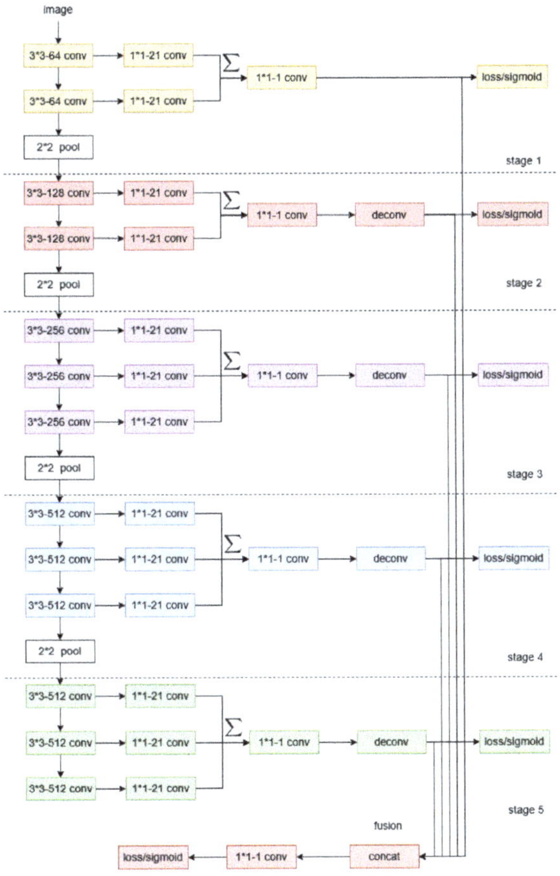

Figure 13. Architecture of the RCF network.

6. Transformer Disassembly Results

6.1. Experimental Results of Fuel Tank Cover Disassembly

We are establishing a new intelligent disassembly factory for electrical equipment, and here we provide a photo of the transformer disassembly area, as shown in Figure 14.

Figure 14. Transformer disassembly area in the new established disassembly factory.

The experiments utilized an RGB-D camera for data acquisition, employing multi-modal fusion to integrate 2D images and 3D point cloud data for cover plate identification and processing. A disassembly robot, equipped with a torque-adjustable robotic arm and a laser cutter, automated the disassembly of various covers. The experimental setup simulated an industrial environment, featuring transformer covers of different sizes and conditions, with 50 samples each of screw-fastened and soldered covers. Each sample underwent surface treatment (such as rust or oil) or was sourced from actual end-of-life transformers to accurately replicate real industrial conditions.

To fully assess the disassembly performance of the fuel tank cover, the following evaluation metrics were employed in the experiments:

(1) Recognition accuracy: Measures the system's ability to classify screw-fastened and welded covers accurately.
(2) Disassembly time: Total time taken from identification to the completion of disassembly.
(3) Success rate: The rate of successful disassembly without causing damage.
(4) Safety assessment: Evaluates the impact on transformer core components during the disassembly process.

The results are illustrated in Table 1.

Table 1. Experimental results of disassembling the fuel tank cover.

Metric	Recognition Accuracy	Disassembly Time	Success Rate	Security Assessment
Screw-fastened cover	99%	186.3 s	98%	Undamaged
Welded cover	99%	265.4 s	96%	Undamaged

The recognition accuracy reached 99% for both screw-fastened and welded covers, demonstrating that the combination of RGB-D cameras and multimodal fusion technology effectively mitigates the adverse effects of contamination, such as oil and rust, on recognition performance. By leveraging both the texture information from 2D images and the depth data from 3D point clouds, the system maintains high accuracy even in complex industrial environments.

The average disassembly time for screw-fastened covers was 186.3 s, compared to 265.4 s for welded covers. The increased time for welded covers stems from the complexity of cutting through welded joints, necessitating a more intricate process. While screw-fastened covers allow for straightforward torque control with a robotic arm, welded covers involve laser cutting, edge recognition, and detailed cutting path planning, making the operation more time-consuming.

The success rates for disassembling screw-fastened and welded covers were 98% and 96%, respectively. The higher success rate for screw-fastened covers was due to precise torque control of the robotic arm, minimizing damage during disassembly. In contrast, the slightly lower success rate for welded covers was linked to issues like melt adhesion from localized melting of the joints. Enhancing laser cutting precision and optimizing laser power could further improve outcomes. In safety assessments, no damage occurred to the transformer core during the disassembly of either cover type, highlighting effective safety measures and the use of an expansion mask to protect critical components. Overall, the system demonstrated strong performance in recognition accuracy, efficiency, safety, and success rate, confirming the feasibility of the proposed approach.

6.2. Experimental Results of Internal Component Disassembly

To validate the effectiveness of the automated disassembly system for transformer internal components, 50 standardized experiments were conducted to evaluate system performance in disassembly time, success rate, and safety. The experiments took place in a controlled laboratory environment, with the transformer designated for disassembly shown in Figure 15.

Figure 15. Transformer interior before disassembly.

A multi-view RGB-D camera was employed to capture 2D images and 3D point cloud data of the transformer interior, ensuring comprehensive coverage of all disassembled parts. The cameras were strategically mounted on the top and four sides of the transformer to effectively acquire data on screws, copper plates, winding studs, and silicon steel sheets.

High-performance computing equipment facilitated data processing, while an automated cutting robot arm performed the disassembly operations. A stable experimental environment was maintained to ensure the accuracy of the cutting process.

To objectively evaluate the system's performance, three key metrics were established: disassembly time, disassembly success rate, and safety assessment. Disassembly time refers to the total duration from system activation to the completion of internal component removal. Disassembly success rate is the proportion of successful disassembly operations relative to the total number of experiments conducted. The safety assessment focuses on detecting any damage to critical transformer components, such as windings and key electronic parts, during the disassembly process.

In the 50 standardized transformer cutting experiments, the system achieved an average disassembly time of 876.6 s, with the fastest recorded at 848.2 s and the slowest at 896.7 s. Out of these operations, 49 were successful, resulting in a disassembly success rate of 98%. The sole failure occurred during silicon steel sheet processing due to a path planning error. Notably, no successful disassembly operation damaged core components, demonstrating effective cutting path planning that mitigated risks to critical parts. The results are visually represented in Figure 16 and summarized in Table 2.

Figure 16. Transformer interior after disassembly.

Table 2. Experimental results of disassembling the transformer interior.

Disassembly Steps	Average Disassembly Time	Disassembly Success Rate	Security Assessment
Cutting cover	290.5 s	100%	Undamaged
Cutting winding studs	305.7 s	98%	Undamaged
Cutting or lifting silicon steel sheets	280.4 s	98%	Undamaged

6.2.1. Visualization of the Disassembly Process

In order to make our experiment appear more comprehensive and to demonstrate the effectiveness of our method, we provide additional disassembly photos, as shown in Figure 17. Figure 17a illustrates the transformer cover and internal component recognition, while Figure 17b shows the process and photos of the dismantling of discarded transformers.

Figure 17. Component recognition and disassembly process. (**a**) Transformer cover and internal component recognition. (**b**) Transformer disassembly process and results.

6.2.2. Analysis of Disassembly Time

The results from the 50 experiments indicate that the system's average disassembly time is 876.6 s, showcasing a significant advantage over traditional methods. This time reduction is largely due to the automated path planning and target detection techniques employed by the system, which prove particularly efficient for handling screws and winding studs. In our experiments, the transformer we used is a 10 KV, 400 KVA oil-immersed transformer. The number of screws is between approximately 150 and 300, the length of the core welds is about 1.5 to 3 m, the length of the oil tank welds is about 5 to 8 m, and the weld length of other components is about 5 to 10 m.

6.2.3. Analysis of Disassembly Success Rate

The system achieved a success rate of 98%, demonstrating its strong adaptability to the complex internal structures of transformers. The sole failure during silicon steel sheet processing highlights the challenges posed by specific transformer designs, suggesting that further optimization of the path planning algorithm could enhance performance in such cases.

6.2.4. Analysis of Safety Assessment

The automated disassembly system has proven effective in safeguarding the core components of the transformer, with no damage reported to the windings or other critical parts during successful operations. This reliability highlights the system's superiority over manual methods, as it minimizes the risk of mishandling and enhances the overall safety during the disassembly process.

The results from the 50 experiments validate the system's effectiveness in disassembly time, success rate, and safety. Its automated path planning and target detection notably enhance disassembly efficiency while protecting core components. Future research should focus on optimizing the path planning algorithm to increase adaptability to complex structures and further improve the success rate of disassembly operations.

7. Conclusions

This paper presents an automated transformer disassembly method leveraging multimodal sensing and cooperative control. By fusing 2D images and 3D point cloud data from a multi-view RGB-D camera, alongside deep learning models and advanced cutting technologies, the system demonstrates high accuracy and efficiency in disassembling transformers. The experimental results highlight the system's impressive disassembly success rate and safety, effectively handling key components like screws, copper plates, winding studs, and silicon steel sheets while preventing damage to critical transformer components.

The experimental results indicate that

- The system achieves an average disassembly time of under 20 min, marking a significant reduction compared to traditional manual methods.
- The disassembly success rate stands at 98%, showcasing the system's adaptability to various complex structures and transformer types.
- Importantly, there was no damage to core components in any successful disassembly experiments, ensuring a safe disassembly process.

The system notably enhances disassembly efficiency and simplifies operations through automated path planning and multimodal feature fusion technology. Its versatility allows it to adapt to various transformer types, presenting promising applications in waste transformer recycling.

Author Contributions: Conceptualization, L.W.; methodology, F.C.; software, Y.H.; validation, L.W.; formal analysis, F.C.; investigation, Z.Z.; resources, Y.H.; data curation, Y.H.; writing—original draft preparation, L.W.; writing—review and editing, Y.H. and K.Z.; visualization, K.Z.; supervision, Y.H. and Z.Z.; project administration, Y.H.; funding acquisition, Z.Z. All authors have read and agreed to the published version of the manuscript.

Funding: This paper is funded by the State Grid Zhejiang Electric Power Science and Technology Project (5211WF240001 Research on Key Technology of Fine Dismantling and Green Full-volume Recovery of Distribution Transformer Based on Artificial Intelligence).

Data Availability Statement: The raw data supporting the conclusions of this article will be made available by the authors on request.

Conflicts of Interest: The authors Li Wang and Feng Chen were employed by the company State Grid Zhejiang Electric Power Co., Ltd. And authors Yujia Hu and Zhiyao Zheng was employed by the company Zhejiang Huadian Equipment Testing and Research Insitute Co. Ltd. The remaining authors declare that the research was conducted in the absence of any commercial or financial relationships that could be construed as a potential conflict of interest

References

1. Santochi, M.; Dini, G.; Failli, F. Disassembly for recycling, maintenance and remanufacturing: State of the art and perspectives. In *Proceedings of the AMST'02 Advanced Manufacturing Systems and Technology: Proceedings of the Sixth International Conference*; Springer: Berlin/Heidelberg, Germany, 2002; pp. 73–89.
2. Han, G.; Ding, G.; Li, C.; Li, S. Case-matched study of pcbs toxiciy effects to women and children case in the areas which disused transformers were dismantled. *J. Hyg. Res.* **2006**, *35*, 791–793.
3. Jia, Z.; Bhatia, A.; Aronson, R.M.; Bourne, D.; Mason, M.T. A Survey of Automated Threaded Fastening. *IEEE Trans. Autom. Sci. Eng.* **2018**, *16*, 298–310. [CrossRef]
4. Rosati, G.; Faccio, M.; Carli, A.; Rossi, A. Fully flexible assembly systems (F-FAS): A new concept in flexible automation. *Assem. Autom.* **2013**, *33*, 8–21. [CrossRef]
5. Cai, H.; Xu, X.; Zhang, Y.; Cong, X.; Lu, X.; Huo, X. Elevated lead levels from e-waste exposure are linked to sensory integration difficulties in preschool children. *Neurotoxicology* **2019**, *71*, 150–158. [CrossRef]
6. Zhang, L.; Sheng, H.; Lei, W. Distribution Transformer Recycling Pathway. *China Electr. Equip. Ind.* **2024**, *6*, 32–35.
7. Zhang, K.; Wen, Q.; Zhang, C.; Cai, R.; Jin, M.; Liu, Y.; Zhang, J.Y.; Liang, Y.; Pang, G.; Song, D.; et al. Self-Supervised Learning for Time Series Analysis: Taxonomy, Progress, and Prospects. *IEEE Trans. Pattern Anal. Mach. Intell.* **2024**, *46*, 6775–6794. [CrossRef]
8. Cai, R.; Gao, W.; Peng, L.; Lu, Z.; Zhang, K.; Liu, Y. Debiased Contrastive Learning With Supervision Guidance for Industrial Fault Detection. *IEEE Trans. Ind. Inform.* **2024**, *20*, 12814–12825. [CrossRef]
9. Cai, R.; Peng, L.; Lu, Z.; Zhang, K.; Liu, Y. DCS: Debiased Contrastive Learning with Weak Supervision for Time Series Classification. In Proceedings of the ICASSP 2024—2024 IEEE International Conference on Acoustics, Speech and Signal Processing (ICASSP), Seoul, Reublic of Korea, 14–19 April 2024; pp. 5625–5629.
10. Kroll, E.; Hanft, T.A. Quantitative evaluation of product disassembly for recycling. *Res. Eng. Des.* **1998**, *10*, 1–14. [CrossRef]
11. Chen, W.; Vongbunyong, S. *Disassembly Automation: Automated Systems with Cognitive Abilities*; Sustainable Production; Springer: Berlin/Heidelberg, Germany, 2015.
12. Jin, L.; Zhang, X.; Fang, Y.; Pham, D.T. Transfer Learning-Assisted Evolutionary Dynamic Optimisation for Dynamic Human-Robot Collaborative Disassembly Line Balancing. *Appl. Sci.* **2022**, *12*, 11008. [CrossRef]
13. Tan, W.J.; Chin, C.M.M.; Garg, A.; Gao, L. A hybrid disassembly framework for disassembly of electric vehicle batteries. *Int. J. Energy Res.* **2021**, *45*, 8073–8082. [CrossRef]
14. Zheran, W.; Jie, Y.; Dongdong, G.; Jianfeng, L. Mechanical Structure Design and Test of Multi Wire Diameter High Voltage Cable Cutting Machine. *J. Sci. Res. Rep.* **2022**, *28*, 1–8. [CrossRef]
15. Yong, Z.; Yugang, Z.; Qian, L.; Ning, L.; Chuanying, Z. Design and Control of Ultrasonic Stripping Device for Waste Wire Based on ARM. In *Modular Machine Tool & Automatic Manufacturing Technique*; Tongfang Knowledge Network (Beijing) Technology Co., Ltd.: Beijing, China, 2020; pp. 147–150. [CrossRef]
16. Tang, X.; Liu, Z.; Yu, P. Detection algorithm for multi-scale and multi-directional bolts. *J. Electron. Meas. Instrum.* **2023**, *37*, 221–231.
17. Shafique, K.; Khawaja, B.A.; Sabir, F.; Qazi, S.; Mustaqim, M. Internet of Things (IoT) for Next-Generation Smart Systems: A Review of Current Challenges, Future Trends and Prospects for Emerging 5G-IoT Scenarios. *IEEE Access* **2020**, *8*, 23022–23040. [CrossRef]
18. Roselli, L.; Carvalho, N.B.; Alimenti, F.; Mezzanotte, P.; Orecchini, G.; Virili, M.; Mariotti, C.; Goncalves, R.; Pinho, P. Smart Surfaces: Large Area Electronics Systems for Internet of Things Enabled by Energy Harvesting. *Proc. IEEE* **2014**, *102*, 1723–1746. [CrossRef]
19. Costanzo, A.; Masotti, D. Energizing 5G: Near- and Far-Field Wireless Energy and Data Trantransfer as an Enabling Technology for the 5G IoT. *IEEE Microw. Mag.* **2017**, *18*, 125–136. [CrossRef]
20. Wu, K.; Kuhlenkoetter, B. Dynamic behavior and path accuracy of an industrial robot with a CNC controller. *Adv. Mech. Eng.* **2022**, *14*, 16878132221082869. [CrossRef]
21. Radanliev, P.; De Roure, D.; Nicolescu, R.; Huth, M.; Santos, O. Artificial Intelligence and the Internet of Things in Industry 4.0. *CCF Trans. Pervasive Comput. Interact.* **2021**, *3*, 329–338. [CrossRef]
22. Liu, H.; Duan, T. Real-Time Multimodal 3D Object Detection with Transformers. *World Electr. Veh. J.* **2024**, *15*, 307. [CrossRef]
23. Duan, J.; Zhuang, L.; Zhang, Q.; Zhou, Y.; Qin, J. Multimodal perception-fusion-control and human–robot collaboration in manufacturing: A review. *Int. J. Adv. Manuf. Technol.* **2024**, *132*, 1071–1093. [CrossRef]
24. Xu, S.; Zhou, D.; Fang, J.; Yin, J.; Bin, Z.; Zhang, L. FusionPainting: Multimodal Fusion with Adaptive Attention for 3D Object Detection. In Proceedings of the 2021 IEEE International Intelligent Transportation Systems Conference (ITSC), Indianapolis, IN, USA, 19–22 September 2021; pp. 3047–3054.
25. Xia, C.; Li, X.; Gao, X.; Ge, B.; Li, K.C.; Fang, X.; Zhang, Y.; Yang, K. PCDR-DFF: Multi-modal 3D object detection based on point cloud diversity representation and dual feature fusion. *Neural Comput. Appl.* **2024**, *36*, 9329–9346. [CrossRef]
26. Guo, K.; Gan, T.; Ding, Z.; Ling, Q. Deformable Feature Fusion Network for Multi-Modal 3D Object Detection. In Proceedings of the 2024 3rd International Conference on Robotics, Artificial Intelligence and Intelligent Control (RAIIC), Mianyang, China, 5–7 July 2024; pp. 363–367.
27. Tan, M.; Le, Q. EfficientNetV2: Smaller Models and Faster Training. *Proc. Int. Conf. Mach. Learn. PMLR* **2021**, *139*, 10096–10106.

28. Avetisyan, A.; Dahnert, M.; Dai, A.; Savva, M.; Chang, A.X.; Nießner, M. Scan2CAD: Learning CAD Model Alignment in RGB-D Scans. In Proceedings of the IEEE/CVF Conference on Computer Vision and Pattern Recognition, Long Beach, CA, USA, 15–20 June 2019; pp. 2614–2623.
29. Qi, C.R.; Yi, L.; Su, H.; Guibas, L.J. PointNet++: Deep Hierarchical Feature Learning on Point Sets in a Metric Space. *Adv. Neural Inf. Process. Syst.* **2017**, *30*, 1–10.
30. Božič, A.; Palafox, P.; Zollhöfer, M.; Dai, A.; Thies, J.; Nießner, M. Neural Deformation Graphs for Globally-consistent Non-rigid Reconstruction. In Proceedings of the IEEE/CVF Conference on Computer Vision and Pattern Recognition, Nashville, TN, USA, 20–25 June 2021; pp. 1450–1459.
31. Wang, G.; Chen, Y.; An, P.; Hong, H.; Hu, J.; Huang, T. UAV-YOLOv8: A Small-Object-Detection Model Based on Improved YOLOv8 for UAV Aerial Photography Scenarios. *Sensors* **2023**, *23*, 7190. [CrossRef] [PubMed]
32. Cheng, B.; Misra, I.; Schwing, A.G.; Kirillov, A.; Girdhar, R. Masked-attention Mask Transformer for Universal Image Segmentation. In Proceedings of the IEEE/CVF conference on Computer Vision and Pattern Recognition, New Orleans, LA, USA, 18–24 June 2022; pp. 1290–1299.
33. Dosovitskiy, A.; Beyer, L.; Kolesnikov, A.; Weissenborn, D.; Zhai, X.; Unterthiner, T.; Dehghani, M.; Minderer, M.; Heigold, G.; Gelly, S.; et al. An Image is Worth 16 × 16 Words: Transformers for Image Recognition at Scale. In Proceedings of the International Conference on Learning Representations, Virtual, 3–7 May 2021.
34. Wainwright, M. Stochastic approximation with cone-contractive operators: Sharp. *arXiv* **2019**, arXiv:1905.06265.
35. Redmon, J. You only look once: Unified, real-time object detection. In Proceedings of the IEEE Conference on Computer Vision and Pattern Recognition, Las Vegas, NV, USA, 27–30 June 2016.
36. Zhou, X.; Wang, D.; Krähenbühl, P. Objects as points. *arXiv* **2019**, arXiv:1904.07850.
37. Zhang, Z. A Flexible New Technique for Camera Calibration. *IEEE Trans. Pattern Anal. Mach. Intell.* **2000**, *22*, 1330–1334. [CrossRef]
38. Jain, A.; Katara, P.; Gkanatsios, N.; Harley, A.W.; Sarch, G.; Aggarwal, K.; Chaudhary, V.; Fragkiadaki, K. ODIN: A Single Model for 2D and 3D Segmentation. In Proceedings of the IEEE/CVF Conference on Computer Vision and Pattern Recognition, Seattle, WA, USA, 16–22 June 2024; pp. 3564–3574.
39. Liu, Z.; Lin, Y.; Cao, Y.; Hu, H.; Wei, Y.; Zhang, Z.; Lin, S.; Guo, B. Swin Transformer: Hierarchical Vision Transformer using Shifted Windows. In Proceedings of the IEEE/CVF International Conference on Computer Vision, Montreal, QC, Canada, 10–17 October 2021; pp. 10012–10022.

algorithms

MDPI

Article

A Scalable Framework for Sensor Data Ingestion and Real-Time Processing in Cloud Manufacturing

Massimo Pacella [1,*], Antonio Papa [2], Gabriele Papadia [1] and Emiliano Fedeli [3]

[1] Department of Engineering for Innovation, University of Salento, 73100 Lecce, Italy; gabriele.papadia@unisalento.it
[2] Department of Science and Information Technology, Pegaso University, 80121 Napoli, Italy; antonio.papa@unipegaso.it
[3] Laser Romae S.r.l., 00144 Roma, Italy; emiliano.fedeli@laserromae.it
* Correspondence: massimo.pacella@unisalento.it

Abstract: Cloud Manufacturing enables the integration of geographically distributed manufacturing resources through advanced Cloud Computing and IoT technologies. This paradigm promotes the development of scalable and adaptable production systems. However, existing frameworks face challenges related to scalability, resource orchestration, and data security, particularly in rapidly evolving decentralized manufacturing settings. This study presents a novel nine-layer architecture designed specifically to address these issues. Central to this framework is the use of Apache Kafka for robust, high-throughput data ingestion, and Apache Spark Streaming to enhance real-time data processing. This framework is underpinned by a microservice-based architecture that ensures a high scalability and reduced latency. Experimental validation using sensor data from the UCI Machine Learning Repository demonstrated substantial improvements in processing efficiency and throughput compared with conventional frameworks. Key components, such as RabbitMQ, contribute to low-latency performance, whereas Kafka ensures data durability and supports real-time application. Additionally, the in-memory data processing of Spark Streaming enables rapid and dynamic data analysis, yielding actionable insights. The experimental results highlight the potential of the framework to enhance operational efficiency, resource utilization, and data security, offering a resilient solution suited to the demands of modern industrial applications. This study underscores the contribution of the framework to advancing Cloud Manufacturing by providing detailed insights into its performance, scalability, and applicability to contemporary manufacturing ecosystems.

Keywords: Cloud Manufacturing; innovative framework; layered architecture; system scalability; resource management; high-demand workloads

1. Introduction

Cloud Manufacturing (CM) represents a significant advancement in the manufacturing sector, combining the power of Cloud Computing (CC) and the Internet of Things (IoT) to create a seamless, interconnected production ecosystem. This innovative approach allows the integration of geographically dispersed manufacturing resources, including equipment, materials, and expertise, into a unified platform. Thus, the CM enables manufacturers to access and utilize resources on demand, similar to how CC services are consumed [1,2]. This paradigm shift not only enhances operational efficiency, but also promotes flexibility and scalability in manufacturing processes.

As illustrated in Figure 1, the pay-per-use model inherent in CM offers manufacturers numerous advantages. This allows companies to access advanced manufacturing capabilities without the need for significant upfront investment in equipment and infrastructure. This model optimizes resource allocation by ensuring that manufacturing assets are utilized more efficiently across different users and projects. Furthermore, it enables smaller enterprises to compete in a more level-playing field with larger corporations by providing access to state-of-the-art manufacturing technologies and expertise. Consequently, CM is poised to revolutionize the manufacturing industry by fostering innovation, reducing costs, and improving overall productivity.

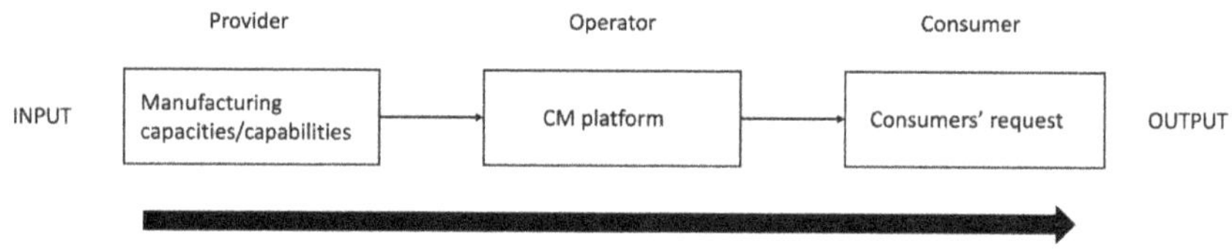

Figure 1. Overview of CM platform architecture. Within this framework, providers produce data regarding their manufacturing capabilities, which are subsequently managed by an operator, whereas consumers receive services customized to their specific requirements.

The integration of CC and IoT technologies facilitates the development of scalable and adaptable production systems, enabling manufacturers to meet the dynamic demands of contemporary manufacturing effectively. Despite their potential, the current CM frameworks encounter significant challenges related to scalability, resource management, and data security, particularly in decentralized and rapidly evolving environments [3]. Addressing these limitations is essential for enhancing the operational efficiency of CM systems.

Recent advancements have highlighted the critical importance of resource optimization and scheduling algorithms for improving overall system efficiency [4]. Advanced scheduling methods, for instance, contribute to optimized resource allocation, reduced production lead times, and improved system performance. However, existing solutions often lack the robustness required to manage the complexities of modern manufacturing, such as volatile demand patterns and integration of diverse heterogeneous resources [5].

To address these challenges, this study proposes an innovative nine-layer framework for CM that incorporates Apache Kafka for high-throughput data ingestion and Apache Spark Streaming for real-time data processing, thereby enhancing operational efficiency and resilience [6]. Additionally, microservice architecture underpins the framework, promoting scalability and reducing latency to facilitate rapid adaptation to market changes, particularly within the manufacturing industry sector [7].

Experimental validation of the framework using sensor data from the University of California-Irvine (UCI) Machine Learning Repository [8] revealed significant improvements in processing time and throughput compared with traditional systems. Notably, RabbitMQ low-latency capabilities, combined with Kafka data durability, optimize the performance for real-time applications. Furthermore, Spark Streaming in-memory processing enables timely insights, making it highly suitable for dynamic data analysis in complex manufacturing scenarios [9]. Therefore, the proposed nine-layer framework enhances operational efficiency, resource optimization, and data security and establishes a resilient solution tailored to the demands of modern industrial applications. This study highlights the potential of this framework to advance CM by presenting practical insights into its performance, scalability, and applicability to contemporary manufacturing ecosystems.

The remainder of this paper is organized as follows. Section 2 presents a review of the recent state-of-the-art CM frameworks and related advanced technologies. Section 3 introduces a novel nine-layer framework designed to enhance CM systems with a modular service-oriented architecture that promotes efficient, secure, and scalable operations, aligned with the recent advancements in CM framework design. Section 4 outlines the evaluation metrics applied to assess the performance of the proposed framework along with a description of the case study utilized in this research. Section 5 presents a numerical analysis of the performance comparison between the two technologies in data ingestion systems. The numerical results are discussed in Section 6, and Section 7 presents the conclusions of the study and directions for future research. An Appendix A section is also provided, which presents a series of algorithms corresponding to the key layers of the proposed framework.

2. State-Of-The-Art Review

CM has transformed the manufacturing sector by shifting from traditional models to flexible service-centric frameworks. This paradigm enables the integration and efficient utilization of distributed manufacturing resources within a cloud ecosystem [10]. CM excels in resource sharing, coordination, and scalability, which are critical for multi-location operations involving diverse stakeholders. However, its implementation poses challenges, such as handling vast data volumes, real-time analytics, security, and collaboration across dynamic manufacturing environments. Effective CM systems require robust data ingestion, processing, and application layers to meet these demands efficiently. Technologies for CM frameworks include Apache Kafka and RabbitMQ for data ingestion, Spark Streaming for real-time analytics, MongoDB for data management, Kubernetes for orchestration, Flask-SocketIO for real-time communication, and microservice architectures for application scalability. We review these technologies as follows:

Apache Kafka
: is a distributed event streaming platform. It enables high-throughput fault-tolerant data pipelines and is a pivotal system for managing large-scale real-time data streams in distributed CM environments. The log-based architecture of the Kafka platform ensures durability and order preservation, which makes it ideal for sequence-sensitive applications [11]. In the framework proposed by [12], Kafka was used to capture and manage IoT data streams, thereby significantly enhancing the scalability and resilience of the CM systems. This design leverages the strengths of Kafka in sequence-sensitive large-scale data management, enabling real-time decision making and operational efficiency within a cloud-based manufacturing context.

RabbitMQ
: offers low-latency messaging, making it effective for real-time notifications and anomaly detection in CM. However, its scalability and durability are limited compared to those of Kafka, which handles continuous, large-scale data streams. The strength of RabbitMQ lies in its latency-sensitive applications, which complement those of Kafka in the hybrid systems.

Spark Streaming
: supports real-time analytics in CM, enabling predictive insights and anomaly detection through continuous data processing [9,13]. Unlike Hadoop, which relies on batch processing, Spark's in-memory architecture delivers low-latency performance essential for quality control and operational intelligence [14].

MongoDB
: is a NoSQL database, which is able to managing unstructured and semi-structured data such as machine logs and sensor outputs. Its scalability and JSON-based architecture make it ideal for diverse CM datasets [15]. MongoDB ensures reliable data storage and retrieval across the distributed cloud resources.

Kubernetes	orchestrates containerized applications, facilitating deployment, scaling, and maintenance of CM services [16]. Its load-balancing and resource-allocation capabilities ensure resilience and scalability under variable operational demands [17], thereby enabling a high performance in dynamic CM environments.
Microservice	architectures are preferred in CM owing to their modular design, which enables independent deployment, scaling, and maintenance [18]. They enhance scalability and flexibility compared to monolithic systems, which face challenges in managing large-scale environments. Microservices support evolving workloads and ensure rapid deployment and update [19].
Flask-SocketIO	extends the capabilities of the Flask Web framework by enabling real-time bidirectional communication between clients and servers. This is particularly beneficial for CM systems that require instantaneous updates such as monitoring production metrics or facilitating interactive dashboards. By leveraging WebSocket protocols, Flask-SocketIO ensures low-latency communication and enhances the responsiveness in dynamic manufacturing environments. Its integration into CM frameworks supports applications such as real-time notifications, collaborative tools, and anomaly detection, further improving operational efficiency [20,21].

Security Issues

Security is a primary concern in CM, where diverse stakeholders operate within a shared cloud infrastructure. Robust security measures are particularly critical for Additive Manufacturing (AM), which is highly data-intensive and relies on intellectual property for three-dimensional (3D) models and design specifications. Unauthorized access, data breaches, and intellectual property theft can severely disrupt AM workflow and CM systems. Advanced access control mechanisms such as Role-Based Access Control (RBAC) are pivotal for addressing these threats. Flask, a lightweight web framework, is frequently used to implement RBAC in order to ensure secure resource access based on user roles. Li et al. [22] demonstrate how Flask supports CM frameworks by restricting access to authorized personnel like operators, managers, or suppliers.

Security and access control layers in CM frameworks should incorporate robust cybersecurity protocols tailored to the AM. These include encryption technologies for safeguarding data during transmission and storage, intrusion detection systems (IDSs) to identify unauthorized activities, and zero-trust architectures to enforce strict verification-based access. Ref. [23] provides a framework for assessing cybersecurity risks in multidisciplinary settings, which is vital for CM systems due to their complex structures.

Safeguarding intellectual property and 3D models in AM is critical. Zafar et al. [24] emphasized that breaches can compromise the entire manufacturing process and advocate solutions, such as digital watermarking and blockchain, for traceability and data integrity. AI-driven real-time threat intelligence further strengthens security by proactively detecting vulnerabilities and mitigating risk. For example, machine learning models can analyze network traffic to flag anomalies that are indicative of cyberattacks. Sriram and Rambabu [25] highlighted the importance of such AI-based approaches in Industry 4.0, where interconnected systems and IoT devices increase the exposure to cybersecurity risks. Their findings also emphasized fostering cybersecurity awareness among personnel to reduce human error-induced breaches. Finally, adopting multifactor authentication (MFA) and advanced cryptographic algorithms can significantly enhance security. Combining these measures with IDS and incident response frameworks establishes comprehensive defenses. Cains et al. [23] underscored the value of contextualized risk assessments for tailoring cybersecurity strategies and enabling CM systems to balance flexibility with rigorous security requirements.

3. The Proposed Framework

Following the recent advancements in CM framework design [26,27], this section presents a novel nine-layer framework designed to enhance CM systems with a modular service-oriented architecture that promotes efficient, secure, and scalable operations. The framework depicted in Figure 2 is organized into nine layers: (1) data collection, (2) communication, (3) data ingestion, (4) data processing and analytics, (5) application, (6) storage, (7) elastic computing and orchestration, (8) security and access control, and (9) user interface and visualization [28].

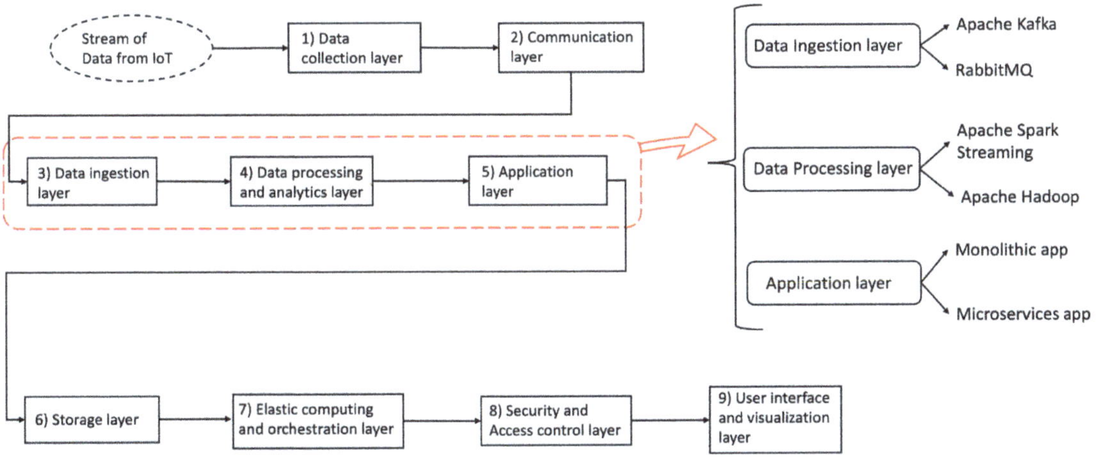

Figure 2. Schematic representation of the proposed framework. The dashed red rectangle highlights the focus of this study.

The data collection layer gathers raw data from various sources, which are then transmitted through the communication layer. The data ingestion, processing, analytics, and application layers form the core of the system, wherein data are transformed into actionable insights. The storage layer ensures data persistence, while the elastic computing and orchestration layers manage resource allocation. The security and access control layers safeguard the entire system, whereas the user interface and visualization layers present processed information in an accessible format.

In existing architectures, tools such as Apache Kafka, Spark Streaming, and microservices have been widely employed to address challenges in CM environments. For instance, frameworks leveraging RabbitMQ or Apache Kafka for data ingestion have demonstrated varying successes in managing high-throughput data streams. However, RabbitMQ often struggles with scalability in distributed systems, whereas the Kafka subscribe architecture offers exceptional scalability and fault tolerance. Similarly, Hadoop-based systems have historically dominated data processing, but have been increasingly replaced by Spark Streaming because of their low-latency, real-time processing capabilities. Microservices have gradually supplanted monolithic architectures, owing to their flexibility in independently scaling, updating, and managing discrete services [29,30].

The proposed nine-layer framework extends the existing solutions by integrating and optimizing these tools to achieve a higher degree of responsiveness, scalability, and modularity. Notably, it introduces a seamless integration of these technologies, paired with innovations, such as enhanced elastic computing mechanisms, advanced orchestration strategies, and comprehensive data privacy and access control policies. This enables the framework to satisfy the critical demands of modern CM systems, such as real-time adaptability, robust security, and user-friendly operations. Specifically, the framework was designed to process the sensor readings generated by devices operating in the AM field, such as 3D printers. These devices produce large datasets that capture critical parameters such as temperature and relative humidity during the material extrusion process when printing polymer filaments. The choice of this dataset highlights the applicability of the framework for optimizing the production workflow in AM.

The data ingestion layer utilizes Apache Kafka, an open-source streaming platform that supports high-throughput real-time data streaming with exceptional scalability and fault tolerance. The publish-subscribe architecture of Kafka enables efficient queuing and seamless data flow to downstream services, making it ideal for CM environments in which IoT devices continuously generate high volumes of data. The experimental findings in Section 5 demonstrate that Kafka significantly outperforms RabbitMQ in handling high-velocity data streams, thereby achieving lower latency and improved scalability within distributed CM systems [31].

In the data processing and analytics layer, Spark Streaming provides real-time analytics capabilities and supports the integration of Machine Learning models for adaptive data-driven decision making. Unlike batch-oriented systems such as Hadoop, Spark Streaming offers low-latency processing, which is essential in dynamic CM environments where immediate insights optimize production workflows. As demonstrated in Section 5, Spark Streaming outperforms Hadoop in managing continuous data flows, yielding substantial reductions in processing time and enhancing operational efficiency [32].

The microservice application layer enables deployment of the framework as a modular service-oriented architecture. This configuration supports the independent scaling, updating, and management of discrete services for specific CM functions. Unlike monolithic architectures, which often encounter scalability limitations and tight inter-component coupling, the microservice approach offers enhanced flexibility and resilience. Each service operates independently, allowing rapid updates without affecting overall system stability [33,34]. Validation results (Section 5) demonstrate that the microservice architecture substantially improves system responsiveness and adaptability in high-demand manufacturing environments [35].

Furthermore, the framework emphasizes the necessity for robust data privacy and user authentication policies within the security and access control layers. These policies include encryption of sensitive data, fine-grained access control, and multifactor authentication mechanisms. Such measures ensure the confidentiality and integrity of the data and safeguard them against unauthorized access and cyber threats, which are critical for trust and compliance in IoT-driven manufacturing systems [36].

By integrating Kafka, Spark Streaming, and a microservice architecture, along with innovations in elastic computing and advanced security protocols, the proposed framework comprehensively addresses the challenges of scalability, responsiveness, and modularity inherent in IoT-driven manufacturing [37]. The experimental validations detailed in the following sections confirm the potential of the framework to significantly advance CM by enabling real-time, adaptable, and secure operations.

4. Materials and Methods

This section outlines the evaluation metrics applied to assess the performance of the proposed framework along with a description of the case study utilized in this article.

4.1. Evaluation Metrics

To assess the effectiveness of the framework, a set of established metrics targeting the system efficiency, scalability, and responsiveness was selected [38]. Based on previous research on real-time data processing, CC, and distributed systems, these metrics provide a comprehensive view of a system's operational capacity and adaptability [1,39,40].

- Throughput measures the number of messages or requests processed per second. Throughput is a key metric for industrial applications such as CM, where a higher throughput indicates an enhanced capacity for handling large-scale data streams.
- Latency defines the delay between data generation and consumption or the response time to an API request. Low latency is critical for real-time applications, where delays can impact decision making and control, especially in time-sensitive manufacturing environments [41].
- Scalability assesses the system ability to sustain performance under increasing workloads by testing with additional message producers, consumers, or concurrent users. This metric is vital for cloud-based architectures, where sensor density or data generation rates can vary significantly over time.
- Resource Utilization: Tracks CPU and memory usage to gauge efficiency. Effective resource utilization ensures high performance and cost efficiency because high utilization may indicate bottlenecks, whereas low utilization and high throughput suggest an optimized system design.

Using these metrics [42], the accuracy and performance of the framework are evaluated using established methodologies in the CC field.

4.2. Case Study

The core layers of the proposed framework, namely the data ingestion, data processing and analytics, and application architecture were validated using real-world sensor data from the "Istanbul Stock Exchange Real-Time Data for Temperature and Humidity Sensors". This dataset was sourced from the "Appliances EnergyPrediction Data Set" on the UCI Machine Learning Repository [43]. It includes temperature and humidity readings from various rooms in a low-energy residential building, with a sample of 100 consecutive readings, as shown in Figure 3.

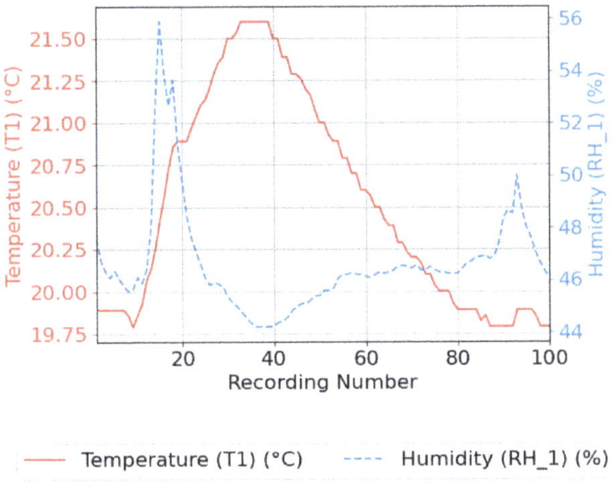

Figure 3. Sample of 100 sequential temperature and humidity readings from real-time sensors.

The data acquisition and preparation process encompassed the following steps (bypassing the framework data collection and communication layers, owing to direct data availability):

1. Retrieved the "Appliances Energy Prediction Data Set" from the UCI Machine Learning Repository.
2. Downloaded the dataset in .csv format.
3. Extracted relevant columns, such as T1 (temperature in the living room) and RH_1 (relative humidity in the living room), along with data from other monitored spaces.
4. Stored the dataset locally in a directory titled Article_dataset for experimental use.

The framework processed these data streams, where each sensor generated readings every second, including the timestamp, temperature (in degrees Celsius °C), and humidity (percentage %). This setup enables real-time ingestion, processing, and analysis across several experimental scenarios to compare different messaging queues, data processing frameworks, and application architectures.

As shown in Figure 4, three experimental campaigns were conducted: the first (left) evaluation of Kafka and RabbitMQ for data ingestion, the second (middle) comparison of Spark Streaming with Apache Hadoop for data processing and analytics, and the third (right) assessment of microservice versus monolithic application architectures.

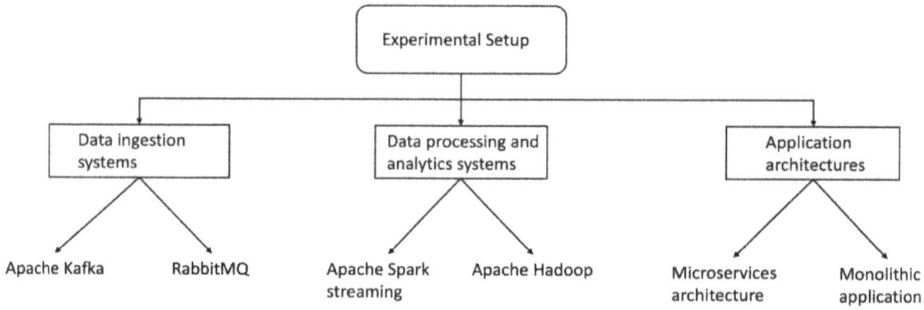

Figure 4. Experimental setup outlining the operational workflow for the considered case study.

4.2.1. Data Ingestion Systems

To assess the data ingestion layer, Apache Kafka and RabbitMQ, which are widely used message queue systems, were deployed in three-node clusters and configured with a replication factor of three for enhanced scalability and fault tolerance. Varying message loads (100, 1000, and 10,000 messages per second) were simulated to reflect different sensor densities in the CM environment. Apache Kafka was set up with temperature and humidity sensors as data producers and data processing systems as consumers. Its distributed fault-tolerant design supports continuous high-volume data streams, which are essential for the CM. The performance metrics for each component were analyzed under various load conditions to confirm the robustness and efficiency of the proposed framework. Conversely, RabbitMQ was configured with sensor data as publishers and consumer applications subscribing to queues using a direct exchange routing configuration to benchmark performance alongside Kafka. Metrics such as the throughput, task duration, and scalability were evaluated across the tested message rates.

4.2.2. Data Processing and Analytic Systems

The tested data processing frameworks included both Apache Spark Streaming and Hadoop, with the former configured with a 5 s sliding window and a 1 s batch interval to compute rolling averages for temperature and humidity. In-memory processing enables low-latency responses for real-time decision making in manufacturing.

Apache Hadoop was used as a batch-processing baseline for calculating temperature and humidity averages. Although it has a higher latency than Spark Streaming, it serves as a reference point for assessing real-time capabilities. The analyzed metrics included the processing latency, resource utilization, and scalability under increased data loads.

4.2.3. Application Architectures

Independent task-based microservices were containerized with Docker and orchestrated with Kubernetes, allowing dynamic scaling and fault isolation, and enabling the scaling of individual services according to load demands. By contrast, a monolithic integrated Flask application manages all tasks (data ingestion, processing, and storage) within one instance. Although simpler to deploy, it lacks fault isolation and scalability, proving that it is more resource-intensive under high loads. The comparison metrics include the response time for request processing, throughput, and scalability.

4.2.4. Experimental Setup

All experiments were conducted on a system with an Intel Core^{TM} i7-6 core processor (Intel Corporation, Santa Clara, CA, USA) and 16 GB RAM. The software versions used were as follows:

- Apache Kafka: 3.8.1.
- RabbitMQ: 4.0.2.
- Apache Spark Streaming: 3.5.2.
- Apache Hadoop: 3.4.1.
- Flask: 3.0.3.
- Docker: 26.0.2.
- Kubernetes: 1.31.2.

The performance metrics for each component were analyzed under various load conditions to confirm the robustness and efficiency of the proposed framework.

5. Results

This section presents an analysis of the performance comparison between Apache Kafka and RabbitMQ in data ingestion systems. This study utilized custom-designed producer and consumer algorithms tailored to each system architecture to evaluate their efficiency under varying message loads. Kafka was integrated with Zookeeper for resource management, while RabbitMQ was deployed using Kubernetes within a Docker environment.

5.1. Data Ingestion Systems

Table 1 summarizes the comparative performance of Apache Kafka and RabbitMQ under various message loads, utilizing both producer (Algorithms A1 and A3) and consumer (Algorithms A2 and A4) components. Kafka was configured with Zookeeper for resource management, while RabbitMQ was orchestrated using Kubernetes within Docker.

The algorithms were optimized specifically for Kafka and RabbitMQ to enhance throughput, latency, and durability by leveraging the architectural advantages of each system. Kafka producer (Algorithm A1) dynamically manages message loads through an adjustable message count parameter (`max_messages`), along with a logging mechanism for progress tracking, which is particularly valuable for handling high data volumes in CM environments. The consumer algorithm (Algorithm A2) focuses on sequential processing with robust error-handling, which is beneficial for applications that require strict data ordering.

For RabbitMQ, the producer (Algorithm A3) employed in-memory messaging to maintain a low-latency dispatch suitable for real-time applications. The consumer

(Algorithm A4) incorporates a callback mechanism for immediate message processing and a prefetch count of one to facilitate rapid adaptability under a dynamic workload. This setup supports high-speed message handling although it does not enforce strict message ordering. The performance metrics for Kafka and RabbitMQ are listed in Table 1.

The Kafka setup demonstrated particular strengths in managing high-volume data streams by leveraging the dynamic message load management and progress-tracking features of the producer algorithm. These abilities make Kafka well suited for CM environments that deal with large-scale data processing. Kafka consumer algorithm emphasizes sequential processing with robust error handling, catering to applications that require strict data ordering. In contrast, the RabbitMQ configuration exhibits advantages in real-time, low-latency applications. The producer algorithm uses in-memory message management for swift dispatch, whereas the consumer algorithm employs a callback mechanism that enables rapid adaptation to changing workloads. This setup allows RabbitMQ to excel in high-speed message-handling scenarios without strict message ordering provided by Kafka.

Table 1. Performance comparison of Apache Kafka and RabbitMQ across varying message loads.

Messages Processed	System Component	Time (s)	Throughput (msg/s)
100	Kafka Producer	0.16	644.87
	Kafka Consumer	2.21	45.28
	RabbitMQ Producer	0.16	644.83
	RabbitMQ Consumer	0.06	1614.62
1000	Kafka Producer	1.40	714.21
	Kafka Consumer	0.47	2137.99
	RabbitMQ Producer	1.49	671.55
	RabbitMQ Consumer	0.46	2161.49
10,000	Kafka Producer	14.02	713.25
	Kafka Consumer	5.27	1895.80
	RabbitMQ Producer	15.97	626.34
	RabbitMQ Consumer	4.61	2169.57

The results of this study, which are graphically represented in Figure 5, demonstrate higher throughput values for Kafka producers than RabbitMQ producers across varying user counts. These findings suggest that Kafka exhibits superior performance in managing structured, sequence-sensitive data, particularly in producer operations, thereby making it more suitable for applications that require ordered message handling. Conversely, RabbitMQ demonstrated higher consumer throughput across all message rates, highlighting its efficacy in real-time high-throughput scenarios where immediate message consumption is prioritized over strict message ordering.

5.2. Data Processing and Analytic Systems

After the evaluation of the two data ingestion systems, a detailed assessment was conducted on the performance of two data processing systems: Spark Streaming and Hadoop Batch Processing. The Kafka producer script was executed with a maximum message count of 10,000, leveraging its favorable throughput and processing time results compared to RabbitMQ under similar input conditions (see Table 1). The comparative performance metrics for Spark Streaming and Hadoop Batch Processing are summarized in Table 2, which serves as a critical reference for analyzing their suitability within the CM framework.

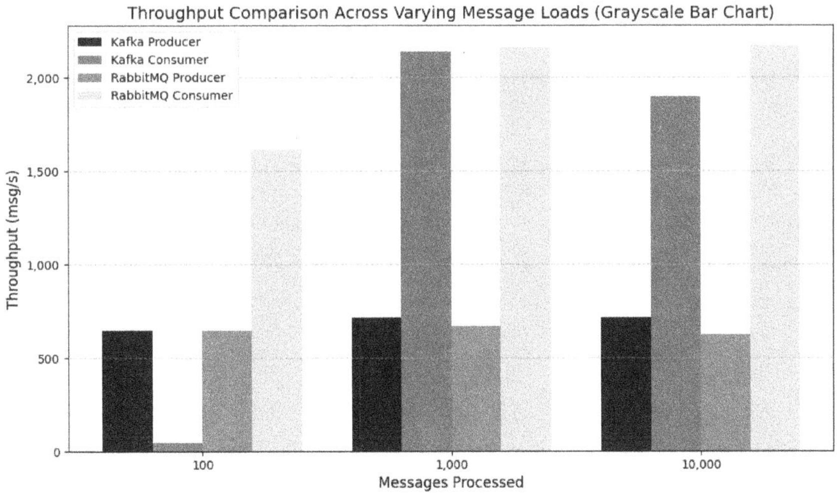

Figure 5. Bar chart of performance comparison of Apache Kafka and RabbitMQ across varying message loads.

Table 2. Performance comparison of Spark Streaming and Hadoop batch processing systems.

Metric	Spark Streaming	Hadoop Batch
Batch ID 0 Record Count	103	-
Batch ID 1 Record Count	2324	-
Batch ID 2 Record Count	161	-
Total Records Processed	2588	10,000
Total Processing Time (s)	4.236	5.976
Throughput (records/s)	612.25 (avg)	1673.45
Average Latency (s)	1.390	-
CPU Usage (Before)	33.5%	28.6%
CPU Usage (After)	39.4% (avg)	33.1%
Memory Usage (Before)	64.1%	63.5%
Memory Usage (After)	64.0% (avg)	63.8%
Average Temperature (avg_T1)	21.68	21.67
Average Relative Humidity (avg_RH_out)	82.43	79.77

An analysis of the metrics presented in Table 2 demonstrates their pivotal role in substantiating the advantages of the proposed framework, as follows:

- Total Records Processed: While Hadoop Batch Processing handles a larger volume of records (10,000 compared to 2588 for Spark Streaming), the discrepancy arises from the batch-oriented nature of Hadoop versus the real-time, continuous nature of Spark Streaming. This distinction reflects the suitability of Spark Streaming for low-latency CM applications, in which immediate insights are prioritized over total volume.
- Total Processing Time (s): Spark Streaming outperforms Hadoop Batch Processing with a shorter processing time (4.236 s vs. 5.976 s). This metric underscores the efficiency of Spark Streaming's in-memory computation model, which reduces the time required to derive actionable insights, and is an essential feature for dynamic and fast-paced manufacturing environments.
- Throughput (records/s): While Hadoop exhibits higher throughput (1673.45 records/s compared to 612.25 records/s of Spark), this metric aligns with its design for batch-

processing scenarios. The relatively low throughput of Spark is a trade-off for its capability to provide real-time processing and immediate feedback.

- Average Latency (s): The 1.390 s average latency of Spark Streaming is a critical metric that highlights its superiority in delivering near-instantaneous data processing. Hadoop, which is inherently batch-oriented, does not support latency measurements in the same sense that its outputs are processed in bulk.
- CPU and Memory Usage: Both systems demonstrate efficient resource utilization, with the average CPU and memory usage of Spark Streaming increasing marginally during operation. This slight increase signifies the ability of Spark to manage resources adaptively in real time, ensuring consistent performance, even under varying workloads.
- Environmental Metrics: The nearly identical values for Average Temperature and Average Relative Humidity across both systems validate the integrity of data processing under similar conditions. However, the real-time aggregation of Spark Streaming offers a temporal advantage for monitoring environmental conditions in CM applications.

The superior performance of Spark Streaming was further bolstered by several innovations embedded in Algorithm A5. Real-time system monitoring enables dynamic adjustments to resource constraints, whereas cumulative tracking of metrics, such as latency and processing times, facilitates iterative process optimization. These features make Spark Streaming an indispensable tool for scenarios that demand continuous, low-latency data processing, operational efficiency, and rapid decision making in CM environments. Conversely, the high throughput of Hadoop Batch Processing remains valuable for prioritizing large-scale data aggregation and offline analytics. The inclusion of enhancements such as batch size optimization and metric logging ensures that Hadoop remains relevant for traditional high-volume data processing needs, albeit at the expense of real-time responsiveness. By integrating these insights, we emphasize the necessity of balancing throughput and latency metrics when selecting data-processing systems for CM applications. The ability of Spark Streaming to deliver low-latency, real-time insights complements the high-throughput capabilities of Hadoop Batch Processing, underscoring its role in optimizing the performance and scalability of our proposed nine-layer CM framework.

5.2.1. Spark Streaming Innovations

In Algorithm A5, several enhancements are introduced to improve the real-time data-processing capabilities of Spark Streaming:

- Real-time system monitoring: the system tracks CPU and memory usage before and after each batch, enabling efficient real-time resource management. This feature is vital for adjusting manufacturing processes based on available resources.
- Adaptive termination mechanism: the algorithm includes an automatic termination feature that stops processing when no new data are received beyond a defined threshold, optimizing resource utilization and enhancing energy efficiency.
- Enhanced aggregation of environmental data: temperature and humidity readings are averaged over time, providing real-time environmental data that are critical for precise manufacturing control.
- Cumulative metrics tracking: the algorithm logs average latencies, processing times, and resource usage, offering a detailed performance log that aids in refining CM processes or scaling for higher demand.
- Configurable query timeout: a flexible timeout parameter is included, allowing adaptability to various manufacturing needs, whether for continuous operation or on-demand scaling.

5.2.2. Hadoop Batch Processing Innovations

In the Hadoop batch processing system, the following enhancements were applied to optimize performance in a batch-oriented context (refer to Algorithm A6):

- Batch limiting for efficient processing: the system processes a set number of records (10,000) to optimize batch sizes for improved performance in a traditional Hadoop setting.
- Artificial delay for simulated batch processing: a controlled delay simulates the time needed to gather and process large data batches, replicating real-world batch intervals in a manufacturing environment.
- System metrics' tracking pre- and post-processing: CPU and memory usage are monitored before and after processing to assess resource utilization throughout the batch processing cycle.
- Throughput and latency calculation: processing time and throughput are recorded to evaluate the batch system's efficiency.
- Logging of aggregate results and performance metrics: key performance metrics and aggregate results are logged, creating a performance record for further analysis and optimization.

These improvements make both systems more efficient and adaptable for CM applications. The analysis (see Table 2) highlights the low-latency and real-time capabilities of Spark Streaming, which offers distinct advantages over traditional Hadoop batch processing. Although Hadoop is effective for large-scale data processing, it introduces higher latency and lower throughput, making Spark Streaming preferable for scenarios that require immediate data insights.

5.3. Application Architecture

This subsection presents a comparative evaluation of monolithic and microservice architectures tested under varying user loads (100, 1000, and 10,000 users) using the Locust tool (an open-source performance/load testing tool). Key metrics, including the user count, average response time (ms), throughput (requests per second), and total requests, were analyzed to assess the scalability and efficiency of each architecture.

5.3.1. Performance Evaluation for the Monolithic Application

The monolithic application developed in Flask was designed to ingest, process, and store the temperature and humidity data. The application includes the following functionalities:

- Data ingestion: the application reads the temperature_humidity_data.csv file using the Pandas library.
- Data processing: real-time calculation of mean temperature and humidity values facilitates immediate data analysis.
- Performance measurement: response times for data processing requests are tracked and integrated into the data processing function, with results returned in JSON format, allowing for easy client-side consumption.

Performance testing was conducted with Locust under user loads from 100 to 10,000 with Table 3, showing the obtained performance metrics.

Algorithms A7 and A8 detail the core functionalities of the monolithic application and load testing scripts, respectively, providing insights into the system's performance under varying loads.

Table 3. Performance metrics for the monolithic application.

User Count	Average Response Time (ms)	Throughput (Requests/s)	Total Requests
100	223.68	44.31	13,239
1000	9372.87	82.66	24,775
10,000	23,086.79	336.61	102,972

5.3.2. Performance Evaluation for the Microservice Architecture

The microservice-based architecture comprises three independent services: ingestion, processing, and storage. Each service was tested with the same user load conditions as the monolithic architecture. Table 4 presents the response time, throughput, and total requests for each of the three services under different user loads.

Table 4. Performance metrics for the microservices architecture.

Service	User Count	Average Response Time (ms)	Throughput (Requests/s)	Total Requests
Ingestion	100	34.90	32.46	19,388
Ingestion	1000	3.65	329.48	197,354
Ingestion	10,000	11,846.57	607.43	366,940
Processing	100	1.94	32.92	19,670
Processing	1000	5.07	329.95	197,656
Processing	10,000	10,608.47	677.91	407,950
Storage	100	1.92	33.10	19,770
Storage	1000	5.27	330.09	197,786
Storage	10,000	10,488.53	687.86	413,726

The microservice architecture was designed to prioritize scalability and flexibility with independent deployment of each service. The following innovations are implemented to optimize performance (see Algorithms A9–A15).

- Modular microservice design: each service (ingestion, processing, and storage) functions independently, promoting scalability and flexibility within the system.
- Integration of Flask with data processing: Flask is used for data ingestion and processing, supporting real-time responses and improving application responsiveness.
- Dynamic data processing: the system dynamically calculates mean temperature and humidity values, enabling immediate data analysis and insights.
- Performance measurement: real-time response tracking is incorporated into data processing functions, providing feedback on performance impacts directly within the application.
- Error handling: robust error-handling mechanisms ensure graceful failure management, enhancing the application's reliability.
- Realistic load simulation: Locust simulates user behavior with varying loads and dynamic wait times, mimicking real-world interactions for accurate performance measurement.
- Flexible session management: the application dynamically manages user sessions, offering a comprehensive understanding of user interactions during testing.
- Real-time performance metrics: metrics are gathered during load tests, delivering immediate insights into potential bottlenecks and system performance under stress.
- Kubernetes deployment: the architecture is deployed on Kubernetes, supporting high availability and scaling of microservices.

The performance metrics, particularly in terms of throughput for 10,000 user counts, as depicted in Figure 6, demonstrate higher values for the three microservices compared to that for the monolithic application, indicating that the design enhancements exemplify the capacity of the microservice architecture to manage increased loads more efficiently than the monolithic system while providing enhanced flexibility and scalability for future expansions.

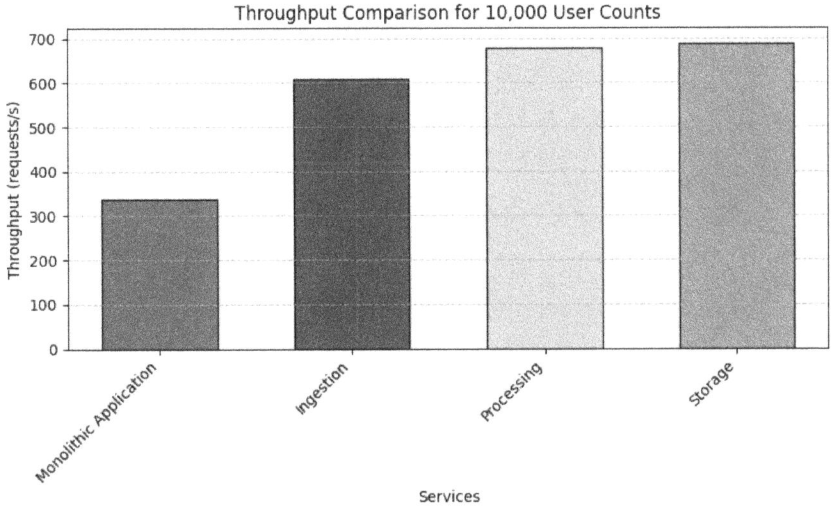

Figure 6. Bar chart of performance metrics for the Monolithic app vs. Microservice architecture.

6. Discussion

The proposed nine-layer framework was designed to address the challenges of scalability, resource orchestration, and data security in modern decentralized manufacturing settings. For this implementation, we use technologies that excel in handling the ingestion and processing of large-scale IoT sensor data with low latency, thereby ensuring real-time responsiveness and long-term operational reliability. This is especially critical for applications in CM and AM, where the ability to monitor and control processing parameters such as temperature and humidity is essential for ensuring the quality and consistency of 3D-printed parts produced through filament material extrusion.

The experimental campaigns clearly demonstrated the performance gains achieved through the integration of Apache Kafka for data ingestion, Spark Streaming for processing, and a microservice architecture for overall framework scalability and resilience. Specifically, the performance evaluation of Kafka and RabbitMQ (Table 1) highlighted the superior capabilities of Kafka in high-throughput, low-latency data ingestion scenarios, which are critical for CM and AM applications. The log-based architecture of Kafka, combined with its durability and fault tolerance, makes it particularly well-suited for handling continuous streams of sensor data generated in AM workflows. For example, Kafka achieved a throughput of 714.21 messages per second for a workload of 1000 messages, outperforming the 671.55 messages per second of RabbitMQ, under the same conditions. This superior throughput, coupled with the consistent performance of Kafka under increased data volumes, ensures that the framework can handle the large-scale datasets required for real-time monitoring of processing parameters such as temperature and humidity in AM. Such capabilities enable immediate fault detection and corrective action, reduce the risk of defects in 3D-printed parts, and enhance the overall operational efficiency.

Similarly, the adoption of Spark Streaming for real-time processing has demonstrated significant advantages over traditional batch processing systems such as Hadoop, as shown in Table 2. The micro-batch architecture of Spark allows for the near-instantaneous ingestion and analysis of IoT sensor data, achieving substantial reductions in processing time and latency. In our experiments, Spark processed equivalent workloads in 4.236 s compared with 5.976 s obtained with Hadoop, achieving a lower average latency of 1.390 s. This real-time processing capability is particularly advantageous for CM and AM scenarios, which require rapid responsiveness to environmental changes during the production of 3D-printed parts. By leveraging Spark's ability to process large volumes of streaming sensor data in real-time, the framework can quickly identify inefficiencies or faults in AM systems, thereby ensuring optimal parameter control and product quality.

The use of microservice architecture further enhances the ability of the framework to support high-throughput, low-latency operations across its layers, as indicated by the comparative results in Tables 3 and 4. Microservices demonstrate superior scalability and fault tolerance under an increasing workload compared with monolithic systems. For instance, under a 10,000 user load, the microservice-based ingestion service processed 366,940 requests compared to the 102,972 requests of the monolithic system. Additionally, microservices maintained sub-10 ms response times for ingestion, processing, and storage tasks, while the monolithic system exhibited response times exceeding 9000 ms. This modularity ensures that failures are isolated into specific components, thereby maintaining the functionality of other parts of the framework during partial disruptions. The scalability of the microservice architecture allows the framework to dynamically adapt to the demands of IoT sensor data streams, which is a critical requirement for CM and AM applications where uninterrupted data flow and rapid analytics are essential.

By integrating Kafka, Spark Streaming, and a microservice architecture, the proposed nine-layer framework delivers unparalleled performance gains for modern industrial applications. The high-throughput durability of Kafka supports seamless data flow across real-time and archival tiers, whereas the in-memory processing of Spark Streaming provides actionable insights in near real time. The microservice architecture ensures that the framework remains robust and scalable, and is capable of handling both real-time alerts and long-term resource planning tasks. These combined features make the framework highly adaptable to the evolving needs of CM, with particular emphasis on the AM sector. By enabling precise control over critical manufacturing parameters, such as temperature and humidity, during the filament extrusion process, the framework ensures the superior quality and consistency of the 3D-printed parts.

Therefore, we demonstrated the effectiveness of the nine-layer framework in addressing the complexities of modern industrial ecosystems. The performance gains achieved through Kafka, Spark Streaming, and microservices underscore the framework's potential to transform decentralized manufacturing systems. Future work could focus on extending the applicability of the framework by incorporating advanced predictive analytics and optimizing cross-tier communication, further validating its role as a transformative solution for CM and AM.

7. Conclusions

Considering the data ingestion processing and real-time analytics in CM, our study confirms that the log-based architecture of the Kafka platform is optimal for robust, scalable, and durable data ingestion. The high throughput and ordered message delivery of the Kafka platform make it particularly effective for real-time monitoring and predictive maintenance, whereas RabbitMQ remains suitable for low-latency small-scale tasks. For data processing, Spark Streaming outperforms Hadoop in latency-sensitive applications, leveraging its in-memory and micro-batch architecture to deliver real-time analytics and actionable insights. This responsiveness is essential for live monitoring and adaptive manufacturing operations, making Spark a preferred solution for dynamic CM environments.

Our analysis also highlights the scalability and efficiency of microservices over monolithic architectures. The modular structure of the microservices supports independent deployment, dynamic scaling, and fault tolerance, thereby enabling superior performance under variable loads. Containerization with Docker and orchestration via Kubernetes further enhance flexibility and resilience, ensuring reliable operations in distributed manufacturing scenarios. These choices collectively form a robust and scalable foundation for real-time CM applications, and they are validated through experimental campaigns that demonstrate high throughput, low latency, and adaptability.

Future research should focus on deploying this framework in industrial case studies to optimize predictive maintenance, real-time quality control, and resource allocation. Incorporating advanced security measures, such as encryption, Role-Based Access Control, and intrusion detection, is critical for addressing cybersecurity challenges inherent in shared CM environments. Techniques such as blockchain and AI-driven threat intelligence can enhance data integrity and resilience against cyber threats, particularly in sensitive applications, such as AM. Additionally, integrating machine learning models for predictive analytics and adaptive system configurations could further optimize performance and responsiveness in real-world scenarios.

In conclusion, the proposed framework integrates Kafka, Spark Streaming, and microservices to address critical CM requirements and achieve high performance, scalability, and resilience. This design establishes a strong foundation for advanced industrial applications with opportunities for future enhancements in security, adaptability, and real-world testing. These advancements have ensured that the framework remains at the forefront of reliable and efficient CM systems in evolving manufacturing environments.

Author Contributions: Conceptualization, M.P.; methodology, M.P. and A.P.; validation, M.P. and A.P.; resources, G.P. and E.F.; writing—original draft preparation, M.P. and A.P.; writing—review and editing, M.P. and A.P.; supervision, M.P and G.P.; project administration, G.P. and E.F.; funding acquisition, G.P. and E.F. All authors have read and agreed to the published version of the manuscript.

Funding: This work was funded by Puglia Region (Italy)—Project "SMILE&SCALETECH" (P.O. PUGLIA FESR 2014-2020).

Data Availability Statement: The data analyzed in this manuscript are available at https://archive.ics.uci.edu/dataset/374/appliances+energy+prediction (accessed on 1 January 2025).

Acknowledgments: The authors express their gratitude for the administrative and technical assistance provided by the company Advantech S.r.l. in Lecce, Italy.

Conflicts of Interest: Author E.F. was employed by the company Laser Romae S.r.l. in Rome, Italy. The remaining authors declare that the research was conducted in the absence of any commercial or financial relationships that could be construed as a potential conflict of interest. The funder had no role in the design of this study; in the collection, analyses, or interpretation of data; in the writing of the manuscript; nor in the decision to publish the results.

Abbreviations

The following abbreviations are used in this manuscript:

AM	Additive Manufacturing
CC	Cloud Computing
CM	Cloud Manufacturing
IoT	Internet of Things
RBAC	Role-Based Access Control

Appendix A

In this appendix section, we presented a series of innovative pseudocodes corresponding to key layers of the proposed framework.

Algorithm A1 outlines the pseudocode for the description of the Kafka producer considering varying input workloads.

Algorithm A1 Kafka Producer Pseudocode

```
Require: Kafka and essential libraries (pandas, json, etc.)
Ensure: Message count, total time, and throughput metrics
  Initialize logger with INFO level and load dataset as data
  for max_messages in {100, 1000, 10000} do
      Sample data_sample of size max_messages from data
      Initialize Kafka producer and start_time
      for each row in data_sample up to max_messages do
          Produce message to 'temp_humidity_topic'; increment message_count
          Log progress every 10 messages; sleep 0.001s for simulation
      end for
      Flush producer, calculate total_time and throughput as message_count / total_time
      Log final metrics: message_count, total_time, and throughput
  end for
```

Algorithm A2 reports the pseudocode defining the Kafka consumer tool, still considering varying numbers of input messages.

Algorithm A2 Kafka Consumer Pseudocode

```
Require: Kafka and essential libraries (json, time, etc.)
Ensure: Processed message count, total time, and throughput metrics
  Initialize logger with INFO level and set consumer_config with Kafka parameters
  Initialize Kafka consumer with consumer_config and subscribe to 'temp_humidity_topic'
  function CONSUME_MESSAGES(max_messages)
      Start timer (start_time); initialize message_count to 0
      while message_count < max_messages do
          Poll for messages with timeout
          if message error then
              Log error and continue polling
          else
              Decode JSON message, log message, and increment message_count
              if message_count is divisible by 10 then
                  Log progress
              end if
          end if
      end while
      Calculate total_time and throughput as message_count / total_time
      Log final metrics and close consumer
  end function
  Run consume_messages for max_messages values {100, 1000, 10000}
```

Furthermore, we described the pseudocodes for, respectively, configuring both RabbitMQ producer and consumer with varying input workloads (Algorithms A3 and A4).

Algorithm A3 RabbitMQ Producer Pseudocode

Ensure: Total messages sent, total time, and throughput metrics
  Initialize `logger` with `INFO` level
  Load dataset as `data`
  for `max_messages` in {100, 1000, 10000} **do**
    Sample `data` with `max_messages` rows as `data_sample`
    Establish RabbitMQ connection and declare durable queue `'temp_humidity_queue'`
    Start timer (`start_time`) and log initial message
    Initialize `message_count` to 0
    for each row in `data_sample` **do**
      Convert `row` to `json` and publish to RabbitMQ queue `'temp_humidity_queue'`
      Increment `message_count` and **sleep** briefly
      if `message_count` is divisible by 10 **then**
        Log progress
      end if
    end for
    Close connection, calculate `total_time`, and compute `throughput`
    Log final metrics and output:
      "Total Messages: `message_count`", "Total Time: `total_time`", "Throughput: `throughput`"
  end for

Algorithm A4 RabbitMQ Consumer Pseudocode

Ensure: Total messages consumed, total time, and throughput metrics
  Initialize `logger` with `INFO` level
  Establish RabbitMQ connection and declare durable queue `'temp_humidity_queue'`
  for `max_messages` in {100, 1000, 10000} **do**
    Set `start_time` and initialize `message_count` to 0
    function CALLBACK(`ch, method, properties, body`)
      Parse `body` as `message_data`; log data and acknowledge message
      Increment `message_count`
      if `message_count` is divisible by 10 **then**
        Log progress
      end if
      if `message_count` $\geq$ `max_messages` **then**
        Stop consuming
      end if
    end function
    Log start; set `prefetch` to 1; register `callback` and start consuming
    On exit, calculate `total_time` and compute `throughput`
    Log final metrics and output:
      "Total Messages: `message_count`", "Total Time: `total_time`", "Throughput: `throughput`"
    Close connection
  end for

The pseudocode for configuring the Data Processing and Analytics layer is detailed in Algorithm A5, with emphasis on the Spark Streaming tool.

Algorithm A5 Spark Streaming Code for Real-Time Monitoring

  Imports and Initial Setup
  Import necessary libraries:
    - Spark SQL libraries
    - System monitoring and time libraries
  Define data schema for incoming temperature and humidity data

Algorithm A5 *Cont.*

Initialization
Start Spark Session for real-time streaming and configure it to read from Kafka
Stream Kafka data by:
- Connecting to Kafka server
- Subscribing to the specified topic
- Loading data stream

Parse and structure data by:
- Converting data to string
- Parsing JSON data based on schema

Define Termination and Metrics Variables
Set termination parameters for detecting a halt in new data
Initialize cumulative metrics dictionary to track performance and data averages over time
Processing Function: Process Each Micro-Batch
function PROCESS_BATCH(`batch_df`, `batch_id`)
    Record start time of processing
    Capture CPU and memory usage before batch processing
    Count records in the batch
    if no new data detected after multiple batches **then**
        Increment empty batch counter
        if counter exceeds limit **then**
            Terminate the streaming job
        end if
    else
        Reset empty batch counter
    end if
    Calculate data averages by:
    - Computing average temperature and humidity values for each sensor
    - Storing these averages in a temporary structure for this batch

    Calculate performance metrics by:
    - Computing processing time, throughput, and latency
    - Recording CPU and memory usage after processing

    Update cumulative metrics with batch statistics (latency, temperature, and humidity averages)
    Log performance data by writing batch ID, record count, processing time, and system metrics to a log file
end function
Streaming Job Execution
Configure streaming query to process each batch with `process_batch` by:
- Using `foreachBatch` to apply the function to each micro-batch
- Setting `outputMode` to update with each new batch

Start and await termination of the streaming query with a timeout

Algorithm A6 reports the pseudocode for the Hadoop batch processing system.

Algorithm A6 Batch Processing Framework Using Hadoop

Ensure: Batch processing results and system metrics
Imports and Initial Setup
Import necessary libraries, including Spark SQL and system monitoring libraries
Define data schema for temperature and humidity
Initialize Spark Session
Start a Spark session with Kafka configuration
Configure Kafka settings by:
- Setting `bootstrap_servers`
- Subscribing to the specified topic
- Setting offset to `earliest` to process all data

Algorithm A6 *Cont.*

Data Loading and Batch Limiting
Load data from Kafka in batch mode
Limit data to first 10,000 records for batch simulation
Introduce artificial delay for simulated batch processing
System Metrics Before Processing
Record CPU and memory usage before processing
Start timer to measure batch processing time
Data Processing and Aggregation
Convert batch data to string format
Parse JSON and extract relevant fields according to schema
Calculate average values for each temperature and humidity sensor
Calculate Performance Metrics
Record total processing time
Count records processed and calculate throughput
System Metrics After Processing
Record CPU and memory usage after processing
Log Output to File
Format log output with batch processing results by:
- Total records processed, processing time, throughput
- CPU and memory usage before and after processing
- Calculated averages for sensor data

Write log output to file
Terminate Spark Session
Stop the Spark session

In Algorithm A7, the data processing for temperature and humidity is implemented for the monolithic app and the performance of the monolithic system is further evaluated through a simulation in Algorithm A8.

For the microservices architecture, the ingestion service is described in Algorithm A9, followed by the processing service in Algorithm A10 and storage service in Algorithm A11. Deployment of these services is handled by Kubernetes, as described in Algorithms A12–A14.

Performance testing using Locust is outlined in Algorithm A15.

Algorithm A7 Data Processing for Temperature and Humidity

Require: CSV file path
Ensure: JSON response containing mean temperature, mean humidity, and response time
Initialize `Flask` application ▷ Innovative integration of `Flask` for data processing and web services
function PROCESS_DATA
`start_time` ← `current_time()`
`data` ← `load_CSV(CSV_file_path)` ▷ Efficient CSV file ingestion for real-time processing
`mean_temp` ← `calculate_mean(data, 'temperature')` ▷ Dynamic calculation of mean temperature
`mean_humidity` ← `calculate_mean(data, 'humidity')` ▷ Dynamic calculation of mean humidity
`response_time` ← `current_time()` - `start_time` ▷ Real-time performance metric
`result` ← { `'mean_temperature'`: `mean_temp`, `'mean_humidity'`: `mean_humidity`, `'response_time'`: `response_time` }
return `JSON(result)` ▷ Response in JSON format for client applications
end function
Error Handling:
if an error occurs **then**
return `JSON({ 'error': error_message })` ▷ Robust error handling for reliable operation

Algorithm A8 Locust User Simulation for Performance Testing

Require: Target URL, number of users, spawn rate
Ensure: Performance metrics collected during load test
  function USERBEHAVIOR
    Initialize `user_session` ▷ Dynamic user session management for flexible testing
    while `session` is active **do**
      `wait_time` ← `random_between(1, 3)` ▷ Dynamic wait times to simulate real-world user behavior
      `sleep(wait_time)`
      `response` ← `send_GET(request_to_url)` ▷ Request simulation to evaluate response times and success rates
    end while
  end function

Algorithm A9 Ingestion Service—Data Loading

Require: CSV file path
Ensure: Row count of the dataset
  Initialize `Flask` application ▷ Modular service for data ingestion via `Flask`
  function INGEST_DATA
    Load CSV file ▷ Efficient and flexible data loading mechanism
    return `success_message` and `row_count`
  end function
  Error **Handling:**
    if an error occurs **then**
      return `error_message` ▷ Robust error handling for seamless operation
  Run `Flask` app on host `0.0.0.0`, port 5001 ▷ Microservice accessibility at defined port

Algorithm A10 Processing Service—Data Computation

Require: JSON data containing temperature and humidity fields
Ensure: Average temperature and humidity
  Initialize `Flask` application ▷ Decoupled microservice for data computation
  function PROCESS_DATA
    Convert JSON data to `DataFrame` ▷ Structured data processing for computation
    Compute average temperature from temperature fields ▷ Real-time analytics on temperature data
    Compute average humidity from humidity fields ▷ Real-time analytics on humidity data
    return results as JSON ▷ JSON response format for easy integration with client applications
  end function
  Error **Handling:**
    if an error occurs **then**
      return `error message` ▷ Error handling for enhanced reliability
  Run `Flask` app on host `0.0.0.0`, port 5002

Algorithm A11 Storage Service—Data Storage and Retrieval

Require: Processed data as JSON
Ensure: Stored data in JSON file, retrieve stored data
  Initialize `Flask` application ▷ Microservice to handle data persistence
  function STORE_DATA
    Write data to file ▷ Innovative approach for storing data in flexible JSON format
    return `success message`
  end function

Algorithm A11 *Cont.*

Error Handling for Storage:
  if an error occurs **then**
    return `error message` ▷ Error handling for smooth data storage
function RETRIEVE_DATA
  Read data from file ▷ Efficient retrieval mechanism for accessing stored data
  return data as JSON
end function
Error Handling for Retrieval:
  if an error occurs **then**
    return `error message` ▷ Graceful error handling for data retrieval
Run `Flask` app on host `0.0.0.0`, port 5003

Algorithm A12 Ingestion Service—Kubernetes Deployment

Require: Docker image `ingestion_service:latest`
Ensure: Deployment and service for ingestion microservice
  Define Deployment with replicas = 3 ▷ Scalable microservice deployment for high availability
  Use Docker image `ingestion_service`
  Expose port 5001 inside the container
  Define `LoadBalancer` service for external access ▷ Easy integration into Kubernetes architecture
  Map port 5001 to the service

Algorithm A13 Processing Service—Kubernetes Deployment

Require: Docker image `processing_service:latest`
Ensure: Deployment and service for processing microservice
  Define Deployment with replicas = 3
  Use Docker image `processing_service`
  Expose port 5002 inside the container
  Define `LoadBalancer` service for external access
  Map port 5002 to the service

Algorithm A14 Storage Service—Kubernetes Deployment

Require: Docker image `storage_service:latest`
Ensure: Deployment and service for storage microservice
  Define Deployment with replicas = 3
  Use Docker image `storage_service`
  Expose port 5003 inside the container
  Define `LoadBalancer` service for external access
  Map port 5003 to the service

Algorithm A15 Locust Performance Testing

Require: Microservice endpoints
Ensure: Response time and success rate measurements
  Define `IngestionServiceUser` ▷ Simulates user interaction with ingestion service
  Task Test ingestion service with GET request
  Define `ProcessingServiceUser` ▷ Simulates user interaction with processing service
  Task Test processing service with GET request
  Define `StorageServiceUser` ▷ Simulates user interaction with storage service
  Task Test storage service with GET request

References

1. Gharibvand, V.; Kolamroudi, M.K.; Zeeshan, Q.; Çınar, Z.M.; Sahmani, S.; Asmael, M.; Safaei, B. Cloud based manufacturing: A review of recent developments in architectures, technologies, infrastructures, platforms and associated challenges. *Int. J. Adv. Manuf. Technol.* **2024**, *131*, 93–123. [CrossRef]
2. Hayyolalam, V.; Pourghebleh, B.; Chehrehzad, M.R.; Pourhaji Kazem, A.A. Single-objective service composition methods in cloud manufacturing systems: Recent techniques, classification, and future trends. *Concurr. Comput. Pract. Exp.* **2022**, *34*, e6698. [CrossRef]
3. Brecko, A.; Kajati, E.; Koziorek, J.; Zolotova, I. Federated learning for edge computing: A survey. *Appl. Sci.* **2022**, *12*, 9124. [CrossRef]
4. Rashidifar, R.; Bouzary, H.; Chen, F.F. Resource scheduling in cloud-based manufacturing system: A comprehensive survey. *Int. J. Adv. Manuf. Technol.* **2022**, *122*, 4201–4219. [CrossRef]
5. Liu, S.; Cheng, H. Manufacturing Process Optimization in the Process Industry. *Int. J. Inf. Technol. Web Eng. (IJITWE)* **2024**, *19*, 1–20. [CrossRef]
6. Ye, Y.; Wang, M.; Yao, S.; Jiang, J.N.; Liu, Q. Big data processing framework for manufacturing. *Procedia CIRP* **2019**, *83*, 661–664. [CrossRef]
7. Wang, J.; Antwi-Afari, M.F.; Tezel, A.; Antwi-Afari, P.; Kasim, T. Artificial Intelligence in Cloud Computing technology in the Construction industry: A bibliometric and systematic review. *J. Inf. Technol. Constr.* **2024**, *29*, 480–502. [CrossRef]
8. Ge, K.; Nguyen, P.; Arnaout, R. *lucie*: An Improved Python Package for Loading Datasets from the UCI Machine Learning Repository. *arXiv* **2024**, arXiv:2410.09119.
9. Kekevi, U.; Aydın, A.A. Real-time big data processing and analytics: Concepts, technologies, and domains. *Comput. Sci.* **2022**, *7*, 111–123. [CrossRef]
10. Chiappa, S.; Videla, E.; Viana-Céspedes, V.; Piñeyro, P.; Rossit, D.A. Cloud manufacturing architectures: State-of-art, research challenges and platforms description. *J. Ind. Inf. Integr.* **2023**, *34*, 100472. [CrossRef]
11. Raptis, T.P.; Passarella, A. A survey on networked data streaming with apache kafka. *IEEE Access* **2023**, *11*, 85333–85350. [CrossRef]
12. Ooi, B.Y.; Lee, W.K.; Shubert, M.J.; Ooi, Y.W.; Chin, C.Y.; Woo, W.H. A flexible and reliable internet-of-things solution for real-time production tracking with high performance and secure communication. *IEEE Trans. Ind. Appl.* **2023**, *59*, 3121–3132. [CrossRef]
13. Kaur, J. Streaming Data Analytics: Challenges and Opportunities. *Int. J. Appl. Eng. Technol.* **2023**, *5*, 10–16.
14. Chen, W.; Milosevic, Z.; Rabhi, F.A.; Berry, A. Real-time analytics: Concepts, architectures and ML/AI considerations. *IEEE Access* **2023**, *11*, 71634–71657 . [CrossRef]
15. Xu, C.; Du, X.; Fan, X.; Giuliani, G.; Hu, Z.; Wang, W.; Liu, J.; Wang, T.; Yan, Z.; Zhu, J.; et al. Cloud-based storage and computing for remote sensing big data: A technical review. *Int. J. Digit. Earth* **2022**, *15*, 1417–1445. [CrossRef]
16. Böhm, S.; Wirtz, G. Cloud-edge orchestration for smart cities: A review of kubernetes-based orchestration architectures. *EAI Endorsed Trans. Smart Cities* **2022**, *6*, e2. [CrossRef]
17. Al Qassem, L.M.; Stouraitis, T.; Damiani, E.; Elfadel, I.M. Containerized microservices: A survey of resource management frameworks. *IEEE Trans. Netw. Serv. Manag.* **2024**, *21*, 3775–3796. [CrossRef]
18. Pontarolli, R.P.; Bigheti, J.A.; de Sá, L.B.R.; Godoy, E.P. Microservice-oriented architecture for industry 4.0. *Eng* **2023**, *4*, 1179–1197. [CrossRef]
19. Yang, H.; Ong, S.; Nee, A.Y.; Jiang, G.; Mei, X. Microservices-based cloud-edge collaborative condition monitoring platform for smart manufacturing systems. *Int. J. Prod. Res.* **2022**, *60*, 7492–7501. [CrossRef]
20. Lathkar, M. *Building Web Apps with Python and Flask: Learn to Develop and Deploy Responsive RESTful Web Applications Using Flask Framework (English Edition)*; BPB Publications: New Delhi, India, 2021.
21. Tantrapirom, K.; Pungrasmi, P.; Tangthavonsirikul, S.; Jitnaknan, T. A Reliable Real-Time Web Interface for an Online Laboratory. In *Online Engineering and Society 4.0: Proceedings of the 18th International Conference on Remote Engineering and Virtual Instrumentation*; Springer: Berlin/Heidelberg, Germany, 2021; Volume 298, p. 35.
22. Li, D.; Han, D.; Crespi, N.; Minerva, R.; Sun, Z. Fabric-scf: A blockchain-based secure storage and access control scheme for supply chain finance. *arXiv* **2021**, arXiv:2111.13538.
23. Cains, M.G.; Flora, L.; Taber, D.; King, Z.; Henshel, D.S. Defining cyber security and cyber security risk within a multidisciplinary context using expert elicitation. *Risk Anal.* **2022**, *42*, 1643–1669. [CrossRef] [PubMed]
24. Zafar, M.Q.; Khan, M.B.; Zhao, H. Cyber Security in Additive Manufacturing. In *Integration of Heterogeneous Manufacturing Machinery in Cells and Systems*; CRC Press: Boca Raton, FL, USA, 2024; pp. 151–160.
25. Sriram, G.; Rambabu, S. IMPORTANCE OF CYBERSECURITY IN ADDITIVE MANUFACTURING IN THE ERA OF INDUSTRY 4.0. *Int. J. Manuf. Mater. Mech. (IJMMME)* **2024**, *2940*, 6442.
26. Chen, J.; He, J.; Chen, F.; Lv, Z.; Tang, J.; Li, W.; Liu, Z.; Yang, H.H.; Han, G. Towards General Industrial Intelligence: A Survey on IIoT-Enhanced Continual Large Models. *arXiv* **2024**, arXiv:2409.01207.

27. Wang, J.; Xu, C.; Zhang, J.; Zhong, R. Big data analytics for intelligent manufacturing systems: A review. *J. Manuf. Syst.* **2022**, *62*, 738–752. [CrossRef]
28. Alshareef, H.N. Current development, challenges, and future trends in cloud computing: A survey. *Int. J. Adv. Comput. Sci. Appl.* **2023**, *14*, 329–338. [CrossRef]
29. Liu, C.; Su, Z.; Xu, X.; Lu, Y. Service-oriented industrial internet of things gateway for cloud manufacturing. *Robot.-Comput.-Integr. Manuf.* **2022**, *73*, 102217. [CrossRef]
30. Yang, Z.; Zhen, L. How to optimize service-oriented cloud manufacturing. *J. Oper. Res. Soc.* **2024**, 1–15. [CrossRef]
31. Vemulapalli, G. Architecting for Real-Time Decision-Making: Building Scalable Event-Driven Systems. *Int. J. Mach. Learn. Artif. Intell.* **2023**, *4*, 1–20.
32. Tian, H.; Zhao, C.; Xie, J.; Li, K. Dynamic Operation Optimization of Complex Industries Based on a Data-Driven Strategy. *Processes* **2024**, *12*, 189. [CrossRef]
33. Hossain, M.D.; Sultana, T.; Akhter, S.; Hossain, M.I.; Thu, N.T.; Huynh, L.N.; Lee, G.W.; Huh, E.N. The role of microservice approach in edge computing: Opportunities, challenges, and research directions. *ICT Express* **2023**, *9*, 1162–1182. [CrossRef]
34. Wang, L.; Jiang, Y.X.; Wang, Z.; Huo, Q.E.; Dai, J.; Xie, S.L.; Li, R.; Feng, M.T.; Xu, Y.S.; Jiang, Z.P. The operation and maintenance governance of microservices architecture systems: A systematic literature review. *J. Softw. Evol. Process* **2023**, *35*, e2433. [CrossRef]
35. Lim, M.K.; Xiong, W.; Wang, C. Cloud manufacturing architecture: A critical analysis of its development, characteristics and future agenda to support its adoption. *Ind. Manag. Data Syst.* **2021**, *121*, 2143–2180. [CrossRef]
36. Xu, C.; Du, X.; Fan, X.; Yan, Z.; Kang, X.; Zhu, J.; Hu, Z. A modular remote sensing big data framework. *IEEE Trans. Geosci. Remote Sens.* **2021**, *60*, 1–11. [CrossRef]
37. Vitorino, J.P.; Simão, J.; Datia, N.; Pato, M. IRONEDGE: Stream processing architecture for edge applications. *Algorithms* **2023**, *16*, 123. [CrossRef]
38. Naghib, A.; Jafari Navimipour, N.; Hosseinzadeh, M.; Sharifi, A. A comprehensive and systematic literature review on the big data management techniques in the internet of things. *Wirel. Netw.* **2023**, *29*, 1085–1144. [CrossRef]
39. Ramezani, S.B.; Cummins, L.; Killen, B.; Carley, R.; Amirlatifi, A.; Rahimi, S.; Seale, M.; Bian, L. Scalability, explainability and performance of data-driven algorithms in predicting the remaining useful life: A comprehensive review. *IEEE Access* **2023**, *11*, 41741–41769. [CrossRef]
40. Al-Jumaili, A.H.A.; Muniyandi, R.C.; Hasan, M.K.; Paw, J.K.S.; Singh, M.J. Big data analytics using cloud computing based frameworks for power management systems: Status, constraints, and future recommendations. *Sensors* **2023**, *23*, 2952. [CrossRef]
41. Zhang, T.; Zhao, Y.; Jia, W.; Chen, M.Y. Collaborative algorithms that combine AI with IoT towards monitoring and control system. *Future Gener. Comput. Syst.* **2021**, *125*, 677–686. [CrossRef]
42. Dapkute, A.; Siozinys, V.; Jonaitis, M.; Kaminickas, M.; Siozinys, M. Digital Twin Data Management: Framework and Performance Metrics of Cloud-Based ETL System. *Machines* **2024**, *12*, 130. [CrossRef]
43. Assadian, C.F.; Assadian, F. Data-Driven Modeling of Appliance Energy Usage. *Energies* **2023**, *16*, 7536. [CrossRef]

algorithms

MDPI

Article

A Multi-Objective Path-Planning Approach for Multi-Scenario Urban Mobility Needs

Zhaohui Wang [1,2], Meng Zhang [1,*], Shanqing Liang [1], Shuang Yu [1], Chengchun Zhang [1] and Sheng Du [3,*]

1 China Satellite Network Digital Technology Co., Ltd., Xiong'an 070001, China; liangshq@chinasatnet.com.cn (S.L.)
2 School of Computer, China University of Geosciences, Wuhan 430074, China
3 School of Automation, China University of Geosciences, Wuhan 430074, China
* Correspondence: zhangm1@chinasatnet.com.cn (M.Z.); dusheng@cug.edu.cn (S.D.)

Abstract: With the development of smart cities and intelligent transportation systems, path planning in multi-scenario urban mobility has become increasingly complex. Traditional path-planning approaches typically focus on a single optimization objective, limiting their applicability in complex urban traffic systems. This paper proposes a multi-objective vehicle path-planning approach tailored for diverse scenarios, addressing multi-objective optimization challenges within complex road networks. The proposed method simultaneously considers multiple objectives, including total distance, congestion distance, travel time, energy consumption, and safety, and incorporates a dynamic weight-adjustment mechanism. This allows the algorithm to provide optimal route choices across four application scenarios: urban commuting; energy-efficient driving; holiday travel; and nighttime travel. Experimental results indicate that the proposed multi-objective planning algorithm outperforms traditional single-objective algorithms by effectively meeting user demands in various scenarios, offering an efficient solution to multi-objective optimization challenges in diverse environments.

Keywords: path planning; urban travel; smart transportation; multi-objective optimization

1. Introduction

The development of smart cities and intelligent transportation has made multi-objective path planning a key technology to meet the demands of efficient traffic management and personalized travel in urban environments. Intelligent transportation systems require path planning to support traffic management, autonomous driving, logistics, and public transportation in finding efficient routes that alleviate traffic congestion, enhance transportation efficiency, and reduce energy consumption. Consequently, real-time dynamic planning, multi-modal travel integration, personalized demand, and big data support are essential requirements for path planning in smart cities. In modern transportation systems, multi-objective path planning can provide customized travel solutions tailored to diverse user needs, enabling them to make optimal choices by balancing factors such as time, cost, comfort, and environmental impact. Additionally, multi-objective path planning offers a scientific basis for the design of public transportation systems, road layouts, and infrastructure planning. By considering the needs of different groups and environmental impacts, urban planners can allocate resources more effectively to improve accessibility and equity in urban transportation, reduce congestion, and mitigate environmental damage.

In recent years, path planning has achieved significant advances across various domains, including intelligent transportation, robotics, logistics management, and urban planning. Traditional algorithms, such as Dijkstra's and A*, remain foundational; however, their applications are limited in complex and dynamic environments. Researchers have worked to optimize these algorithms to enhance computational efficiency and adaptability. For instance, Jin et al. proposed a multi-modal path-planning approach based on a multi-objective A* algorithm [1], meeting the complex requirements of multi-modal transportation. Akopov et al. applied real-coded genetic algorithms in simulation-based optimization for autonomous transportation systems, demonstrating higher accuracy in solving large-scale optimization problems [2]. Wu et al. introduced a 2.5D multi-objective path-planning method based on deep reinforcement learning, achieving an effective trade-off between distance and energy consumption for vehicles in off-road terrain environments [3]. Ren et al. integrated D* Lite with an improved A* algorithm to develop an incremental multi-objective path-planning algorithm [4], addressing efficiency issues in dynamic environments. Wang et al. presented a method that combines an improved A* algorithm with a multi-objective cellular genetic algorithm aimed at emergency resource allocation and path planning in natural disaster chains [5]. Bostelmann-Arp et al. developed a multi-objective evolutionary optimization approach for coverage path planning in precision agriculture, aiming to increase field coverage efficiency while reducing energy consumption [6]. Zhang et al., Huang et al., and Pu et al. employed the ant colony optimization algorithm [7–9], while Cui et al. used the artificial bee colony algorithm [10] to address the multi-objective path-planning challenges for mobile robots. Ntakolia et al. utilized the ant colony optimization algorithm to enhance each Pareto solution, evaluating the optimal solution using a Mamdani fuzzy inference system to achieve multi-objective path planning for unmanned surface vehicles [11]. Zhao et al. proposed an innovative path-planning framework for unmanned surface vessels, which integrates multi-objective optimization with a perceptual vector re-planning strategy [12]. Xin et al. utilized an improved genetic algorithm for path planning of unmanned surface vehicles, achieving an optimal balance between path length and time cost through a multi-domain inversion algorithm [13]. Li et al. developed a multi-objective path-planning method for unmanned aerial vehicle inspection in oilfields, enhancing the efficiency and reliability of route planning [14]. Salhi et al. designed a multi-objective optimization approach to balance connectivity quality and energy consumption in UAV path planning [15]. Zhang et al., Xu et al., and Yu et al. independently introduced novel multi-objective evolutionary algorithms with dual constraint-handling mechanisms [16], dimension exploration, differential evolution [17], and an adaptive evolutionary multi-objective estimation of distribution algorithm [18], respectively. These approaches yield both short and safe routes in UAV path-planning applications.

Single-objective optimization algorithms are limited in their ability to balance multiple conflicting objectives, making them less practical for path planning that requires comprehensive consideration of multiple factors. Multi-objective optimization provides a more comprehensive and flexible path-planning solution suited to diverse application scenarios and user requirements. However, optimizing multiple objectives simultaneously in path planning significantly increases the problem's complexity. Current research lacks in-depth consideration of user-specific requirements for different driving scenarios within urban traffic systems [19–21].

This study employs a genetic algorithm to optimize the A* path-planning method and introduces a dynamic weight-adjustment mechanism. This mechanism enables multi-objective path planning to dynamically prioritize objectives based on specific scenarios and user requirements, thereby providing route options that better align with user preferences. This approach holds significant potential for enhancing the efficiency of transportation systems, reducing environmental pollution, and ensuring driving safety.

2. Preliminaries

To address the multi-objective optimization problem in urban path planning, this study focuses on minimizing five key objectives: total distance; congestion distance; total time; energy consumption; and risk index. These objectives are subject to various constraints, including maximum allowable time, congestion distance limits, energy consumption limits, and safety requirements. By combining the A* algorithm and the genetic algorithm and introducing a dynamic weight-adjustment mechanism, the proposed framework aims to provide efficient solutions to multi-objective optimization challenges. This section outlines the A* algorithm for multi-objective path planning, the genetic algorithm, and the dynamic weight-adjustment mechanism.

2.1. A* Path-Planning Algorithm

The A* algorithm is a heuristic search algorithm widely used in pathfinding and graph traversal. As a heuristic search algorithm, A* iteratively selects the optimal node and expands the search path to find the optimal route globally. By using a comprehensive cost evaluation function, the A* algorithm effectively reduces the number of intermediate nodes that need to be traversed, thus enhancing algorithm efficiency. The formula for the comprehensive cost evaluation function is as follows:

$$f(n) = g(n) + h(n) \tag{1}$$

where $f(n)$ represents the comprehensive priority of node n. $g(n)$ denotes the accumulated path cost from the start node to the current node n. $h(n)$ is the heuristic estimation function, which estimates the cost from node n to the goal node.

Algorithm 1 illustrates the A* path-planning algorithm, a widely used approach for finding an optimal path from a start node to a goal node in a network graph. This algorithm initializes two sets, openSet and closeSet. The openSet contains nodes that are pending exploration, while the closeSet contains nodes that have already been explored.

In each iteration, the algorithm selects the node n from openSet with the lowest priority. If n is the goalNode, the algorithm traces back from goalNode through its parent nodes to construct and return the path from startNode to goalNode, successfully completing the search. If n is not the goalNode, it is removed from openSet and added to closeSet, marking it as explored. The algorithm then examines each neighbor m of n. If m is already in closeSet, it is skipped, as it has already been explored. If m is not in openSet, it is added to openSet, with its parent set to n, and its priority is calculated. The priority of m combines the known cost from startNode to m and the heuristic estimate from m to goalNode, balancing exploration with an efficient path toward the goal.

This process repeats until openSet is empty (indicating that no path is found) or until the goalNode is reached, at which point, the path is returned. If no path is found after all nodes are explored, the algorithm returns a message, "Path not found", signaling that no valid route exists between the start and goal nodes in the given network graph [22].

2.2. Genetic Algorithm

The genetic algorithm is an optimization algorithm based on natural selection and genetic mechanisms, suitable for solving complex global optimization problems. Its core idea is to simulate the process of biological evolution, gradually optimizing the fitness of candidate solutions through operations of "selection", "crossover", and "mutation", leading the population toward the optimal solution [23–25]. The following outlines the specific steps of the genetic algorithm:

Algorithm 1: A* Algorithm

Inputs: Road network graph G, start node n_{start}, goal node n_{goal}
Outputs: Path from n_{start} to n_{goal}, or "Path not found"

Initialize: openSet and closeSet
Add n_{start} to openSet, with priority set to 0
while openSet is not empty **do**
$n \leftarrow$ node in openSet with the highest priority
if n is n_{goal} **then**
return the path traced back from n_{goal} to n_{start}
end if
Remove n from openSet
Add n to closeSet
for each neighbor node m of $n\$m\$$ **do**
if m is in closeSet **then**
Skip this neighbor node
end if
if m is not in openSet **then**
Set m's parent node as n
Calculate m's priority
Add m to openSet
end if
end for
end while
return "Path not found"

In the initial stage of the genetic algorithm, a random population is generated, where each individual α represents a vector encoding a specific solution. Each individual is evaluated based on a fitness function $f(\alpha)$, with the goal of maximizing the fitness function.

In each generation, the selection operation is responsible for selecting individuals with higher fitness from the current population, increasing the probability that these individuals will be passed on to the next generation. The selection process is typically based on proportional selection according to individual fitness, meaning that the probability p_i of selecting an individual is positively correlated with its fitness, as given by the following formula:

$$p_i = \frac{f(x_i)}{\sum\limits_{j=1}^{N} f(x_j)} \tag{2}$$

where $f(x_i)$ represents the fitness of the i-th individual, and N is the total number of individuals in the population. Through the selection operation, individuals with higher fitness are more likely to be retained, guiding the population toward regions of higher fitness.

The crossover operation is used to perform gene recombination within the population to generate new offspring. Typically, two individuals are selected for crossover, exchanging parts of their genes to create new individuals. Assuming a crossover point k, the offspring x_{new} generated from individuals x_i and x_j can be represented as

$$x_{\text{new}} = (x_{i1}, x_{i2}, \ldots, x_{ik}, x_{j(k+1)}, \ldots, x_{jn}) \tag{3}$$

The crossover operation increases the diversity of solutions and explores a broader solution space, thereby enhancing the global search capability.

Subsequently, the mutation operation randomly modifies certain genes of an individual with a certain probability, introducing new genetic variations to maintain population diversity and prevent premature convergence to local optima. For gene x_{nk}, the mutation operation can be expressed as

$$x'nk = xnk + \delta, \text{ with probability } \mu \quad (4)$$

where δ is a small random change, and μ is the mutation rate. The mutation operation increases the exploratory capability of the population, enabling the algorithm to escape local optima and increasing the probability of global convergence.

Through multiple iterations of the above "selection–crossover–mutation" process, the genetic algorithm continuously generates new generations of individuals, gradually improving the population's fitness.

2.3. *Dynamic Weight-Adjustment Mechanism*

To adapt to the needs of different traffic scenarios, we have introduced a dynamic weight-adjustment mechanism based on real-world scenarios. This mechanism adjusts the weights in real time according to changes in the scenario and environment, enabling the path-planning process to meet diverse travel requirements. When assigning weights, we fully consider the potential correlations between different objectives. Generally, total time, congestion distance, and total distance are positively correlated. To avoid the amplification of such correlations affecting the optimization results, the dynamic adjustment mechanism reduces the weight proportions of strongly correlated objectives, ensuring the fairness of multi-objective optimization. The weights for multi-scenario urban mobility needs are shown in Table 1.

Table 1. Weights for multi-scenario urban mobility needs.

Scenario	Total Distance	Congestion Distance	Total Time	Energy Consumption	Safety
Urban Commuting	0.1	0.2	0.6	0.05	0.05
Energy-Efficient Driving	0.2	0.1	0.1	0.5	0.1
Holiday Travel	0.25	0.25	0.2	0.15	0.15
Nighttime Travel	0.2	0.05	0.2	0.15	0.4

2.3.1. Urban Commuting

In urban commuting during peak hours, traffic congestion and commute time are the primary concerns for drivers. Therefore, the dynamic weight-adjustment mechanism assigns higher weights to travel time and congestion distance in the path planning, prioritizing routes that reduce traffic congestion. Through this strategy, path planning can provide efficient travel solutions under congested conditions, helping users avoid congested sections.

2.3.2. Energy-Efficient Driving

In the context of energy-efficient driving, especially for electric vehicles and low-carbon travel demands, energy consumption becomes the primary optimization target. In this scenario, the dynamic weight-adjustment mechanism increases the weight for the energy consumption objective and reduces the weights of other objectives, guiding the algorithm to favor low-energy routes, even if travel time is slightly extended. This strategy effectively reduces overall energy consumption, aligns with the demands for energy-efficient driving, and helps save energy while extending the range of electric vehicles.

2.3.3. Holiday Travel

Holiday travelers typically value comfort and efficiency during their journeys. Users tend to prioritize travel comfort over the shortest possible time. The dynamic weight-adjustment mechanism assigns higher weights to total distance and time, ensuring that trips are both comfortable and efficient.

2.3.4. Nighttime Travel

Safety and traffic efficiency are critical considerations for nighttime travel, particularly for rideshare drivers and emergency responders. The dynamic weight-adjustment mechanism increases the weights for safety and time, ensuring safe and efficient travel in high-risk environments.

3. Multi-Objective Path Planning

In multi-objective path planning, to optimize the driving experience and enhance path-planning efficiency across different scenarios, this study targets the optimization of five objectives across various application contexts. This section introduces the specific methods for optimizing objectives.

3.1. Optimization Objectives

This study adopts the weighted sum method as the core algorithm for multi-criteria decision analysis, primarily due to its low sensitivity to weight variations and low computational complexity, which make it highly applicable to path planning. In contrast, other multi-criteria decision analysis methods have certain limitations. For instance, the multiplicative convolution method may amplify interactions between objectives, reducing the robustness of the algorithm. Similarly, although the TOPSIS method performs well in ranking solutions, its computational cost increases significantly in high-dimensional objective scenarios. Therefore, considering these factors, the weighted sum method is the optimal choice for this study.

The goal of multi-objective path planning is to minimize a weighted comprehensive objective function $F_{\text{total}}(p)$. The path p is defined as a sequence of consecutive nodes $(n_1, n_2, \ldots, n_k)$, where each pair of nodes (n_i, n_{i+1}) forms an edge in the graph G. This function consists of multiple weighting factors and corresponding objective terms, each representing a different optimization requirement. Each weighting factor is dynamically adjusted during the path-planning process based on the demands of real-world scenarios, enabling multi-objective optimization of the path. To ensure comparability among the optimization objectives, each objective needs to be normalized. The normalization method is detailed in Formula (16). The mathematical model for this multi-objective path optimization problem is as follows:

$$\begin{aligned} \min_p F_{\text{total}}(p) &= \alpha(t) \cdot f_{\text{length}}(p) \\ &+\beta(t) \cdot f_{\text{congestion}}(p) + \gamma(t) \cdot f_{\text{time}}(p) \\ &+\delta(t) \cdot f_{\text{energy}}(p) + \epsilon(t) \cdot f_{\text{risk}}(p) \end{aligned} \tag{5}$$

$$\text{s.t.} \begin{cases} f_{\text{time}}(p) \leq T_{\max} \\ f_{\text{congestion}}(p) \leq C_{\max} \\ f_{\text{energy}}(p) \leq E_{\max} \\ f_{\text{risk}}(p) \leq R_{\max} \end{cases} \tag{6}$$

$$\forall i \in \{1,2,\ldots,k-1\},\ (n_i, n_{i+1}) \in E \tag{7}$$

where $\alpha(t)$, $\beta(t)$, $\gamma(t)$, $\delta(t)$, and $\epsilon(t)$ are the weighting coefficients dynamically adjusted according to the scenario. $f_{\text{length}}(p)$ represents the total length of path p; $f_{\text{congestion}}(p)$ is the congestion length of path p; $f_{\text{time}}(p)$ denotes the total time of path p; $f_{\text{energy}}(p)$ represents the energy consumption of path p, and $f_{\text{risk}}(p)$ is the risk index of path p.

Equation (6) describes the constraints of this optimization problem. The path must be composed of consecutive nodes from the start to the destination, meaning that there is an edge between each pair of adjacent nodes n_i and n_{i+1} in graph G. The total travel time $f_{\text{time}}(p)$ has an upper limit $T_{\max}$, representing the maximum acceptable travel time. The congestion length $f_{\text{congestion}}(p)$ has an upper limit $C_{\max}$ to avoid paths passing through severely congested areas. The energy consumption $f_{\text{energy}}(p)$ has an upper limit $E_{\max}$, meeting the demand for energy conservation. The risk index $f_{\text{risk}}(p)$ has an upper limit $R_{\max}$ to ensure driving safety.

Equation (7) describes the decision variable constraints of the optimization problem. The decision variable is the feasibility constraint of the path: the path must consist of consecutive nodes from the start to the end, with an edge connecting each pair of adjacent nodes n_i and n_{i+1}. k represents the total number of nodes in the path, and $(n_i, n_{i+1}) \in E$ indicates that there is an edge between node n_i and node n_{i+1}.

This study selects five optimization objectives: total distance; congestion distance; time; energy consumption; and risk index. These objectives comprehensively assess the feasibility of each path based on the actual needs of users. Each optimization objective is described in detail below.

1. Total Distance

The total distance of the path is defined as the cumulative length from the starting point to the endpoint. Given a path node sequence $n_1, n_2, \ldots, n_k$, where k is the number of nodes in the path, the total distance $f_{\text{length}}(p)$ of the path is expressed as

$$f_{\text{length}}(p) = \sum_{i=1}^{k-1} d(n_i, n_{i+1}) \tag{8}$$

where $d(n_i, n_{i+1})$ represents the distance between nodes n_i and n_{i+1};

2. Congestion Distance

The congestion distance refers to the cumulative length of all congested segments in the path and is used to assess the traffic condition of the path. Congestion status is determined by the "congestion tag" in the path. The congestion distance $f_{\text{congestion}}(p)$ of the path is defined as follows:

$$f_{\text{congestion}}(p) = \sum_{i=1}^{k-1} \begin{cases} d(n_i, n_{i+1}), \text{if congestion}(n_i, n_{i+1}) > 0 \\ 0, \text{otherwise} \end{cases} \tag{9}$$

where congestion(n_i, n_{i+1}) is the congestion value of edge (n_i, n_{i+1}). If the congestion value is greater than zero, the segment distance is included in the cumulative congestion distance;

3. Total Time

The total time $f_{\text{time}}(p)$ of the path comprises the driving time and the waiting time at red lights. In this study, the average vehicle speed is set to v = 60 km/h, and the red light waiting time is assumed to be 1 min per stop. The total time can be expressed as

$$f_{\text{time}}(p) = \frac{f_{\text{length}}(p)}{v} + r \cdot t_r \tag{10}$$

where $f_{\text{length}}(p)$ is the total length of the path; r is the number of red lights along the path, and t_r is the waiting time per red light;

4. Energy Consumption

Based on the phenomenon of increased energy consumption under congested conditions, this study evaluates energy consumption according to the congestion status of the path. Due to frequent acceleration, deceleration, and idling, vehicles experience additional energy consumption. The value of 20% is used as an average to represent the extra impact of congestion on energy consumption. The total energy consumption $f_{\text{energy}}(p)$ of the path can be represented as

$$f_{\text{energy}}(p) = \sum_{i=1}^{k-1} e(n_i, n_{i+1}) \tag{11}$$

where $e(n_i, n_{i+1})$ denotes the unit energy consumption from node n_i to node n_{i+1}, defined as

$$e(n_i, n_{i+1}) = d(n_i, n_{i+1}) \times \begin{cases} 1.2, & \text{ifcongestion}(n_i, n_{i+1}) > 0 \\ 1, & \text{otherwise} \end{cases} \tag{12}$$

When a segment of the path is congested, the energy consumption increases by 20% due to congestion; otherwise, it is calculated at the normal rate;

5. Risk Index;
6. In this study, the risk index is measured by the sum of the "road type score" and "traffic flow score". The risk index $f_{\text{risk}}(p)$ of the path is calculated as

$$f_{\text{risk}}(p) = \frac{d(n_i, n_{i+1})}{f_{\text{length}}} \sum_{i=1}^{k-1} (\text{RL}(n_i, n_{i+1}) + \text{TL}(n_i, n_{i+1})) \tag{13}$$

where $\text{RL}(n_i, n_{i+1})$ represents the road type score from node n_i to node n_{i+1}; $\text{TL}(n_i, n_{i+1})$ represents the traffic flow score from node n_i to node n_{i+1}; $d(n_i, n_{i+1})$ is the length of the edge from node n_i to node n_{i+1}, and $f_{\text{length}}(p)$ is the total length of the path. The road type score is as follows:

$$\text{RL}(n_i, n_{i+1}) = \begin{cases} 5, & \text{Highway} \\ 4, & \text{Urban Main Road} \\ 3, & \text{Urban Secondary Road} \\ 2, & \text{Rural Road, Alley, Side Road} \\ 1, & \text{Other} \end{cases} \tag{14}$$

The traffic flow score is as follows:

$$\text{TL}(n_i, n_{i+1}) = \begin{cases} 1, \geq 2000\text{vehicles/day} \\ 3,\ 500 \sim 2000 \text{ vehicles/day} \\ 5, \leq 500 \text{ vehicles/day} \end{cases} \tag{15}$$

The risk index comprehensively considers the impact of road type and traffic flow on the safety of the path. A higher score indicates a greater potential risk associated with the road. When optimizing the path, the system tends to favor paths with a lower risk index to enhance overall safety.

The selection of the above optimization objectives aims to comprehensively evaluate path quality from multiple dimensions, meeting the diverse requirements of vehicle path planning in intelligent transportation systems. The importance of each optimization objective varies across different scenarios. Through the dynamic weight-adjustment mechanism, the system can provide optimized path selections tailored to each specific scenario.

3.2. Optimization Method

In this experiment, a genetic algorithm is used for multi-objective optimization of path planning. The genetic algorithm is an evolutionary algorithm based on the principles of natural selection and genetics, evolving a population of paths through selection, crossover, and mutation operations to approximate the optimal solution in a multi-objective space. In the genetic algorithm optimization for multi-objective path planning, the diversity and rationality of the initial population are key factors influencing the final optimization effect. To generate an initial population that is both diverse and feasible, this study uses the A* algorithm to generate a set of feasible paths from the start node to the goal node. To avoid excessive concentration or convergence of the generated paths, a dynamic avoidance point strategy is introduced, which enhances the diversity of each path in the population while maintaining feasibility. This approach allows a more comprehensive coverage of the search space, facilitating crossover and mutation operations in subsequent genetic processing. For each generated path, the values of each objective attribute are calculated, which will be used in the subsequent multi-objective optimization process.

Algorithm 2 describes the process of generating an initial population of paths. First, it accepts the road network graph G, the start node n_{start}, the end node n_{end}, and the number of candidate paths M as inputs. To enhance path diversity, the algorithm temporarily removes nodes from the avoidance set P_{avoid} during each path generation to ensure that the generated paths are not completely identical. In each iteration, the algorithm uses the A* algorithm to search for the optimal path b_k from the start node to the end node in the road network graph. Then, the generated path b_k is added to the candidate path set P, and a node from path b_k is selected and added to the avoidance set P_{avoid} to prevent this node from being included in subsequent path generations. After the path generation is completed, the nodes in P_{avoid} are restored to the road network graph G to ensure the integrity of the graph for the next path generation. Finally, the algorithm returns the initial population P, which contains M paths.

Algorithm 2: A* Initial Path Generation

Input: G: Road network graph, n_{start}: Start node, n_{end}: End node, M: Number of candidate paths to generate in the population
Output: P: Set of candidate paths in the initial population

1. Initialize population count: population $\leftarrow 0$
2. $P \leftarrow \varnothing$
3. $P_{\text{avoid}} \leftarrow \varnothing$
4. **for each** $k = (1, \ldots, M)$ **do**
5. Temporarily remove nodes in P_{avoid} from G
6. Use the A* algorithm in G to search for the optimal path b_k from n_{start} to n_{end}
7. Add the generated path b_k to the path set P
8. Select a node from b_k and add it to P_{avoid}
9. Restore nodes in P_{avoid} to G
10. **end for**
11. **return** P

Algorithm 3 describes the process of using a genetic algorithm on the road network graph G to find the optimal path from the start node n_{start} to the end node n_{end}. Unlike traditional genetic algorithms that rely on fixed weights, Algorithm 3 employs dynamic weights $\alpha(t)$, $\beta(t)$, $\gamma(t)$, $\delta(t)$, and $\epsilon(t)$, allowing the algorithm to adapt to varying optimization priorities. In addition, the use of the A* algorithm ensures that paths generated during mutation remain valid and connected. The algorithm begins by generating an initial population of paths. For each path b_k, its cost is calculated as the weighted sum of multiple objectives, including path length, congestion, time, energy consumption, and risk. The paths are then sorted by their costs, and the lowest-cost half is selected as parents for reproduction.

Algorithm 3: Path Optimization Algorithm

Inputs: Road network graph G, start node n_{start}, end node n_{end}, initial population size N, maximum iterations T, mutation rate k.
Output: B: Optimal path after crossover and mutation.

$globalBest \leftarrow$ None
$minCost \leftarrow \infty$
for each candidate path b_k in the initial population P **do**
$cost \leftarrow \alpha(t) \cdot f_{\text{length}}(b_k) + \beta(t) \cdot f_{\text{congestion}}(b_k) + \gamma(t) \cdot f_{\text{time}}(b_k) + \delta(t) \cdot f_{\text{energy}}(b_k) + \epsilon(t) \cdot f_{\text{risk}}(b_k)$
end for
$selected \leftarrow$ Select top $N/2$ paths based on $cost$
$P_{\text{new}} \leftarrow \varnothing$
for each pair of paths (path1, path2) in *selected* **do**
Select random crossover point c
child1 ← path1[0:c] + path2[c+1:]
child2 ← path2[0:c] + path1[c+1:]
Add child1 and child2 to P_{new}
end for
for each path in P_{new} **do**
if random probability < mutation rate
Select path[m] as mutation point
Select new node connected to path[m] and insert after path[m]
if path[m+1] and new node are not directly connected
Generate *pathlink* ←A*$_{\text{search}}$ (G, new node, path[m+1])
Insert *pathlink* into path
end if
end if
end for
$B \leftarrow$ Select the path with the minimum $cost$ in P_{new}
if $cost(B) < minCost$
$globalBest \leftarrow B$
$minCost \leftarrow cost(B)$
end if
$generation \leftarrow generation + 1$
if $generation \geq T$
return $globalBest$
end if.

Next, the selected paths are shuffled and paired for crossover operations. For each pair of parent paths, path1 and path2, a random crossover point c along the path length is selected. Two child paths are created by combining the first half of path1 with the second half of path2 to form child1 and the first half of path2 with the second half of path1 to form child2. These child paths are added to the new population P_{new} to increase diversity.

Subsequently, each path in P_{new} undergoes a mutation operation with a certain probability. If a mutation occurs, a random node m in the path is selected as the mutation point, and a new node connected to m is selected as the insertion node. If the new node is not adjacent to the next node in the path, the A* algorithm is used to generate a sub-path (referred to as "pathlink") connecting the insertion node to the subsequent node in the original path, ensuring the connectivity and validity of the path. After each iteration, the path B with the minimum cost in the population is selected. If B's cost is lower than the global minimum cost minCost, B is marked as the global best path, referred to as "globalBest". The algorithm continues until the maximum number of iterations T is reached, at which point, it outputs the globalBest path.

This algorithm ensures diversity in the optimized paths through crossover and mutation operations, enabling the generation of solutions that satisfy multi-objective constraints. It ensures the generated paths meet the required targets while exhibiting optimal trade-offs and characteristics.

4. Experimental Design

This study adopts a multi-objective optimization approach for path planning by combining the A* algorithm with a genetic algorithm and applying weighted objectives to achieve optimal solutions. This section provides a detailed explanation of this experimental scheme for multi-objective path planning. The specific experimental scheme is shown in Figure 1.

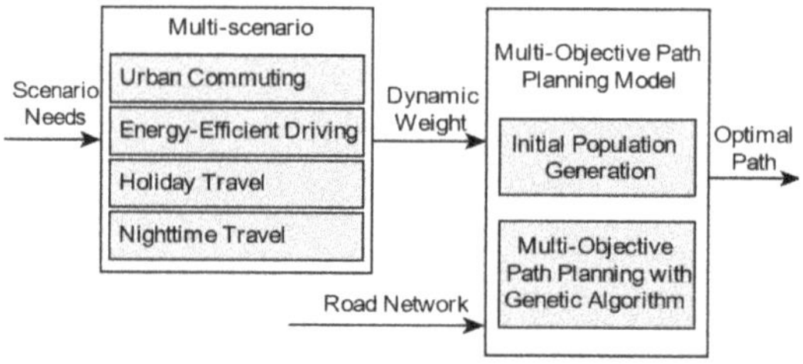

Figure 1. Multi-objective path-planning scheme.

This study uses open-source road network data obtained from OpenStreetMap [26]. The road network data are converted into a graph structure, and graph search algorithms are applied for path planning. Each intersection is treated as a node, and the segments between adjacent intersections serve as edges. The node information includes geographic coordinates and other details, while edges represent road segments and contain attributes such as length and road type. Additionally, to better simulate real traffic conditions, this study introduces randomly generated traffic lights and congestion attributes in the experimental design. Traffic light attributes include red and green signals, simulating the signal control characteristics of real-world traffic intersections. Furthermore, each edge is randomly assigned a congestion attribute to mimic the impact of varying vehicle densities on traffic speed, making path planning more aligned with actual requirements.

In this experiment, an initial population is generated using Algorithm 1, consisting of paths with the same start and end points but different routes. To evaluate the quality of each path individual, a comprehensive fitness function is designed. The fitness function is based on the weighted sum of the following five optimization objectives: total path length, length of congested segments, total time, energy consumption, and safety. To avoid the influence of scale differences between the various objectives on optimization and to make each objective comparable in fitness calculations, each objective is normalized.

This normalization ensures that indicators with different units have a consistent basis for comparison. Let x be the raw value of a certain objective, and let x_{min} and x_{max} be the minimum and maximum values of this objective within the current population, respectively. The normalized value x_{norm} is calculated as follows:

$$x_{\text{norm}} = \frac{x - x_{\text{min}}}{x_{\text{max}} - x_{\text{min}}} \quad (16)$$

Through this normalization, the range of each objective is unified within the interval [0, 1], ensuring a balanced influence of different objectives on fitness during the optimization process. The normalized initial population data are then processed by Algorithm 2, where continuous crossover and mutation operations are applied to find the optimal path under multi-objective constraints.

5. Discussion

The performance of the multi-objective path-planning algorithm is presented across different experimental scenarios, with a detailed analysis of each experimental result. By comparing the optimization effectiveness of paths generated by different algorithms, the effectiveness of the proposed method is verified.

This experiment selected road network data within Wuhan as the study area, setting two geographical coordinates within Wuhan as the start and end points for path planning, with latitude and longitude coordinates of (114.2547391, 30.632697) and (114.3286448, 30.3069509), respectively. The geographic area of this experiment covers various road types, including highways, main roads, secondary roads, and residential roads, allowing the influence of different road types on various indicators to be reflected, thereby providing a more comprehensive test of the algorithm's performance in multi-objective trade-offs.

In this experiment, 10 initial paths were generated using the A* algorithm with dynamic avoidance points, and optimized paths were selected using the multi-objective optimization algorithm. In different scenarios, the requirements and focus of path planning vary. Therefore, to evaluate the effectiveness of the algorithm in the multi-objective optimization process, we compared the changes in each indicator between the optimized paths and the initial population and conducted statistical analysis, as shown in Table 2. The path maps for each scenario are shown in Figure 2, where the red curve represents the optimized path, and the other colored curves represent the paths from the initial population.

From the distribution of paths in each scenario shown in Figure 2, it can be observed that the dynamic avoidance point strategy significantly enhances the diversity of the population, providing a broad search space for the genetic algorithm. Table 2 presents the weighted cost and the three lowest-cost initial population paths, along with the optimized path for each scenario. In the "Urban Commuting" scenario, the optimized path has a total length of approximately 69 km, significantly shorter than the paths in the initial population. The total time of the optimized path is also lower than that of the initial population paths, meeting the primary requirement for speed and smooth traffic flow during peak hours. In the "Energy-Efficient Driving" scenario, the energy consumption of the optimized path is significantly lower than the average energy consumption level of the initial population, with fewer congested segments, further reducing energy usage. In the "Holiday Travel" scenario, the optimized path exhibits excellent performance in terms of total length, risk index, and energy consumption, balancing the trip's cost-effectiveness with driving safety. In the "nighttime travel" scenario, the optimized path performs well in terms of risk index and path length, ensuring safety while reducing congested segments.

Table 2. Result of the multi-objective path-planning approach.

Scenario	Path Type	Total Length (km)	Congestion Length (km)	Total Time (hours)	Risk Index	Energy Consumption	Weighted Cost
Urban Commuting	Initial Population 5	75.5	7.657	1.258	4.674	77,030.846	0.276
	Initial Population 1	74.517	7.318	1.242	4.605	75,980.633	0.21
	Initial Population 2	70.533	8.113	1.176	4.93	72,155.424	0.079
	Optimized Path	**69.442**	**4.077**	**1.391**	**4.623**	**70,257.355**	**0.075**
Energy-Efficient Driving	Initial Population 5	75.5	7.657	1.258	4.674	77,030.846	0.269
	Initial Population 1	74.517	7.318	1.242	4.605	75,980.633	0.204
	Initial Population 2	70.533	8.113	1.176	4.93	72,155.424	0.075
	Optimized Path	**65.458**	**4.872**	**1.474**	**4.974**	**66,432.146**	**−0.192**
Holiday Travel	Initial Population 7	76.499	9.229	1.275	4.608	78,344.574	0.410
	Initial Population 5	75.500	7.657	1.258	4.674	77,030.846	0.393
	Initial Population 1	74.517	7.318	1.242	4.605	75,980.633	0.304
	Optimized Path	**73.622**	**12.218**	**1.560**	**4.136**	**76,066.184**	**0.196**
Nighttime Trave	Initial Population 7	76.499	9.229	1.275	4.608	78,344.574	0.420
	Initial Population 1	74.517	7.318	1.242	4.605	75,980.633	0.355
	Initial Population 10	83.014	16.924	1.384	4.361	86,398.536	0.350
	Optimized Path	**70.99**	**8.955**	**1.483**	**4.095**	**72,781.000**	**−0.133**

(**a**) (**b**) (**c**) (**d**)

Figure 2. Multi-Scenario Path-Planning Results: (**a**) Urban Commuting Scenario; (**b**) Energy-Efficient Driving Scenario; (**c**) Holiday Travel Scenario; (**d**) Nighttime Travel Scenario.

To further demonstrate the multi-objective optimization advantages of this algorithm in path-planning tasks, we designed a set of comparative experiments. Using the same initial path population, we compared the performance of our algorithm with single-objective optimization algorithms. The single-objective optimization algorithms selected were simulated annealing [27] and a greedy algorithm [28]. Table 3 summarizes the optimization results of each algorithm.

From the experimental results, while our algorithm shows a slight disadvantage in the total travel time of the paths, it exhibits significant advantages in multiple dimensions, including path length, congestion avoidance, energy consumption control, and safety. First, the total length and congestion length in each scenario for our algorithm are almost universally lower than those of the single-objective optimization algorithms, indicating that multi-objective optimization can more efficiently avoid congested areas and find shorter paths. Second, the energy-saving effect of the multi-objective optimization algorithm is significantly better than that of the single-objective algorithms, making it an ideal choice for environmentally conscious users and those with long-distance driving needs. Additionally, the risk index of the paths planned by our algorithm is generally lower than that of the single-objective optimization algorithms, effectively enhancing the safety of users during driving. Finally, despite balancing multiple objectives, our algorithm demonstrates a shorter execution time compared to other methods like simulated annealing and greedy algorithms, highlighting its efficiency and practicality in real-world applications.

This fully demonstrates the effectiveness and superiority of our algorithm in meeting diverse path-planning requirements, providing an ideal path-planning solution for future real-world applications.

Table 3. Comparison results with other optimization methods.

Path Type	Total Length	Congestion Length	Total Time	Risk Index	Energy Consumption	Execution Time (s)
Genetic Algorithm Multi-Objective Optimization (Urban Commuting)	69.442	**4.077**	1.391	4.623	70,257.355	144.33
Genetic Algorithm Multi-Objective Optimization (Energy-Efficient Driving)	**65.458**	4.872	1.474	4.974	**66,432.146**	152.21
Genetic Algorithm Multi-Objective Optimization (Holiday Travel)	69.532	**4.077**	1.409	4.621	70,347.685	148.17
Genetic Algorithm Multi-Objective Optimization (Nighttime Travel)	73.63	12.218	1.56	**4.174**	76,073.595	**140.94**
Simulated Annealing Single-Objective Optimization	75.493	8.199	1.258	4.691	77,133.551	173.14
Greedy Algorithm Single-Objective Optimization	75.117	8.199	**1.251**	4.701	76,756.651	165.49

6. Conclusions

This study proposes a multi-objective path-planning method for vehicles in urban transportation tailored for various scenarios. The method introduces a dynamic weight-adjustment mechanism to accommodate the requirements of different traffic scenarios. Experiments conducted on the road network data from OpenStreetMap validate the effectiveness of this approach in meeting the demands of various scenarios, including urban commuting, energy-efficient driving, holiday travel, and nighttime travel. Compared with traditional single-objective optimization algorithms, the proposed method balances multiple conflicting objectives in path planning, resulting in more reasonable routes. This study provides a practical solution to the problem of multi-scenario, multi-objective path planning and demonstrates strong potential for application in urban transportation system optimization. As traffic networks expand and demands become more diverse, future research could further enhance the computational efficiency of the algorithm and introduce additional constraints to improve its applicability in real-time traffic environments. This study highlights the flexibility of the proposed method in addressing diverse traffic conditions, paving the way for its integration and application in intelligent transportation systems. Future research should explore the application of this method in more complex and dynamic traffic networks, such as multi-modal transportation systems or scenarios with highly variable traffic flow. Additionally, efforts could be made to further enhance the algorithm's real-time computational performance and incorporate more optimization objectives or constraints to expand its practical applicability.

Author Contributions: Conceptualization, Z.W. and M.Z.; methodology, Z.W.; software, M.Z.; validation, Z.W., M.Z., and C.Z.; formal analysis, S.Y.; investigation, S.L.; resources, C.Z.; data curation, S.D.; writing—original draft preparation, Z.W. and M.Z.; writing—review and editing, Z.W. and S.D.; visualization, S.L.; supervision, S.D.; project administration, Z.W.; funding acquisition, C.Z. All authors have read and agreed to the published version of the manuscript.

Funding: This research was funded by the Industry–University–Research Cooperation Project, grant number 2024-P-01-00001536-07-1453.

Data Availability Statement: No new data were created or analyzed in this study. Data sharing is not applicable to this article.

Conflicts of Interest: Authors Zhaohui Wang, Meng Zhang, Shanqing Liang, Shuang Yu and Chengchun Zhang were employed by the company China Satellite Network Digital Technology Co., Ltd. The remaining authors declare that the research was conducted in the absence of any commercial or financial relationships that could be construed as a potential conflict of interest.

References

1. Jin, B. Multi-objective A* algorithm for the multimodal multi-objective path planning optimization. In Proceedings of the 2021 IEEE Congress on Evolutionary Computation (CEC), Kraków, Poland, 28 June–1 July 2021; pp. 1704–1711.
2. Akopov, A.S.; Beklaryan, L.A.; Beklaryan, A.L. Simulation-Based Optimisation for Autonomous Transportation Systems Using a Parallel Real-Coded Genetic Algorithm with Scalable Nonuniform Mutation. *Cybern. Inf. Technol.* **2021**, *21*, 127–144. [CrossRef]
3. Wu, X.; Huang, S.; Huang, G. Deep reinforcement learning-based 2.5D multi-objective path planning for ground vehicles: Considering distance and energy consumption. *Electronics* **2023**, *12*, 3840. [CrossRef]
4. Ren, Z.; Rathinam, S.; Likhachev, M.; Choset, H. Multi-objective path-based D* lite. *IEEE Robot. Autom. Lett.* **2022**, *7*, 3318–3325. [CrossRef]
5. Wang, F.; Xie, Z.; Liu, H.; Pei, Z.; Liu, D. Multiobjective emergency resource allocation under the natural disaster chain with path planning. *Int. J. Environ. Res. Public Health* **2022**, *19*, 7876. [CrossRef] [PubMed]
6. Bostelmann-Arp, L.; Steup, C.; Mostaghim, S. Multi-objective seed curve optimization for coverage path planning in precision farming. In Proceedings of the Genetic and Evolutionary Computation Conference, Lisbon, Portugal, 15–19 July 2023; pp. 1312–1320.
7. Zhang, D.; Luo, R.; Yin, Y.; Zou, S. Multi-objective path planning for mobile robot in nuclear accident environment based on improved ant colony optimization with modified A*. *Nucl. Eng. Technol.* **2023**, *55*, 1838–1854. [CrossRef]
8. Huang, S.; Wu, X.; Huang, G. Deep reinforcement learning-based multi-objective path planning on the off-road terrain environment for ground vehicles. *arXiv* **2023**, arXiv:2305.13783.
9. Pu, X.; Song, X.; Tan, L.; Zhang, Y. Improved ant colony algorithm in path planning of a single robot and multi-robots with multi-objective. *Evol. Intell.* **2024**, *17*, 1313–1326. [CrossRef]
10. Cui, Q.; Liu, P.; Du, H.; Wang, H.; Ma, X. Improved multi-objective artificial bee colony algorithm-based path planning for mobile robots. *Front. Neurorobotics* **2023**, *17*, 1196683. [CrossRef]
11. Ntakolia, C.; Kladis, G.P.; Lyridis, D.V. A fuzzy logic approach of Pareto optimality for multi-objective path planning in case of unmanned surface vehicle. *J. Intell. Robot. Syst.* **2023**, *109*, 21. [CrossRef]
12. Zhao, L.; Bai, Y.; Paik, J.K. Achieving optimal-dynamic path planning for unmanned surface vehicles: A rational multi-objective approach and a sensory-vector re-planner. *Ocean. Eng.* **2023**, *286*, 115433. [CrossRef]
13. Xin, J.; Zhong, J.; Yang, F.; Cui, Y.; Sheng, J. An Improved Genetic Algorithm for Path-Planning of Unmanned Surface Vehicle. *Sensors* **2019**, *19*, 2640. [CrossRef] [PubMed]
14. Li, K.; Yan, X.; Han, Y.; Ge, F.; Jiang, Y. Many-objective optimization-based path planning of multiple UAVs in oilfield inspection. *Appl. Intell.* **2022**, *52*, 12668–12683. [CrossRef]
15. Salhi, M.; Delavernhe, F. Multiobjective UAV path planning: Connectivity quality and energy consumption. In Proceedings of the GLOBECOM 2023—2023 IEEE Global Communications Conference, Kuala Lumpur, Malaysia, 4–8 December 2023; pp. 746–751.
16. Zhang, W.; Peng, C.; Yuan, Y.; Cui, J.; Qi, L. A novel multi-objective evolutionary algorithm with a two-fold constraint-handling mechanism for multiple UAV path planning. *Expert Syst. Appl.* **2024**, *238*, 121862. [CrossRef]
17. Xu, X.; Xie, C.; Luo, Z.; Zhang, C.; Zhang, T. A multi-objective evolutionary algorithm based on dimension exploration and discrepancy evolution for UAV path planning problem. *Inf. Sci.* **2024**, *657*, 119977. [CrossRef]
18. Yuhang, R.; Liang, Z. An adaptive evolutionary multi-objective estimation of distribution algorithm and its application to multi-UAV path planning. *IEEE Access* **2023**, *11*, 50038–50051. [CrossRef]
19. Jeddisaravi, K.; Alitappeh, R.J.; Guimarães, F.G. Multi-objective mobile robot path planning based on A* search. In Proceedings of the 6th International Conference on Computer and Knowledge Engineering, Edinburgh, Scotland, 25–29 April 2016; pp. 7–12.
20. He, Y.; Liao, N.; Lin, K. Can China's industrial sector achieve energy conservation and emission reduction goals dominated by energy efficiency enhancement? A multi-objective optimization approach. *Energy Policy* **2021**, *149*, 112108. [CrossRef]
21. Guo, X.; Ji, M.; Zhao, Z.; Wen, D.; Zhang, W. Global path planning and multi-objective path control for unmanned surface vehicle based on modified particle swarm optimization (PSO) algorithm. *Ocean Eng.* **2020**, *216*, 107693. [CrossRef]
22. Tang, G.; Tang, C.; Claramunt, C.; Hu, X.; Zhou, P. Geometric A-Star algorithm: An improved A-Star algorithm for AGV path planning in a port environment. *IEEE Access* **2021**, *9*, 59196–59210. [CrossRef]
23. Shivgan, R.; Dong, Z. Energy-efficient drone coverage path planning using genetic algorithm. In Proceedings of the 2020 IEEE 21st International Conference on High Performance Switching and Routing (HPSR), Newark, NJ, USA, 11–14 May 2020; pp. 1–6.
24. Pehlivanoglu, Y.V.; Pehlivanoglu, P. An enhanced genetic algorithm for path planning of autonomous UAV in target coverage problems. *Appl. Soft Comput.* **2021**, *112*, 107796. [CrossRef]

25. Pan, Y.; Yang, Y.; Li, W. A deep learning trained by genetic algorithm to improve the efficiency of path planning for data collection with multi-UAV. *IEEE Access* **2021**, *9*, 7994–8005. [CrossRef]
26. OpenStreetMap. About OpenStreetMap. Available online: https://wiki.openstreetmap.org/wiki/Main_Page (accessed on 1 October 2024).
27. Ait-Saadi, A.; Meraihi, Y.; Soukane, A.; Ramdane-Cherif, A.; Gabis, A.B. A novel hybrid chaotic aquila optimization algorithm with simulated annealing for unmanned aerial vehicles path planning. *Comput. Electr. Eng.* **2022**, *104*, 108461. [CrossRef]
28. Xiang, D.; Lin, H.; Ouyang, J.; Huang, D. Combined improved A* and greedy algorithm for path planning of multi-objective mobile robot. *Sci. Rep.* **2022**, *12*, 13273. [CrossRef] [PubMed]

algorithms

MDPI

Article

Grounding Grid Electrical Impedance Imaging Method Based on an Improved Conditional Generative Adversarial Network

Ke Zhu *, Donghui Luo, Zhengzheng Fu, Zhihang Xue and Xianghang Bu

State Grid Sichuan Electric Power Research Institute, Chengdu 610041, China; dhluo@foxmail.com (D.L.); cathygold@foxmail.com (Z.F.); zhihangxue2024@163.com (Z.X.); xianghangbu2024@163.com (X.B.)
* Correspondence: kez2024@163.com

Abstract: The grounding grid is an important piece of equipment to ensure the safety of a power system, and thus research detecting on its corrosion status is of great significance. Electrical impedance tomography (EIT) is an effective method for grounding grid corrosion imaging. However, the inverse process of image reconstruction has pathological solutions, which lead to unstable imaging results. This paper proposes a grounding grid electrical impedance imaging method based on an improved conditional generative adversarial network (CGAN), aiming to improve imaging precision and accuracy. Its generator combines a preprocessing module and a U-Net model with a convolutional block attention module (CBAM). The discriminator adopts a PatchGAN structure. First, a grounding grid forward problem model was built to calculate the boundary voltage. Then, the image was initialized through the preprocessing module, and the important features of ground grid corrosion were extracted again through the encoder module, decoder module and attention module. Finally, the generator and discriminator continuously optimized the objective function and conducted adversarial training to achieve ground grid electrical impedance imaging. Imaging was performed on grounding grids with different corrosion conditions. The results showed a final average peak signal-to-noise ratio of 20.04. The average structural similarity was 0.901. The accuracy of corrosion position judgment was 94.3%. The error of corrosion degree judgment was 9.8%. This method effectively improves the pathological problem of grounding grid imaging and improves the precision and accuracy, with certain noise resistance and universality.

Keywords: grounding grid; electrical impedance tomography; generative adversarial network; corrosion detection

1. Introduction

Due to lightning, equipment failure and other problems, abnormal currents in substations may increase rapidly. At such times, the buried grounding grid provides a discharge channel for those abnormal currents. At the same time, the grounding grid also serves as a common grounding point for primary and secondary equipment in the substation to ensure the safety of the equipment [1]. In high-voltage substations and power systems, most of the grounding grid materials used are galvanized flat steel or round steel, which are prone to corrosion or fracture to varying degrees, posing a great threat to the safe operation of the power system [2,3]. Traditional detection methods generally require the substation to shut down, and then it is excavated to find the branches of the grounding grid that are corroded or broken. The whole process is cumbersome, the measurement is complex and blind, and it also affects the normal operation of the power system [4]. Electrical impedance tomography (EIT) is one of the main methods for non-invasive detection of grounding grids. It can reconstruct the on-site image of the grounding grid without large-scale excavation [5]. In recent years, many scholars have applied EIT technology to the field of grounding grid corrosion diagnosis and have made certain progress, but it still cannot intuitively display the corrosion status of the grounding grid [6,7]. References [8,9] have achieved good imaging results by optimizing the iterative algorithm of grounding grid impedance imaging, but they cannot accurately display the degree of corrosion. At present, the EIT inverse problem reconstruction algorithm based on deep learning has been widely studied and has shown its unique advantages in large-scale nonlinear reconstruction. The problem solved has a high degree of nonlinearity and it is solved with a fast solution speed thanks to easy access to simulation training datasets [10–12].

In the research on grounding grid corrosion imaging, reference [13] proposed a transient electromagnetic method for grounding grid detection using artificial neural networks to perform resistivity imaging, providing fast and accurate calculation capabilities. Reference [14] used laser-induced breakdown spectroscopy (LIBS) combined with machine learning to evaluate the degree of grounding grid corrosion, improving the accuracy of predicting the degree of corrosion. Reference [15] developed a multi-point synchronous temporary grounding wire detection device based on convolutional neural networks to accurately classify the corrosion status of the grounding grid. Most current studies use intelligent algorithms combined with electromagnetic imaging or electrical network theory to image the grounding grid [16–18]. The contribution of this paper is to demonstrate the application of impedance imaging theory combined with deep learning algorithms to image the grounding grid, which improves the precision and accuracy of grounding grid corrosion detection, and promote further research on impedance imaging of grounding grids.

Compared with traditional methods and other deep learning models, CGAN performs better in dealing with noise and nonlinearity, resulting in more accurate and stable corrosion pattern reconstruction [19–21]. The CGAN is able to learn the complex mapping between the measured voltage and the conductivity distribution from large-scale simulation data. Therefore, this paper proposes a grounding grid electrical impedance imaging method based on an improved CGAN, to improve the precision and accuracy of grounding grid corrosion detection. First, a grounding grid simulation model is established, and the boundary voltage is obtained by solving the forward problem. Then, an improved CGAN algorithm is designed, and the boundary voltage value is input for grounding grid electrical impedance imaging. The generator of this method mainly consists of four modules: the preprocessing module, encoder module, decoder module and attention module. The discriminator is a PatchGAN structure, and the grounding grid electrical impedance image is reconstructed through adaptive training and optimization of the loss function. Finally, the generated image is segmented into branches to detect the corroded branches of the grounding grid and their corrosion degree.

The main contributions of this paper are as follows:

1. This paper innovatively introduces a CGAN framework specifically for grounding grid corrosion detection based on EIT technology, which combines a preprocessing module, encoder module, decoder module and attention module to improve the imaging accuracy.

2. This paper presents a comprehensive analysis of the performance of the proposed model, proving that compared with traditional methods, not only is the reconstruction accuracy significantly improved, but also the degree of grounding grid corrosion can be more accurately judged.

3. The effectiveness of the method proposed in this paper is proven through extensive simulation and experimental data, showing that it also has good noise resistance and stability in an actual grounding grid corrosion detection task.

2. Grounding Grid Boundary Voltage Calculation

Electrical impedance tomography (EIT) has the advantages of being non-invasive, simple in structure, easy to operate and low in cost. The forward problem to be solved is the boundary voltage under a known conductivity distribution. In this paper, the finite element method (FEM) is used to decompose the grounding grid detection area into multiple grid elements and discretize them into triangular units. Taking the grounding grid model 3 × 3 as an example, the total calculation area is an area of 18 m × 18 m, including the grounding grid and the surrounding soil area. The cross-sectional area of each branch is 0.5 m × 0.05 m, the length is 5 m and the distance between adjacent nodes is 4 m. In order to ensure accurate simulation of the grounding grid, the calculation area is discretized into 31,757 triangular elements with a minimum element size of 0.01288 m^2. The mesh is finer at the nodes and around the electrode area to better capture the potential distribution. The mesh diagram after segmentation is shown in Figure 1. The node coordinate information of the triangle is then used to solve the interpolation point of the function. Finally, the linear expression is solved through the equivalent variation theory.

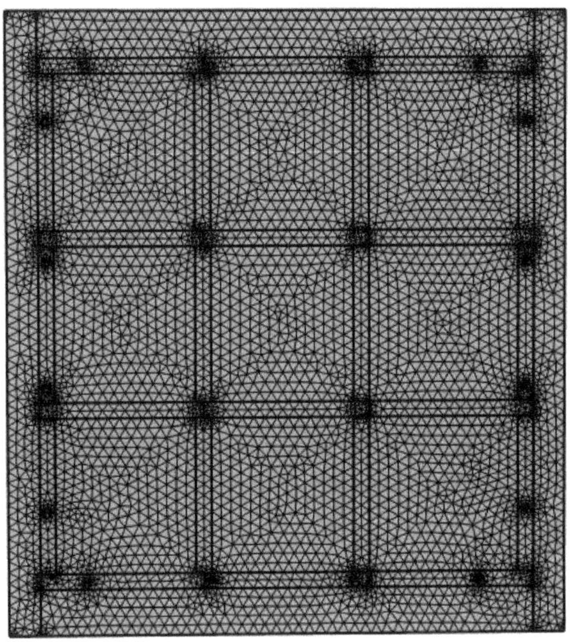

Figure 1. Schematic diagram of grounding grid model segmentation.

In a two-dimensional quasi-static field, the boundary problem of the grounding grid field can be equivalent to a variational problem. The total area S of the field is converted into the sum of the areas of the subdivided triangular units, and the boundary problem can be written as follows:

$$\begin{aligned} F(\phi) &= \int_s \frac{1}{2}\sigma\left[\left(\frac{\partial\phi}{\partial x}\right)^2 + \left(\frac{\partial\phi}{\partial y}\right)^2\right]dxdy \\ &= \sum_{n=1}^{n_0} \int_{s_n} \frac{1}{2}\sigma\left[\left(\frac{\partial\phi_n}{\partial x}\right)^2 + \left(\frac{\partial\phi_n}{\partial y}\right)^2\right]dxdy \end{aligned} \tag{1}$$

Among them, σ represents the conductivity, ϕ represents the potential distribution in the electric field, n_0 represents the total number of segmented units and s_n represents the area of the nth segmented unit. By solving the unit coefficient matrix, all unit coefficient matrices are merged into the total coefficient matrix K [22]. The linear finite element equations of the measured area can be expressed as follows:

$$K\phi = 0 \tag{2}$$

Assume that the current injected into and out of the grounding grid is I, and the nodes correspond to the m and n nodes of the finite element model, respectively, while other nodes are not processed. To establish a reference potential, a node is chosen as the ground node and its potential is set to 0. At this time, the above equation can be written as follows:

$$\begin{bmatrix} K_{11} & K_{12} & \cdots & 0 & \cdots & K_{1N} \\ K_{21} & K_{22} & \cdots & 0 & \cdots & K_{2N} \\ \vdots & \vdots & & \vdots & & \vdots \\ K_{m1} & K_{m2} & \cdots & 0 & \cdots & K_{mN} \\ \vdots & \vdots & & \vdots & & \vdots \\ K_{m1} & K_{n2} & \cdots & 0 & \cdots & K_{nN} \\ \vdots & \vdots & & \vdots & & \vdots \\ K_{l1} & K_{l2} & \cdots & 1 & \cdots & K_{lN} \\ \vdots & \vdots & & \vdots & & \vdots \\ K_{N1} & K_{N2} & \cdots & 0 & \cdots & K_{NN} \end{bmatrix} \begin{bmatrix} \phi_1 \\ \phi_2 \\ \vdots \\ \phi_m \\ \vdots \\ \phi_n \\ \vdots \\ \phi_l \\ \vdots \\ \phi_N \end{bmatrix} = \begin{bmatrix} 0 \\ 0 \\ \vdots \\ I \\ \vdots \\ -I \\ \vdots \\ 0 \\ \vdots \\ 0 \end{bmatrix} \tag{3}$$

Then, the Gaussian elimination method is used to calculate the node potential of the subdivided unit $U(\rho) = [\phi_1, \phi_2 \ldots\ldots \phi_N]$.

Based on the finite element method, this paper uses COMSOL Multiphysics 6.1 and MATLAB R2024a software to jointly simulate and establish a simulation model of 3×3 and 2×3 grounding grids with different corrosion positions, numbers and corrosion degrees. The simulation example is shown in Figure 2. The conductivity of the normal uncorroded flat steel material is 1×10^7 S/m, and the conductivity of the soil part is 5×10^{-3} S/m. This paper adopts a 16-electrode adjacent excitation model. The electrodes surround the measured area, inject the current in turn and measure the voltage value of the adjacent electrodes, and the injection current density is set to 1 A/m. The principle of adjacent excitation cycle measurement is to select 16 accessible nodes around the measured grounding grid, inject the current from adjacent nodes, $P_1 - P_2$, $P_2 - P_3$, …… $P_{15} - P_{16}$, $P_{16} - P_1$, in turn, and cyclically measure the adjacent potentials of the remaining 13 nodes except the measured node, that is, 208 boundary voltage values are obtained, and then the voltage values are reconstructed through the improved CGAN algorithm.

The conductivity ratio of grounding grid materials under normal conditions and under corrosion conditions is generally within 10 times, so this paper mainly diagnoses the corrosion of grounding grids with conductivity of 1×10^6 S/m to 1×10^7 S/m. The dataset includes 4500 sets of boundary voltage values obtained by simulation and the corresponding real conductivity distribution images, of which 80% are randomly selected as training sets, 10% as validation sets and 10% as test sets. Each pair consists of a set of boundary voltage measurements and the corresponding true conductivity map. The boundary voltage values are input into the generator to generate a conductivity distribution map, and the corresponding true conductivity distribution map is input into the discriminator to determine whether the generated image is correct or not.

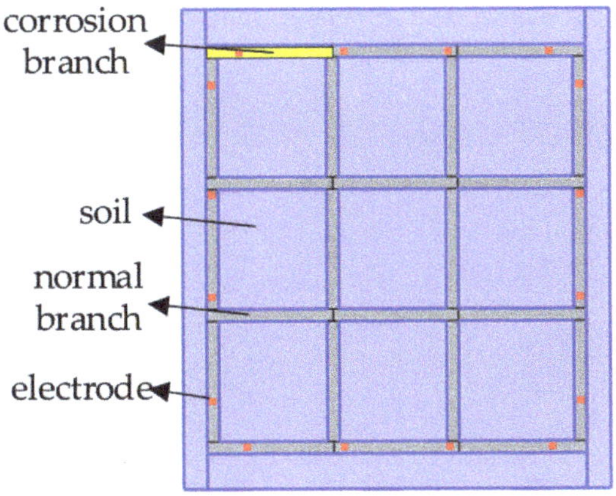

Figure 2. Simulation diagram of the forward problem of the grounding grid.

Since the traditional EIT imaging method struggles to effectively reconstruct the regular structure and corrosion conditions of each branch of the grounding grid, this paper uses the color coding method to diagnose the corrosion conditions. The defined real corrosion diagnosis image is shown in Figure 3, which is used to guide the supervised learning of the CGAN to generate the grounding grid electrical impedance imaging map. Taking the 3 × 3 structure as an example, the conductivity value and the color value are linearly mapped, and the conductivity imaging map is smoothly transitioned from blue to yellow. In the figure, the blue area indicates lower conductivity, and the yellow area indicates higher conductivity, which is conducive to image analysis after imaging the CGAN grounding grid in order to solve its corrosion location and corrosion degree.

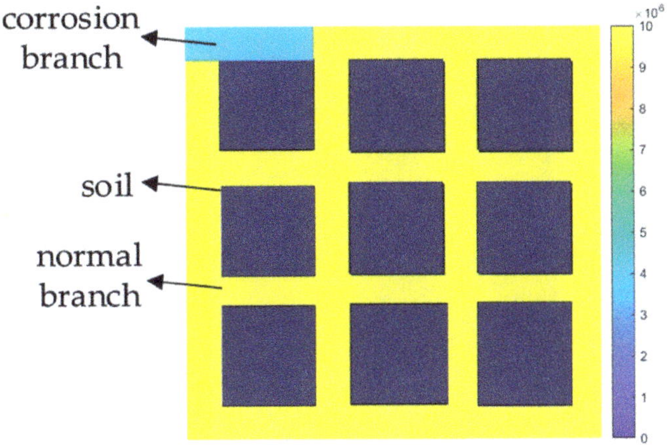

Figure 3. Real corrosion diagram of grounding grid.

3. Research on an Improved CGAN Ground Grid Imaging Algorithm

This paper designs an improved CGAN algorithm. The algorithm flow is shown in Figure 4. The generator inputs 208 voltage values obtained by the finite element method, and it generates the conductivity distribution map of the grounding grid through supervised learning. The discriminator inputs the boundary voltage and the generated or real image, and it establishes the L1 combined with CGAN loss function. The generator effect is improved through adversarial training, so that it can directly generate a real grounding grid image without the need for discriminant model reconstruction.

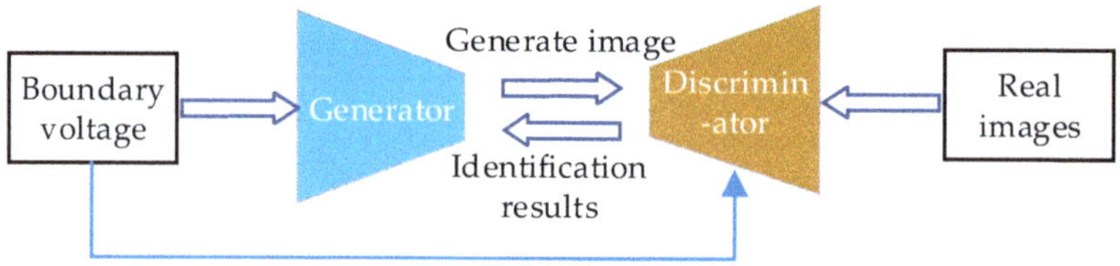

Figure 4. Improved CGAN algorithm flow chart.

3.1. Improved CGAN Structure

3.1.1. Generator Design

The generator of this method is mainly composed of four modules: the preprocessing module, encoder module, decoder module and attention module. Its structure is shown in Figure 5. First, the input layer receives the boundary voltage value, and the preliminary feature map of the ground grid electrical impedance imaging is obtained after passing through the preprocessing module. Then, the high-level features are extracted for imaging through a U-shaped structure network with a depth of 5 layers. The encoder module of U-Net consists of multiple down-sampling layers, each of which contains two convolutional layers with a convolution kernel size of 4 × 4. The stride of the first convolutional layer is 1, which is used for fine feature extraction; the stride of the second convolutional layer is 2, which replaces the traditional pooling layer to better preserve the detail information in image reconstruction. In order to speed up network training and prevent overfitting, batch normalization, a dropout layer and a leaky-ReLU activation function are introduced in the encoder. Its batch normalization is as shown in Equation (4):

$$y = \gamma\left(\frac{x-\mu}{\sqrt{\sigma^2+\varepsilon}}\right)+\beta \tag{4}$$

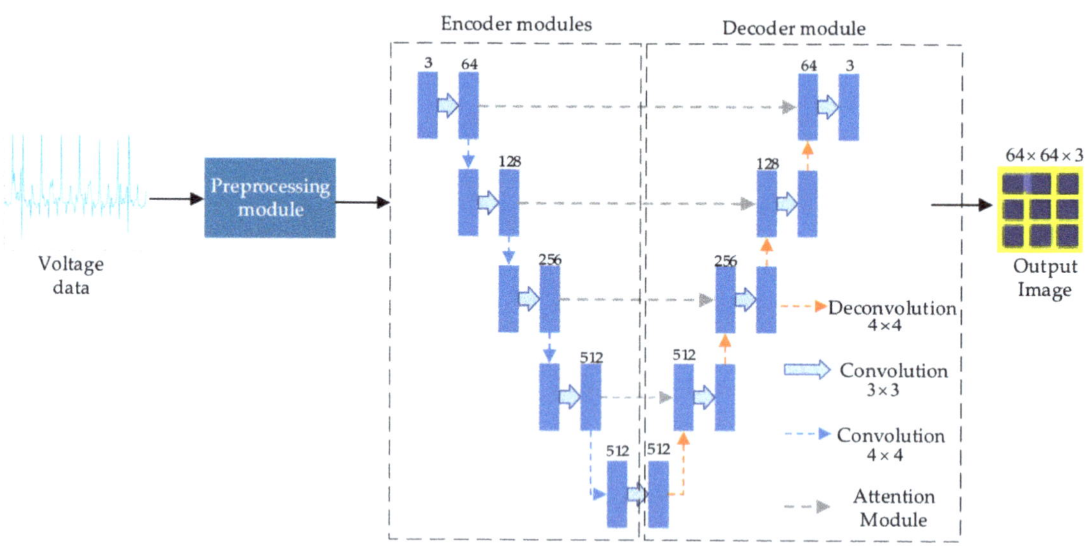

Figure 5. Generator structure diagram.

The decoder module gradually restores the spatial size of the feature map through multiple up-sampling layers and deconvolutional layers. The structure of the deconvolutional network is similar to that of the encoder, using the same convolution kernel size and stride to gradually enlarge the resolution of the feature map and finally generate a ground grid corrosion image. The size of the generated image is consistent with the input to ensure the spatial consistency of the image.

The preprocessing module is responsible for learning the nonlinear mapping relationship between the boundary voltage and the target impedance image to form a preliminary grounding grid impedance image. As shown in Figure 6, the input layer accepts 208 boundary voltage values, and the boundary voltage data sequence is converted into a 13 × 16 matrix through the fully connected layer and the deformation layer for further two-dimensional feature extraction. Its expression is given in Equation (5).

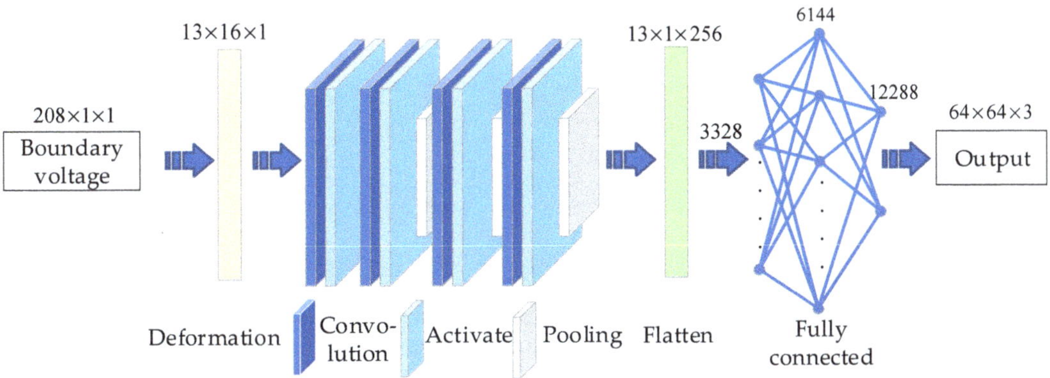

Figure 6. Preprocessing module diagram.

$$Z = reshape(\sigma(W_1 \cdot x + b_1)) \in R^{16\times13} \tag{5}$$

Then, the network extracts high-order features through a four-level convolutional network, and it finally outputs the conductivity imaging topology of the grounding grid through a deformation and fully connected network. In the first layer of the convolution structure, 32 convolution kernels of size 3 × 3 and step size 1 are used. The second, third, and fourth convolutional layers are basically the same, containing 64, 128, and 256 convolution kernels of 3 × 3 size, respectively, gradually obtaining higher-level feature information. The activation function after the convolution operation uses Leaky ReLU. After each convolutional layer, a pooling layer is used to reduce the feature size, and the pooling kernel size is 2 × 2. The activation function is Equation (6):

$$f(x) = \begin{cases} x \quad , if\ x > 0 \\ 0.01x\ , if\ x \leq 0 \end{cases} \tag{6}$$

Then, the two-dimensional information features extracted by the convolutional neural network are converted into one-dimensional information through the deformation layer, further information features are learned through two layers of fully connected layers and the Tanh function is used for normalization to generate preliminary feature information of the grounding grid. The Tanh function is Equation (7).

$$f(x) = \tanh(x) = \frac{e^x - e^{-x}}{e^x + e^{-x}} \tag{7}$$

The attention module fuses the features extracted by the encoder with the features in the decoder to better preserve details and important information. This paper adopts the CBAM (Convolutional Block Attention Module) attention mechanism to independently infer the attention map through the channel attention and spatial attention modules, thereby enhancing the transmission of feature information. As shown in Figure 7, the channel attention mechanism calculates the importance of different channels of the input feature map through global average pooling and maximum pooling, while the spatial attention mechanism assigns weights through the local information of the feature map.

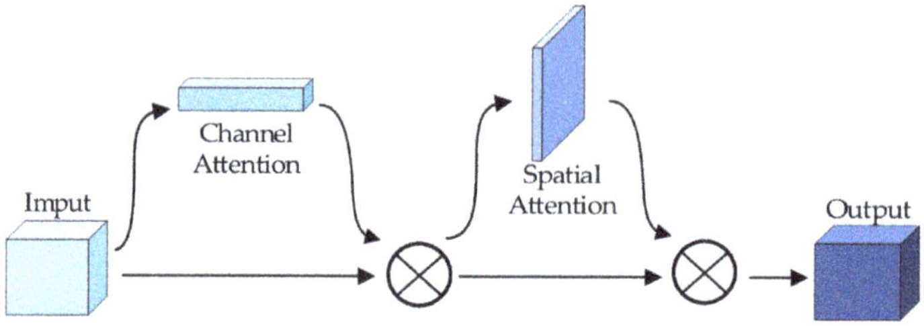

Figure 7. Attention module diagram.

For the input feature map F, the channel attention map M_c is calculated as follows:

$$M_c(F) = \sigma(MLP(AvgPool(F)) + MLP(MaxPool(F))) \tag{8}$$

Among them, $AvgPool$ and $MaxPool$ distributions are the global average pooling and average maximum pooling operations, σ is the sigmoid activation function and MLP is a multi-layer perceptron with shared weights. The spatial attention map M_s is calculated by the 7×7 convolution kernel, and the specific expression is as follows:

$$M_s(F) = \sigma\left(f^{7\times 7}([AvgPool(F); MaxPool(F)])\right) \tag{9}$$

where $f^{7\times 7}$ represents the 7×7 convolution operation of size, and ";" represents feature concatenation. Finally, by multiplying the input features point by point, CBAM can effectively strengthen the weight distribution of conductivity change features, thereby optimizing the EIT reconstruction effect under the complex distribution of grounding grid corrosion.

$$X_{out} = X + (M_c(F)) \odot (M_s(F) \odot X)) \tag{10}$$

$\odot$ represents element-wise multiplication.

3.1.2. Discriminator Design

The discriminator uses the PatchGAN structure, which can effectively capture the high-frequency features at the patch (local area) level in the image. Compared with the global discriminator, PatchGAN divides the input image into several small blocks and judges the authenticity of these small blocks one by one to ensure that the model can learn the local texture and high-frequency information in the image [23]. Its expression is Equation (11).

$$D(I) = \sum_i L(D(\hat{x}_i), y_i) \tag{11}$$

$\hat{x}_i$ is the i th patch in the image I. $D(\hat{x}_i)$ is the judgment result of the discriminator on the i th patch, outputting a scalar value indicating the probability that the patch is a real image, and y_i is the label of each patch (1 for real images and 0 for generated images).

The discriminator D uses the convolutional network as its core structure. First, it constructs a fully connected layer and a deformation layer to convert the 13 × 16 voltage sequence into a feature map of 64 × 64, which is combined with the generated image or the real image into a multi-channel feature map and then input into a four-level convolutional network structure. Each layer of the convolutional network consists of convolution, pooling and activation layers. The convolution kernel size is 5 × 5 and the step size is 2, which gradually reduces the spatial dimension of the feature map to extract high-level feature information. The four-level convolutional layers contain 64, 64, 128 and 256 filters, respectively, and a batch normalization layer is used to normalize small batches of data to accelerate the training process and improve the stability of the model. After structured analysis, the data are flattened by the flattening layer, connected to two fully connected layers for further decision-making and mapped by the Sigmoid activation function in the output layer to judge the authenticity of the image. The Sigmoid function is Equation (12):

$$\sigma(x) = \frac{1}{1+e^{-x}} \tag{12}$$

3.2. Objective Function and Training Process

The loss function of the improved CGAN algorithm in this paper is mainly composed of the L1 loss and the adversarial loss. The weighted combination of the two losses constitutes the final total loss value. The L1 loss is defined as the average value of the absolute error between the generated sample and the real sample. Compared with the L2 loss, the L1 loss has better robustness and can generate smoother images, which is more suitable for ground grid corrosion imaging tasks [24]. Considering the objective functions of G and D, the objective function of the network structure proposed in this paper is expressed as follows:

$$\begin{gathered} L = \lambda_1 \arg\min_G \max_D L_{CGAN}(D,G) + \lambda_2 L_I \\ \begin{cases} L_{CGAN}(D,G) = E_{x,y\sim p_{data}(x,y)}[\log D(x,y)] \\ \qquad + E_{x\sim p_{data}(x)}[\log(1 - D(x,G(x)))] \\ L_1 = E_{(x,y)\sim p_{data}(x,y)}[\| y - G(x) \|_1] \end{cases} \end{gathered} \tag{13}$$

In Equation (13), x represents the conditional input image, y is the target real image and p_{data} represents the distribution of data.

The entire training process is shown in Figure 8. During the training process, the training data and test data are first normalized, and then the structural parameters of the generative network and the discriminative network are set, including loss function parameters, activation function parameters, batch size parameters, number of iterations, etc., and initialized. The Adam optimizer is used for network training. The training process is mainly divided into two stages. First, the parameters of the discriminator D are fixed, and the EIT image data generated by G and the true conductivity distribution are combined with the conditional information, respectively, and input into the discriminator D to optimize the parameters of G and improve the image generation ability of the generative network; then, the parameters of the generator G are fixed, and the parameters of D are updated according to the output of G to enhance the ability of the discriminative network to identify true and false samples. The two are optimized alternately to continuously improve the overall performance.

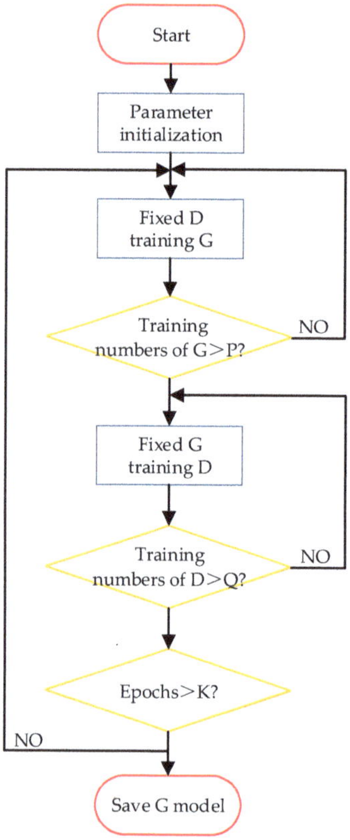

Figure 8. Training flow chart.

4. Grounding Grid Imaging Results and Evaluation Analysis

4.1. Ground Grid Imaging Results

After the dataset was constructed, 100 rounds of training were conducted. Figure 9 shows the loss curves of the generator and discriminator during the training process. The generator loss is composed of adversarial loss and L1 regularization, while the discriminator loss reflects the performance when distinguishing between real samples and generated samples. The curve shows stable convergence at around 50 rounds of training, indicating that the training is balanced and feature learning is effective, without problems such as mode collapse or over-strengthening of the discriminator.

In order to verify the effectiveness of the algorithm, this paper carried out experimental verification on a large number of test sets of grounding grid boundary voltages, analyzed the potential maps of different corrosion locations and corrosion degrees, and compared the conductivity topology maps obtained by the Tikhonov algorithm, NORSE algorithm, TV algorithm and CGAN imaging algorithm. A representative corrosion model was selected for simulation imaging, and the conductivity of the corrosion site was 2.0×10^6 S/m. The imaging effect is shown in Figure 10. According to the definition of conductivity value of image color mapping above, red, yellow and blue in turn represent the decrease of conductivity. The bluer represents lower conductivity, which is usually corrosive location or land. It is not difficult to find that the traditional EIT algorithm struggles to accurately determine the corrosion location due to its morbidity and underdetermination when solving nonlinear inverse problems. The branch edge of the conductivity topology map presented in its imaging is poor, and there are artifacts in the branch. The actual conductivity difference between the corrosion site and the soil cannot be distinguished. It can only roughly reflect the corrosion location, and it is even more difficult to determine the degree of corrosion. Although the imaging of the improved CGAN algorithm proposed in this paper has conductivity color errors and a small amount of noise, it can accurately determine the corrosion location.

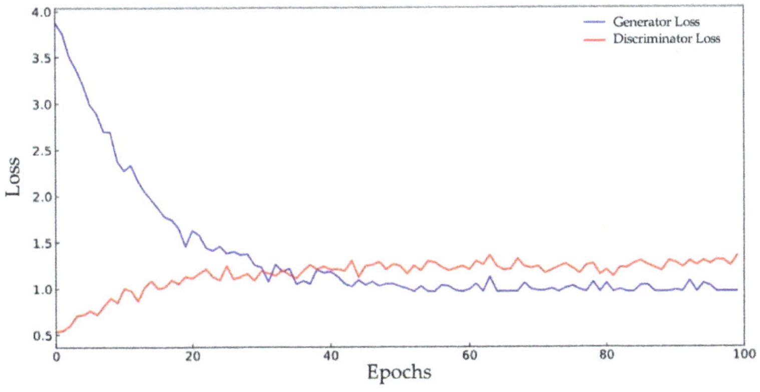

Figure 9. Generate adversarial training loss graph.

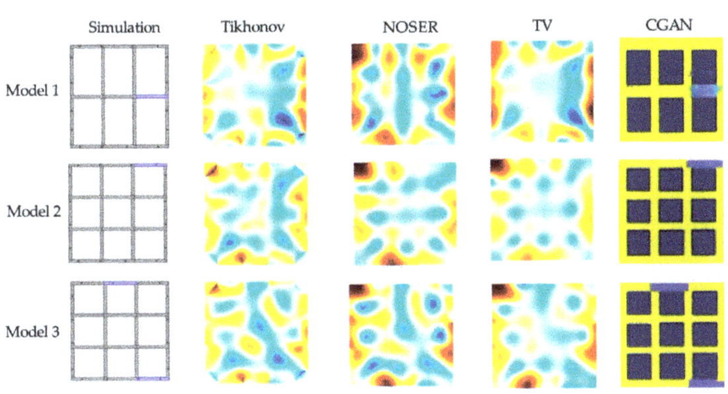

Figure 10. Comparison of traditional algorithm imaging.

The proposed CGAN-based approach introduces moderate complexity during the training phase, and once training is complete, its inference time is significantly faster than that of conventional methods. The significant improvement in reconstruction quality and noise immunity shown in Table 1 justifies the increased complexity, making it a viable approach for corrosion imaging of actual ground grids.

Table 1. Comparison table of algorithm complexity.

Model	Reasoning Time (s)	Performance
Tikhonov	6.3	Poor quality, sensitive to noise
Noser	4.5	Moderate quality, limited robustness
TV	7.8	Good quality, prone to artifacts
CGAN	2.3	Excellent quality, robust to noise

In order to verify the improvement effect of the improved CGAN algorithm, experimental comparisons were made with the generative network using CNN and U-net. Here, 100 rounds of training were conducted under the same conditions. The test set used typical single corrosion and double corrosion models. The imaging effect is shown in Figure 11. The green part of model 1 and 3 represents grounding grid corrosion, and the conductivity of the actual corrosion part is 6.1×10^6 S/m and 5.3×10^6 S/m. Model 2 is corroded at the blue position, and the conductivity at the actual corrosion position is 2.8×10^6 S/m. It can be seen that the improved CGAN imaging algorithm has made great progress in the diagnosis of grounding grid corrosion. Due to the simple structure of the CNN generator model, the image details of the generated image at the corrosion site are not clear enough, the color space information is not captured and there are artifacts at the corrosion site. The generation network composed of U-Net better retains the spatial information and local features, and the generated image quality is better than the traditional CNN. After adding the CBAM attention mechanism, the network can more adaptively select important channel features, improve the generator's ability to capture the global structure and details of the image and reduce artifacts and distortion.

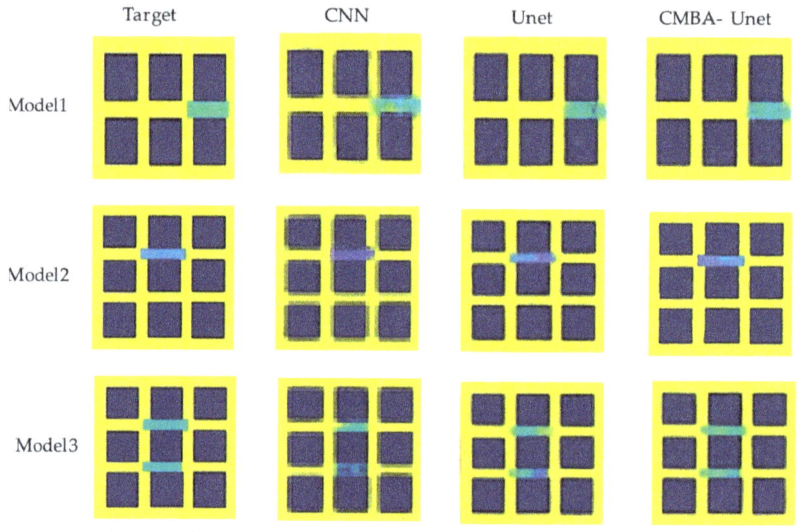

Figure 11. Comparison of secondary imaging using different algorithms.

Due to the inevitable deviations in voltage measurements caused by environmental and equipment factors, this paper introduces sufficient Gaussian noise into the boundary voltage measurement results to evaluate the noise resistance and generalization performance of the algorithm. The noise is added as shown in Equation (14).

$$X_{noisy} = X + N\left(0, \sigma^2\right) \tag{14}$$

After adding Gaussian noise of different sizes, grounding grid impedance imaging is performed. As shown in Figure 12, the blue part of model 1 represents grounding grid corrosion, and the conductivity of the actual corrosion part is 2.2×10^6 S/m. Model 2 is corroded at the green position, and the conductivity at the actual corrosion position is 5.8×10^6 S/m.As the noise level increases, particularly when the standard deviation of the noise exceeds 5% of the voltage values, the imaging quality is significantly affected. However, when introducing low to moderate noise, the imaging results remain largely unaffected.

Even with moderate levels of noise, the algorithm is still able to accurately detect the corrosion location and corrosion state, demonstrating the robustness and noise resilience of the proposed method. This indicates that the model can maintain a reliable performance under practical, noisy conditions, making it suitable for real-world applications where measurement noise is inevitable.

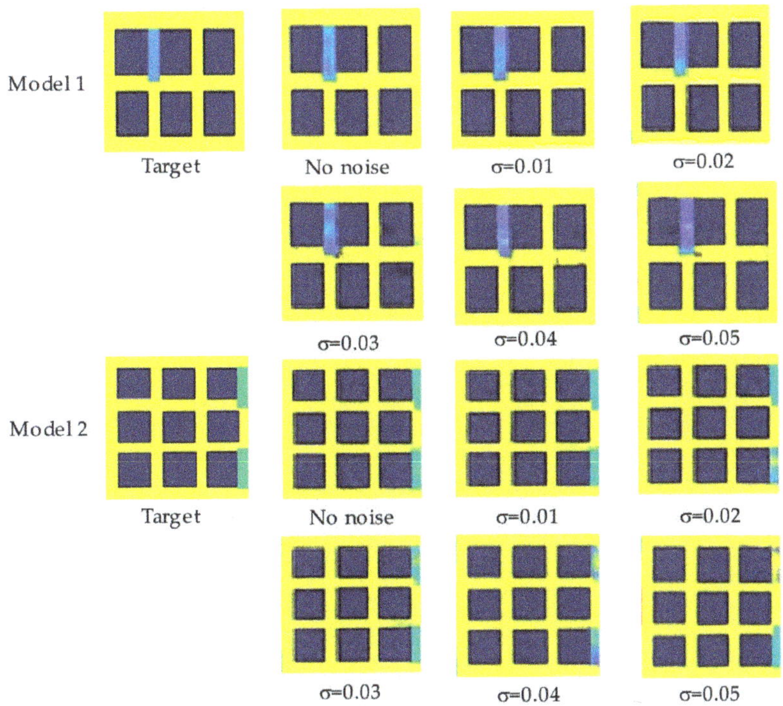

Figure 12. Algorithmic imaging after adding different noises.

4.2. Ground Grid Imaging Evaluation Index

In order to intuitively reflect the effectiveness and superiority of this algorithm, this paper analyzes the imaging results of simulation data from a quantitative perspective, using the structural similarity index (SSIM) and peak signal to noise ratio (PSNR) to evaluate the effect of image reconstruction. The equation is as follows:

$$S(x,y) = \frac{(2\mu_x\mu_y + c_1)(2\sigma_{xy} + c_2)}{(\mu_x^2 + \mu_y^2 + c_1)(\sigma_x^2 + \sigma_y^2 + c_2)} \quad (15)$$

where u_x and σ_x represent the mean and standard deviation of the x image, u_y and σ_y represent the mean and standard deviation of the y image, σ_{xy} represents the covariance of the x and y images, and c_1 and c_2 are constants, usually 6.5025 and 58.5225. The SSIM value is between 0 and 1, where 1 means that the two images are exactly the same.

When solving the PSNR value, you need to first calculate the mean square error (MSE) of each target image, as follows:

$$M(i,j) = \frac{1}{mn}\sum_{i=0}^{m-1}\sum_{j=0}^{n-1} I((i,j) - K(i,j))^2 \quad (16)$$

In Equation (16), $I(i,j)$ and $K(i,j)$ represent the pixel values of the original image and the contrast image, respectively. Then, the peak signal-to-noise ratio is expressed as follows:

$$P = 10\log_{10}(\frac{MAX^2}{M}) \tag{17}$$

MAX is the maximum pixel value of the image, $MAX = 2^n - 1$; the higher the image peak signal-to-noise ratio, the better the image quality and the less distortion.

Based on the relatively regular characteristics of the grounding grid branches, this paper segmented the conductivity images after CGAN imaging to better diagnose corrosion. The conductivity value and corrosion degree of the corroded branch can be calculated based on the divided branches. The conductivity value is solved as Equation (18):

$$\sigma = \frac{1}{N}\sum_{i=1}^{N}(k\cdot(C_i - C_{\min}) + \sigma_{\min}) \tag{18}$$

N is the total number of branch units, C_i is the unit color value, $C_{\min}$ is the minimum color reference value, k is the mapping ratio coefficient, $\sigma_{\min}$ is the minimum conductivity value, which is 1×10^6 S/m, and $\sigma_{\max}$ is the corrosion upper limit conductivity value, which is 1×10^7 S/m. The corrosion degree can be calculated based on the solved conductivity value ξ:

$$\xi = \frac{\sigma - \sigma_{\min}}{\sigma_{\max} - \sigma_{\min}} \times 100\% \tag{19}$$

According to the determined corrosion branch and corrosion degree, the judgment accuracy A and judgment error R are obtained:

$$A = \frac{TP}{TP + FN} \tag{20}$$

$$R = \sqrt{\frac{1}{N}\sum_{i=1}^{N}(\xi_x - \xi_y)^2} \tag{21}$$

TP represents the correctly detected corroded branch, FN represents the missed corroded branch, ξ_x represents the calculated corrosion degree and ξ_y is the actual corrosion degree.

4.3. Analysis of Ground Grid Imaging Evaluation

The conductivity value of each branch can be calculated by Equation (18), and then the corrosion situation can be further obtained. According to the corrosion situation after imaging of model 3 in Figure 13, it can be concluded that branch 2 and branch 24 are severely corroded. The conductivity of branch 2 is calculated to be 1.8×10^6 S/m, and its corrosion degree is 82%. The conductivity of branch 24 is 1.5×10^6 S/m, and its corrosion degree is 85%.

To further verify the grounding grid corrosion detection performance of this algorithm on different model test sets, the following figure shows a randomly selected part of the test data. The scatter plot of the measured corrosion degree ξ_x at the corroded location and the actual corrosion degree ξ_y at the corroded location are shown in Figure 14. It can be concluded that the corrosion degree of the corroded branch of the grounding grid detected by it is basically consistent with the actual one, and the error is small. This verifies that the proposed algorithm is highly accurate in assessing the degree of corrosion and shows that it can reliably detect corrosion in grounding grid systems with small errors, confirming its robustness and practical applicability in real-world scenarios.

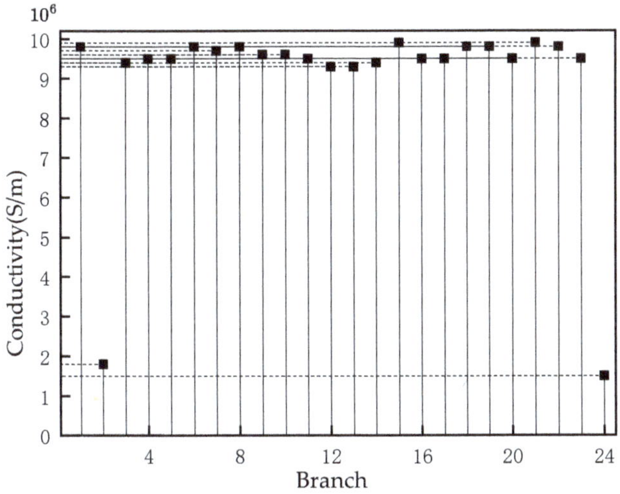

Figure 13. Corrosion of each branch of model 3.

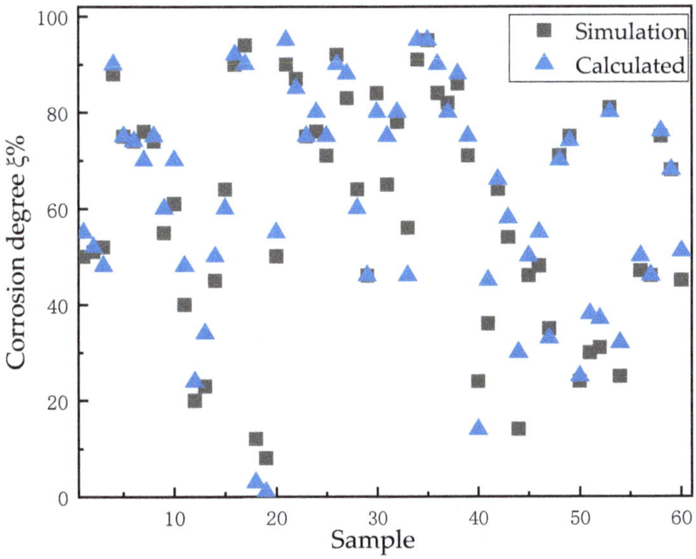

Figure 14. Comparison of measured corrosion levels.

Then, the grounding grids were imaged with different grid sizes and single-branch corrosion and double-branch corrosion to study the influence of corrosion position identification accuracy and corrosion degree error. From the results of Table 2, it can be concluded that the improved CGAN imaging method proposed in this paper has the highest accuracy when the corrosion branch is a single branch in the single corrosion case of the 2×3 and 3×3 grids, and it needs to be improved under the double branch. In the case of double-branch corrosion, the different corrosion degrees lead to subtle changes in potential characteristics, making it difficult to extract features and thus increasing the error in imaging corrosion degree and decreasing the accuracy of corrosion position judgment. Compared with the traditional EIT imaging method, this method still has great advantages and is conducive to the application of grounding grid corrosion diagnosis.

Table 2. One-shot imaging accuracy and error of different models.

Model	A	R
2 × 3 (Single corrosion)	96.3%	7.6%
3 × 3 (Single corrosion)	95.5%	8.1%
2 × 3 (Double corrosion)	91.2%	12.6%
3 × 3 (Double corrosion)	88.7%	15.8%

In Table 3, the evaluation index table of different algorithms shows that the average P of the image generated by the improved CGAN is 1.7407 higher than that of the image generated by U-Net, and it is 3.4809 higher than that generated by the CNN. The SSIM value is increased by 0.0445 and 0.0904 compared with U-Net and the CNN. This fully demonstrates the effectiveness of the improved method in better retaining accurate feature representations such as structural details. The increased PSNR and SSIM values indicate that the proposed method and its improved generator can provide more accurate and reliable conductivity images for grounding grid analysis, and thus they may play a greater role in the study of grounding grid conductivity imaging.

Table 3. Evaluation index table of different algorithms.

	Model 1 (2 × 3)		Model 2 (3 × 3)	
	S	P	S	P
CNN	0.8146	16.4524	0.8065	16.6654
U-Net	0.8476	18.1468	0.8654	18.4514
U-Net-CBAM	0.8975	20.4465	0.9044	19.6332

The accuracy A of the corrosion branch judgment of each algorithm on the test set is calculated, and the R between the corrosion degree of the corrosion site and the actual degree is obtained, as shown in Table 4. It can be concluded that the improved CGAN imaging algorithm proposed in this paper has an accuracy increase of 9.1% compared with the CNN structure after improving the generation network, and the corrosion degree judgment error is reduced by 15.4%. Compared with the U-Net network, the accuracy is increased by 5.7% and the error is reduced by 8.8%. This shows that the improvements made to the generator network in the CGAN architecture produce more accurate and reliable corrosion detection, and its attention module effectively extracts features, highlighting the effectiveness of this method in improving imaging accuracy and corrosion assessment accuracy, which is more conducive to the research of grounding grid corrosion diagnosis.

Table 4. Accuracy and diagnostic error of different algorithms.

	A	R
CNN	85.2%	25.2%
U-Net	88.6%	18.6%
U-Net-CBAM	94.3%	9.8%

This algorithm performs ground grid imaging after adding different Gaussian noises, as shown in Figure 15. Although noise is added to the data, the noise has little effect on the imaging quality, and the accuracy of the model only slightly decreases. This shows that even in the presence of noise, the detection method can still identify the corrosion area well, indicating that the model is noise robust to a certain extent, and the decrease in accuracy is small, indicating that the interference of noise in the imaging results does not significantly affect the final detection performance.

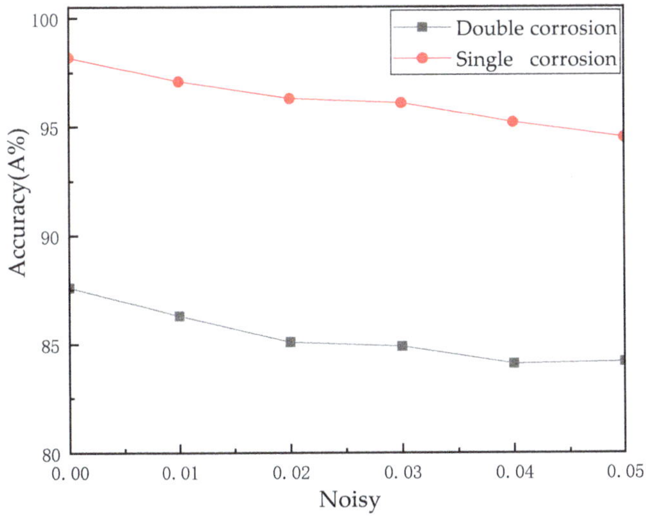

Figure 15. Imaging accuracy after different noises.

5. Conclusions

In order to solve the morbidity problem of traditional algorithms in grounding grid impedance imaging, this paper proposes a grounding grid impedance imaging method based on the improved CGAN. The input measured boundary voltage value is imaged through the improved CGAN algorithm. The algorithm generator is mainly composed of four modules: the preprocessing module, encoder module, decoder module and attention module. The discriminator is a PatchGAN structure. The grounding grid impedance image is reconstructed through adversarial training and optimization of the objective function. Through simulation experiments of different corrosion positions and different corrosion degrees of the grounding grid, it is proven that this method significantly improves the precision and accuracy of the grounding grid corrosion diagnosis image and obtains the grounding grid image with complete boundaries and clear corrosion conditions.

The accuracy of this method in detecting double-branch corrosion is lower than that of single-branch corrosion. The reason is that there are more types of double-branch corrosion, and it is difficult to extract voltage characteristics. The error in detecting slight corrosion is larger than that in moderate corrosion. Considering that the cause of the problem is that the voltage characteristics in complex and slight cases do not change significantly, error in judging the degree of corrosion occurs.

Future work will integrate feature detail extraction and expand the dataset to improve the model's weak recognition performance when imaging slight corrosion and multiple corroded branches, optimize the imaging resolution of the CGAN imaging network and more accurately display the corrosion status of the grounding grid. In summary, the method proposed in this paper provides a new idea for grounding grid impedance imaging, which is expected to be applied in grounding grid corrosion diagnosis and inspection.

Author Contributions: Conceptualization, K.Z.; methodology, K.Z.; software, D.L.; validation, D.L.; data curation, Z.X.; investigation, Z.F.; writing—original draft preparation, D.L.; writing—review and editing, K.Z.; visualization, X.B. All authors have read and agreed to the published version of the manuscript.

Funding: The research was funded by the Science and Technology Project of the State Grid Sichuan Electric Power Company: Research on online monitoring technology and system development of grounding grid operation status (52199723001M).

Data Availability Statement: The data supporting the reported results are not publicly available due to privacy or ethical restrictions. Please contact the corresponding author for more information.

Conflicts of Interest: The authors declare no conflicts of interest. The funders had no role in the design of this study; in the collection, analyses or interpretation of data; in the writing of the manuscript; or in the decision to publish the results.

References

1. Hu, H.; Fang, M.; Hu, F.; Zeng, S.; Deng, X. A new design of substation grounding based on electrolytic cathodic protection and on transfer corrosion current. *Electr. Power Syst. Res.* **2021**, *195*, 107174. [CrossRef]
2. Wang, Y.; Jiang, J.; Huang, Y.; Wang, J. Design of substation grounding grid in CFETR. *Sci. Rep.* **2024**, *14*, 25009. [CrossRef]
3. Zhang, C.; Liao, Y.; Gao, X.; Zhao, J.; Yuan, Y.; Liao, R. Research Advances of Soil Corrosion of Grounding Grids. *Micromachines* **2021**, *12*, 513. [CrossRef]
4. Zhao, J.; Meng, X.; Ren, X.; Li, S.; Zhang, F.; Yang, X.; Xu, J.; Yuan, Y. Review on soil corrosion and protection of grounding grids. *Materials* **2024**, *17*, 507. [CrossRef]
5. Li, X.; Yang, F.; Ming, J.L.; Jadoon, A.; Han, S. Imaging the corrosion in grounding grid branch with inner-source electrical impedance tomography. *Energies* **2018**, *11*, 1739. [CrossRef]
6. Li, X.; Yang, F.; Yu, X.; Dong, M.; Yao, D. Research on the inverse problem of grounding grid fault diagnosis based on inner-source EIT. *Trans. China Electrotech. Soc.* **2019**, *34*, 902–909.
7. Hu, J.-Y.; Hu, J.-G.; Lan, D.-L.; Ming, J.-L.; Zhou, Y.-T.; Li, Y.-W. Corrosion evaluation of the grounding grid in transformer substation using electrical impedance tomography technology. In Proceedings of the Annual Conference of the IEEE Industrial Electronics Society, Beijing, China, 29 October 2017.
8. Yan, X.; Huang, S.; Smolik, W.T.; Chen, W.; Yang, S. A detection method for fast electrical impedance imaging of grounding grid based on optimized differential-multigrid-homotopy algorithm. *IEEE Trans. Instrum. Meas.* **2023**, *72*, 3528714. [CrossRef]
9. He, L.; Yang, L.; Yan, X.; Chen, W.; Huang, S. Research on the grounding grid electrical impedance imaging algorithm based on improved Tikhonov and Lp regularization. *Prog. Electromagn. Res. B* **2024**, *106*, 1–16. [CrossRef]
10. Wang, H.; Liu, K.; Wu, Y.; Wang, S.; Zhang, Z.; Li, F.; Yao, J. Image reconstruction for electrical impedance tomography using radial basis function neural network based on hybrid particle swarm optimization algorithm. *IEEE Sens. J.* **2021**, *21*, 1926–1934. [CrossRef]
11. Jeon, D.; Kim, M.K.; Jeong, Y.; Oh, J.E.; Moon, J.; Kim, D.J.; Yoon, S. High-accuracy rebar position detection using deep learning–based frequency-difference electrical resistance tomography. *Autom. Constr.* **2022**, *135*, 104116. [CrossRef]
12. Shi, Y.; Li, Y.; Fu, F.; Wang, M.; Yang, B.; Lou, Y.; Tian, Z. A fully connected neural network-based voltage compensation method for accurate reconstruction in brain electrical impedance tomography. *Biomed. Signal Process. Control* **2023**, *86*, 105252. [CrossRef]
13. Qin, S.; Wang, Y.; Tai, H.-M.; Wang, H.; Liao, X.; Fu, Z. TEM apparent resistivity imaging for grounding grid detection using artificial neural network. *IET Gener. Transm. Distrib.* **2019**, *13*, 3932–3940. [CrossRef]
14. Huang, Z.; Xia, L.; Zhang, H.; Liu, F.; Tu, Y.; Yang, Z.; Wei, W. Evaluation of grounding grid corrosion extent based on laser-induced breakdown spectroscopy (LIBS) combined with machine learning. *Comput. Electr. Eng.* **2024**, *120*, 109849. [CrossRef]
15. Yin, L.; Li, Y. Multi-point synchronous temporary grounding wire detection device based on convolutional neural networks. *Int. J. Electr. Power Energy Syst.* **2024**, *158*, 109955. [CrossRef]
16. Fu, Z.; Song, S.; Wang, X.; Li, J.; Tai, H.-M. Imaging the topology of grounding grids based on wavelet edge detection. *IEEE Trans. Magn.* **2018**, *54*, 6200808. [CrossRef]
17. Noroznia, H.; Gandomkar, M.; Nikoukar, J. Pipeline failure evaluation and prediction using failure probability and neural network based on measured data. *Heliyon* **2024**, *10*, e26837. [CrossRef]
18. Adail, A.S.; Saad, M.H.; Said, A. Evaluation of the optimum safety performance of the nuclear reactor compact grounding system under lightning strikes and ground fault. *Kerntechnik* **2023**, *89*, 1–14. [CrossRef]
19. Hui, X.; Xu, Y.; Niu, J.; Zhang, W. Rapid evaluation and prediction of cure-induced residual stress of composites based on cGAN deep learning model. *Compos. Struct.* **2024**, *330*, 117827. [CrossRef]
20. Yang, B.; Arshad, M.H.; Zhao, Q. Packet-level and flow-level network intrusion detection based on reinforcement learning and adversarial training. *Algorithms* **2022**, *15*, 453. [CrossRef]
21. Du, X.; Qi, J.; Kang, J.; Sun, Z.; Wang, C.; Xie, J. Partial discharge data augmentation and pattern recognition method based on DAE-GAN. *Algorithms* **2024**, *17*, 487. [CrossRef]

22. Yan, X.; Lyu, Q.; Lin, X.; Chen, W. Research on grounding grid electrical impedance tomography algorithm based on Tikhonov and TV hybrid regularization. *Chin. J. Sci. Instrum.* **2021**, *42*, 160–171.
23. Wang, Z.; Zhang, F.; Zhang, T.; Yang, Y.; Fu, Y. High-Resolution Image Generation with Enhanced PatchGAN Discriminator. *Pattern Recognit.* **2023**, *142*, 109337.
24. Han, B.; Guo, L.; Wang, J.; Zhang, Z.; Zhang, G.; Jia, S. Fast general normalized convolutional sparse filtering via L1-L2 mixed norm for rotating machinery fault diagnosis. *Measurement* **2022**, *198*, 111136. [CrossRef]

algorithms

MDPI

Article

Generating Job Recommendations Based on User Personality and Gallup Tests

Shakhmar Sarsenbay [1,2], Asset Kabdiyev [3], Iraklis Varlamis [4,*], Christos Sardianos [4], Cemil Turan [1], Bobir Razhametov [3] and Yermek Kazym [3]

1 Computer Science Department, SDU University, 040900 Kaskelen, Kazakhstan; shakhmar.sarsenbay@sdu.edu.kz (S.S.); cemil.turan@sdu.edu.kz (C.T.)
2 School of Digital Technologies, Narxoz University, 050035 Almaty, Kazakhstan
3 Tanu.ai, 050063 Almaty, Kazakhstan; assetkabdiyev@gmail.com (A.K.); baburrazhametov@gmail.com (B.R.); kazym777@gmail.com (Y.K.)
4 Department of Informatics and Telematics, Harokopio University of Athens, GR-17778 Athens, Greece; sardianos@hua.gr
* Correspondence: varlamis@hua.gr; Tel.: +30-210-9549-405

Abstract: This paper introduces a novel approach to job recommendation systems by incorporating personality traits evaluated through the Gallup CliftonStrengths assessment, aiming to enhance the traditional matching process beyond skills and qualifications. Unlike broad models like the Big Five, Gallup's CliftonStrengths assesses 34 specific talents (e.g., 'Analytical', 'Empathy'), enabling finer-grained, actionable job matches. While existing systems focus primarily on hard skills, this paper argues that personality traits—such as those measured by the Gallup test—play a crucial role in determining career satisfaction and long-term job retention. The proposed approach offers a more granular and actionable method for matching candidates with job opportunities that align with their natural strengths. Leveraging Gallup tests, we develop a job-matching approach that identifies personality traits and integrates them with recommendation algorithms to generate a list of the most suitable specializations for the user. By utilizing a GPT-4 model to process job descriptions and rank relevant personality traits, the system generates more personalized recommendations that account for both hard and soft skills. The empirical experiments demonstrate that this integration can improve the accuracy and relevance of job recommendations, leading to better career outcomes. The paper contributes to the field by offering a comprehensive framework for personality-based job matching and validating its effectiveness, paving the way for a more holistic approach to recruitment and talent management.

Keywords: job recommendation systems; personality traits; career satisfaction; hard skills; soft skills; personalized recommendations; personality-based job matching

1. Introduction

Job recommendation systems have become increasingly useful in modern recruitment processes, offering a more efficient and personalized way to match candidates with suitable job opportunities. The trend towards personalization in recommendation systems is particularly pronounced in job markets, where understanding individual preferences and characteristics can significantly enhance the effectiveness of these systems. Traditional job recommendation systems often focus on skills, qualifications, and past behavior, but they frequently overlook deeper personal factors such as personality traits [1]. This oversight is significant because personality plays a pivotal role in determining career satisfaction, productivity, and long-term job retention. Job recommendation systems have become increasingly useful in modern recruitment processes, offering a more efficient and personalized way to match candidates with suitable job opportunities. The trend towards personalization in recommendation systems is particularly pronounced in job markets, where understanding individual preferences and characteristics can significantly enhance the effectiveness of these systems. Traditional job recommendation systems often focus on skills, qualifications, and past behavior, but they frequently overlook deeper personal factors such as personality traits [1]. This oversight is significant because personality plays a pivotal role in determining career satisfaction, productivity, and long-term job retention. In this work, we propose a novel approach to job recommendations that leverages the Gallup CliftonStrengths personality assessment to enable more meaningful job–candidate matches. We apply GPT-4 and distance-based ranking methods to produce interpretable and fair recommendations, validated in a real-world setting.

The Big Five personality traits—openness, conscientiousness, extraversion, agreeableness, and neuroticism—have been shown to influence user behavior and preferences in various contexts, including recommendation systems [2,3]. By integrating personality traits into job recommendation systems, we can address the shortcomings of traditional systems and potentially improve career satisfaction and long-term job retention. This approach could also help employers identify candidates who are more likely to thrive in their work environment, leading to better talent acquisition and retention strategies. While prior work has largely relied on broad personality constructs like the Big Five (e.g., [2]), our use of Gallup's 34 themes enables finer-grained recommendations by mapping specific strengths to job requirements. For instance, a role requiring 'Relationship Building' may prioritize traits like 'Empathy' or 'Includer', which are not captured by generic extraversion or agreeableness measures.

The Gallup Personality Test, specifically the CliftonStrengths assessment (https://www.gallup.com/cliftonstrengths/en/home.aspx, accessed on 1 May 2025), offers a unique approach to evaluating personality traits by focusing on 34 distinct strengths or talents that individuals naturally exhibit. This assessment is based on the premise that understanding and leveraging these strengths can enhance personal and professional performance. Unlike traditional personality assessments, like the Big Five, which categorize individuals into broad traits, the Gallup test provides a more nuanced view by identifying specific talents that can be developed and utilized effectively in various contexts. This granularity makes it particularly useful for job recommendation systems, as it allows for more precise matching of individuals with job roles that align with their natural strengths. Throughout this paper, we use the term *traits* to refer to the 34 distinct themes identified by the CliftonStrengths assessment, which Gallup often refers to interchangeably as talents or strengths depending on the context. We do not use traits in the broader sense defined by psychological models like the Big Five.

To avoid confusion between commonly used psychological constructs and the terminology of the CliftonStrengths framework, we clarify the following distinctions. In this work we use the following terms:

- *Personality traits* refer to broad, stable dispositions that influence behavior across situations. This includes models like the Big Five (e.g., extraversion, conscientiousness), which provide a general psychological profile.
- *Strengths* are defined, following the Gallup CliftonStrengths framework, as a person's consistent near-perfect performance in a specific activity. Strengths emerge when innate talents are refined through practice and knowledge.

- *Talents* are naturally recurring patterns of thought, feeling, or behavior that can be productively applied. They represent the raw potential that, when invested in, develops into a strength.

By incorporating the Gallup test's insights into job matching, our method seeks to provide a more holistic and personalized approach to recruitment. This integration can help ensure that job seekers are matched with roles that not only align with their skills and qualifications but also resonate with their natural strengths and talents. Ultimately, this novel approach has the potential to enhance career satisfaction, productivity, and long-term job retention by creating a better fit between individuals and their work environments.

This paper makes several key contributions to the field of job recommendation systems. Firstly, it introduces a unique approach for incorporating personality traits, as evaluated by the Gallup CliftonStrengths assessment, into job recommendation systems. This framework provides a more nuanced approach to matching candidates with job opportunities by considering their natural strengths and talents. In contrast to traditional methods that rely on manual trait–job pairing, our work employs GPT-4 to dynamically infer rankings, adapting to evolving job markets. In addition, it applies a bias detection/mitigation technique to the LLM-based results to ensure fairness across demographics. Secondly, the paper validates the effectiveness of the proposed method through empirical experiments, demonstrating how integrating personality traits can improve the accuracy and relevance of job recommendations. It integrates different distance metrics, including a sigmoid-weighted Manhattan distance to prioritize mismatches in high-impact traits. Last and most importantly, it incorporated the proposed approach in an actual job recommendation platform in Kazakhstan that is used by several companies and hundreds of candidates.

The paper is structured to provide a comprehensive overview of our novel method for integrating personality traits into job recommendation systems. Following this introduction, Section 2 discusses related work and the role of personality in job recommendations, highlighting the importance of personalization and the limitations of existing systems. Section 3 presents the proposed method, including data processing and model design, detailing how the Gallup CliftonStrengths assessment is integrated into the recommendation framework. Section 4 details the experimental setup and provides an overview of the application that currently supports our approach. Section 5 presents the results, providing an analysis of the effectiveness of our approach compared to traditional methods. Finally, Section 6 concludes the paper and outlines future work, discussing potential extensions and applications of our framework in broader recruitment contexts.

2. Related Work

The literature on recommender systems and their various applications is full of variations of collaborative filtering, such as content-based or hybrid methods [4], which take advantage of the available information expressed as user or item content, user-to-item preferences, etc. to recommend the most appropriate choices for each individual user or group of users [5]. Content-based approaches, in the case of job recommendations, try to match resume information with job descriptions by quantifying the similarity of the respective texts. This was traditionally performed using cosine similarity at the high-dimensional vector space of keywords [6]. However, recent advances in transformers and embeddings allow more proficient semantic-based matching to be employed and improve matching performance [7].

A recent survey on e-recruitment recommendation systems [8] examines the more practical aspects of job recommendations and focuses on the challenges that e-recruitment systems have to resolve. As shown in the survey, job recommendation systems differ significantly from traditional general-purpose recommender systems due to several distinct characteristics. Unlike traditional systems, job recommenders adhere to the "one worker, one job" principle, where job seekers and positions are typically limited to singular matches, creating competition and necessitating a small, highly selective set of recommendations. These systems also operate on a two-sided engagement model, requiring mutual actions from job seekers and employers, unlike unilateral user actions in traditional domains like movie recommendations. Additionally, job recommenders emphasize both suitability and user preferences, integrating multi-faceted data such as skills, experience, and cultural fit, while addressing challenges like fairness and trustworthiness in this high-stakes domain. Furthermore, the transient nature of job listings and episodic engagement of users result in short interaction histories, making it harder to gather and utilize data compared to other domains. According to the same survey, job recommendation systems face challenges, including data quality issues like noise, semantic gaps, multilingual data, and sparsity, which complicate feature extraction and matching.

A different group of recommender systems in the recruitment industry comprises works that aim to generate career improvement recommendations via upskilling or reskilling actions based on user profiles and their desired positions [9–11]. The various methods used for tackling this task comprise content-based matching between user profiles and training courses [11], the use of knowledge graphs in order to perform information-rich matching [10], or even dynamic programming [9] and other matching optimization techniques. Another recent survey [12] summarizes the techniques that can be employed for recommending skills for upskilling or reskilling, to Content-Based Filtering (CBF), which identifies skills similar to a user's profile by analyzing their history and preferences; Collaborative Filtering (CF), which leverages the preferences of other users, either through memory-based approaches using similarity measures or model-based methods for predicting new skills; Knowledge-Based techniques (KB), which infer skills based on predefined rules and user preferences; Utility-Based techniques (UB), which calculate the utility of skills based on multi-attribute preferences; Rule-Based techniques (RB) that use if–then rules to match users with relevant skills; and Hybrid Filtering (HF), which combines these methods to enhance accuracy and address limitations like sparsity, scalability, and cold-start issues.

According to another recent survey [13], deep learning techniques in job recommendation systems include Convolutional Neural Networks (CNNs) for extracting features like keywords from job descriptions, Recurrent Neural Networks (RNNs) for analyzing sequential text data to predict user preferences, Autoencoders for creating compact representations of job descriptions to identify similar roles, and Generative Adversarial Networks (GANs) for generating new job descriptions aligned with user interests, offering sophisticated, personalized, and adaptable recommendations at the cost of higher computational and training complexity. Finally, Graph Neural Networks (GNNs) combined with knowledge-graph-based techniques [14] are gaining hype for providing better skills, experience, and education matching between candidates and positions.

Recommending a job that matches the user's profile is very important since it can reduce underemployment or unemployment and, indirectly, contribute to social and economic development. In this direction, the work of [7] presents an interesting approach that employs Large Language Models and, more specifically, BERT to generate content-based job recommendations based on user resumes and job descriptions. Simpler NLP techniques have been employed in [15] to find matching between user profiles and job descriptions. However, these approaches stick to the matching of hard skills and ignore soft skills and personality traits that can either be hidden behind the words of a job description text or a user resume. The importance of soft skills is recognized by the CareProfSys system [16], which collects demographic and personality data from users, along with skill information from the user's CV and professional social media (i.e., LinkedIn). Manual extraction of text segments from the above sources is performed, and rule-based and BERT-based mapping is employed to map texts into specific skill codes from a manually compiled lexicon. Some filtering steps limit the candidates that match each job, and finally, an ontology is employed to perform the matching between the positions' requirements and the candidate profiles. Another job recommendation engine, JobFit [17], processes job descriptions and applicants' profiles and generates a JobFit score indicating how well the applicant fits a position. Once again, the job inputs comprise required skills, experience, and qualification, and while experience and qualification act as filters, skills are matched to the applicant's skills using NLP techniques. The system also considers the applicant's personality (the big 5 traits) by measuring the correlation of the user's personality with the personality of employees who work in this job and by using it to measure the possible satisfaction from the job. Prior work on personality-aware job recommendations (e.g., [17]) often relies on the Big Five model, which, while useful for broad trait alignment, lacks granularity for specific strength-based matching. In contrast, Gallup's 34 themes—such as 'Achiever', 'Communication', or 'Strategic'—provide actionable insights into how innate talents align with role-specific demands (e.g., 'Strategic' for consulting roles). This fine-grained approach bridges a gap left by broader psychological models and manual skill-mapping methods (e.g., [16]), enabling dynamic, scalable recommendations.

In recent years, transparent and explainable recommender systems have attracted considerable attention. He et al.'s TriRank [18] models aspect-level interactions in a tripartite graph to enable users to inspect, which review-derived aspects drive each recommendation, thus improving transparency and scrutability. Chen et al.'s GREASE [19] generates both factual and counterfactual explanations for GNN-based recommenders by optimizing adjacency perturbations, offering concise, user-understandable reasons for item rankings. More recently, Mohammadi et al. [20] highlighted the need to incorporate recommender performance metrics when evaluating explanation methods, demonstrating that ignoring recommendation accuracy can lead to misleading assessments of explainer quality.

The use of Gallup tests that we adopt in our study allows us to better understand user personality, since it provides a more fine-grained analysis than the big 5 traits, and also covers several soft skills, which are of equal, if not higher, importance than the hard skills that are explicitly stated in a job description and can be easily used to filter out non-relevant candidates. In addition, we automate the process of skill matching, as well as the mapping of textual descriptions to skills, using a Large Language Model (i.e., chatGPT).

In summary, while prior work has extensively explored various techniques for job recommendations—including content-based and collaborative filtering methods, deep learning approaches, knowledge graphs, and hybrid systems—most approaches primarily focus on hard skill matching or leverage user preferences in a limited way. Recent efforts have begun to consider soft skills and personality traits, yet often rely on coarse models like the Big Five or manual extraction and mapping processes which lack scalability and granularity for strength-based role alignment. Our work distinguishes itself by integrating Gallup's 34 themes (e.g., 'Achiever', 'Strategic') as first-class features, enabling fine-grained matching of innate talents to job demands. Furthermore, we employ Large Language Models to automate semantic matching, overcoming the limitations of manual ontology-based systems while offering richer trait-to-role alignment than traditional content-based methods. This combination enables a more nuanced and holistic recommendation process that addresses key limitations in existing systems, particularly around dynamic soft skill identification and scalable trait-aware recommendations.

3. Proposed Approach

The proposed approach has been designed to generate job recommendations for graduate students who perform the Gallup test in order to evaluate their skills and help them find the most appropriate jobs out of a wide range of positions. The input it considers is the graduates' evaluation using the CliftonStrengths test and a text that describes each job position. The overall process is depicted in Figure 1.

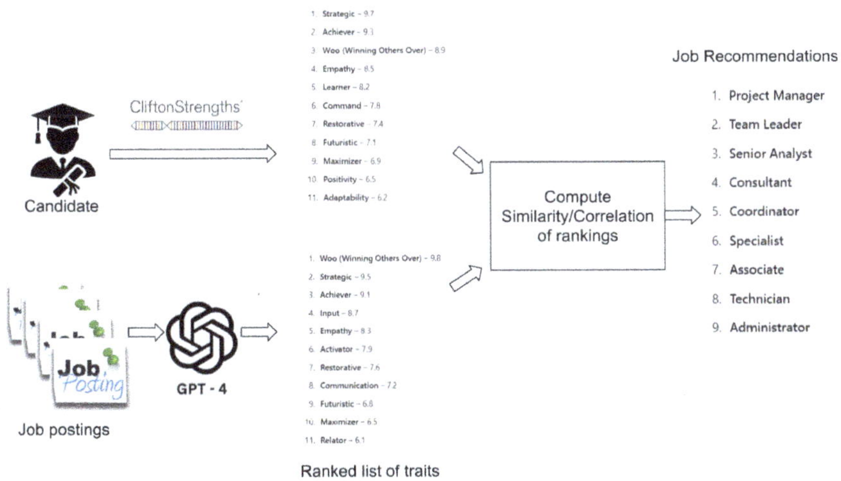

Figure 1. The main flow of data in the proposed approach.

The first step in the proposed approach is to utilize the GPT-4 model to process job positions within specific sectors of a broader industry and identify the most important personality traits from the 34 official CliftonStrengths themes. This is achieved by constructing a precise and context-aware prompt (see Figure 2) designed to simulate the role of a Career Counselor. The prompt incorporates detailed information about the job title, sector, and industry, asking the AI to rank the CliftonStrengths themes from most relevant to least relevant for the specific role.

The ranking process considers the job's specific requirements, necessary personality traits, and the strengths typically associated with success in the given position. By iteratively evaluating each of the traits in a step-by-step manner, the AI provides a ranked list in a standardized format, ensuring that every skill is used exactly once. This ranking is then used to assign a weight to each of the 34 CliftonStrengths traits, reflecting their relative importance for the given role. These weighted traits serve as the foundation for further processing and analysis in the workflow.

```
"role": "user",
"content": f"""You are a Career Counselor utilizing the CliftonStrengths34
assessment test to offer insightful analysis for a professional who is working
as a {profs.loc[inx]} within the {spec.loc[inx]} sector of the broader {sphere.loc[inx]}
industry. Rank the 25 {clifton_strengths} CliftonStrengths34 official themes from most relevant to
least relevant for the {profs.loc[inx]}. Start by selecting the theme you believe
is most crucial for success in this role. From the remaining 33, select the next
most essential, and continue this process until all themes are ranked. Consider
the specific job requirements, necessary skills, and strengths typically needed
for the career.\nPlease provide the ranking list only, without any other information
or reasonings. Let's think step-by-step. Give the answer in 34 rows. Each row's
format: 'number. theme'. For example: '10. Analytical'.\nConsider only 34 official
themes from the CliftonStrengths34 test, which are: {clifton_strengths}.
Incorporate all 34 themes into your answer, each used exactly once for accuracy."""
```

Figure 2. The GPT-4 prompt generates the importance of each personality trait for each job title.

The next step is to evaluate whether the LLM-based extraction process introduces any bias in the weighting of CliftonStrengths traits across all job positions. To achieve this, we construct a 34 × 34 matrix, where each element represents the cumulative weight of a specific trait across all analyzed job positions. This matrix provides a comprehensive overview of how each trait is ranked and weighted on a global scale.

By analyzing the matrix, we identify cases where certain traits have a total weight that exceeds a predefined threshold, indicating a potential bias introduced by the LLM-based ranking process. For such traits, a normalization function is applied to adjust the weights, smoothing out the overemphasis and ensuring that the distribution of trait importance aligns more evenly across the dataset.

Let $M \in \mathbb{R}^{34\times 34}$ be the cumulative weight matrix, where $M_{i,j}$ is the total weight of trait i across all job positions. We first compute, for each trait i,

$$\begin{aligned} m_i &= \max_{1\leq j\leq 34} M_{i,j}, \\ n_i &= \min_{1\leq j\leq 34} M_{i,j}. \end{aligned} \tag{1}$$

We then identify any trait i for which $m_i > 100$ (our chosen bias threshold). For these "overemphasized" traits, we apply a min–max rescaling to cap the maximum at 100:

$$M'_{i,j} = \begin{cases} \dfrac{M_{i,j} - n_i}{m_i - n_i} \times 100 & \text{if } m_i > 100, \\ M_{i,j} & \text{otherwise.} \end{cases} \tag{2}$$

This transformation ensures $\max_j M'_{i,j} = 100$ and $\min_j M'_{i,j} = 0$, preserving relative differences while smoothing extreme peaks. We selected simple min–max scaling for its transparency and ease of reproduction and because it retains monotonicity—ensuring that more important traits remain more heavily weighted even after correction.

The impact of this normalization process is visualized in two plots (see Figure 3): the "before" figure, which illustrates the raw cumulative weights of the traits, and the "after" figure, which shows the adjusted weights following normalization. These visualizations provide insight into the effectiveness of the bias correction process and ensure that the workflow maintains a fair and balanced assessment of the CliftonStrengths traits.

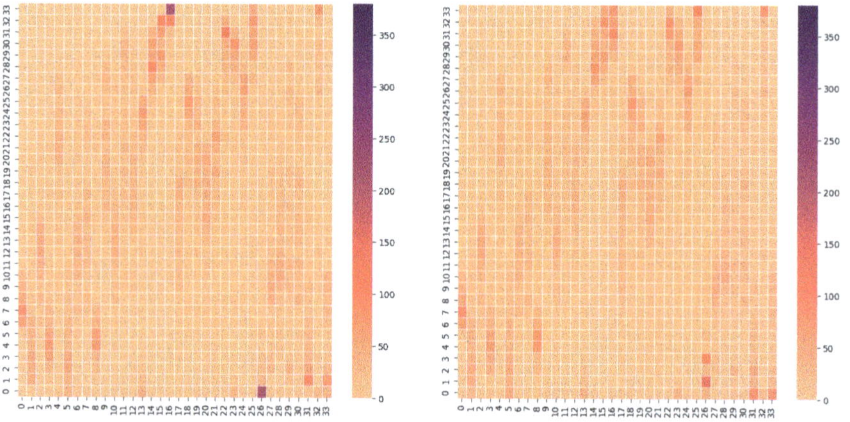

Figure 3. Comparison of cumulative weights before and after normalization.

The third step of the process is to employ the CliftonStrengths questionnaire and analyze all the candidate profiles. The result of this process is that every candidate is associated with a vector of 34 weights that correspond to the importance of each trait in the candidate's personality. In this step, we take advantage of the power of the Gallup test methodology in capturing the importance of each trait in a person's character.

The final step of the recommendation process is to compare the job description traits with the candidate traits and rank jobs accordingly for each candidate. This step employs a vector similarity metric to compute the similarity (or distance) between the job and the candidate vector. Any of the common metrics (e.g., cosine similarity, manhattan, or Euclidean distance) can be applied at this step. Alternatively, we could rank the traits by their importance for the candidate and the position and compare the correlation of the two rankings using a correlation metric.

When the process finishes, each candidate gets as an output a ranked list of positions that match their personality traits. Algorithm 1 summarizes the main steps of our approach.

Algorithm 1 Job Recommendation Based on Gallup Test Scores

Require: Set of job descriptions J, Set of candidate profiles C
Ensure: Ranked job list for each candidate

Initialize trait matrix $T_{jobs} \leftarrow \{\}$ ▷ Store trait weights per job
Initialize global trait bias matrix $M \in \mathbb{R}^{34 \times 34} \leftarrow 0$
for all job j in J **do**
    Construct GPT-4 prompt with job title, sector, and industry
    $R_j \leftarrow$ GPT4_RankCliftonStrengths(j) ▷ Return ranking of 34 traits
    $W_j \leftarrow$ ConvertToWeights(R_j) ▷ Assign weights based on ranking
    $T_{jobs}[j] \leftarrow W_j$
end for
$T_{jobs} \leftarrow$ NormalizeBias(T_{jobs}) ▷ Apply normalization if bias threshold is exceeded
for all candidate c in C **do**
    $V_c \leftarrow$ GallupTestVector(c) ▷ Obtain vector of 34 weighted traits
    Initialize $R_c \leftarrow \{\}$ ▷ Recommended job scores
    for all job j in J **do**
        $V_j \leftarrow T_{jobs}[j]$
        $D \leftarrow$ DistanceMetric(V_c, V_j) ▷ Use weighted Manhattan, Euclidean or cosine
        $R_c[j] \leftarrow D$
    end for
    RankJobs$[c] \leftarrow$ SortBySimilarity(R_c)
end for
return RankJobs

3.1. *Similarity/Distance Metrics*

To compare the matching between the weighted traits of the candidate and a position, several metrics were used. Below are a few of these metrics, including their equations and brief descriptions.

3.1.1. Weighted Manhattan Distance

Manhattan distance, also known as the L1 distance, measures the absolute difference between corresponding elements of two vectors. In our problem, it is defined as:

$$\text{Manhattan Distance} = \sum_{i=1}^{34} w_i \cdot |U_i - P_i| \tag{3}$$

where **U** is the user profile vector, and **P** is the respective position profile vector. Both vectors are of size 34, and U_i and P_i represent the i-th components of the vectors **U** and

P, respectively. w_i is the weight assigned to the i-th trait. The weights are assigned to each trait depending on how high it ranks for the user U, using a sigmoid function, as depicted in Figure 4 and Equation (4). The differences in highly ranked traits for the user are weighted more than those in lower ranked personality traits.

$$w_i = \frac{1}{1 + e^{-\frac{(x_i - 17)}{\pi}}} \quad (4)$$

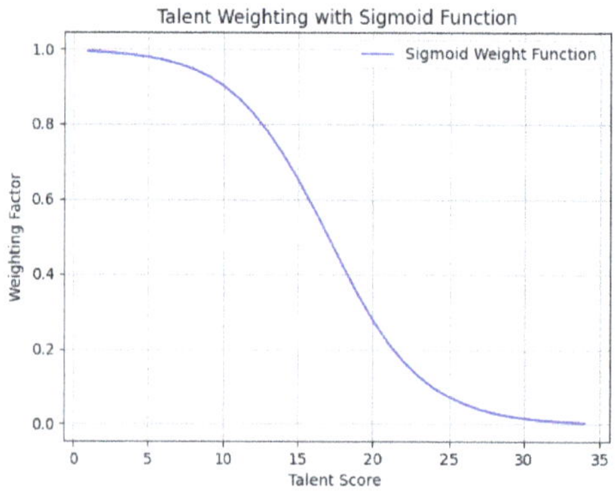

Figure 4. The function used to weigh the importance of differences in each personality trait in the distance metrics.

A smaller Manhattan distance indicates higher similarity between the vectors.

3.1.2. Weighted Euclidean Distance

Euclidean distance is a straight-line distance between two points (vectors) in a multi-dimensional space. It is commonly used to measure the dissimilarity between two weight vectors. The formula with weights used in our case is:

$$\text{Euclidean Distance} = \sqrt{\sum_{i=1}^{34} [w_i \cdot (U_i - P_i)]^2} \quad (5)$$

where U_i and P_i represent the i-th components of the vectors **U** and **P**, for the user and the position profile respectively, and w_i is the corresponding weight, based on the importance of the trait for the user, as before. A smaller Euclidean distance indicates a higher similarity between the vectors.

3.1.3. Cosine Similarity

Cosine similarity measures the cosine of the angle between two vectors, which gives an indication of how similar they are in direction. The formula is defined as:

$$\text{Cosine Similarity} = \frac{\mathbf{A} \cdot \mathbf{B}}{||\mathbf{A}||||\mathbf{B}||} \quad (6)$$

where **A** and **B** are the weight vectors of the two trait lists, and $\mathbf{A} \cdot \mathbf{B}$ is the dot product of the vectors. The magnitude of each vector is represented by $||\mathbf{A}||$ and $||\mathbf{B}||$.

This metric gives a value between -1 (completely opposite directions) and 1 (completely similar directions), with 0 indicating orthogonality (no similarity).

These metrics provide diverse ways to analyze the relationship between the two lists, whether focusing on vector similarity, or distance of rankings. Depending on the application, one metric may be more suitable than another based on the specific nature of the data and the desired outcome.

The three distance/similarity metrics each have distinct characteristics that make them suitable for different aspects of trait-based matching:

- Manhattan distance (L1 norm) provides a linear, robust measure of absolute differences between corresponding trait weights. Its weighted variant (Equation (2)) can emphasize specific trait mismatches through customizable weighting functions (Figure 4), making it particularly suitable for rank-sensitive comparisons, where the magnitude of individual trait discrepancies matters.
- Euclidean distance (L2 norm) measures the straight-line distance between trait vectors in the multidimensional space. While sensitive to large individual differences (due to its quadratic nature), it provides a comprehensive view of overall vector dissimilarity that accounts for both the direction and magnitude of trait weight variations.
- Cosine similarity evaluates the angular alignment between trait vectors, focusing purely on their directional similarity regardless of magnitude. This makes it effective for identifying patterns in relative trait importance while being invariant to absolute weight scaling differences.

Each metric offers unique advantages: Manhattan distance's robustness to outliers, Euclidean distance's comprehensive dissimilarity measurement, and cosine similarity's focus on directional alignment. The choice between them depends on whether the matching process prioritizes individual trait discrepancies (Manhattan), overall dissimilarity (Euclidean), or proportional similarity (cosine).

The experimental evaluation that follows demonstrates the differences between these metrics.

4. Experimental Evaluation

In order to evaluate the performance of the proposed approach, we collected descriptions for 256 job postings and passed 100 graduates from the CliftonStrength test. Then, we run the process presented in Section 3 using Euclidian and Manhattan distance to measure the similarity of lists.

4.1. Participant Demographics

To better understand our evaluation sample, we collected and analyzed demographic information from all participants, who are recent graduates from various disciplines in Kazakhstan.

Study and Profession Backgrounds: Participants' fields of study spanned 45 unique disciplines. The most common study backgrounds were *Teacher* (10 participants), and *Translator* (4). Their current professions were equally diverse, with top roles including *English Teachers* (8) and *Other Teachers* (5).

Age and Gender Distribution: The sample consisted of 59 female and 41 male graduates, with ages ranging from 16 to 44 years (mean = 24.4, SD = 5.54). Figure 5 illustrates the age distribution by gender.

Job Matching and Experience: Only 5% of participants reported prior work experience outside their current roles. Additionally, 46 participants (48%) are employed in the same profession they studied, which may influence their evaluation of job recommendations.

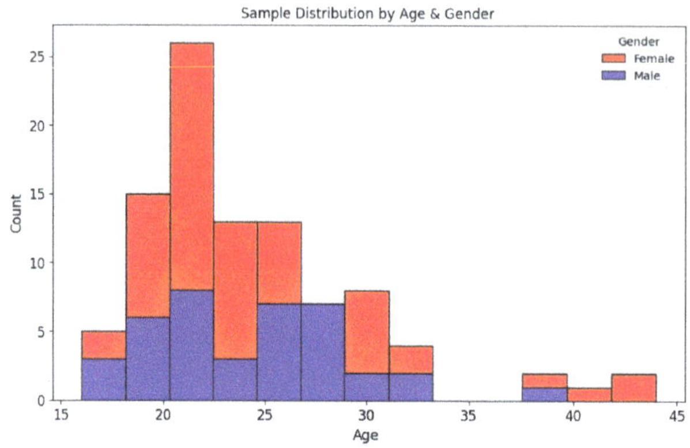

Figure 5. Age distribution of participants, separated by gender.

4.2. Pre-Processing

Before analysis, input data undergoes rigorous preprocessing:

- **Job Descriptions**:
  - Raw text is cleaned (stopword removal, lemmatization) and structured into (title, sector, industry) tuples.
  - GPT-4 processes these tuples using the prompt in Figure 2 to produce a ranked list of the 34 CliftonStrengths traits per job.
  - Trait weights are min–max scaled to [1, 100] to prevent magnitude dominance in Euclidean distance calculations.
- **Gallup Test Results**:
  - Global trait weights are monitored via a 34 × 34 matrix tracking cumulative weights across jobs.
  - Traits exceeding $\pm 2\sigma$ from the mean undergo log-normalization (Equation (2)) to mitigate skew that could disproportionately affect Euclidean distances.
  - Corrected weights are clipped to [5, 95] to preserve ordinal relationships while limiting extreme values.

We also have a baseline method that follows a different approach: First, it collects user test responses to the Strengths Assessment Test and sends them to GPT-4, which generates a concise personality summary. This summary is then converted into a numerical embedding using SentenceTransformers. Each profession's description is also converted to vector embeddings. We then calculate the cosine similarity between the user's embedding and the embedding of each profession to measure how closely they match. The professions are ranked by similarity, allowing the system to suggest careers based on a deep semantic understanding. By comparing our proposed method with this baseline, we aim to assess the benefits of incorporating personality traits into job recommendations using different distance metrics.

The preprocessing pipeline was designed to ensure equitable performance across all distance metrics. For instance, min–max scaling and outlier clipping mitigate Euclidean distance's sensitivity to magnitude variations, while L2 normalization of baseline embeddings guarantees cosine similarity and focuses solely on angular similarity. These steps enable meaningful comparisons between our trait-based method and the semantic-search baseline.

4.3. Experiments' UI

In order to compare the three alternatives and evaluate the overall performance of the proposed approach, we developed a web-based application that streamlines the job recommendation process. Career counselors must first login through the Login Page (Figure 6) using their credentials. Once authenticated, they are redirected to the Dashboard (Figure 7), which serves as the main hub for managing users and career reports. From the dashboard, counselors can add new users, access completed career tests, and navigate to individual user profiles.

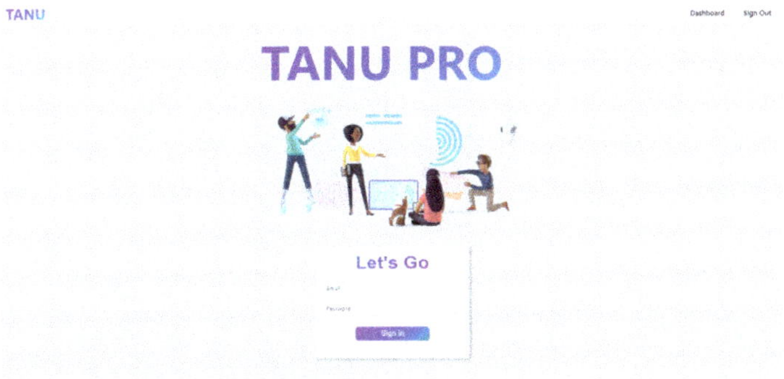

Figure 6. The login page of the application.

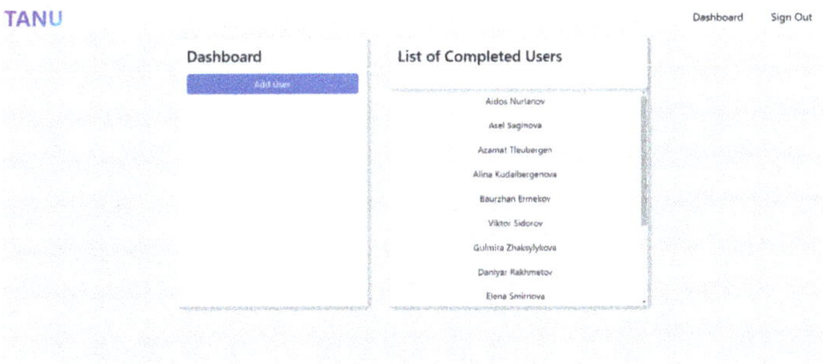

Figure 7. The dashboard used for the evaluation.

Each candidate begins the process by entering their name on the Information Page (Figure 8) before proceeding to the Upload Page (Figure 9), where they submit their Gallup test results (PDF) and Strengths Assessment Test results (Excel file). Upon successful submission, the system automatically processes the data and redirects the user to the Career Report Page.

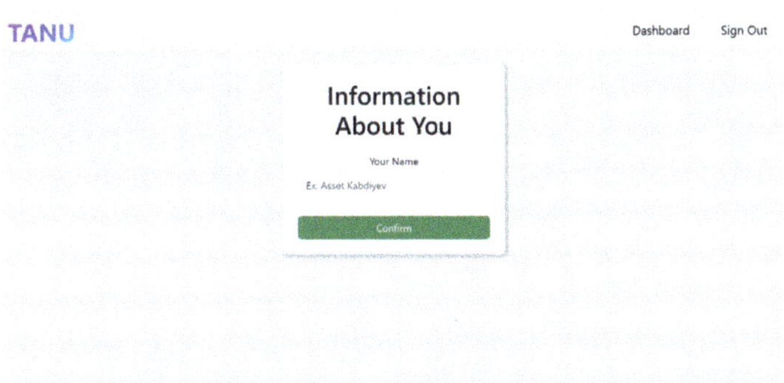

Figure 8. The user information page.

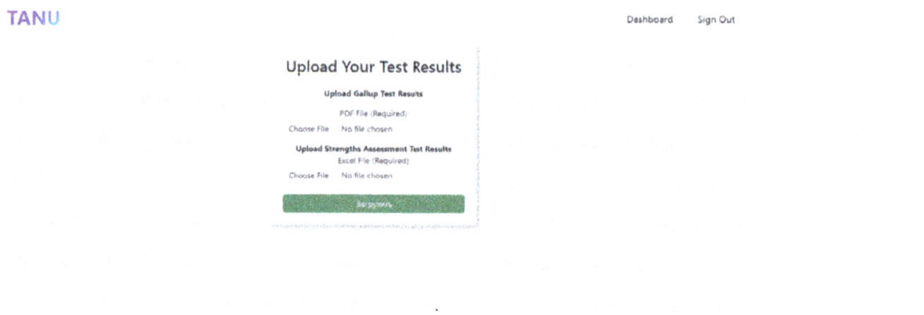

Figure 9. The page where the user uploads their evaluation results.

On the career report page (Figure 10), candidates are presented with three separate lists of potential job recommendations, generated using different similarity metrics (Cosine Similarity, Euclidean Distance, and Manhattan Distance). These lists are displayed in a randomized order to minimize selection bias and prevent candidates from being influenced by list positioning. Users can interact with the recommendations by filtering career fields, adjusting match scores, and exploring detailed profession descriptions through embedded links.

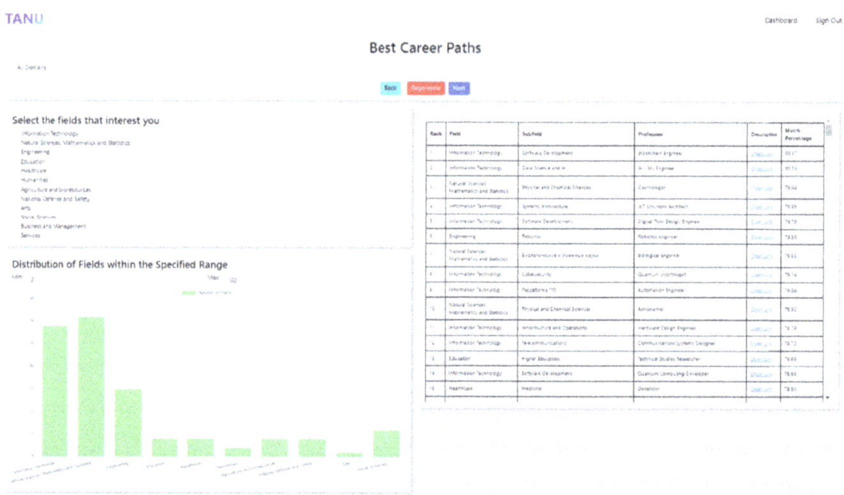

Figure 10. The job recommendations page.

To assess the effectiveness of each similarity method, candidates are asked to review all three lists and select the one they believe best represents their career preferences and aspirations. This structured process allows for a more objective comparison of the different methods while providing career counselors with insights into which metric yields the most relevant recommendations. The navigation features within the application also allow users to refine their selections, revisit results, or proceed to further career exploration, ensuring a seamless and user-friendly experience.

4.4. Computational Efficiency Analysis

While our approach prioritizes recommendation quality over training speed, we evaluate its computational demands:

- **GPT-4 Processing**: Requires ~3 s per job description (256 jobs = ~13 min. total).

- **Bias Correction**: The 34 × 34 matrix normalization adds negligible overhead (<1 min).
- **Recommendation Generation**: Scales linearly with candidates (100 candidates × 256 jobs = 25,600 comparisons at ∼0.1 ms each = ∼2.5 s total).

The numbers above demonstrate practical deployability despite not being optimized purely for training speed.

5. Results and Discussion

The evaluation process engaged 100 university graduates who took the personality test. This section presents and discusses the main results of the evaluation process in a comparative manner, highlighting the overall performance of the method using different metrics and the respective performance in various user subgroups depending on the domain of studies.

Specifically, the graduates evaluated three distinct job recommendation methods—Weighted Manhattan, Weighted Euclidean, and Baseline—by scoring each method on a scale from 1 to 10. The analysis focuses on comparing the performance of the three approaches by examining their score distributions across participants. The dataset also includes additional attributes such as the graduates' current specialty, the broader area of their work, their initial field of study, and whether their current job aligns with their studied specialty. The analysis that follows aims to uncover patterns, strengths, and weaknesses of each method across different graduate subgroups and provide actionable insights for improving job recommendation systems. This comparative assessment provides insights into the effectiveness of each approach in capturing meaningful patterns related to personality traits and professional alignment and satisfaction.

The first comparison examines the performance of the two proposed alternatives versus the baseline method. As shown in Figure 11, which displays the average score and the standard deviation for each method, the two proposed alternatives outperform the baseline. The weighted Manhattan method is almost 0.5 degrees better than the baseline, on average, based on the evaluation of the 100 graduates. This means that the method is statistically significantly better than the baseline, almost at the 90% confidence interval.

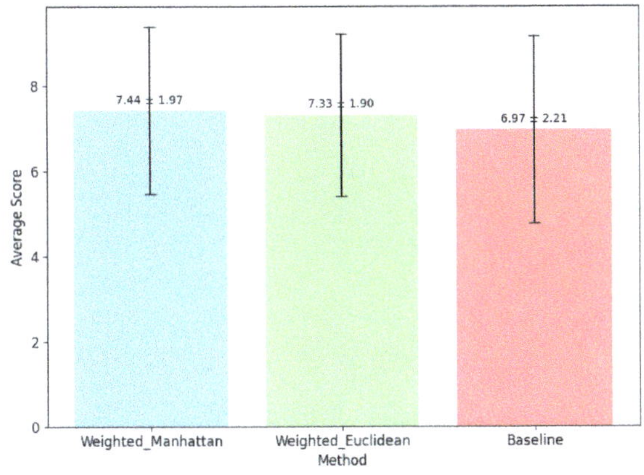

Figure 11. The distribution of ratings per method for graduates who work in the specialization they studied and those who do not.

Following the overall performance comparison, we would like to examine the differences in the distribution of scores to the three methods between graduates who are working on the specialization they studied and those who do not. As shown in Figure 12 the scores are more dispersed for all metrics among graduates working outside their specialty (interquartile range [IQR]: 3.5–6.5 for Manhattan, 3–6 for Euclidean) compared to those within their specialty (IQR: 6–8 for Manhattan, 5–7 for Euclidean). The average score for the two proposed methods is higher than the baseline.

The group of graduates who work in the same domain that they studied has a more clear opinion of the quality of the results of each method and a more cohesive evaluation. Apart from a few outliers, they rank the weighted Manhattan-based alternative higher than the other two methods, giving scores that are either 7 or 8 out of 10. More specifically, in the within-specialty group, the weighted Manhattan method achieved a median score of 7.5 (IQR = 6–8), with 75% of ratings being 7 or higher. The weighted Euclidean method showed a slightly lower consensus with a median of 6 (IQR = 5–7). Baseline scores were consistently the lowest with a median of 4 (IQR = 3–5). In the outside-specialty group, both proposed methods outperformed the baseline (median scores of 5 vs. 3 respectively), but exhibited wider score distributions (Manhattan IQR = 3.5–6.5; Euclidean IQR = 3–6). The baseline method showed the poorest performance with a median of 3 (IQR = 2–4). The greater variance in scores for this group suggests more variability in how relevant the recommendations were perceived to be. These numerical results demonstrate that graduates working in their field of study showed both higher satisfaction and greater consensus in their evaluations, particularly favoring the weighted Manhattan approach. The wider score ranges among those working outside their specialty may reflect more diverse career trajectories or differing expectations from the recommendation system.

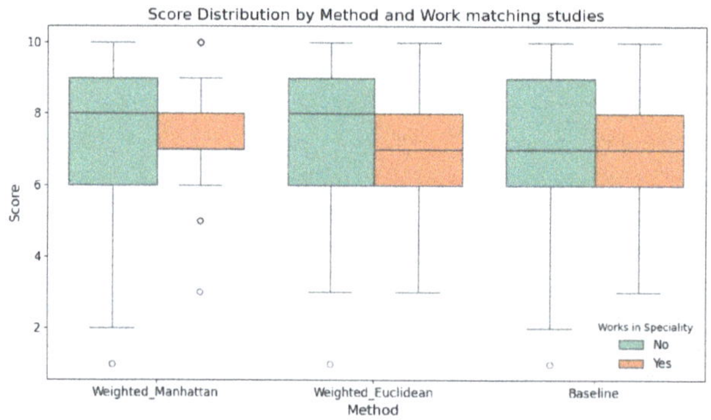

Figure 12. The distribution of ratings per method for graduates who work in the specialization they studied and those who do not.

The next set of results highlights whether certain methods perform better than others for specific work specializations. From what is shown in Figure 13, our proposed approach outperforms the text similarity-based baseline in all specialization areas. However, the weighted Manhattan method is preferred among graduates who work in Business and Management, Education, and Services, whereas the weighted Euclidian method is preferred among graduates who work in Engineering, Information Technology, and Social Sciences. The two methods are equally valued among graduates who work in Natural Sciences, Mathematics, and Statistics.

Similar results are found in the radar plot of Figure 14, which displays the respective average score per group of graduates, based on the area they have studied. Once again, the two proposed alternatives outperform the baseline in all areas apart from the group of graduates of Information Technology for which the three methods have comparable performance.

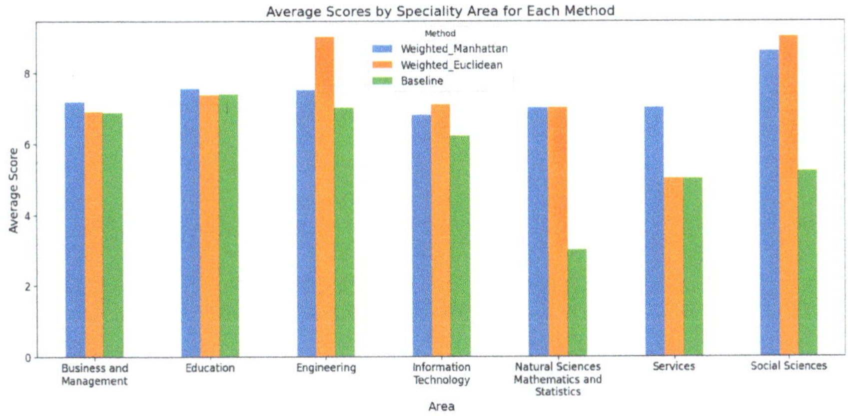

Figure 13. The performance of the proposed methods against the baseline across the different areas of specialization that graduates work in.

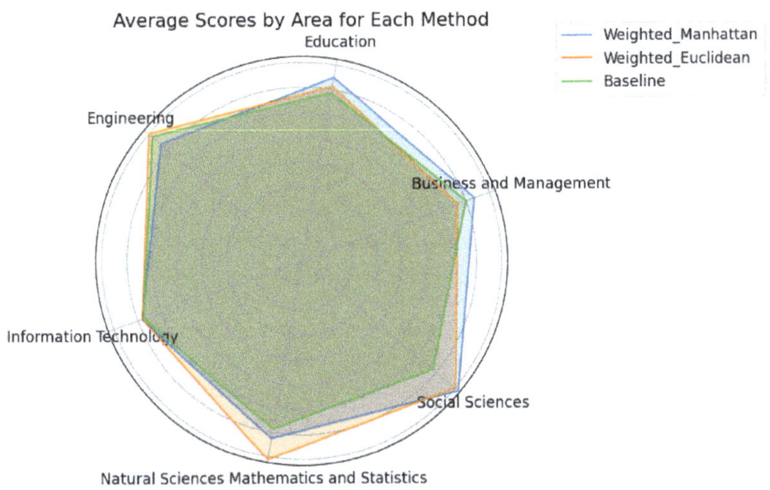

Figure 14. The performance of the proposed methods against the baseline across the different areas of specialization that the graduates have studied.

While the study provides valuable insights into the performance of job recommendation methods, several limitations should be acknowledged. First, the sample size of 100 graduates, though sufficient for initial comparisons, may lack the diversity and statistical power to generalize findings across broader populations or niche specializations. For instance, subgroups like graduates in Natural Sciences or Information Technology were underrepresented, potentially skewing results (e.g., the comparable performance of methods in IT). Second, the evaluation relied on self-reported scores, which may introduce subjective bias, and the analysis focused narrowly on specialty alignment and domain areas, overlooking other factors like demographic diversity, job market dynamics, or longitudinal satisfaction. Finally, while the proposed methods outperformed the baseline, their reliance on Manhattan and Euclidean metrics may oversimplify the complexity of personality–job alignment.

To address these limitations, future work could expand the participant pool to include more graduates across diverse specializations and geographic regions, ensuring robust subgroup analyses. Testing advanced similarity methods (e.g., machine learning-driven metrics, hybrid models combining personality traits with contextual job-market data) could enhance recommendation accuracy. Additionally, incorporating objective metrics (e.g., job retention rates, employer feedback) and longitudinal studies would strengthen validity, while explainability frameworks could clarify why certain methods succeed in specific domains (e.g., Manhattan's dominance in Business vs. Euclidean in Engineering).

6. Conclusions and Future Work

This study introduced a novel job recommendation system that integrates personality traits evaluated through the Gallup CliftonStrengths assessment, offering a more holistic approach to career matching by aligning users' natural strengths with job requirements. Empirical evaluations involving 100 graduates demonstrated that the proposed methods significantly outperformed the baseline text-similarity approach, showing a 0.5-point average improvement in user satisfaction. Notably, graduates working in their studied specializations exhibited more cohesive evaluations, consistently favoring the proposed approach, while the performance of the two proposed variants varied across domains. These results underscore the value of incorporating personality traits into recommendation systems, particularly for enhancing alignment between users' intrinsic strengths and job roles.

However, the study has several limitations. First, the sample size, though sufficient for initial validation, limits generalizability to niche specializations (e.g., underrepresented groups in IT or Natural Sciences). Second, reliance on self-reported scores introduces potential subjective bias, and the analysis focused narrowly on specialty alignment rather than demographic or job-market dynamics.

Future work should expand the participant pool to include diverse specializations and geographic regions to validate robustness. Testing advanced similarity methods, such as machine learning-driven metrics or hybrid models integrating contextual job-market data, could further refine accuracy. As part of future work, we plan to conduct a rigorous ablation study to isolate and quantify the impact of each pipeline component—especially the CliftonStrengths-derived personality vectors—on recommendation performance. In addition, we plan to incorporate comparisons with other recommendation techniques, such as collaborative filtering and hybrid recommenders, to further validate our approach in a broader algorithmic context. We also aim to explore the use of standard evaluation metrics, including AUC and precision/recall, to provide a more comprehensive view of accuracy and performance trade-offs.

Furthermore, recognizing the importance of adaptability in both individuals and systems, we aim to investigate how dynamic, future-oriented strengths—such as those captured by the Gallup Adaptability, Learner, and Strategic themes—can be leveraged to match users with roles that are themselves evolving. This may include hybridizing narrow strength-based models with broader frameworks like the Big Five to better address the multidimensional nature of jobs that demand both technical precision and socio-emotional intelligence. Incorporating objective metrics like job retention rates or employer feedback, alongside longitudinal studies, would strengthen validity. For this reason, we plan to conduct a longitudinal follow-up incorporating objective indicators such as job placement outcomes, employer feedback, and career retention rates, to more robustly evaluate the long-term impact of the proposed method. Additionally, explainability frameworks could clarify why certain methods excel in specific domains. By addressing these challenges, personality-based recommendation systems can evolve into indispensable tools for fostering career satisfaction and talent retention.

Author Contributions: Conceptualization, S.S., A.K. and C.T.; methodology, A.K. and C.S.; software, A.K.; validation, S.S., A.K. and C.S.; formal analysis, S.S. and Y.K.; investigation, I.V.; resources, S.S. and A.K.; data curation, S.S. and A.K.; writing—original draft preparation, S.S., C.S. and I.V; writing—review and editing, C.S. and I.V.; visualization, A.K. and I.V.; supervision, I.V.; project administration, I.V.; funding acquisition, B.R. and Y.K. All authors have read and agreed to the published version of the manuscript.

Funding: This research received no external funding.

Informed Consent Statement: Informed consent was obtained from all subjects involved in the study.

Data Availability Statement: Data will be made available by the authors upon request.

Acknowledgments: We would like to extend our deepest gratitude to the team at Tanu AI for their invaluable assistance in data collection and methodology development. Their dedication, expertise, and collaborative efforts played a crucial role in the successful completion of this research. We truly appreciate their support and commitment throughout the entire process.

Conflicts of Interest: Author Asset Kabdiyev, Bobir Razhametov and Yermek Kazym were employed by the company Tanu.ai. The remaining authors declare that the research was conducted in the absence of any commercial or financial relationships that could be construed as a potential conflict of interest.

References

1. Potash, P.; Rumshisky, A. Recommender System Incorporating User Personality Profile through Analysis of Written Reviews. In Proceedings of the EMPIRE@ RecSys, Boston, MA, USA, 15–19 September 2016; pp. 60–66.
2. Dhelim, S.; Aung, N.; Bouras, M.A.; Ning, H.; Cambria, E. A survey on personality-aware recommendation systems. *Artif. Intell. Rev.* **2022**, *55*, 2409–2454. [CrossRef]
3. Hassan, R.H.; Hassan, M.T.; Sameem, M.S.I.; Rafique, M.A. Personality-Aware Course Recommender System Using Deep Learning for Technical and Vocational Education and Training. *Information* **2024**, *15*, 803. [CrossRef]
4. Mulay, A.; Sutar, S.; Patel, J.; Chhabria, A.; Mumbaikar, S. Job recommendation system using hybrid filtering. In *Proceedings of the ITM Web of Conferences*; EDP Sciences: Paris, France, 2022; Volume 44, p. 02002.
5. Roy, D.; Dutta, M. A systematic review and research perspective on recommender systems. *J. Big Data* **2022**, *9*, 59. [CrossRef]
6. Zhang, Y.; Yang, C.; Niu, Z. A research of job recommendation system based on collaborative filtering. In Proceedings of the 2014 Seventh International Symposium on Computational Intelligence and Design, Hangzhou, China, 13–14 December 2014; Volume 1, pp. 533–538.
7. Panchasara, S.; Gupta, R.K.; Sharma, A. AI Based Job Recommedation System using BERT. In Proceedings of the 2023 7th International Conference On Computing, Communication, Control And Automation (ICCUBEA), Pune, India, 18–19 August 2023; pp. 1–6.
8. Mashayekhi, Y.; Li, N.; Kang, B.; Lijffijt, J.; De Bie, T. A challenge-based survey of e-recruitment recommendation systems. *ACM Comput. Surv.* **2024**, *56*, 1–33. [CrossRef]
9. Umemoto, K.; Milo, T.; Kitsuregawa, M. Toward recommendation for upskilling: Modeling skill improvement and item difficulty in action sequences. In Proceedings of the 2020 IEEE 36th International Conference on Data Engineering (ICDE), Dallas, TX, USA, 20–24 April 2020; pp. 169–180.
10. Weichselbraun, A.; Waldvogel, R.; Fraefel, A.; van Schie, A.; Kuntschik, P. Building knowledge graphs and recommender systems for suggesting reskilling and upskilling options from the web. *Information* **2022**, *13*, 510. [CrossRef]
11. Parida, M.; Saxena, V.S.; Supraja, P. Job Profile Upskilling Through Content-based Course Recommendation System using Hadoop MapReduce. *Grenze Int. J. Eng. Technol. (GIJET)* **2023**, *9*, 513.
12. Zou, Z.; Huspi, S.H.; Nuar, A.N.A. A Review on Job Recommendation System. *J. Adv. Res. Appl. Sci. Eng. Technol.* **2024**, *41*, 113–124. [CrossRef]
13. Patil, A.; Suwalka, D.; Kumar, A.; Rai, G.; Saha, J. A survey on artificial intelligence (AI) based job recommendation systems. In Proceedings of the 2023 International Conference on Sustainable Computing and Data Communication Systems (ICSCDS), Erode, India, 23–25 March 2023; pp. 730–737.
14. Patel, R.; Mishra, S.; Ailani, N.; Mirani, S.; Ren, Z.; Mohammed, S. Personalized Context-Oriented Job Recommendation System Based On Knowledge Graph. *Authorea Prepr.* **2024**. [CrossRef]
15. Alsaif, S.A.; Sassi Hidri, M.; Ferjani, I.; Eleraky, H.A.; Hidri, A. NLP-based bi-directional recommendation system: Towards recommending jobs to job seekers and resumes to recruiters. *Big Data Cogn. Comput.* **2022**, *6*, 147. [CrossRef]

16. Dascălu, M.I.; Hang, A.; Puskás, I.F.; Bodea, C.N. CareProfSys: A job recommender system based on machine learning and ontology to support learners' employability at regional level. *Issues Inf. Syst.* **2023**, *24*, 71–82.
17. Appadoo, K.; Soonnoo, M.B.; Mungloo-Dilmohamud, Z. Job Recommendation System, Machine Learning, Regression, Classification, Natural Language Processing. In Proceedings of the 2020 IEEE Asia-Pacific Conference on Computer Science and Data Engineering (CSDE), Gold Coast, Australia, 16–18 December 2020; pp. 1–6. [CrossRef]
18. He, X.; Chen, T.; Kan, M.Y.; Chen, X. TriRank: Review-aware explainable recommendation by modeling aspects. In Proceedings of the 24th ACM International on Conference on Information and Knowledge Management, Melbourne, Australia, 18–23 October 2015; pp. 1661–1670.
19. Chen, Z.; Silvestri, F.; Wang, J.; Zhang, Y.; Huang, Z.; Ahn, H.; Tolomei, G. Grease: Generate factual and counterfactual explanations for gnn-based recommendations. *arXiv* **2022**, arXiv:2208.04222.
20. Mohammadi, A.R.; Peintner, A.; Müller, M.; Zangerle, E. Are We Explaining the Same Recommenders? Incorporating Recommender Performance for Evaluating Explainers. In Proceedings of the 18th ACM Conference on Recommender Systems, Bari, Italy, 14–18 October 2024; pp. 1113–1118.

algorithms

MDPI

Article

Comprehensive Risk Assessment of Power Grids Using Fuzzy Bayesian Networks Through Expert Elicitation: A Technical Analysis

Yasir Mahmood [1,*], Nof Yasir [2], Nita Yodo [1], Ying Huang [1,*], Di Wu [2] and Roy A. McCann [3]

1 Civil, Construction, and Environmental Engineering Department, North Dakota State University, Fargo, ND 58102, USA; nita.yodo@ndsu.edu
2 Electrical and Computer Engineering Department, North Dakota State University, Fargo, ND 58102, USA; nof.yasir@ndsu.edu (N.Y.); di.wu.3@ndsu.edu (D.W.)
3 Electrical Engineering Department, University of Arkansas, Fayetteville, AR 72701, USA; rmccann@uark.edu
* Correspondence: yasir.mahmood@ndsu.edu (Y.M.); ying.huang@ndsu.edu (Y.H.)

Abstract: Power grid infrastructures, essential to modern societies for electricity distribution, are prone to vulnerabilities due to their numerous sensitive components, necessitating a comprehensive risk assessment. Uncertainty in historical failure data often compromises accurate risk quantification, leading to the integration of expert elicitation as a solution. This study develops a Bayesian network (BN) risk assessment model integrated with fuzzy set theory (FST), referred to as the fuzzy Bayesian network (FBN). By incorporating expert insights, this model quantifies internal and external risk variables more comprehensively. Crisp probabilities (CPr), derived from regional transmission operator (RTO) failure incident data, are complemented by fuzzy probabilities (FPr) from expert elicitation. The findings indicate that equipment conditions, specifically transmission lines and circuit breakers, are critical threats to power grids. Environmental factors, particularly storms, emerge as vulnerability risks. A comparison of results using both CPr plus FPr versus FPr alone underscores the utility of expert elicitation in risk assessment. This research demonstrates the effectiveness of FBNs through expert elicitation, providing a comprehensive and accurate framework for power grid risk assessment. To improve risk evaluation in critical infrastructure, integrated data collection techniques are recommended.

Keywords: external and internal risk factors; fuzzy set theory; environmental factors; equipment conditions; critical infrastructure; crisp probabilities; fuzzy probabilities

1. Introduction

Electricity has a major role and significant impact on modern life activities. Various economic sectors worldwide depend heavily on the electric power industry, and generated energy is used to meet industry and domestic needs [1]. Due to large-scale urbanization and settlement, electricity demand has increased, and maintaining power is crucial for everyday life and economic vitality [2]. Critical power infrastructure, also known as the power grid, is required to generate and distribute electricity based on four fundamental functions, i.e., electricity generation, transmission, distribution, and finally, consumption by end users [3]. These critical infrastructures are susceptible to various natural and man-made risks that threaten their integrity [4]. Natural hazards include weather-related factors, such as rainfall, high winds, and extreme temperatures, and environmental factors, such as earthquakes, storms, fires, lightning, tornadoes, and vegetation [5,6]. There are numerous man-made risk factors, such as operational parameters, which include maintenance issues, disconnects, current flow, voltage level, and power factors [2]. Equipment conditions are also critical for assessing the associated risks, and commonly known equipment failures include malfunctioning capacitors, transformers, circuit breakers, generators, reactors, and transmission lines. Some specialized risk factors also threaten the reliability of power grids, including cyberattacks, unauthorized access, and the failure of the supervisory control and data acquisition (SCADA) system [7]. These potential risks are severe concerns for operating agencies and all stakeholders, potentially leading to prolonged blackouts that could have a significant impact on the country's economy. One of the motivations for conducting this study is the recent blackout in Europe, particularly in Spain and Portugal, which underscores the importance and timeliness of power grid risk assessment and resilience. This event, which affected millions of people across the region, emphasizes the practical relevance of the proposed model, underscoring the need for enhanced infrastructure resilience in the face of such widespread failures [8,9]. Similarly to these, the blackout serves as a reminder of the vulnerabilities in power grids. Furthermore, it underscores the need for advanced risk assessment approaches, such as the fuzzy Bayesian network model proposed in this study, to more accurately predict and mitigate the effects of future failures. There are numerous techniques to quantify these risk factors and suggest mitigation measures. One of these promising methods is the quantitative risk assessment approach (QRA), which is commonly used when adequate historical data for past failure incidents are available [10]. The most commonly known QRA methods are fault tree analysis (FTA), event tree analysis (ETA), Monte Carlo simulation (MCS), and Bayesian networks (BNs) [11]. In newly developed or less-documented infrastructures, historical data may be unavailable or unreliable due to certain inherent factors, such as incomplete maintenance records [12]. Qualitative risk assessment techniques are often used in power grid risk assessment to evaluate potential risks and vulnerabilities objectively. These methods may not provide precise numerical values but offer valuable insights into risk characteristics and help prioritize future analyses [13]. A few commonly known qualitative risk assessment techniques are failure modes and effects analysis (FMEA), risk matrices, bowtie analysis, the Delphi method, and expert elicitation [14]. These techniques convert qualitative data into quantitative numbers, and risk is assessed for the facility under consideration [15]. Researchers have conducted numerous studies to assess the risks posed to power grids by suggesting mitigation strategies for the stability of power flow to end users. In the next paragraph, a few important studies are discussed, followed by the research gap and focus of this research.

Using the QRA approach, Li et al. [16] proposed a model using hierarchical Bayesian analysis (HBA) to quantify the risks associated with submarine pipelines. The methodology used accounts for uncertainty in the data and model, and an industrial case study is used to demonstrate the use of this approach. Borenius et al. [15] adopted a qualitative risk assessment approach and conducted expert interviews across Europe and the US to identify significant risks to power grids. Based on the results, it is concluded that false data injection, denial of services, and malware attacks are significant threats. Dong et al. [17] proposed a risk assessment model combining the data-driven analytical hierarchy process (D-AHP) and grey theory for smart grids. To obtain comprehensive assessment values and risk grades, 5 first-level and 13 second-level indices were combined using an empirical dataset for the Suzhou Smart Grid Demonstration Project in China. To evaluate the impact of cyber systems on power grid dispatching systems, Chen et al. [18] proposed a risk assessment model and calculated the power grid risk probabilities and consequences through risk index levels. To highlight the IT vulnerabilities and cyber threats to power grids, Canbolat et al. [19] proposed a hybrid risk assessment model using fuzzy theory. This study provides meaningful insights into ensuring power grid stability by combining linguistic and numerical analyses. Zhu et al. [20] proposed a novel approach for accessing cascading failure sequences in AC/DC hybrid power grids using a game model and quantitative indices. Although the model was validated on China's provincial AC/DC hybrid power grid, its scalability and practical implications must be considered. By applying graph theory to identify the communities at risk of power loss due to wildfires, Jones et al. [21] proposed a novel approach. Fire probability data and betweenness centrality and minimum cut analyses highlight vulnerable areas. Potential limitations to the method include the difficulty of practical implementation and the need for further validation with larger, more complex grids. Bian et al. [22] proposed an innovative technique for assessing and mitigating risks in large-scale power grids, specifically transmission line trips caused by natural hazards. The proposed risk analysis method combines FTA and BN modeling to assess and predict tripping accidents caused by wildfires, lightning, strong winds, and ice storms. However, real-world interactions and uncertainties may be distorted by modeling simplifications. In recent years, several methodologies have been proposed to assess risks in power grid systems, such as intelligent inspection models based on edge computing (e.g., RepYOLO for power line inspection) and data collection protocols for smart grids [23]. These approaches primarily focus on improving operational efficiency and security in specific aspects of grid management, such as data integrity and defect detection. Additionally, studies like the one focusing on cascading failures through risk-graph analysis examine network vulnerabilities but fail to address the probabilistic nature of uncertainty and expert elicitation, which is critical for effective risk management [24]. Our work proposes a novel fuzzy Bayesian network approach that integrates expert opinions and weather-related risks, providing a more comprehensive model for assessing power grid vulnerabilities, including the impact of cascading failures and external disturbances.

After conducting a detailed literature review, we confidently state that while previous research has addressed significant threats to power grid systems, most studies focus primarily on a limited range of risks. In particular, cyber threats and transmission line failures are often the primary areas of concern, leaving many other potential risks underexplored. To highlight the practical significance and relevance of our proposed risk assessment model, we compare it with existing methods from the recent literature. These methods, which include power line intelligent inspection, secure data collection in smart grids, and cascading failure vulnerability analysis, focus on different aspects of infrastructure risk. Although these methods provide valuable insights, they focus on specific types of risks or heavily rely on historical data and traditional engineering models. In contrast, our proposed model offers a more comprehensive approach by integrating FBNs and expert elicitation. Our model identifies a broader range of risk factors, including equipment failure, human error, and weather-related risks such as extreme temperatures, flooding, and lightning. Including these weather-related factors, which are increasingly critical for infrastructure resilience, provides a more holistic view of risk. Through this comparison, we demonstrate that our methodology offers enhanced adaptability, precision, and reliability in assessing the risks to power grid systems, proving its practical significance and superiority over existing approaches. Additionally, the lack of historical data and the vagueness of existing datasets can lead to under- or overestimating risk assessments [25]. Furthermore, due to the unavailability of incident data for certain risk factors, such as floods or earthquakes, existing models may struggle to generate results when new threats emerge.

To bridge these gaps, this study combines fuzzy set theory (FST) through expert elicitation and the BN, commonly known as the fuzzy Bayesian network (FBN). The BN incorporates fuzzy logic because it aligns with the intricacies and uncertainties inherent to power grid systems, giving it distinct advantages [26]. Expert elicitation will provide a more comprehensive risk assessment, accounting for external and internal factors [27].

Using the BN, ongoing risk assessment will remain relevant, and the model will be updated as new evidence is acquired. Integrating an FBN in this study enables a comprehensive risk assessment of power grids by combining quantitative data and expert opinions. Due to changing environmental conditions, evolving cyber threats, and the dynamic nature of power grids, the FBN is exceptionally well suited for handling imprecise, incomplete, or uncertain information, which is common in power grid risk assessments [28]. Another novelty of this study is that it compares root causes, also known as basic events (BEs), identified through expert elicitation with those identified through historical data only.

Expert opinions gathered through surveys enhance the efficacy of this risk assessment model. These insights provide valuable complements to the quantitative data, making them essential for a comprehensive understanding of power grid risks. Applying this methodology enhances the comprehensiveness of our risk assessment and ensures that our findings benefit the stakeholders involved in ensuring power grid stability and security.

The remainder of this paper is organized as follows: Section 2 provides an overview of the fuzzy Bayesian network (FBN), introducing Bayesian networks, fuzzy set theory, and the role of expert elicitation in risk assessment. Section 3 outlines the methodology for applying the FBN to power grid risk assessment, detailing the identification of risk factors, data collection, and the construction of the FBN. Section 4 presents the model implementation using both crisp and fuzzy probabilities to assess power grid risks. Section 5 discusses the results, including a comparison of models and a sensitivity analysis. Finally, Section 6 concludes the paper, summarizing the findings and suggesting directions for future research.

2. Overview of the FBN

2.1. Bayes' Theorem and the BN

The BN is based on the Bayes theorem presented by Thomas Bayes in the 18th century. The main concept of the Bayes theorem revolves around addressing the uncertainty encountered in daily life [29]. It can be used to determine the probability of an event based on the occurrence of a previous event. The Bayes theorem is a fundamental principle of probability theory underpinning the BN to update the probability of a variable based on evidence from its parent node, making it valuable for decision-making and machine-learning applications [22]. The Bayes theorem can be expressed using Equation (1).

$$P(B/A) = \frac{P(A/B) \times P(B)}{P(A)} \quad (1)$$

In Equation (1), P(A) is the probability of event A, P(B) is the probability of event B, P(B/A) is the probability of event B given that event A has already occurred, and P(A/B) is the probability of event A given that event B has already occurred.

BNs are mathematical models representing the causal relationship for different risk variables using CPTs. In a BN, nodes are connected through directed acyclic graphs (DAGs), and edges represent causal relationships between risk variables [30]. A variable's probability can be updated based on the new evidence that the parent's node acquired. The BN approach is a powerful tool for modeling complex systems, decision-making, and machine-learning applications where updating probabilities in response to updated information is crucial to the model's accuracy [31]. A simple description of the BN is shown in Figure 1. Nodes A, B, and C are parent nodes or BEs, Nodes X and Y are child nodes, also known as intermediate events (IEs), and Node Z is the top event (TE) or the outcome of this network.

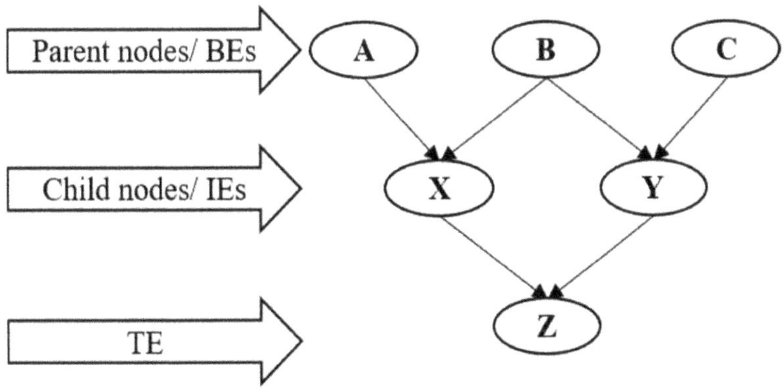

Figure 1. A sample BN structure with a causal relationship among different risk levels.

2.2. Expert Elicitation

Expert elicitation is a crucial element in power grid risk assessment, enabling the quantification of uncertainty and imprecision associated with various factors [32]. Power grids are complex and influenced by multiple risk factors, including component reliability, environmental conditions, and external factors, which are not fully captured by historical data alone. Expert elicitation enables the incorporation of subjective judgments from individuals with extensive experience and knowledge in the power grid sector [33].

To ensure the reliability of the expert inputs and minimize potential biases, we have carefully selected domain experts based on specific attributes that are important for providing accurate insights into the risk factors associated with power grid failures. The experts selected for this study are based on position, experience, education, and age. The roles of the experts within the industry, including senior engineers, risk analysts, and safety specialists, are considered. Seniority in the field serves as a proxy for experience and depth of knowledge in power grid risk management. A higher weight is assigned to those with more experience in power grid integrity, failure modes, and risk mitigation. Educational qualification is another critical factor, as experts with advanced degrees (e.g., M.S. or Ph.D.) in relevant fields, such as risk management, are more likely to be aware of existing and emerging threats. Although age is not a direct measure of expertise, age is included as a rough indicator of career length and accumulated knowledge in the industry. Experts with a balance of practical field experience and academic grounding are more professional and give an added advantage. The scoring system ensures that all attributes are considered proportionately while minimizing subjective biases in the selection process. For position, the score varies from 1 to 5, with 5 representing the highest level of expertise (e.g., senior manager or director). The score for experience also varies from 1 to 5, with 5 indicating more than 20 years of experience in the power industry. For education, scores range from 1 to 5, with 5 representing a Ph.D. or equivalent in a relevant field. Lastly, the score for age ranges from 1 to 5, with 5 indicating 50 years of age or older. The total score for each expert was computed as the sum of the individual scores, normalized to ensure consistency across the expert pool.

2.3. Fuzzy Set Theory

Fuzzy set theory (FST) is a mathematical framework that extends traditional set theory by incorporating degrees of membership to represent uncertainty and imprecision [34]. In conventional set theory, elements are classified as binary, meaning they are either True or False or Yes or No. In contrast, FST allows elements with membership values ranging from 0 to 1, reflecting varying degrees, making it an ideal tool for modeling uncertainty in systems like power grid risk assessment [35]. Experts express their input using linguistic variables (e.g., "low", "medium", "high"), later converted into fuzzy numbers that represent the degree of membership of various risk factors. This fuzzy representation enables the incorporation of vagueness and uncertainty in expert knowledge, thereby making the model more flexible and robust [36].

In power grid risk assessment, FST is applied to model uncertainties in key parameters, such as component reliability, environmental conditions, and operational performance. FST, through expert elicitation, enables domain experts to provide subjective judgments about risk levels, which are then converted into fuzzy numbers [27]. The application of FST in power grid risk assessment follows a structured, three-step process to calculate fuzzy probabilities (FPr) based on expert input:

- The first step involves converting expert-provided linguistic terms (e.g., "low", "medium", "high") into fuzzy numbers. These numbers represent the degree of membership of a particular risk factor within each category, allowing for a more nuanced representation of expert knowledge [37].
- In the second step, the opinions of multiple experts are aggregated into a collective membership function. This ensures that the model accounts for the diversity of expert judgments, effectively reflecting the uncertainty and variability in expert knowledge [37].
- The third step involves converting the aggregated membership function into FPr, representing the likelihood of specific risk events. These FPr consider expert input and the inherent uncertainty in the data.

This approach integrates expert knowledge by providing a more adaptive, robust, and flexible model for assessing power grid risks. Using fuzzy probabilities in the Bayesian network (BN) framework enables the more comprehensive modeling of complex, uncertain relationships within power grids, thereby enhancing the model's ability to predict and manage risks. By integrating expert elicitation with Bayesian networks, a fuzzy Bayesian network (FBN) framework can be formed that is more adaptable for analyzing complex relationships among variables in power grids [38]. Expert judgments help the model to handle uncertainties related to environmental and operational factors, such as weather events, equipment failures, and third-party interference. The FBN methodology is more effective in modeling and managing the dynamic and uncertain nature of power grid systems, enabling more informed risk management and resilience planning decision-making [39].

2.4. Construction of the BN for Transformation to the FBN

For constructing the BN, CPTs are the foundation for representing the conditional relationships between variables. CPTs describe the probability of outcomes for a child node, given the states of its parent nodes. Traditional BNs derive these probabilities using historical data or expert opinions when data are scarce or incomplete. However, this conventional approach struggles to capture real-world data's inherent vagueness and uncertainty, particularly in complex systems such as power grids [39]. To address these challenges, FBNs extend BNs by integrating fuzzy logic, which provides a robust mechanism to handle vague or uncertain data [40]. The following steps outline the process of constructing a BN and transforming it into an FBN:

1. Development of the BN. The initial step involves creating the BN by identifying critical variables influencing the system, such as environmental factors, external interferences, and operational parameters. The second step establishes dependencies among nodes based on the literature and expert knowledge. The last step is constructing CPTs to

represent conditional probabilities derived from historical data and expert elicitation. The general structure of the BN is shown in Figure 1.

2. Integration of fuzzy logic into BNs. The transition to an FBN begins by integrating fuzzy logic principles to handle the uncertainties in node relationships. The variables in the BN are transformed into fuzzy variables characterized by linguistic terms such as "Low", "Medium", or "High". These terms are represented using fuzzy sets with defined membership functions (e.g., triangular or trapezoidal functions) [41]. For all nodes without CPTs through historical data, traditional CPTs are replaced with FPr due to the unattainability of CPr. These values reflect the degree of possibility for each outcome under uncertain conditions.
3. Aggregation of expert opinions using fuzzy logic. As discussed, expert opinions are critical in constructing CPTs when historical data are scarce. To address inconsistencies or subjective biases among experts, each input is assigned a weighting factor based on their expertise level and the relevance of their knowledge to the variable in question. Expert opinions, provided as linguistic terms, are aggregated using fuzzy operations such as weighted averages or fuzzy intersections. This ensures a complete and unbiased representation of the underlying uncertainties.
4. Probabilistic inference in FBNs. Inference in FBNs is carried out through probabilistic and fuzzy reasoning. The process involves propagating evidence across the network and updating node probabilities as fuzzy values, allowing dynamic model adjustment in response to new information. When precise numerical values are required for decision-making, defuzzification techniques are applied to convert fuzzy results into crisp outputs.
5. Validation and Sensitivity Analysis. The last steps are validation and sensitivity analyses to ensure the reliability of the FBN. The impact of variations in input fuzzy sets on output probabilities is assessed, identifying the critical factors influencing system behavior. The model is tested using real-world scenarios to confirm its predictive accuracy and robustness.

3. Methodology

Figure 2 shows the proposed framework for power grid risk assessment using the FBN. The proposed framework can be explained in three steps. Step I includes consultation with experts from the power grid industry/academia and a related literature review to identify the risk factors or BEs. After identifying the BEs, cause-and-effect relations are established using nodes and edges to show the relationships of all variables leading to the TE of the power grid shutdown. Step II involves two key activities: cleaning historical failure incident data and formulating a survey questionnaire for experts. The questionnaire aimed to gather opinions on identified risk variables expressed in linguistic terms. Once the data are analyzed, they are utilized to calculate CPTs. In Step III, the processed data from Step II are fed to the FBN to obtain the failure probability of the TE, and SA is performed to identify the most influential risk factors. Diagnosis inference is also conducted to check the FBN's validity and the proposed model's failure propagation. In the same step, the developed framework is compared with the FBN constructed using FPr only, and conclusions are drawn. In subsequent paragraphs, all steps are explained in detail.

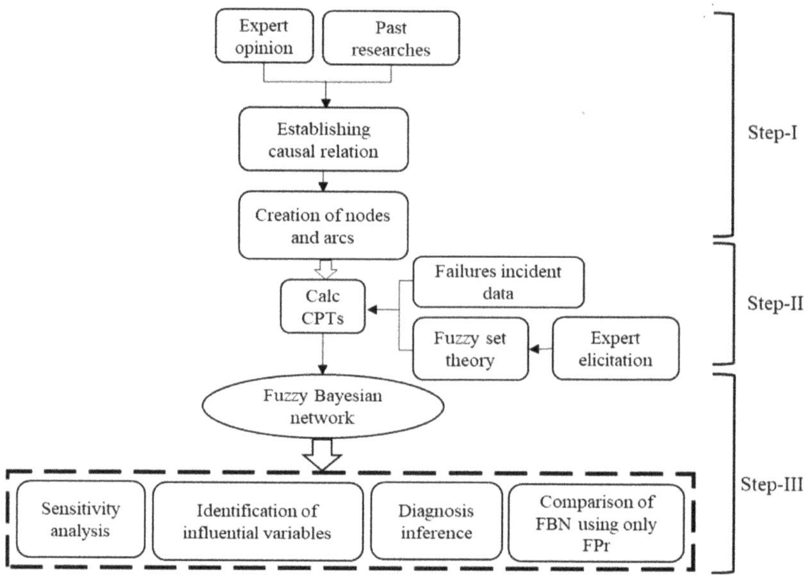

Figure 2. A framework of FBN application for power grid risk assessment.

3.1. *Step I: Identification and Establishment of Causal Relationships Among Risk Factors*

3.1.1. Identification of Risk Factors

In this step, the most influential BEs are identified, leading to the likelihood of TE. The identification of BEs is performed in two phases. During the first phase, two experts were consulted, one with more than 30 years of experience in academia with extensive research on power grids and a second expert with more than ten years of experience working in the power grid industry. Second, based on past research through a comprehensive literature review [2,22,40–48], twenty-six BEs were identified as the root cause of the most critical risk factors, as shown in Figure 3. The focus of this research study, with "power grid shutdown" as TE, is intended to capture the overall system failure, aggregating the contributing factors into a single analysis for clarity. However, examining how shutdowns at specific generating stations and their associated load curtailments influence the grid's resilience is pertinent. In interconnected networks, the failure of a particular generating station can cascade across the power grid. For instance, the inability of a high-capacity station in a critical location could disproportionately impact the grid compared to a smaller, less strategically located station. When a generating station shuts down, the load it previously supplied is redistributed to other operational stations or transmission lines. This redistribution may exceed the operational limits of certain lines or transformers, creating system-wide imbalances, triggering additional outages, propagating through the network, and escalating the risk of a complete grid shutdown. Similarly, load curtailments also serve as a critical operational measure to mitigate the impact of generating station outages. By reducing demand on the grid during a station's failure, operators can maintain system balance and prevent cascading failures. This study uses historical incident failure data from an RTO to calculate CPr. The provided RTO data contain only sixteen BEs; the remaining ten BEs were identified by consulting experts and a literature review.

Figure 3. BEs and their causal relation to intermediate events.

3.1.2. Determination of Causal Relationships Among Risk Factors

Past research and experts have assisted in establishing the causal relationships among BEs. Based on a literature review and discussion with experts, five IEs are identified: equipment conditions, weather conditions, environmental factors, operational parameters, and cybersecurity. These IEs are the child nodes directly influenced by the parent nodes or BEs, leading to TEs.

3.1.3. Creation of Nodes and Edges

After identifying BEs and establishing causal relationships, the next step is to connect BEs and IEs to TEs using edges. Figure 3 explains the creation of nodes and edges, showing the cause-and-effect relationships of all BEs leading to IEs. For instance, transmission line tripping is a BE related to equipment condition failure leading to TE (power grid shutdown). Similarly, the voltage level and current flow are operational parameters leading to the TE.

3.2. Step II: Data Collection

3.2.1. Application of Expert Elicitation

For this study, a survey questionnaire was formulated using Qualtrics and sent for approval by the Institutional Review Board (IRB). Figure 4 describes the process employed to obtain the expert elicitation.

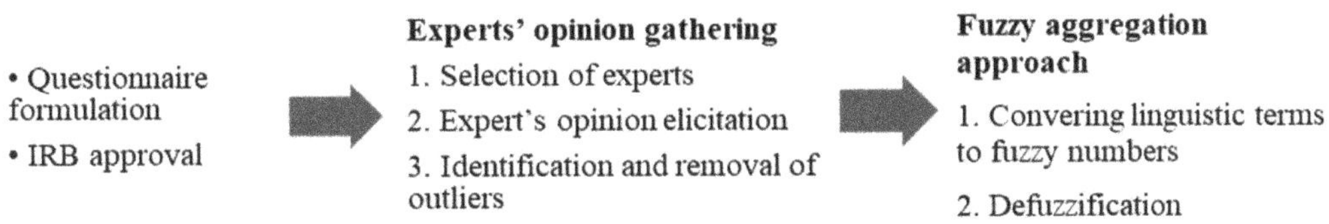

Figure 4. Application of FST for the calculation of FPr.

The selection process for the experts remained very strict. They were selected based on their professional position (PP), experience (Exp), education (EdU), and age. The weights given to the experts based on their PP, EdU, Exp, and age are shown in Table 1.

Table 1. Expert selection criterion and related scores [49].

Criterion	Description	Score	Criterion	Description	Score
Professional Position	Sr./Jr. academic	5	Experience	<5	2
	Engineer	4		5–9	2
	Technician	3		10–19	3
	Operator	3		20–30	4
	Other	2		>30	5
Education	Ph.D.	5	Age	<30	2
	Masters	4		30–39	3
	Bachelor	3		40–50	4
	Social degree	3		>50	5
	High school	2			
	Other	2			

The weighting score for each expert is calculated using Equation (2) [37].

$$\text{Weight score of expert i} = \text{Score(PP)} + \text{Score(Edu)} + \text{Score(Exp)} + \text{Score (Age)} \quad (2)$$

$$W_i = \frac{W_i}{\sum_{i-1}^{n} W_i} \quad (3)$$

Here, W_i is the weight score of expert i based on PP, EdU, Exp, and age.

For this study, a seven-point fuzzy membership function is used, with very low (VL), low (L), fairly low (FL), medium (M), fairly high (FH), high (H), and very high (VH) remaining the highest scores used to quantify the BEs. The descriptions of the scores, along with a description of the linguistic variables, are shown in Figure 5.

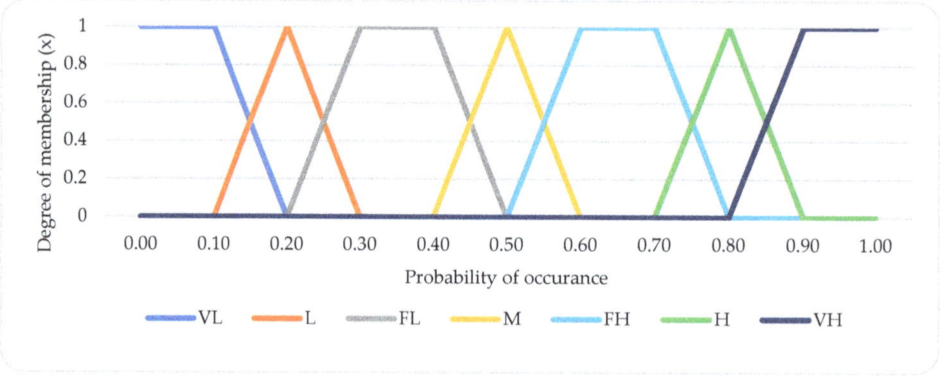

Figure 5. Linguistic terms with corresponding fuzzy membership functions [50].

3.2.2. Calculating Fuzzy Possibilities

Calculating FPs involves converting linguistic terms into FPs by incorporating expert weights. Many techniques exist for calculating FPs, but for this study, a fuzzy linear opinion pool (FLOP), an effective and simple method, is employed [51]. Equation (4) explains the aggregation of FPs.

$$FPs = \sum_{j=1}^{n} Wij \times Aij \; j = 1, 2, \ldots\ldots, n \tag{4}$$

where FPs are the fuzzy possibilities for BEi, and W_{ij} is the expert's weighting factor for expert j for BEi. A_{ij} represents the linguistic opinion provided by expert j for the BE i. These linguistic terms are expressed as fuzzy sets to capture the expert opinions' inherent uncertainty and vagueness. To compute A_{ij}, the experts provide their opinions using predefined linguistic terms such as "Low", "Medium", "High", etc. Each linguistic term corresponds to a fuzzy set defined by a membership function (e.g., triangular or trapezoidal fuzzy numbers). The fuzzy numbers associated with these linguistic terms are directly used in the calculation as A_{ij}. These fuzzy sets provide a numerical representation of linguistic terms, enabling their inclusion in the fuzzy possibility computation.

3.2.3. Calculating Fuzzy Probabilities

Defuzzification plays a crucial role in converting FPs into FPr, facilitating an effective decision-making process for risk assessment in power grid systems [48]. For this study, we employ the widely used Center of Area (CoA) technique, which extracts a crisp value from fuzzy sets by calculating the center of the area under the membership function curve. The formula for the defuzzified output X is

$$X = \frac{\int \mu(x)dx}{\int \mu i(x)} \tag{5}$$

where

- X is the defuzzification output of i;
- x is the output variable;
- i(x) is the aggregated membership function representing the degree of membership for each value of x.

In our model, converting FPs to FPr is essential for assessing risks such as equipment failure, human error, and environmental factors. We utilize trapezoidal and triangular membership functions to represent fuzzy sets, as these functions effectively capture the imprecision inherent in expert judgments and uncertain data [27]. The trapezoidal function is beneficial for risk factors with well-defined thresholds, while the triangular function is more suited for risks that exhibit gradual transitions. Trapezoidal and triangular membership functions can be calculated using Equation (6).

$$\mu A(x) = \begin{cases} 0, & x < a1 \\ \frac{x - a1}{a2 - a1}, & a1 \le x \le a2 \\ 1, & a2 \le x \le a3 \\ \frac{a4 - x}{a4 - a3}, & a3 \le x \le a4 \\ 0, & x > a4 \end{cases} \tag{6}$$

where

- μA(x) is the membership function for fuzzy set A;
- x is the output variable;
- a1, a2, a3, and a4 are the parameters defining the trapezoidal membership function.

Figure 6 illustrates the shapes of these membership functions. These functions map expert inputs, represented as linguistic variables, to a numerical scale, integrating subjective expert opinions with FPr. This provides a robust framework for risk assessment.

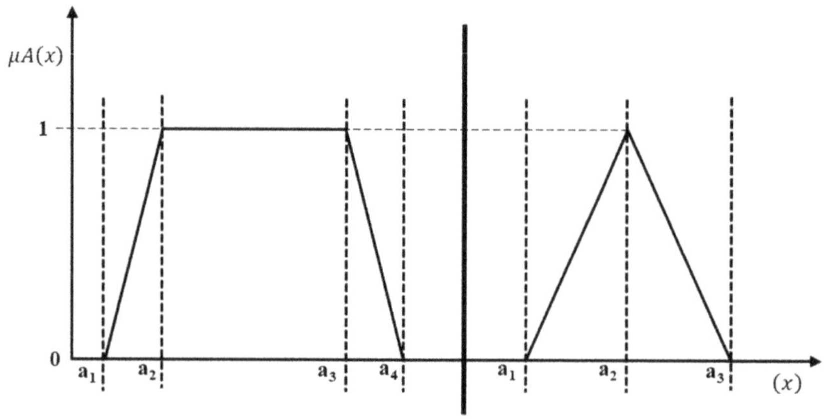

Figure 6. Trapezoidal and triangular membership functions.

In this study, FPs are defuzzified using the CoA method to obtain FPr, ensuring that fuzzy outputs from expert elicitation and fuzzy membership functions are translated into actionable, precise values. Additionally, FPr are not static and can be dynamically adjusted, allowing for flexibility as new risks emerge in power grid systems.

To enhance the precision and adaptability of the model, hyperparameters such as the fuzzy membership function ranges (e.g., VL range) can be manually adjusted or optimized using methods like Bayesian optimization. This optimization enables the continuous refinement of the fuzzy sets, ensuring that the model accurately captures relevant risk factors and expert insights, resulting in more precise predictions of power grid failures.

3.2.4. Determination of FPr

FPr represent the expert's opinion on the final outcome for BEs that are either vague or for which no historical data are available. It can be substituted for nodes instead of CPr. For this study, a simple method proposed by Osinawa in 1998 was employed [52].

$$\mathrm{FPr} = \begin{cases} \frac{1}{10^{\mathrm{K}}} \text{ if FPs } \neq 0 \\ 0 \text{ if FPs } = 0 \end{cases} \quad (7)$$

where $K = \left[\left(\frac{1-\mathrm{FPs}}{\mathrm{FPs}}\right)\right]^{\frac{1}{3}} \times 2.301$

The FPs calculated through Equation (7) are used to determine FPr. Here, K is the Onisawa constant, and this function uses the exponent 1/3 to introduce nonlinearity, which is desirable for some applications and demonstrates direct one-to-one mappings between possibility and probability. A constant of 2.301 is selected based on empirical rules for specific scaling or normalization.

3.3. Step III: Construction of the FBN and Failure Predictions

Following the calculation of CPr and FPr in Step II, this step explains the construction of the FBN using CPTs as input to the model. The primary purpose of this step is to estimate the likelihood of TEs, checking the chances of failure using prior probabilities. Using the prior probabilities, different scenarios can be created to check the influence of different BEs on the entire network. Diagnosis inference is performed to determine the most critical parent nodes by taking the TE with a confirmed 100% failure case. The last part of this step compares the FBN constructed through CPr plus FPr and the model constructed exclusively using FPr.

4. Model Implementation

4.1. Determination of CPr Using RTO Data

CPr depict the likelihood of a BE based on historical failure data. The historical failure incident data obtained from the RTO are utilized for this study. The data are divided into different categories based on the BE distribution explained in Section 3.1. After categorization, the data were reviewed carefully to ensure preprocessing, including cleansing and filling in the missing values. At this stage, the consistency of the values is also verified. The RTO data consist of power grid failure data from 14 states, which include Arkansas, Colorado, Iowa, Kansas, Louisiana, Minnesota, Missouri, Montana, Nebraska, New Mexico, North Dakota, Oklahoma, South Dakota, Texas, and Wyoming. Table 2 shows the calculations for CPr based on the RTO data.

Table 2. CPr based on historical RTO data.

Intermediate Event	Basic Event	Occurrences	CPr
Equipment conditions	Capacitor	16	0.0159
	Transformers	42	0.0417
	Circuit breakers	188	0.1867
	Generators	No historical data	
	Reactor	1	0.0010
	Transmission lines	300	0.2979
Weather conditions	Rain	9	0.0089
	Wind speed	37	0.0367
	Weather	62	0.0616
	Temperature	28	0.0278
Environmental factors	Vegetation management	5	0.0050
	Earthquakes	No historical data	
	Storms	176	0.1748
	Fire risks	31	0.0308
	Floods	No historical data	
	Lightning	54	0.0536
	Tornados	26	0.0258
Operational parameters	Power factor	No historical data	
	Voltage levels	8	0.0079
	Frequency	No historical data	
	Current flow	No historical data	
	Maintenance	5	0.0050
	Disconnect	11	0.0109
Cybersecurity	SCADA (supervisory control and data acquisition) systems	8	0.0079
	Unauthorized access	No historical data	
	Cyberattacks	No historical data	

4.2. Weighting Score for Expert Elicitation

The CPr calculated through the RTO data are validated by assessing their coherence with domain expert knowledge. After IRB approval, the survey questionnaire was sent to at least 45 experts. These experts are from academia and the power industry and have vast experience with research in power grid systems. The selection of these experts was based on consultation with a panel of researchers assisting the authors of this study. After two reminders in one month of surveying, twenty-one responses were received, with only eighteen being completed in all aspects. These eighteen responses were analyzed using statistical techniques for completeness and coherence. Three responses were declared outliers due to inconsistent points outside the $\sigma \pm 1$. To ensure a comprehensive analysis that incorporates diverse perspectives and expertise on power grid failures, only fifteen responses were selected for a final evaluation. Outliers were excluded using the interquartile range (IQR) technique to maintain the integrity and reliability of the data. These responses were chosen from a group of experts with varied backgrounds in industry and academia, each bringing unique knowledge and experience to the power grid failure mechanism. This selection process ensures that the analysis reflects a broad range of viewpoints, addressing the complex nature of power grid failures and enhancing the overall depth of the findings.

The weight for each variable received in linguistic terms was added to the total weight using Equation (2), and the weighted values were calculated using Equation (3). The results of expert elicitation from experts showing their PP, Exp, EdU, and age are shown in Table 3.

Table 3. The weighting scores of fifteen experts.

Expert	PP	EdU	Exp	Age	Weighting Score
E1	4	4	5	5	0.4390
E2	4	5	3	3	0.3659
E3	4	4	5	5	0.4390
E4	4	5	2	2	0.3171
E5	5	5	2	3	0.3659
E6	4	5	2	2	0.3171
E7	2	3	2	2	0.2195
E8	4	5	2	3	0.3415
E9	4	5	2	2	0.3171
E10	2	4	2	2	0.2439
E11	4	4	2	2	0.2927
E12	4	5	3	3	0.3659
E13	2	5	4	3	0.3415
E14	4	5	2	3	0.3415
E15	4	4	2	2	0.2927

4.3. Discussion on Calculated FPr

This section addresses the results generated using the calculated crisp and fuzzy probabilities. CPr measure the risk level based on historical failure incident data, and FPr measure the risk frequency and impact by adjusting for uncertainty and ambiguity via expert elicitation. The risk profile can be enhanced significantly by integrating FPr and CPr through a comprehensive analysis of identified risk factors and failure modes. Table 4 shows FPr calculations for all BEs, and the corresponding CPr are in the last column. It is evident from the calculations that FPr values vary from CPr. The reasons for these variations can be explained by the fact that, because of objective and subjective uncertainties, real-world scenarios are rarely crisp and deterministic in risk analysis, and insufficient and vague data may result in an under- or overestimation of process risk. Another reason is that the RTO databases present constant failure data over time and do not reflect recent component reliability improvements. For these reasons, the results obtained using FPr for BEs were expected to differ from those obtained using CPr. It is pertinent to mention here that the calculated probabilities are intended to be dynamic in the proposed fuzzy-aggregation approach, reflecting the evolving condition of the risk factors associated with the power grid. As power grid infrastructure degrades or new environmental risks emerge (such as extreme weather), these probabilities will be periodically recalculated using updated data, including expert opinions, maintenance records, and real-time data. The updated probabilities ensure that the model remains accurate and relevant to the current state of the power grid and its vulnerabilities. Moreover, the calculated probabilities are region-specific, as we recognize that the risks faced by power grids can differ significantly depending on geographical location. Our expert survey questionnaire asked respondents to consider regional risk factors, such as wildfires in California, snowstorms in the Midwest, and flooding risks in coastal regions. This approach ensures that the probabilities are tailored to the local environmental conditions and are not generalized across different regions. The model reflects the specific risks associated with each region by incorporating region-specific inputs.

Table 4. FST is applied to obtain FPr through expert elicitation.

Intermediate Event	Basic Event	FPs	K	FPr
Equipment conditions	Capacitor	0.1081	4.6491	0.0062
	Transformers	0.1130	4.5735	0.0074
	Circuit breakers	0.1483	4.1203	0.0209
	Generators	0.2115	3.5676	0.0747
	Reactor	0.0921	4.9335	0.0032
	Transmission lines	0.2020	3.6378	0.0636
Weather conditions	Rain	0.1720	3.8849	0.0360
	Wind speed	0.1796	3.8179	0.0420
	Weather	0.1391	4.2246	0.0165
	Temperature	0.1852	3.7704	0.0468
Environmental factors	Vegetation management	0.1323	4.3074	0.0136
	Earthquakes	0.1396	4.2189	0.0167
	Storms	0.1900	3.7307	0.0513
	Fire Risks	0.1650	3.9505	0.0309
	Floods	0.1648	3.9524	0.0308
	Lightning	0.1892	3.7373	0.0505
	Tornados	0.2039	3.6229	0.0658

Table 4. *Cont.*

Intermediate Event	Basic Event	FPs	K	FPr
Operational parameters	Power factor	0.1582	4.0174	0.0265
	Voltage levels	0.1467	4.1385	0.0201
	Frequency	0.1970	3.6760	0.0582
	Current flow	0.1827	3.7915	0.0446
	Maintenance	0.1621	3.9784	0.0290
	Disconnect	0.2004	3.6498	0.0618
Cybersecurity	SCADA (supervisory control and data acquisition) systems	0.2437	3.3561	0.1216
	Unauthorized access	0.1760	3.8496	0.0390
	Cyberattacks	0.1508	4.0936	0.0223

5. Results and Discussion

5.1. Calculation of CPTs and Construction of the FBN

Once CPr and FPr have been quantified, the next step is to calculate the CPTs. For this study, CPr calculated from RTO data are used for sixteen BEs, and for the remaining ten BEs, FPr are used (refer to Figure 3). For the second case (C-2), CPT calculations are based on FPr for all twenty-six BEs, and the results are compared to determine the effects of using expert elicitation. Table 5 shows the two cases developed to compare the FBN using CPr and FPr. It is important to highlight that this comparison excludes cases where only historical data are utilized. This exclusion is due to limitations in the availability of historical data for all basic events; only 16 out of 26 BEs have historical records. It is also crucial to recognize that using incomplete data for this analysis may lead to unreliable risk assessment results.

Table 5. Comparison of the FBN using CPr and FPr.

Case	Data	Basic Events
C-1	Historical + Expert's elicitation	Sixteen BEs (CPr) Ten BEs (FPr)
C-2	Expert's elicitation	Twenty-six BEs (FPr)

5.2. C-1: Construction of the FBN Using CPr Plus FPr

To develop the FBN, a cause-and-effect relation was established, and CPr and FPr were fed to the GiNIe software 5.0 [53], as shown in Figure 7. Using this innovative approach, the model delineates accident scenario modeling based on CPr from RTO data and FPr calculated by experts. All twenty-six BEs lead to TEs through IEs, showing the likelihood of a power grid shutdown as a TE. Here, it is evident that the significant factors leading to power grid shutdown are external factors, which include the tripping of transmission lines with a 30% failure probability, faults due to circuit breakers with a 19% failure probability, and generators with a 7% failure probability. Weather conditions and wind speeds are also disruptions caused by prior probabilities of 6% and 4%, respectively. Internal factors, i.e., cybersecurity and operational parameters, significantly lead to TE. Operating parameters such as frequency fluctuation and current flow may lead to disruptions in the power grid system. In addition, cybersecurity vulnerabilities, such as unauthorized access, increase the likelihood of TE occurrence. Although prior probabilities of transmission line tripping and malfunctioning circuit breakers are the major contributors, the simulation results show that the chances of TE occurrence are very low, with a failure probability of only 3%. However, the likelihood of equipment conditions being affected is 36%, and the likelihood of environmental factors being affected is 11%, much greater than that of BEs. The lower likelihood of a TE of 3% can be attributed to good safety and maintenance practices that maintain a smooth electricity supply to users. External risk factors must be considered and mitigated to maintain a resilient and robust power grid system.

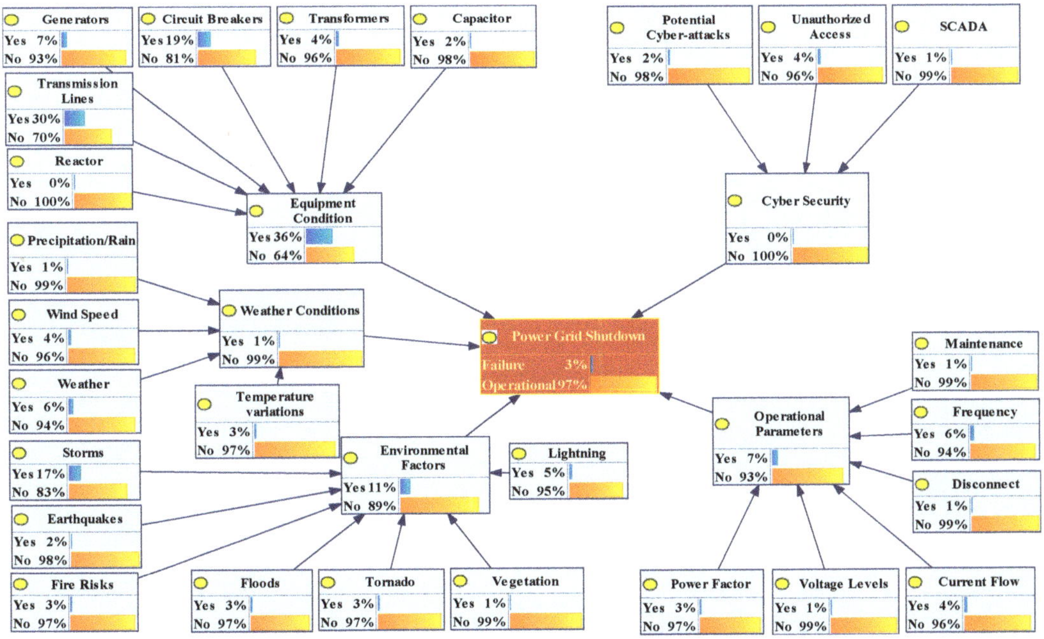

Figure 7. Power grid shutdown scenario modeled using the FBN.

5.3. C-2: Construction of the FBN Using Expert Elicitation (FPr) Only

This subsection addresses the construction of the FBN for the likelihood of TEs using the FPr for all twenty-six BEs. Figure 8 shows the results obtained using FPr. The IEs have low failure probabilities compared to case C-1. Figure 9 compares the failure probabilities for cases C-1 and C-2. By comparing risk variables, notable differences emerge between CPr and FPr. Specifically, the failure probabilities for the equipment conditions and environmental factors are 23% and 3% greater, respectively, for CPr than for FPr. Conversely, the failure probabilities for weather conditions, operational parameters, and cybersecurity are 8%, 2%, and 8% lower for CPr than for FPr. Despite the difference in CPr and FPr IEs, the failure probability for TE remains the same for both cases. It is crucial to carefully distinguish that the failure of the power grid remains consistent regardless of whether historical failure data are used or expert elicitation is employed.

CPr are based on historical failure data, which may lack important updates or safety and maintenance measures compared to expert elicitation. For instance, the probability of failure in cybersecurity is 0% when historical data are used. This finding seems implausible in real-world scenarios, given the increasing likelihood of cyberattacks due to technological advancements. Similarly, the significance of SCADA failure is given 12% weight when assessed by experts, compared to 1% extracted from RTO data, a critical BE that threatens the integrity of power grids. Such discrepancies highlight the importance of incorporating expert insights to capture nuanced risk factors and potential threats more accurately. The results of our fuzzy-aggregation approach offer valuable insights for informed maintenance and design decisions in power grid infrastructure. By identifying areas at higher risk of failure due to weather-related events, aging infrastructure, or environmental threats, the model helps prioritize maintenance resources and targeted interventions. For instance, regions prone to wildfires or extreme storms can benefit from strengthening grid infrastructure, while regions with aging equipment may require upgrades or replacement. The model's output can also enhance design strategies for new power grids, ensuring their resilience in the face of local environmental risks.

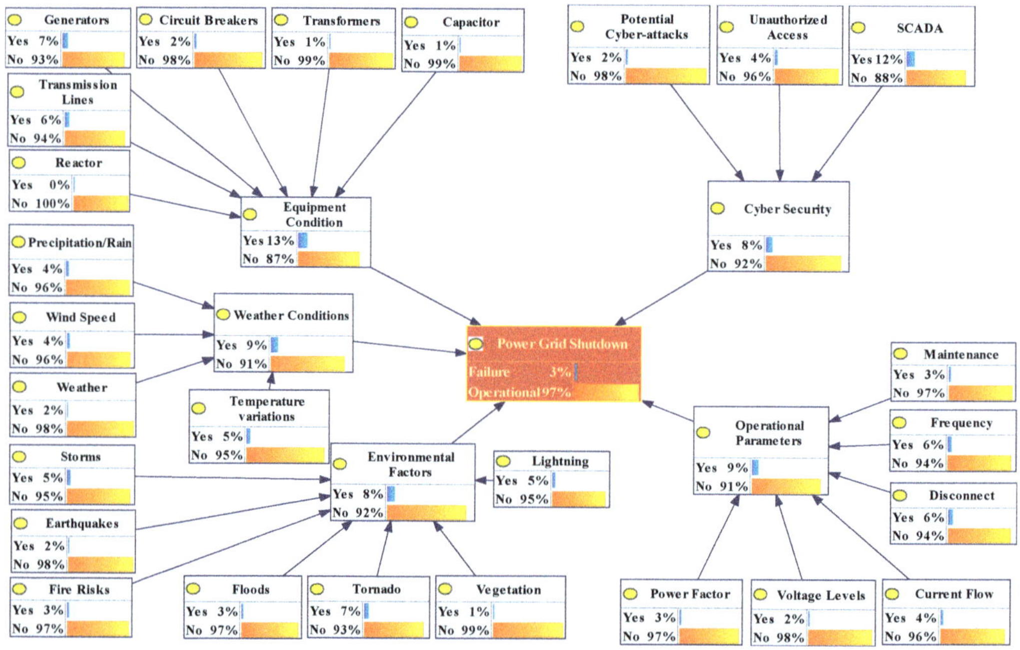

Figure 8. Modeled FBN using expert elicitation (FPr) only.

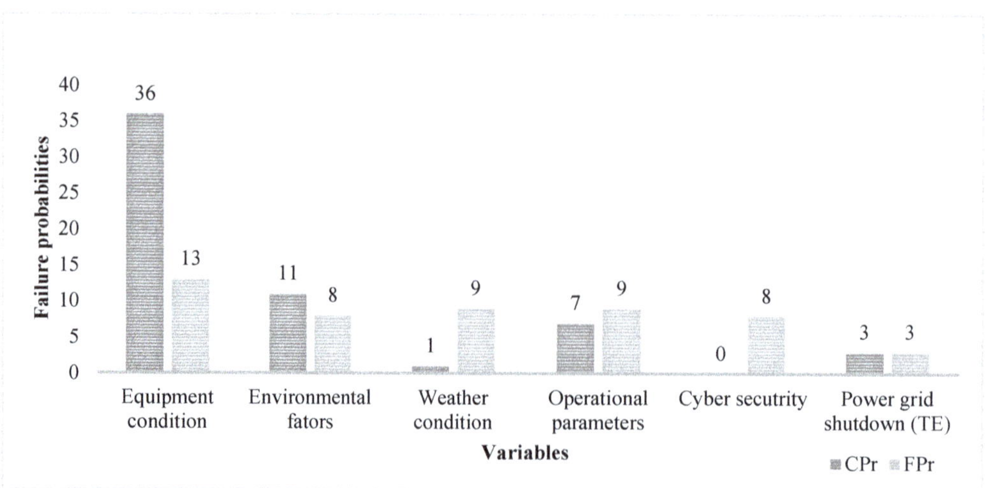

Figure 9. Comparison of failure probabilities of the IEs using CPr and FPr.

5.4. Sensitivity Analysis

Performing a sensitivity analysis (SA) is crucial in the BN framework. This approach provides a valuable technique for scrutinizing uncertainty by observing how alterations in influencing factors represented by parent nodes impact the child nodes. The key influencing elements are revealed by identifying the most sensitive factors. Consequently, this information establishes pertinent emergency plans, preventive measures, and regulatory actions. For this study, following the construction of the FBN, SA is performed to check whether the probabilities in the FBN impact the overall TE outcomes.

Figure 10a shows the sensitivity of BEs. Environmental factors are the most crucial root causes for the occurrence of TEs, with storms being the most sensitive factor (0.019), followed by lightning and earthquakes (0.015), and tornadoes and floods (0.014). The sensitivity to equipment conditions is also a significant factor for the likelihood of TEs, with significant values of 0.005 and 0.004 for transmission lines and earthquakes, respectively. For the remaining BEs related to the equipment conditions of the capacitor, transformer, and generator, the sensitivity is 0.003, which is relatively less sensitive to the occurrence of TEs.

Sensitivity tornado diagrams are used in risk analysis to determine the most significant risks associated with an infrastructure due to the potential impact of different variables. It is easier to visualize how various factors influence the success or failure of a system when information is organized in a digestible manner. Figure 10b shows the sensitivity tornado diagram of the power grid risk assessment. Environmental factors are the most sensitive factors for a power grid to shut down as a TE. Storms are the most crucial variable environmental factors, and transmission lines are the most sensitive variable for equipment conditions.

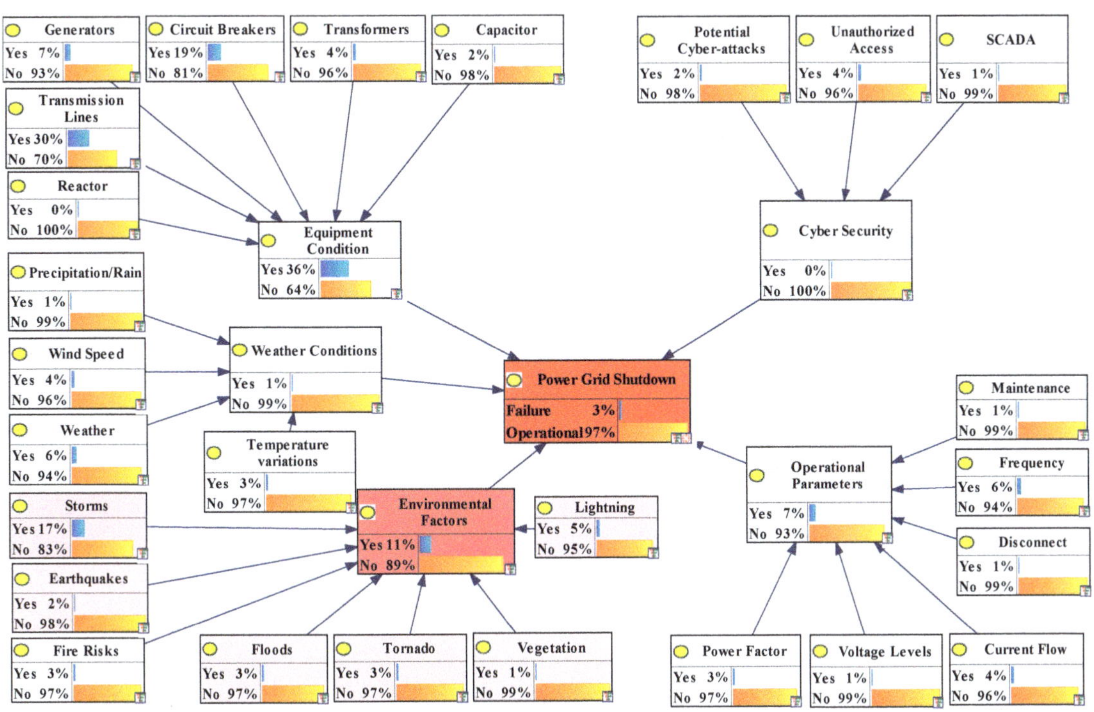

(**a**) Sensitivity Analysis of BEs

Figure 10. *Cont.*

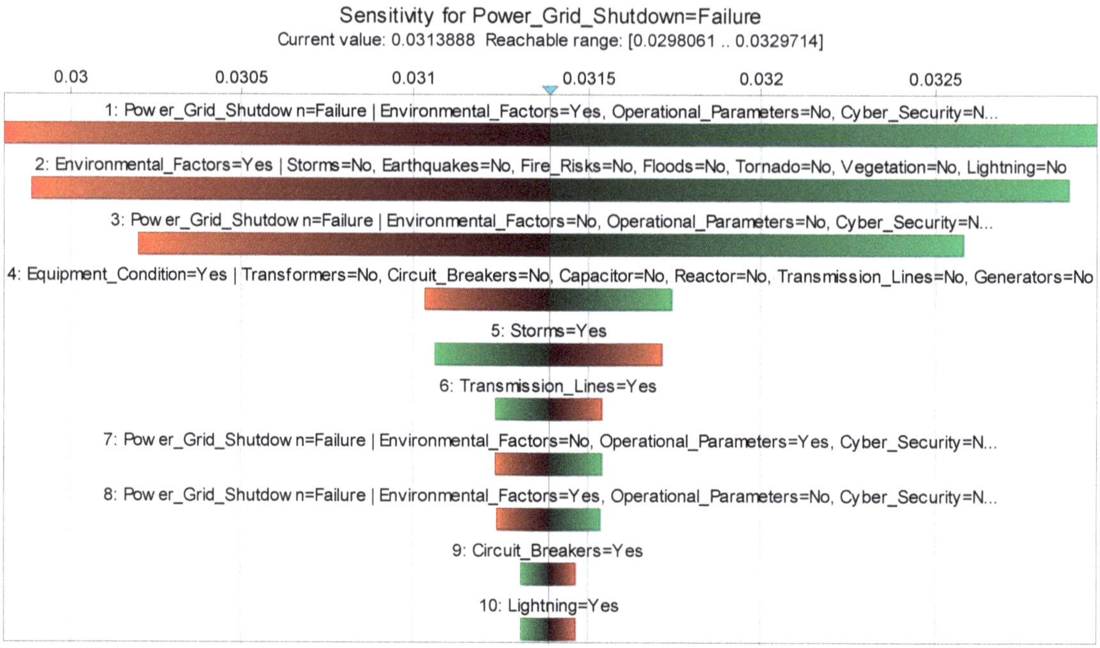

(**b**) Sensitivity Tornado Diagram

Figure 10. (**a**) Sensitivity analysis to identify the most critical variables, and (**b**) sensitivity tornado diagram.

5.5. Diagnosis Inference

In FBNs, diagnosis inference is a valuable technique for determining posterior probabilities based on new, updated information. When new evidence is available, it can be applied to the model to trigger the IEs and root causes to determine the effect on the entire network. It begins by assessing the impact of the evidence provided for the power grid failure node on its parent nodes. It is possible to propagate the impact of such evidence backward and forward to determine which parent nodes affect the likelihood of TE. In this study, the evidence has been propagated—a confirmed power grid shutdown (assuming a failure probability of 100%)—illustrating the FBN model with the failure evidence inserted. There was a significant increase in the probable occurrence of environmental factors from a baseline probability of 11% to 59%, and the significant BE fire risk increased from 3% to 35%. Similarly, the posterior probabilities of equipment conditions decreased from 36% to 22% with BE circuit breakers, generators, and transmission lines, with new probabilities of 19%, 20%, and 24%, respectively. The results from the diagnosis inference are shown in Figure 11, with a TE failure probability of 100%.

The results indicate a significant increase in the likelihood of environmental factors and equipment conditions for the parent nodes. The baseline probabilities of 11% and 36% for these variables increased to 56% and 44%, respectively. The posterior probabilities primarily affected two parent nodes: storms and transmission lines. This highlights these nodes as the most influential factors, emphasizing the need to implement mitigation strategies to address external influences in power grid risk assessment.

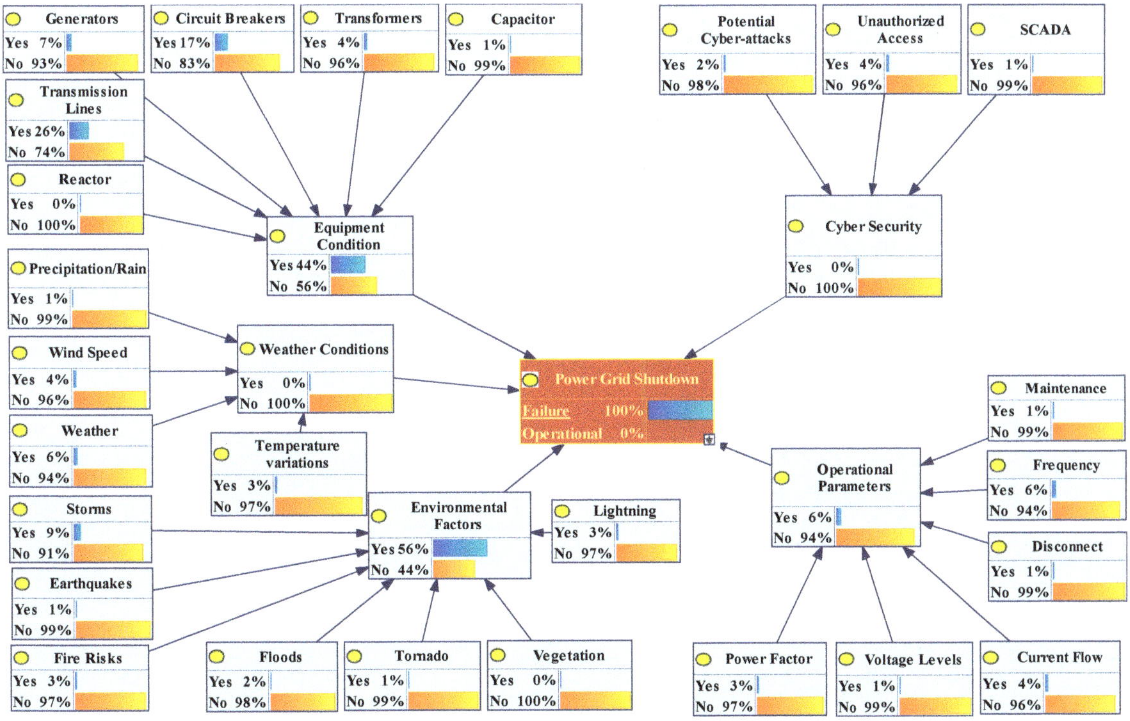

Figure 11. Diagnosis inference using 100% failure probability as TE.

6. Conclusions

This study presents an FBN for the risk assessment of power grids based on historical failure incident data and expert elicitation. RTO data are utilized for calculating CPr, and experts from the power industry and academia are consulted for calculating FPr. The main contributions of this research are summarized below.

- This study identifies twenty-six external and internal critical risk variables responsible for power grid shutdowns by presenting a comprehensive risk level spectrum. To offset the vagueness and uncertainty in historical data, the FST using expert elicitation is integrated with a BN to present a more nuanced risk assessment approach.
- The initial risk assessment with sixteen BEs using CPr and ten BEs using FPr shows that the probability of TE (power grid shutdown) is 3%. Environmental factors account for 11% of TE failure rates, followed by equipment conditions, which account for 36%. A higher failure probability from equipment conditions confirmed that the root causes are the tripping of transmission lines and circuit breakers. A failure probability of 11% from environmental factors endorsed the increased risk of the likelihood of TEs because of storms and weather conditions.
- Expert elicitation is endorsed as a nuanced approach to integrating a BN and FST. For instance, based on RTO historical data, SCADA is less likely to disrupt the power grid's functionality, with a failure probability of only 1%. However, results from expert opinion confirmed it as a serious threat with a 12% probability of failure.
- Diagnosis inference with 100% confirmation of TE highlights the most critical IEs as environmental factors and equipment conditions, with 59% and 22% failure probabilities, respectively. Environmental factors remain the most significant IE, with the root cause of fire risk as the most influential BE, with a failure rate of 35%, followed by storms

(13%). Equipment conditions are also a critical IE with root causes of transmission lines (24%), generators (20%), and circuit breakers (19%). Diagnosis inference confirmed the authenticity of the FBN for cybersecurity and operational parameters, with leading root causes for the likelihood of TEs being unauthorized access (10%) and frequency changes (9%).

- A comparison of an FBN constructed through CPr plus FPr versus FBN (FPr only) yields similar results for the likelihood of TEs (3%). Still, significant variations exist in the failure probabilities of BEs and IEs. Expert elicitation confirmed that the equipment condition is the most critical IE (13%), followed by weather conditions and operational parameters with a failure probability of 9%, and cybersecurity and environmental factors with 8%.
- The expert's opinions yielded different results than historical failure data since the latest safety and maintenance strategies altered the threat levels, which can be captured through expert elicitation, as historical data remained constant over time. Moreover, due to improved mitigation strategies, there are fewer chances of failure incidents of the same type in the future, making CPr less relevant than expert opinions.

Integrating FBNs using expert elicitation is an effective risk assessment technique for evaluating these viable assets. However, certain limitations when using an expert's opinion, such as long distances and unpredictable environmental conditions, may lead to the under- or overestimation of risk levels. To counter these challenges, robotic inspection and intelligent perception may be incorporated to complement the proposed approach for future studies.

Author Contributions: Y.M.: Methodology, Investigation, Writing—Original Draft, Visualization, Validation, Software, Resources, Formal Analysis, Data Curation, Conceptualization. N.Y. (Nof Yasir): Validation, Software, Resources, Formal Analysis, Data Curation. N.Y. (Nita Yodo): Writing—Review and Editing, Visualization, Validation, Methodology, Investigation, Formal Analysis. Y.H.: Supervision, Writing—Review and Editing, Validation, Supervision, Resources, Project Administration, Funding Acquisition, Conceptualization. D.W.: Writing—Review and Editing. R.A.M.: Writing—Review and Editing. All authors have read and agreed to the published version of the manuscript.

Funding: This research was funded by National Science Foundation (NSF) EPSCoR-RII Track-2 Program under NSF award No. OIA-2119691, U. S. Department of Transportation PHMSA under Grant No. 693JK3250009CAAP, and the APC was funded by MDPI. The findings and opinions presented in this manuscript are those of the authors only and do not necessarily reflect the sponsors' perspective.

Data Availability Statement: The data that have been used are confidential.

Conflicts of Interest: The authors declare no conflicts of interest.

Abbreviations

The following abbreviations are used in this manuscript:

BN	Bayesian Network
FST	Fuzzy Set Theory
FBN	Fuzzy Bayesian Network
CPr	Crisp Probabilities
RTO	Regional Transmission Operator
FPr	Fuzzy Probabilities
SCADA	Supervisory Control And Data Acquisition
QRA	Quantitative Risk Assessment
FTA	Fault Tree Analysis
ETA	Event Tree Analysis
MCS	Monte Carlo Simulation

FMEA	Failure Modes and Effects Analysis
HBA	Hierarchical Bayesian Analysis
D-AHP	Data-Driven Analytical Hierarchy Process
BEs	Basic Events
CPTs	Conditional Probability Tables
IEs	Intermediate Events
TE	Top Event
SA	Sensitivity Analysis
FLOP	Fuzzy Linear Opinion Pool

References

1. Hossain, N.U.I.; Jaradat, R.; Hosseini, S.; Marufuzzaman, M.; Buchanan, R.K. A framework for modeling and assessing system resilience using a Bayesian network: A case study of an interdependent electrical infrastructure system. *Int. J. Crit. Infrastruct. Prot.* **2019**, *25*, 62–83. [CrossRef]
2. Zhang, J.; Bian, H.F.; Zhao, H.H.; Wang, X.X.; Zhang, L.L.; Bai, Y.P. Bayesian Network-Based Risk Assessment of Single-Phase Grounding Accidents of Power Transmission Lines. *Int. J. Environ. Res. Public Health* **2020**, *17*, 1841. [CrossRef]
3. energy.gov. The Flow of Electrical Power. Available online: https://www.energy.gov/electric-power (accessed on 23 February 2025).
4. Lin, Y.; Bie, Z.; Qiu, A. A review of key strategies in realizing power system resilience. *Glob. Energy Interconnect.* **2018**, *1*, 9. [CrossRef]
5. Xu, Y.H.; Xing, Y.K.; Huang, Q.H.; Li, J.; Zhang, G.D.; Bamisile, O.; Huang, Q. A review of resilience enhancement strategies in renewable power system under HILP events. *Energy Rep.* **2023**, *9*, 200–209. [CrossRef]
6. Ji, C.Y.; Wei, Y.; Mei, H.; Calzada, J.; Carey, M.; Church, S.; Hayes, T.; Nugent, B.; Stella, G.; Wallace, M.; et al. Large-scale data analysis of power grid resilience across multiple US service regions. *Nat. Energy* **2016**, *1*, 16052. [CrossRef]
7. Wang, J.; Zuo, W.D.; Rhode-Barbarigos, L.; Lu, X.; Wang, J.H.; Lin, Y.L. Literature review on modeling and simulation of energy infrastructures from a resilience perspective. *Reliab. Eng. Syst. Saf.* **2019**, *183*, 360–373. [CrossRef]
8. Reed, B. What caused the blackout in Spain and Portugal and did renewable energy play a part? *The Guardian*, 29 April 2025.
9. @Reuters. Spain, Portugal switch back on, seek answers after biggest ever blackout. *Reuters*, 30 April 2025.
10. Jufri, F.H.; Widiputra, V.; Jung, J. State-of-the-art review on power grid resilience to extreme weather events: Definitions, frameworks, quantitative assessment methodologies, and enhancement strategies. *Appl. Energy* **2019**, *239*, 1049–1065. [CrossRef]
11. He, R.; Li, X.H.; Chen, G.M.; Wang, Y.C.; Jiang, S.Y.; Zhi, C.X. A quantitative risk analysis model considering uncertain information. *Process Saf. Environ. Prot.* **2018**, *118*, 361–370. [CrossRef]
12. Lin, S.S.; Shen, S.L.; Zhou, A.; Xu, Y.S. Risk assessment and management of excavation system based on fuzzy set theory and machine learning methods. *Autom. Constr.* **2021**, *122*, 103490. [CrossRef]
13. Rahman, M. The Advantages and Disadvantages of Using Qualitative and Quantitative Approaches and Methods in Language "Testing and Assessment" Research: A Literature Review. *J. Educ. Learn.* **2020**, *6*, 10. [CrossRef]
14. Park, S.J.; Seo, H.J.; Park, S.M.; Park, S.H. Establishment of a Risk-Assessment System for Coastal Activities Based on Statistical Data. *J. Coast. Res.* **2024**, *1*, 458–462. [CrossRef]
15. Zúñiga, A.A.; Fernandes, J.F.P.; Branco, P.J.C. Fuzzy-Based Failure Modes, Effects, and Criticality Analysis Applied to Cyber-Power Grids. *Energies* **2023**, *16*, 3346. [CrossRef]
16. Li, X.H.; Chen, G.M.; Khan, F.; Xu, C.H. Dynamic risk assessment of subsea pipelines leak using precursor data. *Ocean Eng.* **2019**, *178*, 156–169. [CrossRef]
17. Dong, H.; Zhao, J.; Yang, X.Y.; Yang, K. Combination of D-AHP and Grey Theory for the Assessment of the Information Security Risks of Smart Grids. *Math. Probl. Eng.* **2020**, *2020*, 3517104. [CrossRef]
18. Chen, B.Y.; Chen, H.Y.; Zhang, Y.Y.; Zhao, J.H.; Manlab, E. Risk Assessment for the Power Grid Dispatching Process Considering the Impact of Cyber Systems. *Energies* **2019**, *12*, 1084. [CrossRef]
19. Canbolat, S.; Elbez, G.; Hagenmeyer, V. A new hybrid risk assessment process for cyber security design of smart grids using fuzzy analytic hierarchy processes. *Automatisierungstechnik* **2023**, *71*, 779–788. [CrossRef]
20. Zhu, D.R.; Cheng, W.J.; Duan, J.D.; Wang, H.F.; Bai, J. Identifying and assessing risk of cascading failure sequence in AC/DC hybrid power grid based on non-cooperative game theory. *Reliab. Eng. Syst. Saf.* **2023**, *237*, 109359. [CrossRef]
21. Jones, C.B.; Bresloff, C.J.; Darbali-Zamora, R. Electric Grid Vulnerability Analysis to Identify Communities Prone to Wildfires. *IEEE Access* **2023**, *11*, 35630–35638. [CrossRef]
22. Bian, H.F.; Zhang, J.; Li, R.X.; Zhao, H.H.; Wang, X.X.; Bai, Y.P. Risk analysis of tripping accidents of power grid caused by typical natural hazards based on FTA-BN model. *Nat. Hazards* **2021**, *106*, 1771–1795. [CrossRef]

23. Liu, M.; Li, Z.; Li, Y.; Liu, Y. A Fast and Accurate Method of Power Line Intelligent Inspection Based on Edge Computing. *IEEE Trans. Instrum. Meas.* **2022**, *71*, 1–12. [CrossRef]
24. Jin, H.; Uludag, S.; Lui, K.-S.; Nahrstedt, K. Secure data collection in constrained tree-based Smart Grid environments. In Proceedings of the 2014 IEEE International Conference on Smart Grid Communications (SmartGridComm), Venice, Italy, 3–6 November 2014. [CrossRef]
25. Kumari, P.; Halim, S.Z.; Kwon, J.S.I.; Quddus, N. An integrated risk prediction model for corrosion-induced pipeline incidents using artificial neural network and Bayesian analysis. *Process Saf. Environ. Prot.* **2022**, *167*, 34–44. [CrossRef]
26. De Iuliis, M.; Kammouh, O.; Cimellaro, G.P.; Tesfamariam, S. Quantifying restoration time of pipelines after earthquakes: Comparison of Bayesian belief networks and fuzzy models. *Int. J. Disaster Risk Reduct.* **2021**, *64*, 102491. [CrossRef]
27. Zarei, E.; Khakzad, N.; Cozzani, V.; Reniers, G. Safety analysis of process systems using Fuzzy Bayesian Network (FBN). *J. Loss Prev. Process Ind.* **2019**, *57*, 7–16. [CrossRef]
28. Zhang, L.M.; Wu, X.G.; Skibniewski, M.J.; Zhong, J.B.; Lu, Y.J. Bayesian-network-based safety risk analysis in construction projects. *Reliab. Eng. Syst. Saf.* **2014**, *131*, 29–39. [CrossRef]
29. Ding, Y.; Ye, X.W.; Guo, Y.; Zhang, R.; Ma, Z. Probabilistic method for wind speed prediction and statistics distribution inference based on SHM data-driven. *Probabilistic Eng. Mech.* **2023**, *73*, 103475. [CrossRef]
30. MacLeod, J.; Tan, S.; Moinuddin, K. Reliability of fire (point) detection system in office buildings in Australia-A fault tree analysis. *Fire Saf. J.* **2020**, *115*, 103150. [CrossRef]
31. Davila-Frias, A.; Yodo, N.; Le, T.; Yadav, O.P. A deep neural network and Bayesian method-based framework for all-terminal network reliability estimation considering degradation. *Reliab. Eng. Syst. Saf.* **2023**, *229*, 108881. [CrossRef]
32. Mahmood, Y.; Afrin, T.; Huang, Y.; Yodo, N. Sustainable Development for Oil and Gas Infrastructure from Risk, Reliability, and Resilience Perspectives. *Sustainability* **2023**, *15*, 4953. [CrossRef]
33. Landquist, H.; Norrman, J.; Lindhe, A.; Norberg, T.; Hassellöv, I.M.; Lindgren, J.F.; Rosén, L. Expert elicitation for deriving input data for probabilistic risk assessment of shipwrecks. *Mar. Pollut. Bull.* **2017**, *125*, 399–415. [CrossRef]
34. Moein Younesi Heravi, A.Y.S.B.R. Using Fuzzy Approach in Determining Critical Parameters for Optimum Safety Functions in Mega Projects. *Front. Nat.-Inspired Ind. Optim.* **2023**, *1*, 183–200. [CrossRef]
35. Zhang, D.B.; Chu, Z.W.; Gui, Q.J.; Wu, F.; Yang, H.J.; Ma, Y.H.; Tao, W.Q. Transformer maintenance decision based on condition monitoring and fuzzy probability hybrid reliability assessment. *IET Gener. Transm. Distrib.* **2023**, *17*, 976–992. [CrossRef]
36. Weng, Z.X.; Shi, L.B.; Xu, Z.; Lu, Q.; Yao, L.Z.; Ni, Y.X. Fuzzy power flow solution considering wind power variability and uncertainty. *Int. Trans. Electr. Energy Syst.* **2015**, *25*, 547–572. [CrossRef]
37. Suh, Y.A.; Song, K.; Cho, J. Fuzzy-technique-based expert elicitation on the occurrence probability of severe accident phenomena in nuclear power plants. *Nucl. Eng. Technol.* **2021**, *53*, 3298–3313. [CrossRef]
38. Guan, L.; Liu, Q.; Abbasi, A.; Ryan, M.J. Developing a Comprehensive Risk Assessment Model Based on Fuzzy Bayesian Belief Network (FBBN). *J. Civ. Eng. Manag.* **2020**, *26*, 614–634. [CrossRef]
39. Sun, H.; Yang, Z.L.; Wang, L.C.; Xie, J. Leakage failure probability assessment of submarine pipelines using a novel pythagorean fuzzy bayesian network methodology. *Ocean Eng.* **2023**, *288*, 115954. [CrossRef]
40. Lu, Q.; Zhang, W. Integrating dynamic Bayesian network and physics-based modeling for risk analysis of a time-dependent power distribution system during hurricanes. *Reliab. Eng. Syst. Saf.* **2022**, *220*, 108290. [CrossRef]
41. Liu, H.; Li, Y.; Cao, Y.J.; Zeng, Z.L.; Sidorov, D. Operational Risk Assessment of Electric-Gas Integrated Energy Systems Considering N-1 Accidents. *Energies* **2020**, *13*, 1208. [CrossRef]
42. Mensah, A.F.; Dueñas-Osorio, L. Efficient Resilience Assessment Framework for Electric Power Systems Affected by Hurricane Events. *J. Struct. Eng.* **2016**, *10*, 142. [CrossRef]
43. Wang, M.Z.; Li, C.; Wang, X.H.; Piao, Z.Y.; Yang, Y.S.; Dai, W.T.; Zhang, Q. Research on Comprehensive Evaluation and Early Warning of Transmission Lines' Operation Status Based on Dynamic Cloud Computing. *Sensors* **2023**, *23*, 1469. [CrossRef]
44. Abedi, A.; Gaudard, L.; Romerio, F. Review of major approaches to analyze vulnerability in power system. *Reliab. Eng. Syst. Saf.* **2019**, *183*, 153–172. [CrossRef]
45. Yu, S.; Wang, C.; Geng, H.; Fan, H. Review on Risk Assessment of Power System. *Procedia Comput. Sci.* **2017**, *109*, 6. [CrossRef]
46. Machado, P.G.; Ribeiro, C.D.; do Nascimento, C.A.O. Risk analysis in energy projects using Bayesian networks: A systematic review. *Energy Strategy Rev.* **2023**, *47*, 101097. [CrossRef]
47. AlMajali, A.; Wadhawan, Y.; Saadeh, M.S.; Shalalfeh, L.; Neuman, C. Risk assessment of smart grids under cyber-physical attacks using Bayesian networks. *Int. J. Electron. Secur. Digit. Forensics* **2020**, *12*, 357–385. [CrossRef]
48. Mo, L.G.; Wei, L. Risk assessment method for power grid communication link failure based on fuzzy comprehensive assessment. *Int. J. Internet Protoc. Technol.* **2022**, *15*, 69–75. [CrossRef]
49. Ramzali, N.; Lavasani, M.R.M.; Ghodousi, J. Safety barriers analysis of offshore drilling system by employing Fuzzy Event Tree Analysis. *Saf. Sci.* **2015**, *78*, 49–59. [CrossRef]

50. Guo, X.X.; Jie, J.; Khan, F.; Ding, L. Fuzzy Bayesian network based on an improved similarity aggregation method for risk assessment of storage tank accident (vol 144, pg 242, 2020). *Process Saf. Environ. Prot.* **2021**, *149*, 1031. [CrossRef]
51. Fatemi, S.A.; Kuh, A.; Fripp, M. Parametric methods for probabilistic forecasting of solar irradiance. *Renew. Energy* **2018**, *129*, 666–676. [CrossRef]
52. Onisawa, T. An Approach to Human Reliability in Man-Machine Systems Using Error Possibility. *Fuzzy Sets Syst.* **1988**, *27*, 87–103. [CrossRef]
53. BayesFusion, L. BayesFusion Artificial Intelligence Modeling and Machine Learning Software. Available online: https://www.bayesfusion.com/contact/ (accessed on 14 February 2025).

algorithms

MDPI

Article

Plugging Small Models in Large Language Models for POI Recommendation in Smart Tourism

Hong Zheng [1,2], Zhenhui Xu [3], Qihong Pan [1,2], Zhenzhen Zhao [1,2] and Xiangjie Kong [1,2,*]

1 College of Computer Science and Technology, Zhejiang University of Technology, Hangzhou 310023, China; 201806062028@zjut.edu.cn (H.Z.); qihongpan@zjut.edu.cn (Q.P.); zhenzzhao97@zjut.edu.cn (Z.Z.)
2 Zhejiang Key Laboratory of Visual Information Intelligent Processing, Hangzhou 310023, China
3 Zhejiang Supcon Information Co., Ltd., Hangzhou 310053, China; xuzh@supconit.com
* Correspondence: xjkong@zjut.edu.cn; Tel.: +86-158-4090-1926

Abstract: Point-of-interest (POI) recommendation is a crucial task in location-based social networks, especially for enhancing personalized travel experiences in smart tourism. Recently, large language models (LLMs) have demonstrated significant potential in this domain. Unlike classical deep learning-based methods, which focus on capturing various user preferences, LLM-based approaches can further analyze candidate POIs using common sense and provide corresponding reasons. However, existing methods often fail to fully capture user preferences due to limited contextual inputs and insufficient incorporation of cooperative signals. Additionally, most methods inadequately address target temporal information, which is essential for planning travel itineraries. To address these limitations, we propose PSLM4ST, a novel framework that enables synergistic interaction between LLMs and a lightweight temporal knowledge graph reasoning model. This plugin model enhances the input to LLMs by making adjustments and additions, guiding them to focus on reasoning processes related to fine-grained preferences and temporal information. Extensive experiments on three real-world datasets demonstrate the efficacy of PSLM4ST.

Keywords: smart tourism; POI recommendation; large language model; temporal knowledge graph; plugin model; human mobility pattern

1. Introduction

As cities are constantly developing and innovating, smart tourism—a crucial part of smart cities—is gaining more attention. With the diversification of tourism options, it uses cutting-edge technology such as IoT, big data, and AI [1]. Its aim is to connect and manage urban areas and tourism resources in a smart way. In this way, it offers personalized services to tourists, making tourism more convenient and satisfying [2]. In particular, the rise of location-based social networks (LBSNs) such as Yelp (https://www.yelp.com/) and Foursquare (https://foursquare.com/) has led to explosive growth in spatiotemporal data. These rich data present great opportunities for the advancement of point-of-interest (POI) recommendation, an important task in smart tourism. POI recommendation aims to recommend POIs that users may be interested in according to their historical data, so as to achieve a more user-friendly smart tourism service. Recent advances [3] in POI recommendation are shifting from classical neural network models to new LLM-based frameworks.

In addition to early methods [4], existing mainstream classic models based on deep learning mainly have two directions. Firstly, sequence-based approaches are harnessed for trajectory modeling. Secondly, graph-based methods for learning complex relations.

Moreover, a handful of recent studies [5,6] have begun to shift their focus to mining time information to capture time slot preferences. Some studies [6,7] have further introduced target time to provide users with recommendations for specific time slots, which better meet their daily needs. Recently, LLMs have attracted significant attention. Existing research [8–10] has proven that LLMs can acquire and represent spatiotemporal knowledge from training corpora, as well as exhibit strong capabilities for time series prediction, thus laying a theoretical foundation for the next POI recommendation. Wang et al. [11] have made preliminary attempts. They primarily rely on users' check-in history records to execute zero-shot prompting. Based on extensive common sense [12,13], LLMs can perform robust predictions even for cold-start users. Moreover, LLMs can provide corresponding explanations while predicting, thus addressing the issue of poor interpretability in classic DL-based methods [14].

However, the aforementioned existing research still has some limitations. First, unlike LLMs that possess a lot of common sense, classic models need to extend proprietary modules to solve specific problems. For example, users frequently check in various affordable stores, we can realize that users have poor economic ability and recommend affordable POIs, while classic models need to expand an economic preference module. More critically, classic models lack the ability to directly explain their predictions, which limits their interpretability and practicality in real-world applications. Second, LLMs' limited context window hinders their ability to process complete trajectory datasets simultaneously, restricting comprehensive analysis of macro-level user behavior patterns. And it also introduces an important issue, that is, due to the random sampling and extraction of partial trajectories, the target POI may not appear in the current context. Moreover, many LLM-based models perform only simple in-context learning (ICL). Therefore, although LLM-based models have extensive common sense and can eliminate many unreasonable candidate POIs, it is difficult to fully capture the various fine-grained preferences of users.

To address the aforementioned limitations, we propose PSLM4ST, a novel framework that Plugs Small Models into Large Language Models for POI recommendation in Smart Tourism. As shown in Figure 1, small models can finely adjust and supplement the input of LLMs and guide LLMs to focus on the reasoning process of various fine-grained preferences, thereby more accurately capturing changes in user preferences across different temporal and spatial contexts, and thus significantly improve the accuracy and degree of personalization of the recommended results. In conclusion, the contributions of this paper are as follows:

- To our knowledge, we are the first to use DL-based models as LLM plugins, combining their strengths for the next POI recommendation. By introducing target time and fully exploring time slot preferences, PSLM4ST can provide users with more accurate and user-friendly recommendations.
- The plugin model is a temporal knowledge graph reasoning model, built on multiple lightweight modules designed to capture fine-grained preferences. Hence, it generates more precise candidate sets for LLMs, derived from various preference sources.
- Extensive experiments on three real-world datasets demonstrate the superiority of our proposed PSLM4ST.

The rest of this paper is organized as follows: Section 2 discusses related work. Section 3 provides the problem definition and analyzes the check-in data. Section 4 introduces our proposed PSLM4ST in detail. Our experiments and results are described in Section 5. In Sections 6 and 7, we discuss and conclude our work.

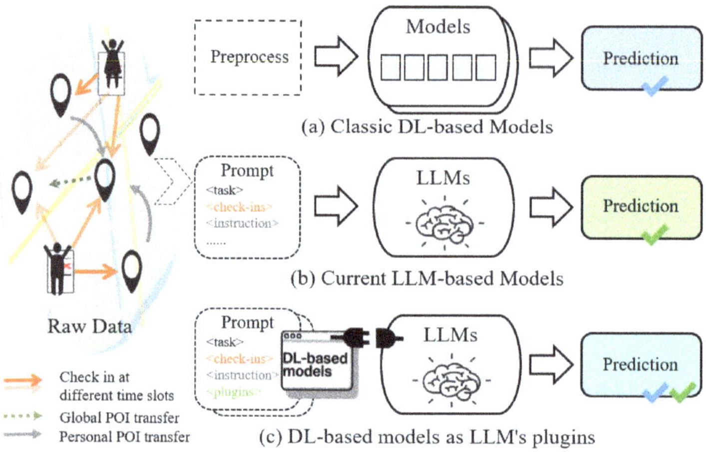

Figure 1. Comparison between classic DL-based models, current LLM-based models, and using DL-based models as LLM plugins.

2. Related Work

2.1. Next POI Recommendation

2.1.1. Classic Methods

Mainstream research treats the next POI recommendation as a sequence prediction task. Earlier studies proposed RNN-based models [15–18] to fully model long- and short-term patterns. Moreover, inspired by Transformer, some studies proposed Transformer-based models [19–21], resulting in stronger sequence modeling capabilities. Researchers then introduced graph structures to alleviate the limitations of sequence-based approaches designed to enhance the global collaboration signal [22–25]. For example, GETNext [19] innovatively proposes a global trajectory graph, which aims to mine the global collaborative information of user trajectories. This design cleverly addresses the limitation of merely treating the point-of-interest recommendation as a sequential prediction task, enabling the model to understand user behavior patterns and interest preferences from a more macroscopic perspective. In contrast, STHGCN [26] takes an alternative approach by employing hypergraphs to capture trajectory–granularity information. It can learn from both the historical trajectories of individual users (intra-user) and the collaborative trajectories among different users (inter-user). The introduction of hypergraphs allows the model to effectively capture the high-order relationships between fine-grained and coarse-grained user movement patterns.

2.1.2. Time-Aware Methods

In the development of POI recommendation systems, numerous studies [27,28] have highlighted the significant impact of temporal factors on user behavior patterns. Time-aware POI recommendation methods aim to provide precise suggestions based on specific time slots, making it easier for users to plan their schedules and better aligning recommendations with their needs. Although some studies [29,30] have incorporated additional temporal information, such as periodic patterns, transition costs, and time preferences, most research fails to explicitly consider the target time when predicting the next location, resulting in recommendations that do not meet personalized needs in practical scenarios. For example, MTNet [5], which employs a tree-structured LSTM, captures time preferences but still has room for improvement in considering the target time. Recently, TPG [7] developed a time-aware framework based on the Transformer architecture, using target timestamps as prompt information. ROTAN [6] introduced time rotation techniques, encoding time periods as rotations to naturally capture periodic patterns without altering the original embedding space, thus significantly improving the accuracy of the recommendation.

2.1.3. LLM-Based Methods

Recently, some studies [11,31,32] have begun to explore novel LLM-based frameworks, which offer advantages that are difficult to match with classic DL-based methods. In particular, an LLM-based model also easily utilizes target time information as context and provides recommendation reasons, enabling more user-friendly recommendations, such as [11]. Specifically, LLMMob [11] leverages individual users' check-in data and target check-in times to perform the next POI recommendation using zero-shot prompting. LLM-ZS [31], a simplified version of LLMMob, delves into the effects of zero-shot, one-shot, and few-shot prompting. LLMMove [14] further integrates geographical information of POIs. However, simple prompt engineering methods have limitations in effectively extracting fine-grained user preferences. LLM4POI [33], which is based on fine-tuning large language models, identifies states similar to the current trajectory from historical data by computing trajectory similarity. However, this approach requires substantial training data and computational resources. In contrast, GenUP [32] saves significant computational resources by periodically updating user profiles instead of frequently computing trajectory similarity.

2.2. Temporal Knowledge Graph Reasoning

A temporal knowledge graph (TKG) is a dynamic knowledge graph that contains facts that change over time, making it an ideal data structure to describe check-in behavior. TKG reasoning refers to the process of predicting future facts based on historical facts in the TKG. Therefore, we can easily transform the next time-specific POI recommendation task into the TKG reasoning task. The two main patterns of facts in TKGs are as follows: the repetition or circulation of facts and the evolution of adjacent facts. For example, refs. [34,35] adopted a copy-generation mechanism to identify global repetition patterns of facts.

3. Preliminaries

3.1. Problem Definition

This section introduces the definitions and preliminary concepts pertinent to the time-specific next POI recommendation problem. Specifically, we define $\mathcal{U} = \{u_1, u_2, \ldots, u_{|\mathcal{U}|}\}$ as the set of users, $L = \{l_1, l_2, \ldots, l_{|L|}\}$ as the set of locations, i.e., POIs, $\mathcal{T} = \{t_1, t_2, \ldots, t_{|\mathcal{T}|}\}$ as the set of types of temporal relationships, $\mathcal{C} = \{c_1, c_2, \ldots, c_{|\mathcal{C}|}\}$ as the set of categories, and $\mathcal{A} = \{a_1, a_2, \ldots, a_{|\mathcal{A}|}\}$ as the set of regions obtained by clustering coordinates using the k-means method.

Definition 1 (Check-in Record). *A check-in record is denoted by $c = (u, l, c, a, t, d)$, where user u visits POI l during the time slot t on the date d, and POI l belongs to the category c, located in the region a.*

Definition 2 (Trajectory). *A trajectory is an ordered sequence of check-in records sorted chronologically by timestamp, represented as $T_{u_i} = \{c_1, c_2, \ldots, c_m\}$. Here, c_k represents the k-th check-in on the trajectory, and c_m is the most recent check-in record for the user u_i.*

Definition 3 (Temporal knowledge graph, TKG). *A TKG, symbolized by $\mathcal{G} = \{\mathcal{G}_1, \mathcal{G}_2, \ldots, \mathcal{G}_d\}$, is constructed from a set of factual quadruples arranged in ascending order according to their timestamps. A quad $(s, r, o, t) \in \mathcal{G}_t$ represents a fact with s (subject), r (relation), o (object), and t* *(timestamp). Each $\mathcal{G}_t$ represents a TKG snapshot, and all events within a snapshot occur at the same time.*

Definition 4 (Time-Specific Next POI Recommendation). *Consider the historical trajectory T_{u_i} of the user u_i, as well as a new query $q = (u_i, t, ?, d)$, with u_i belonging to the set of users $\mathcal{U}$. The objective of the time-specific next POI recommendation task is to identify and recommend the top k POIs that are most likely to pique the interest of the user u_i at the specific time t on the date d.*

3.2. Check-In Behavior Data Analysis

In order to explore the rationality of the POI recommendation in mining time slot patterns and POI transfer relationships, we performed data analysis based on the NYC dataset from the Foursquare platform and the CA dataset from the Gowalla platform. Firstly, we investigated the activity of user check-in behavior under different check-in periods. Dividing the data into 24 groups based on user check-in times in UTC, we calculated the check-in proportion for each time slot. As shown in Figure 2, the changes in check-in activity across different time slots are evident in both the NYC and CA datasets. Obviously, the frequency of check-in behavior is closely related to the users' daily routines.

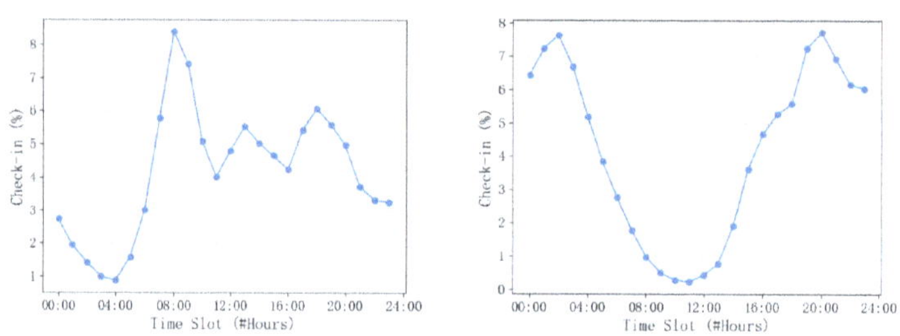

(a) (b)

Figure 2. (**a**) Proportion of check-ins at different time slots in the NYC dataset. (**b**) Proportion of check-ins at different time slots in the CA dataset.

Furthermore, based on common knowledge, different POI categories correspond to different peak visit hours. For instance, bars have their peak visiting hours concentrated between midnight and early morning locally, while restaurants typically experience peak times during local lunch and dinner hours. Therefore, we further analyze the impact of different time slots on the popularity of various POIs, as shown in Figure 3. It can be observed that, regardless of the dataset, there is a significant variation in user preferences for POIs across different time slots. Consequently, incorporating visiting hours into recommendations can lead to more targeted and accurate suggestions for POIs.

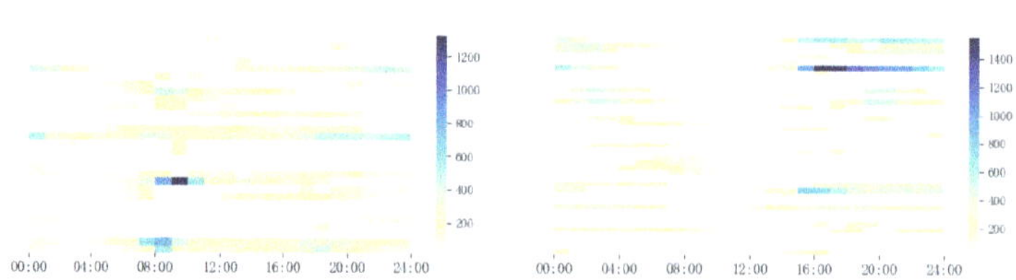

(a) (b)

Figure 3. (**a**) Check-in frequency of some POIs at different time slots in the NYC dataset. (**b**) Check-in frequency of some POIs at different time slots in the CA dataset.

Finally, we analyze the potential transfer patterns of successive check-in pairs. Specifically, on the one hand, we select the 50 most frequent POIs from the NYC dataset and analyze their transfer heat values, as shown in Figure 4a, where the heat values are the results of a logarithmic transformation using $\log_{10}(n+1)$. We can draw the following two conclusions: First, the heat values along the main diagonal are significantly higher compared to the surrounding heat values, indicating that users generally exhibit a pronounced tendency for repeated check-ins. Second, the transfer preferences for POIs are not uniformly distributed, but show a higher preference for certain types of POIs or specific POIs. On the other hand, we analyze the temporal relationship between two successive check-ins, as shown in Figure 4b. It can be clearly observed that the heat values near the main diagonal are relatively higher, meaning that the transfer heat values for POIs in similar time slots are higher. Furthermore, the transfer heat values are generally lower or higher during specific time slots, for example, showing lower transfer heat values between time slot 9 and time slot 12.

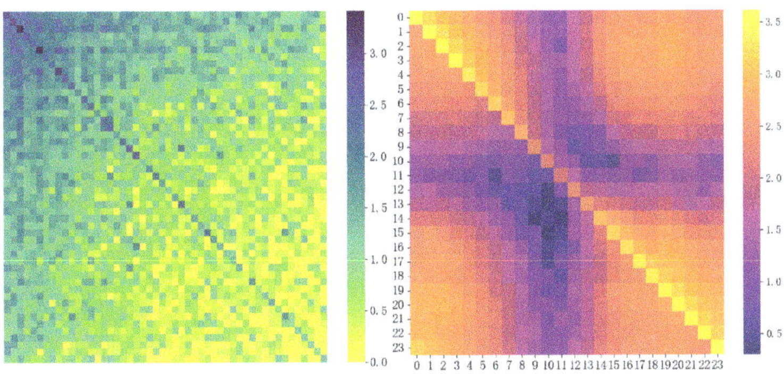

(**a**) (**b**)

Figure 4. (**a**) Distribution of POI category transfers for successive check-in pairs in the NYC dataset. (**b**) Temporal transfer distribution of successive check-in pairs in the CA dataset.

4. Methodology

In this section, we detail our proposed PSLM4ST model. As shown in Figure 5, PSLM4ST mainly includes the following four steps: user check-in data processing, user profile generation, plugin model implementation, and LLM fine-tuning and prediction. In the following sections, we will detail the individual modules of PSLM4ST.

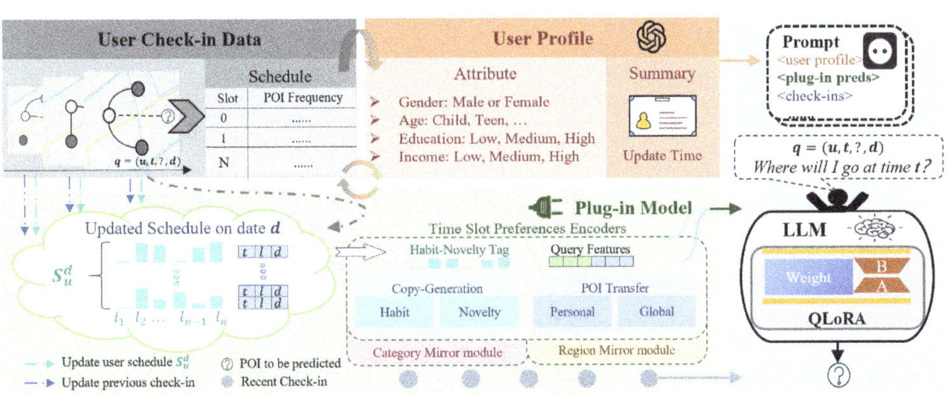

Figure 5. Framework of PSLM4ST.

4.1. TKG and Schedule

Since TKG emphasizes the importance of temporal information, it serves as the foundation for capturing dynamic temporal patterns effectively. Additionally, its extrapolation tasks align well with POI recommendations, and extracting specific quadruple structures is particularly well-suited for recommendation scenarios in specific time slots. Therefore, we incorporate TKG and utilize its reasoning model as a crucial component of our work. Concretely, a day is divided into $|\mathcal{T}|$ time slots. Then all check-in records are generated into corresponding fact quads (u, t, l, d) based on their time information and divided into different snapshots by date d. Each $\mathcal{G}_d = \{(u, t, l, d) \mid u \in \mathcal{U}, t \in \mathcal{T}, l \in L, d \in \mathbb{N}\}$ represents a TKG snapshot on the date, d, with all check-ins within a snapshot occurring on the same date, d. The time slot relation t represents the relationship of checking in at a specific time slot within a day, as shown in Figure 6. We formulate a schedule based on our TKG to depict users' daily check-in patterns. First, we calculate the frequency of check-ins at all POIs within each time slot for each user and update these frequencies for each date. Then, we construct the schedule matrix $S_u^d \in \mathbb{R}^{|\mathcal{T}| \times |L|}$ for each user, u, by

$$S_u^{d_i} = S_u^{d_{i-1}} + \dot{S}_u^{d_i}, S_u^{d_0} = 0 \quad (1)$$

where $\dot{S}_u^{d_i}$ is the schedule change matrix on the date d_i. 0 denotes the zero matrix with dimensions $|\mathcal{T}| \times |L|$.

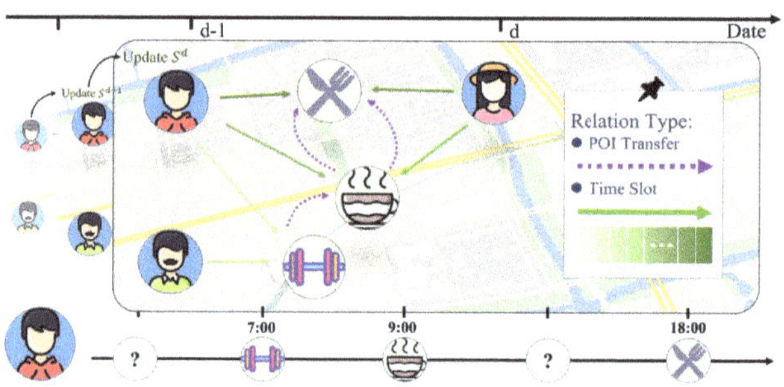

Figure 6. An example of our TKG with three snapshots and the POI transfer reflecting global patterns. 'POI Transfer' means the potential crowd movement patterns between POIs. 'Time Slot' means the user's check-in in a specific time slot. '?' indicates that the current user did not check in or was missing check-in data during that time slot.

4.2. User Profile

Inspired by [32], to generate a far more lifelike user profile, we construct two forms of input data with distinct organizational structures from historical check-in data. The first involves the historical trajectories of users, T_u, which are used mainly to identify user transfer preferences between various POIs. A check-in within T_u is organized as follows: At the time, the user uid visited the POI pid, which is a poi category name with the category id cid. The second is the daily user behavior schedule S_u^d, which is applied primarily to statistically analyze the patterns of user interests during different times. The ten most frequently checked-in POIs and their categories are used for each time slot. Subsequently, these two forms of data are fed into GPT-4o Mini (https://chat.openai.com) to generate the user profile. Due to the anonymity of user data, the user profile predicted by the LLM includes the following two parts, as follows:

- Attributes. Some basic user attributes are intricately linked to their preferences with respect to POIs. For example, restaurants with different price ranges are tailored to customers who have diverse economic capacities. Chen et al. [36] found evidence that a chatbot develops internal representations of its users' states, including the following basic attributes. Specifically, we use LLMs to predict the following four basic attributes: gender, age, education, and income level. Gender is categorized as male or female. Age is segmented into the following five groups: child, teen, young adult, middle-aged, and elderly. Education and income levels are classified into the following three levels: low, medium, and high.

- Summary. To more comprehensively capture the subtleties of user preferences, we instruct the LLM to generate a 200-word summary that simulates user check-in behavior for another LLM. The summary should include information on user behavior patterns, preferences, schedules, etc., such as whether the user tends to explore unfamiliar points of interest or prefers consistently checking in at familiar locations. This empowers the second LLM to simulate the user's thought processes with greater depth and precision.

4.3. *Plugin Model*

4.3.1. User Personal Habit and Novelty Preferences

A user's personal preferences are pivotal in personalizing the next POI recommendation. Within this module, our aim is to discern each user's habitual preference and novelty preference based on a copy-generation mechanism [34]. Users usually show their habitual behavior patterns in different time slots and may be interested in unfamiliar POIs at any time. For example, Bob drinks a cup of coffee at his favorite coffee shop at 2 p.m. almost every weekday, but occasionally tries other activities. Therefore, we can capture user preferences during specific time slots through user embeddings and the time slot embeddings of the current query context $q = (u, t, ?, d)$. First, we transform S_u^d into $\check{S}_u^d$ by

$$\check{S}_u^d = f(S_u^d),\ f(x) = \begin{cases} +\lambda, & \text{if } x > 0. \\ -\lambda, & \text{if } x = 0. \end{cases} \tag{2}$$

Then, with the help of $\check{S}_u^d$, the set of familiar POIs is extracted through the copy mode to mine habit preferences, v_{hab}, and unfamiliar POIs are identified through the generation mode to mine novelty preferences, v_{nov}.

$$v_{hab} = tanh(W_{hab}[u, t] + b_{hab})L^\top + \check{S}_u^d, \tag{3}$$

$$v_{nov} = tanh(W_{nov}[u, t] + b_{nov})L^\top - \check{S}_u^d, \tag{4}$$

where $tanh(\cdot)$ is the activation function. And $W_{hab}, W_{nov} \in \mathbb{R}^{2d \times d}$ and $b_{hab}, b_{nov} \in \mathbb{R}^{d \times d}$ are trainable parameters. L represents all location embeddings. $[\cdot]$ denotes concatenation.

4.3.2. Personal and Global POI Transfer Preferences

Users' check-in behaviors are highly susceptible to their recent check-in situations. From a macroscopic perspective, there exists a significant causal relationship among numerous event pairs formed by users' check-in behaviors in adjacent time slots. Therefore, we need to capture the personal POI transfer preference between different time slots. For each check-in record $c_i = (u, l_i, t_i, d_i)$, we retain the previous check-in record to achieve $(u, l_i, t_i, d_i, l_j, t_j, d_j)$.

$$v_{ptf} = tanh(W_{ptf}[u, t_i, t_j, l_j] + b_{ptf})L^\top. \tag{5}$$

From a global perspective, POI transfer patterns contain global collaborative signals. We can obtain the global POI transfer preference v_{gtf} by

$$\Delta d = (d_i - d_j) \times d_u, \tag{6}$$

$$v_{gtf} = tanh(W_{gtf}[t_i, t_j, l_j, \Delta d] + b_{gtf})L^{\top}, \tag{7}$$

where d_u is the unit date embedding. We use linear layers with the $tanh(\cdot)$ activation function to aggregate information from the query. The output of the linear layers is then multiplied by the transpose of L to obtain $|L|$-dimensional vectors, where each element represents the similarity between the query and the corresponding POI.

4.3.3. Mirror Modules

The user's temporal preferences are also reflected in the potential regions they may be in (e.g., different regions during working hours versus off-hours) and the categories of POIs they are interested in (as shown in the data analysis in Section 3). Therefore, we aim to capture multi-dimensional preferences to enhance the representation. Similar to the various POI preference modules mentioned above, we further constructed mirror modules for POI categories and regions. Specifically, first, since the check-in data do not contain regional division information, we cluster the coordinates of all POIs using the K-means method, dividing them into 60 regions. Second, we construct corresponding schedules for users' check-in behaviors regarding different categories and regions during each time slot, using the same approach as mentioned earlier. Then, we capture the various preferences mentioned above using the corresponding learnable parameters, the transpose of the embedding matrix, and the tail entity embeddings from the previous query. Finally, in addition to the preference vectors (v^l) for POIs, we can also obtain preference vectors for POI categories (v^c) and regions (v^a).

4.4. Next POI Recommendation

4.4.1. Model Inference and Optimization

We apply the activation function $softmax(\cdot)$ to estimate the output of the preference vectors for each module. Each module can output its own predictions. Then, the plugin model will select the top-N locations with the highest probability as the preliminary prediction. For our independent plugin model, we use the hyperparameter α to balance users' habit preferences and novelty preferences, thereby reflecting their needs for POIs (categories or regions) in each time slot. Subsequently, we integrate the personal location transfer preference and the global location transfer preference. These two types of preferences are derived from the internal logic of location transfer as reflected in personal habits and global regularities. We utilize the hyperparameter β to regulate the balance between them.

$$\hat{y}_{hn} = \alpha \cdot softmax(v_{hab}) + (1 - \alpha) \cdot softmax(v_{nov}), \tag{8}$$

$$\hat{y}_{tf} = \beta \cdot softmax(v_{ptf}) + (1 - \beta) \cdot softmax(v_{gtf}), \tag{9}$$

where both α and β are hyperparameters ranging from 0 to 1. Then, we adopt the same method to combine the above preferences. $\hat{y}$ denotes the prediction probabilities in all locations by adding $\hat{y}_{hn}$ and $\hat{y}_{tf}$. And $\hat{y}_{hn}$ represents the prediction results modeled through a copy-generation mechanism for user behavior patterns, whereas $\hat{y}_{tf}$ denotes the prediction results based on location transfer modeling.

The plugin model serves as a temporal knowledge graph reasoning model for the next POI (category or region) recommendation. When given the user's historical check-in trajectory T_u and current query $q = (u, t, ?, d)$, predicting the target POI (category or region) can be regarded as a multi-category classification task, where each category corresponds to a POI. The learning objective is to minimize the following cross-entropy loss $\mathcal{L}_{CE}$ on all check-in records of our TKG snapshots that exist during training.

$$\mathcal{L}_{CE} = -\sum_{d=1}^{|\mathcal{D}|}\sum_{u=1}^{|\mathcal{U}|}\sum_{t=1}^{|\mathcal{T}|}\sum_{k=1}^{K} y(x_k^{(u,t,d)})\log(\hat{y}_k^{(u,t,d)}), \tag{10}$$

where $y(\cdot)$ is an indicator function that is equal to 1 if $x_k^{(u,t,d)}$ is the ground truth POI (category or region) of the k-th query $(u, t, ?, d)$ in the snapshot $\mathcal{G}_d$ and 0 otherwise.

Next, in order to promote the model to learn robust representations, we jointly learn three prediction subtasks through a multi-task training framework. The overall loss function is as follows:

$$\mathcal{L}_{final} = \frac{1}{2\sigma_l^2}\mathcal{L}_{CE}^{l} + \frac{1}{2\sigma_c^2}\mathcal{L}_{CE}^{c} + \frac{1}{2\sigma_a^2}\mathcal{L}_{CE}^{a} + log\sigma_l\sigma_c\sigma_a, \tag{11}$$

where σ_l, σ_c, and σ_a are learnable parameters, and the last term serves as a regularization term for denoising. $\mathcal{L}_{CE}^{l}$, $\mathcal{L}_{CE}^{c}$, and $\mathcal{L}_{CE}^{a}$ are the cross-entropy losses for the three subtasks of POI recommendation, category recommendation, and region recommendation, respectively.

4.4.2. Plugin-Enhanced Prompt

We take the preliminary prediction results generated by the plugin model, along with the user profile and the check-in trajectory, as the given data for the plugin-enhanced prompt. Specifically, we construct the prompt by designing different sentence blocks for various purposes. As shown in Figure 7, a key part of the prompt consists of the user profile block, the trajectory block, the plugin block, and the instruction block. In addition, the hint block and target block are used to explain data formats and obtain results. The POI preliminary prediction results from the plugin block are organized into a list of entries (POI ID, distance, category, region), in descending order of probability, and with the overall historical confidence of the preference module. In addition, preliminary predictions for categories and regions are also included.

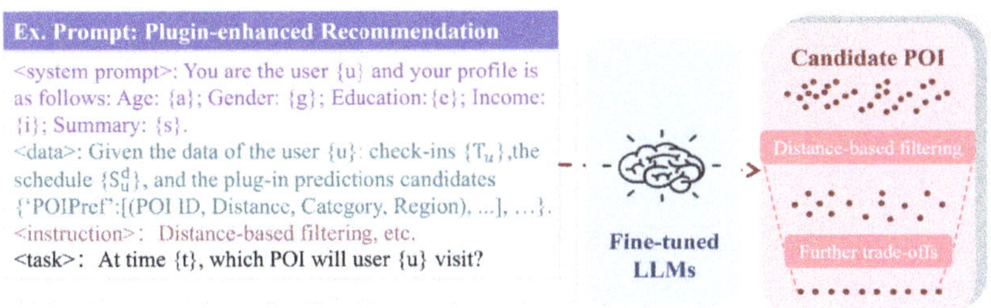

Figure 7. Plugin-enhanced recommendations.

Subsequently, the LLM can conduct in-depth reasoning based on the given data and follow the instructions at the prompt. Specifically, first, we combine the previous check-in location to calculate the distance of the candidate POIs from the preliminary predictions. By evaluating the time gap between successive check-ins, we eliminate candidates with insufficient time feasibility, narrowing the analysis scope and enhancing prediction accuracy. Second, the plugin model's preliminary predictions for categories and regions serve as auxiliary information for POI prediction. Then, the LLM conducts an in-depth analysis of user behavior patterns using the user profile, integrating context information and preliminary predictions from plugin models. Through multi-dimensional evaluation—such as whether the user has checked in at the POI before, whether there is a habitual check-in pattern during the time slot, or whether the user tends to explore new POIs—the POIs that best match the user's behavior pattern are selected as the recommendation. This process fully leverages personalized user profile information and combines spatiotemporal features of check-in trajectories to achieve precise optimization of POI prediction.

4.4.3. Supervised Fine-Tuning

Following [32], we apply parameter-efficient fine-tuning (PEFT) technology during the fine-tuning phase to avoid excessive costs, where we use Llama-2-7b-longlora-32k as our base LLM.

5. Experiments

In this section, we introduce experiments that demonstrate the validity of our proposed model.

5.1. Datasets and Experimental Settings

We evaluate our PSLM4ST model on three widely adopted real-world datasets: Foursquare (https://sites.google.com/site/yangdingqi/home)-NYC (accessed on 5 May 2025), Foursquare-TKY, and Gowalla (http://snap.stanford.edu/data/loc-gowalla.html)-CA (accessed on 5 May 2025). During preprocessing, we follow previous studies. We sort the records chronologically and split the datasets; 80% of the check-ins form the training set, 10% form the validation set, and 10% form the test set. The validation and test sets must include all users and POIs in the training set. And we filter out POIs and users with fewer than 10 check-in records and divide check-in records into 24-h trajectories. Table 1 shows the statistics of the three datasets.

Table 1. Statistics of the datasets.

Dataset	#Users	#POIs	#CATs	#COOs	#Check-ins	#Time Slots
NYC	978	4959	318	60	91,872	96
TKY	2267	7831	289	60	364,408	96
CA	3695	9680	295	60	201,524	12

We use the Xavier initialization method to initialize the model parameters and then optimize using the Adam optimizer with a learning rate of 0.001 and 50 epochs. We set the weight decay to 1×10^{-5}, the embedding dimension to 200, and the batch size to 4096.

5.2. Baselines and Evaluation Metrics

We use the following methods as baselines for our experiment. In addition to a traditional method, `FPMC` [4], an RNN-based method, `STGN` [16], and GCN-based methods, `GETNext` [19] and `STHGCN` [26], we also use the following methods:

- `UTopRec` counts the check-in frequency of each user for all POIs within each time slot according to our TKG.
- `MTNet` [5] is a time-aware state-of-the-art method that introduces a hierarchical check-in description method named Mobility Tree.
- `ROTAN` [6] is a time-aware method that proposes Time2Rotation, which encodes the given time slots as rotations.

- LLM-ZS [31] considers long- and short-term dependencies, solving the time-aware prediction problem by using temporal information.
- GenUP [32] is an LLM-based state-of-the-art model that focuses on user profile generation and fine-tuning.

5.3. Results and Analysis

5.3.1. Overall Comparison

Table 2 presents the experimental results of our model compared to mainstream classic models. Table 3 shows the results of the comparison between our model and LLM-based models. The results show that PSLM4ST outperforms the baselines in most cases, validating our model's advantages.

Table 2. Performance comparison against baselines on three datasets.

Methods	NYC				TKY				CA			
	Acc@1	Acc@5	Acc@10	MRR	Acc@1	Acc@5	Acc@10	MRR	Acc@1	Acc@5	Acc@10	MRR
UTopRec	0.1654	0.3350	0.3588	0.2464	0.1490	0.3269	0.3590	0.2314	0.1311	0.2591	0.2983	0.1938
FPMC	0.1003	0.2126	0.2970	0.1701	0.0814	0.2045	0.2746	0.1344	0.0383	0.0702	0.1159	0.0911
STGN	0.1716	0.3381	0.4122	0.2598	0.1689	0.3391	0.3848	0.2422	0.0982	0.3167	0.4064	0.2040
GETNext	0.2435	0.5089	0.6143	0.3621	0.2254	0.4417	0.5287	0.3262	0.1357	0.2852	0.3590	0.2103
STHGCN	0.2734	0.5361	0.6244	0.3915	0.2950	0.5207	0.5980	0.3986	0.1730	0.3529	0.4191	0.2558
MTNet	0.2620	0.5381	0.6321	0.3855	0.2575	0.4977	0.5848	0.3659	0.1453	0.3419	0.4163	0.2367
ROTAN	0.3106	0.5281	0.6131	0.4104	0.2458	0.4626	0.5392	0.3475	**0.2199**	0.3718	0.4334	**0.2931**
PSLM4ST	**0.3388**	**0.5894**	**0.6787**	**0.4464**	**0.3059**	**0.5596**	**0.6493**	**0.4172**	0.1948	**0.3794**	**0.4581**	0.2855

Table 3. Performance comparison against LLM-based baselines in terms of Acc@1 on three datasets.

Method	Base Model	#params	NYC	TKY	CA
LLM-ZS	GPT-3.5 Turbo	N/A	0.192	0.199	N/A
GenUP	Llama 2	7B	0.2575	0.1699	0.1094
PSLM4ST	Llama 2	7B	0.3388	0.3059	0.1948

It is worth noting that, from the variations in suboptimal models across different datasets, recent research competition in the field of POI recommendation has been quite intense. For instance, on the NYC dataset, MTNet and ROTAN—both of which focus on temporal awareness—achieved suboptimal results on different metrics. This indicates that users in the NYC dataset exhibit more regular temporal patterns, and the optimal-performing PSLM4ST is capable of effectively capturing the time slot preferences. On the TKY dataset, STHGCN, based on hypergraph Transformers, achieved suboptimal results, while MTNet and ROTAN performed relatively worse. This might be due to the fact that users in the TKY dataset had relatively richer check-in trajectories, and both STHGCN and PSLM4ST demonstrated strong capabilities in capturing global collaborative signals. Although ROTAN also considers point-of-interest transition relationships, it only incorporates them as pre-trained embeddings, and subsequent extensive learning through sequence models does not lead to significant final performance. On the final CA dataset, PSLM4ST and ROTAN engaged in intense competition. Similar to the situation in the NYC dataset, PSLM4ST performed relatively better in the Acc@5 and Acc@10 metrics. This suggests that PSLM4ST possesses strong generalization capabilities when expanding the prediction scope, enabling it to cover correct results more comprehensively.

Compared to LLM-based methods, the related work only adopts Acc@1 evaluation, and we maintain consistency. GenUP achieves higher accuracy by utilizing supervised fine-tuning and constructing user profiles, outperforming LLM-ZS's basic ICL approach. Due to the limited context length of LLMs, the actual POI visited by the user may not be present in their context. This means that the true POI may not have been included in the candidate set determinable by the LLM (e.g., through random sampling or by selecting the preceding segment of historical check-in data). Our plugin model can provide a more accurate candidate set. Therefore, PSLM4ST achieves significant performance improvements with the help of the plugin model.

Overall, the advantages of the PSLM4ST model mainly stem from the following reasons: (a) Our plugin model effectively captures users' behavioral preferences within each time slot and their POI transfer preferences across different time slots, thereby providing LLMs with more accurate candidate sets derived from diverse preferences. By mining global POI transfer preferences, it can capture global collaborative signals. (b) LLMs can effectively analyze user profiles and simulate user behaviors based on extensive common knowledge, which is an ability that classic DL-based models do not possess. (c) Synergy between LLM and the plugin model combines the advantages of both.

5.3.2. Analysis of Preliminary Predictions' Top-N Picks

The preliminary prediction result of the plugin model module is a long list with a length equivalent to the total number of POIs. Given the constraint on the length of the prompt, it is essential to select a sub-list from the preliminary prediction result to serve as the plugin's preliminary prediction chunk for the prompt. The temporal knowledge graph plugin model can extract the following five modules: the personal POI transfer preference module (PTF), the global POI transfer preference module (GTF), the user habit preference module (HAB), the user novelty preference module (NOV), and the user check-in frequency statistics module based on the user's schedule S_u^d (UTOP).

Figure 8 shows the accuracy of the top-N prediction results for each module. It can be seen that as N increases, the prediction accuracy in the three datasets initially experiences a rapid improvement, followed by a gradual slowdown in the rate of improvement, maintaining a relatively slower upward trend. PSLM4ST should consider both the accuracy of the top-N predictions and the prompt length constraints to select an appropriate N value. For example, we set N to 60. Additionally, it can be seen that compared to the results of the NYC and TKY datasets, the GTF module achieves the highest accuracy in the CA dataset, while other modules related to specific users exhibit lower performance. The CA dataset has the fewest average check-ins, which means that the model finds it more challenging to capture preferences related to specific users. However, relatively richer global check-in data can support the GTF module in achieving relatively better performance. The UTOP module only mechanically responds to users' habits. It can be seen that its prediction accuracy is almost stable. After N = 10, the accuracy barely improves, so only the first 10 items in each time slot on the schedule need to be used.

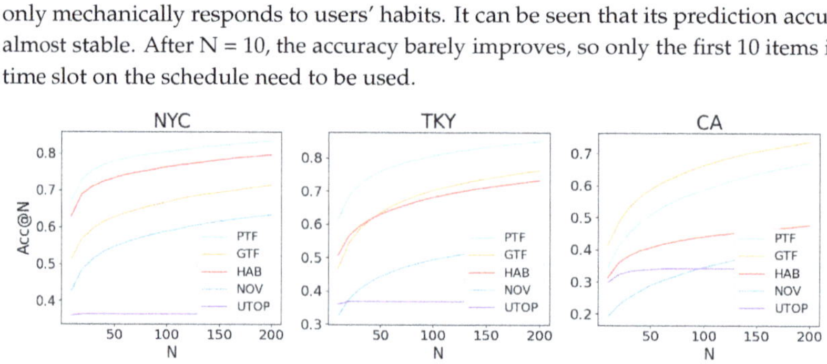

Figure 8. The top-N accuracy of the plugin model's preliminary predictions.

Figure 9 shows the prediction accuracies of mirror modules in the plugin model for points of interest (POIs), categories (CAT), and regions (COO). Since the number of POI categories or regions is significantly smaller than the number of POIs, the corresponding prediction tasks are far less challenging than the POI prediction tasks. Therefore, the mirror modules perform well in POI category prediction and region prediction tasks, achieving satisfactory levels of accuracy. In particular, on the TKY dataset, the mirror modules demonstrate relatively better performance in the two subtasks, with POI category prediction accuracies of Acc@1 = 0.4958 and Acc@20 = 0.9212, and region prediction accuracies of Acc@1 = 0.5235 and Acc@20 = 0.9629. Through joint multitask prediction, valuable semantic information can be provided to the subsequent predictive LLM.

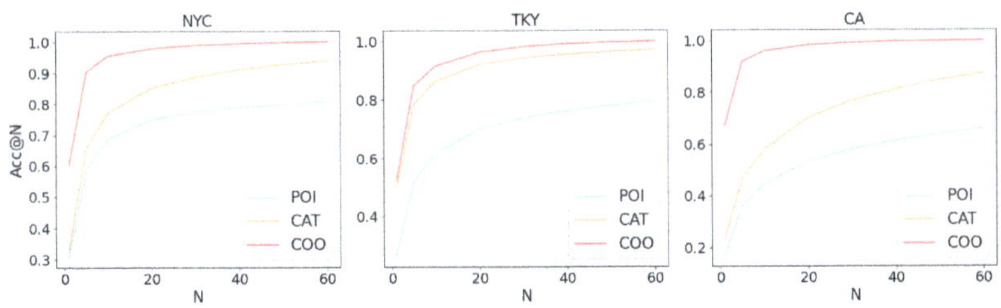

Figure 9. Top-N accuracy analysis in each module for three tasks.

5.3.3. Sensitivity Analysis

To evaluate the impact of weight balance within the preference modules, we conducted a sensitivity analysis on the hyperparameters α and β for specific preference modules on three datasets. As shown in Figure 10, performance trends exhibit an initial increase followed by a decrease as hyperparameters increase across all three datasets. For instance, setting α to 0 causes the model to consider only the user's novelty preference, while setting α to 1 makes the model consider only the user's habit preference. And setting β to 0 causes the model to consider only the user's personal POI transfer preference, while setting β to 1 makes the model consider only the user's global POI transfer preference. In both extreme cases, performance is lower than when both preferences are considered simultaneously. This shows that users are affected by multiple preferences, and different preference modules can generate different effective candidate sets.

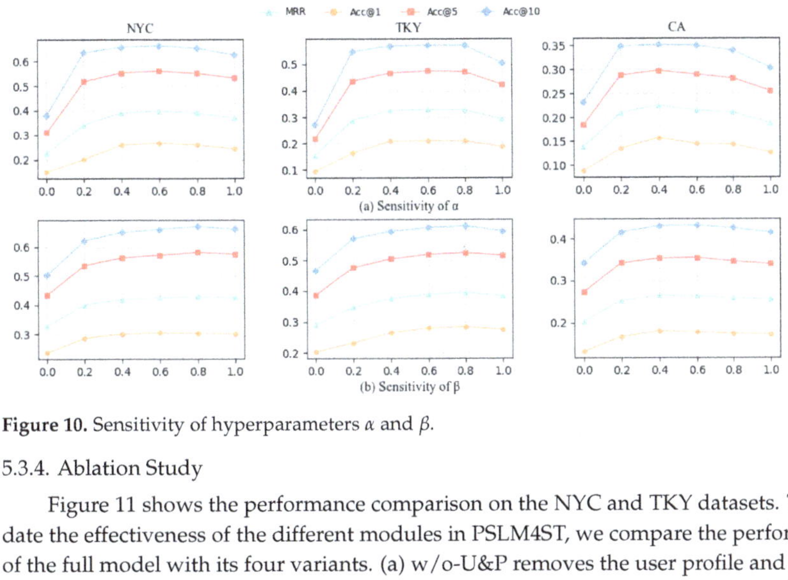

Figure 10. Sensitivity of hyperparameters α and β.

5.3.4. Ablation Study

Figure 11 shows the performance comparison on the NYC and TKY datasets. To validate the effectiveness of the different modules in PSLM4ST, we compare the performance of the full model with its four variants. (a) w/o-U&P removes the user profile and plugin model; (b) w/o-S&P adds the user profile to w/o-U&P, but removes the user summary in the system prompt; (c) w/o-A&P adds the user profile to w/o-U&P, but removes user attributes in the system prompt; (d) w/o-PG adds the user profile to w/o-U&P; (e) w/o-TF removes personal and global POI transfer preferences in the plugin model; (f) w/o-HN removes the personal habits and novelty preferences in the plugin model; (g) w/o-MR removes the mirror modules for the category and region. We can see that the performance of the full model is generally higher than the rest of the variants, so we can say that each module in PSLM4ST contributes to the performance improvement.

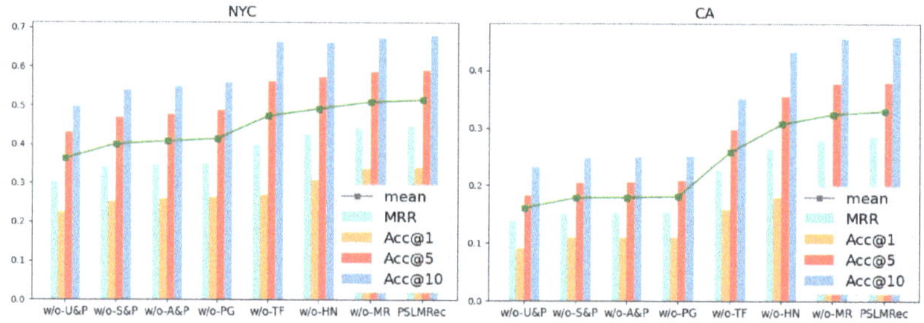

Figure 11. Performance comparison from the ablation study. The green line indicates a relative increase in the mean metric values.

After removing the plugin model, the model's performance dropped significantly. This indicates that the plugin model has a substantial impact on overall performance, particularly due to its preliminary prediction candidate set. Furthermore, the summary section of the user profile has a greater impact on the model than the basic attributes of the user. This is likely because the summary describes the user's life status and personality traits, which reflect and summarize the underlying impact of the user's basic attributes. Finally, it can be seen that the preference modules of the plugin model provide valuable candidate sets. As shown in Figure 8, differences in users' latent preferences across datasets affect the prediction accuracy of the various preference modules.

6. Discussion

Section 5 discusses the experimental results and the phenomena we observed. In this section, we discuss the complexity of the model and other limitations.

Since the main working mechanism of PSLM4ST involves collaboration between the LLM and plugin models for recommendations, its time consumption reflects the sum of the costs of both the LLM and plugin models. Thus, work based on this architecture requires plugin models to have relatively higher inference efficiency. Specifically, the PSLM4ST plugin model is a simple yet effective network, and we analyze its complexity in the training and inference stages. For a minibatch M, the time complexity of learning the preferences is $O(|M||L|)$, and the inference complexity for a single query is $O(L)$ since we only need to calculate the final distribution. The total space complexity is $O(|\mathcal{T}| + |\mathcal{U}| + |L| + N)$, where N is the number of layers in the neural modules.

Regarding the limitations of our model, the approach employing empirical hyperparameters, such as the balance coefficients between multiple preference modules and the granularity of time-slot division, is a common practice in related studies [5,34,35]. However, this approach often necessitates targeted adjustments for different datasets, thus significantly increasing the complexity of model debugging and the overall cost of the application. Consequently, it is imperative to explore adaptive mechanisms in future work that can enable models to automatically adapt to the characteristics of diverse datasets, thereby mitigating the reliance on empirical parameter tuning. In addition, we plan to integrate more multimodal data sources, including text reviews, images, videos posted by users on social platforms, users' social relationships, and detailed POI descriptions. By extracting relevant features from these multimodal data sources, we can enrich the POI information and achieve a more comprehensive understanding of users' needs and preferences.

7. Conclusions

In this paper, we propose a novel framework that aims to facilitate the collaborative work between the plugin model and the pre-trained LLM. Using their complementary strengths, we can predict the POIs at which users will check in during specific time slots with greater precision. Among them, the lightweight plugin model based on TKG reasoning can deeply capture users' various multi-dimensional fine-grained preferences. Meanwhile, the LLM can effectively filter preliminary predictions based on common sense and conduct reasonable reasoning by integrating various sources of information. The efficacy of our proposed method was validated through extensive experiments on three datasets.

Author Contributions: Conceptualization and methodology, H.Z.; data curation and formal analysis, H.Z.; experiments and analysis, H.Z., Z.X., Q.P. and Z.Z.; investigation, Z.X.; validation and visualization, Z.X., Q.P. and Z.Z.; writing—original draft preparation, H.Z., Z.X. and Q.P.; writing—review and editing, X.K. and H.Z.; resources and supervision, X.K.; funding acquisition, X.K. All authors have read and agreed to the published version of the manuscript.

Funding: This research was supported in part by the National Natural Science Foundation of China under Grant 62476247, 62073295 and 62072409, in part by the "Pioneer" and "Leading Goose" R&D Program of Zhejiang under Grant 2024C01214, and in part by the Zhejiang Provincial Natural Science Foundation under Grant LR21F020003.

Institutional Review Board Statement: Not applicable.

Informed Consent Statement: Not applicable.

Data Availability Statement: Data will be available upon reasonable request.

Conflicts of Interest: Author Zhenhui Xu was employed by the company "Zhejiang Supcon Information Co., Ltd.". The remaining authors declare that the research was conducted in the absence of any commercial or financial relationships that could be construed as a potential conflict of interest.

References

1. Wang, W.; Kumar, N.; Chen, J.; Gong, Z.; Kong, X.; Wei, W.; Gao, H. Realizing the potential of the internet of things for smart tourism with 5G and AI. *IEEE Netw.* **2020**, *34*, 295–301. [CrossRef]
2. Zhang, Y.; Sotiriadis, M.; Shen, S. Investigating the impact of smart tourism technologies on tourists' experiences. *Sustainability* **2022**, *14*, 3048. [CrossRef]
3. Zhang, Q.; Yang, P.; Yu, J.; Wang, H.; He, X.; Yiu, S.M.; Yin, H. A Survey on Point-of-Interest Recommendation: Models, Architectures, and Security. *IEEE Trans. Knowl. Data Eng.* **2025**. [CrossRef]
4. Rendle, S.; Freudenthaler, C.; Schmidt-Thieme, L. Factorizing personalized markov chains for next-basket recommendation. In Proceedings of the 19th International Conference on World Wide Web, Raleigh, NC, USA, 26–30 April 2010; pp. 811–820.
5. Huang, T.; Pan, X.; Cai, X.; Zhang, Y.; Yuan, X. Learning time slot preferences via mobility tree for next poi recommendation. In Proceedings of the AAAI Conference on Artificial Intelligence, Vancouver, BC, Canada, 26–27 February 2024; Volume 38, pp. 8535–8543.
6. Feng, S.; Meng, F.; Chen, L.; Shang, S.; Ong, Y.S. Rotan: A rotation-based temporal attention network for time-specific next poi recommendation. In Proceedings of the 30th ACM SIGKDD Conference on Knowledge Discovery and Data Mining, Barcelona, Spain, 25–29 August 2024; pp. 759–770.
7. Luo, Y.; Duan, H.; Liu, Y.; Chung, F.L. Timestamps as prompts for geography-aware location recommendation. In Proceedings of the 32nd ACM International Conference on Information and Knowledge Management, Birmingham, UK, 21–25 October 2023; pp. 1697–1706.
8. Manvi, R.; Khanna, S.; Mai, G.; Burke, M.; Lobell, D.; Ermon, S. Geollm: Extracting geospatial knowledge from large language models. *arXiv* **2023**, arXiv:2310.06213.
9. Gurnee, W.; Tegmark, M. Language models represent space and time. *arXiv* **2023**, arXiv:2310.02207.

10. Harte, J.; Zorgdrager, W.; Louridas, P.; Katsifodimos, A.; Jannach, D.; Fragkoulis, M. Leveraging large language models for sequential recommendation. In Proceedings of the 17th ACM Conference on Recommender Systems, Singapore, 18–22 September 2023; pp. 1096–1102.
11. Wang, X.; Fang, M.; Zeng, Z.; Cheng, T. Where would i go next? large language models as human mobility predictors. *arXiv* **2023**, arXiv:2308.15197.
12. Brown, T.; Mann, B.; Ryder, N.; Subbiah, M.; Kaplan, J.D.; Dhariwal, P.; Neelakantan, A.; Shyam, P.; Sastry, G.; Askell, A.; et al. Language models are few-shot learners. *Adv. Neural Inf. Process. Syst.* **2020**, *33*, 1877–1901.
13. Zhao, W.X.; Zhou, K.; Li, J.; Tang, T.; Wang, X.; Hou, Y.; Min, Y.; Zhang, B.; Zhang, J.; Dong, Z.; et al. A survey of large language models. *arXiv* **2023**, arXiv:2303.18223.
14. Feng, S.; Lyu, H.; Li, F.; Sun, Z.; Chen, C. Where to move next: Zero-shot generalization of llms for next poi recommendation. In Proceedings of the 2024 IEEE Conference on Artificial Intelligence (CAI), Singapore, 25–27 June 2024; pp. 1530–1535.
15. Liu, Q.; Wu, S.; Wang, L.; Tan, T. Predicting the next location: A recurrent model with spatial and temporal contexts. In Proceedings of the AAAI conference on Artificial Intelligence, Phoenix, AZ, USA, 12–17 February 2016; Volume 30.
16. Zhao, P.; Luo, A.; Liu, Y.; Xu, J.; Li, Z.; Zhuang, F.; Sheng, V.S.; Zhou, X. Where to go next: A spatio-temporal gated network for next poi recommendation. *IEEE Trans. Knowl. Data Eng.* **2020**, *34*, 2512–2524. [CrossRef]
17. Xu, C.; Zhao, P.; Liu, Y.; Xu, J.; Sheng, V.S.S.; Cui, Z.; Zhou, X.; Xiong, H. Recurrent convolutional neural network for sequential recommendation. In Proceedings of the The World Wide Web Conference, San Francisco, CA, USA, 13–17 May 2019; pp. 3398–3404.
18. Yang, D.; Fankhauser, B.; Rosso, P.; Cudre-Mauroux, P. Location prediction over sparse user mobility traces using rnns. In Proceedings of the Twenty-Ninth International Joint Conference on Artificial Intelligence, Yokohama, Japan, 11–17 July 2020; pp. 2184–2190.
19. Yang, S.; Liu, J.; Zhao, K. GETNext: Trajectory flow map enhanced transformer for next POI recommendation. In Proceedings of the 45th International ACM SIGIR Conference on Research and Development in Information Retrieval, Washington, DC, USA, 14–18 July 2022; pp. 1144–1153.
20. Lim, N.; Hooi, B.; Ng, S.K.; Wang, X.; Goh, Y.L.; Weng, R.; Varadarajan, J. STP-UDGAT: Spatial-temporal-preference user dimensional graph attention network for next POI recommendation. In Proceedings of the 29th ACM International Conference on Information & Knowledge Management, Virtual, 19–23 October 2020; pp. 845–854.
21. Xia, J.; Yang, Y.; Wang, S.; Yin, H.; Cao, J.; Yu, P.S. Bayes-enhanced multi-view attention networks for robust POI recommendation. *IEEE Trans. Knowl. Data Eng.* **2023**, *36*, 2895–2909. [CrossRef]
22. Zhang, J.; Li, Y.; Zou, R.; Zhang, J.; Jiang, R.; Fan, Z.; Song, X. Hyper-relational knowledge graph neural network for next POI recommendation. *World Wide Web* **2024**, *27*, 46. [CrossRef]
23. Liu, S.; Qi, Y.; Li, G.; Chen, M.; Zhang, T.; Cheng, J.; Lei, J. STGIN: Spatial-Temporal Graph Interaction Network for Large-scale POI Recommendation. In Proceedings of the 32nd ACM International Conference on Information and Knowledge Management, Birmingham, UK, 21–25 October 2023; pp. 4120–4124.
24. Han, H.; Zhang, M.; Hou, M.; Zhang, F.; Wang, Z.; Chen, E.; Wang, H.; Ma, J.; Liu, Q. STGCN: A spatial-temporal aware graph learning method for POI recommendation. In Proceedings of the 2020 IEEE International Conference on Data Mining (ICDM), Virtual, 17–20 November 2020; pp. 1052–1057.
25. Wang, Z.; Zhu, Y.; Liu, H.; Wang, C. Learning graph-based disentangled representations for next POI recommendation. In Proceedings of the 45th International ACM SIGIR Conference on Research and Development in Information Retrieval, Madrid, Spain, 11–15 July 2022; pp. 1154–1163.
26. Yan, X.; Song, T.; Jiao, Y.; He, J.; Wang, J.; Li, R.; Chu, W. Spatio-temporal hypergraph learning for next POI recommendation. In Proceedings of the 46th International ACM SIGIR Conference on Research and Development in Information Retrieval, Taipei, Taiwan, 23–27 July 2023; pp. 403–412.
27. Liu, Y.; Pham, T.A.N.; Cong, G.; Yuan, Q. An experimental evaluation of point-of-interest recommendation in location-based social networks. *Proc. VLDB Endow.* **2017**, *10*, 1010–1021. [CrossRef]
28. Sánchez, P.; Bellogín, A. Point-of-interest recommender systems based on location-based social networks: A survey from an experimental perspective. *ACM Comput. Surv. (CSUR)* **2022**, *54*, 1–37. [CrossRef]
29. Wang, X.; Sun, G.; Fang, X.; Yang, J.; Wang, S. Modeling Spatio-temporal Neighbourhood for Personalized Point-of-interest Recommendation. In Proceedings of the IJCAI, Vienna, Austria, 23–29 July 2022; pp. 3530–3536.
30. Chen, W.; Wan, H.; Guo, S.; Huang, H.; Zheng, S.; Li, J.; Lin, S.; Lin, Y. Building and exploiting spatial–temporal knowledge graph for next POI recommendation. *Knowl.-Based Syst.* **2022**, *258*, 109951. [CrossRef]
31. Beneduce, C.; Lepri, B.; Luca, M. Large language models are zero-shot next location predictors. *arXiv* **2024**, arXiv:2405.20962. [CrossRef]
32. Wongso, W.; Xue, H.; Salim, F.D. GenUP: Generative User Profilers as In-Context Learners for Next POI Recommender Systems. *arXiv* **2024**, arXiv:2410.20643.

33. Li, P.; de Rijke, M.; Xue, H.; Ao, S.; Song, Y.; Salim, F.D. Large language models for next point-of-interest recommendation. In Proceedings of the 47th International ACM SIGIR Conference on Research and Development in Information Retrieval, Washington, DC, USA, 14–18 July 2024; pp. 1463–1472.
34. Zhu, C.; Chen, M.; Fan, C.; Cheng, G.; Zhang, Y. Learning from history: Modeling temporal knowledge graphs with sequential copy-generation networks. In Proceedings of the AAAI Conference on Artificial Intelligence, Virtual, 19–21 May 2021; Volume 35, pp. 4732–4740.
35. Xu, Y.; Ou, J.; Xu, H.; Fu, L. Temporal knowledge graph reasoning with historical contrastive learning. In Proceedings of the AAAI Conference on Artificial Intelligence, Washington, DC, USA, 7–14 February 2023; Volume 37, pp. 4765–4773.
36. Chen, Y.; Wu, A.; DePodesta, T.; Yeh, C.; Li, K.; Marin, N.C.; Patel, O.; Riecke, J.; Raval, S.; Seow, O.; et al. Designing a dashboard for transparency and control of conversational AI. *arXiv* **2024**, arXiv:2406.07882.

algorithms

MDPI

Article

Self-Supervised Keypoint Learning for the Geometric Analysis of Road-MarkingTemplates

Chayanon Sub-r-pa and Rung-Ching Chen *

Department of Information Management, Chaoyang University of Technology, Taichung 413310, Taiwan; t5220317@gm.cyut.edu.tw
* Correspondence: crching@cyut.edu.tw

Abstract: Robust visual perception and geometric alignment are crucial for intelligent automation in various domains, such as industrial processes and infrastructure monitoring. Accurately aligning structured visual elements, such as floor markings or road-marking templates, is essential for tasks like automated guidance, verification, and condition assessment. However, traditional feature-based methods struggle with templates that feature simple geometries and lack rich textures, making reliable feature matching and alignment difficult, even under controlled conditions. To address this, we propose GeoTemplateKPNet, a novel self-supervised deep-learning framework, built upon Convolutional Neural Networks (CNNs), designed to learn robust, geometrically consistent keypoints specifically in synthetic template images. The model is trained exclusively in a synthetic template dataset by enforcing equivariance to geometric transformations and utilizing self-supervised losses, including inside mask loss, peakiness loss, repulsion loss, and keypoint-driven image reprojection loss, thereby eliminating the need for manual keypoint annotations. We evaluate the method in a synthetic template test set, using metrics such as a keypoint-matching comparison, the Inside Mask Rate (IMR), and the Alignment Reconstruction Error (ARE). The results demonstrate that GeoTemplateKPNet successfully learns to predict meaningful keypoints on template structures, enabling accurate alignment between templates and their transformed counterparts. Ablation studies reveal that the number of keypoints (K) impacts the performance, with $K = 3$ providing the most suitable balance for the overall alignment accuracy, although the performance varies across different template geometries. GeoTemplateKPNet offers a foundational self-supervised solution for the robust geometric analysis of templates, which is crucial for downstream alignment tasks and applications.

Keywords: marking sign; industrial floor marking; road-marking sign; image registration; image alignment; CNN

1. Introduction

Intelligent automation, monitoring, and optimization are increasingly critical in industrial processes. These systems rely heavily on robust visual perception, including accurately interpreting and aligning critical visual cues, like floor markings, for autonomous-guided-vehicle (AGV) navigation [1], equipment labels, safety signs, and quality control markers. Understanding and aligning these real-world visual elements with their digital twins, templates, or reference models is crucial for providing automated guidance, tracking assets, verifying processes, and monitoring conditions. However, just like external transportation infrastructure, real-world industrial environments present significant challenges to visual perception due to variations in lighting, dust accumulation, wear and tear, partial occlusion, and changes in viewpoint.

These challenges are highly analogous to those faced when analyzing external road markings. Road markings are fundamental elements of transportation infrastructure, playing critical roles in ensuring road safety [2], guiding traffic flows, and enabling navigation for both human drivers and autonomous vehicles (AVs). Maintaining the visibility and integrity of these markings is paramount. Consequently, efficient and accurate methods for monitoring their condition, verifying their type and placement against standards or maps, and assessing potential damage are increasingly vital for road authorities and AV developers.

As illustrated in Figure 1, industrial and road-marking signs share fundamental visual characteristics and are susceptible to similar degradation processes, viewpoint changes, diverse lighting, and potential motion blur. These factors severely impact the appearance of real-world instances. Furthermore, even clean, canonical template images of these elements, such as the road-marking templates we study, often have simple structures, like straight lines and few distinct corners. This characteristic makes them particularly challenging for classical computer vision techniques, such as hand-crafted feature detectors (e.g., SIFT [3] and ORB [4]). Traditional methods designed to find complex, textured features often detect only a limited number of points on these plain templates, frequently resulting in fewer than the minimum required correspondences (e.g., four for affine transformations) for robust geometric alignment using methods like RANSAC [5]. This limitation applies not only to aligning templates with degraded real-world instances but also to the simpler task of aligning a template with its geometrically transformed version.

(a) (b)

Figure 1. Example of real-world visual cues: (**a**) an underground parking area with marking signs on the floor and walls at Chaoyang University of Technology, Taichung, Taiwan. These markings can mimic those used in factory settings to guide and automate machinery in transportation and other processes, and (**b**) a road-marking arrow on a road surface in Taichung City, Taiwan. Both types of markings are essential for guidance and safety but are subject to environmental degradation and variations in appearance, posing challenges for robust visual analysis and alignment.

In addressing the fundamental need for a robust geometric understanding of these visual elements, particularly their template structures, we propose utilizing deep-learning techniques to learn reliable keypoints that overcome the limitations of traditional feature detection in feature-poor templates. The manual annotation of keypoints in extensive datasets is often unfeasible. Consequently, focusing on road-marking templates as representative structured elements, we introduce GeoTemplateKPNet. This innovative framework utilizes self-supervised learning to accurately predict robust, geometrically consistent keypoints tailored to the distinct geometries or structures of specific visual element classes, using only synthetic template data for training and experimentation. This eliminates the need for manual keypoint labels and avoids reliance on real-world instance data during experimental training and evaluation.

Our core idea is that meaningful keypoints or features can be learned by enforcing equivariance and consistency constraints under various relevant transformations applied to input template data. Uniquely, GeoTemplateKPNet is trained and experimentally evaluated exclusively on synthetic template images, enabling the model to learn features that are robust to geometric transformations of the template itself. We employ a multi-head architecture where a shared backbone extracts common visual features, and class-specific heads learn to predict K keypoints tailored to the distinct geometry or structure of each visual element class, focusing on five arrow-based road-marking template types in this work.

Despite advancements in image alignment, a persistent issue remains: aligning structured, feature-poor templates accurately to their transformed versions. This challenge is critical in areas like road-marking analysis, where templates (e.g., arrow shapes and crosswalks) lack distinctive textures and are geometrically simple and and symmetrical. Traditional feature-based methods, such as SIFT or ORB, fail due to the unreliability of their features. Moreover, creating comprehensive datasets with manually labeled ground-truth keypoints for all road-marking variants is impractical and often undefined. This gap—lacking a reliable method for self-supervised keypoint learning on these templates—hinders applications needing precise geometric analysis, such as automated condition assessment and maintenance planning. This paper proposes a novel framework to learn geometrically consistent keypoints in a self-supervised manner on these challenging template structures.

The keypoints learned by GeoTemplateKPNet on the template serve as a foundation for robust geometric analysis. By detecting corresponding keypoints on a template and its transformed version (using the class ID to select the appropriate class head) and establishing correspondences, we can estimate the transformation that aligns the template. Achieving such robust and accurate alignment on templates, where traditional methods often fail due to insufficient features, demonstrates the significant potential of our method. This capability is a crucial step toward the larger goal of robust template-to-real-world instance alignment, which, in turn, enables a range of critical downstream analysis tasks in infrastructure monitoring and analogous industrial applications, such as transferring segmentation masks or performing condition assessments, by analyzing discrepancies between the aligned template and the real-world instance. While our method demonstrates significant potential and succeeds in learning robust keypoints for most of the tested classes, it is essential to note that it was not successful with every class, highlighting areas for future improvement.

The main contributions of this paper are as follows:

1. A self-supervised deep-learning technique for detecting robust, geometrically meaningful keypoints on synthetic templates of visual element classes (demonstrated on road-marking templates) and trained without manual keypoint annotations by enforcing equivariance to geometric transformations applied to the template data;
2. The successful application and evaluation of a multi-head architecture for class-specific keypoint prediction within this self-supervised framework, tailoring feature learning to different template geometries;
3. The demonstration and quantitative evaluation of a robust template-to-transformed-template alignment pipeline leveraging the learned keypoints on synthetic data, highlighting its effectiveness compared to the failure of classical feature-based methods (like ORB) on these templates, thereby showcasing the method's potential for future template-to-real-world instance alignment.

This paper is structured as follows: Section 2 reviews related work. Section 3 describes the proposed GeoTemplateKPNet methodology, covering the model architecture, self-supervised loss functions, training strategy, and datasets. Section 4 outlines the experimental setup and results, with comparisons and ablation studies. Section 5 offers a discussion. Lastly, Section 6 wraps up the paper and proposes directions for future research.

2. Related Work

Robust visual perception, including the accurate analysis and alignment of critical visual cues (like floor markings, labels, or infrastructure elements), is fundamental for intelligent automation, monitoring, and optimization in industrial processes and civil infrastructure management. However, real-world environments in both domains present significant challenges due to variations in viewpoint, lighting, degradation, and occlusion, which severely impact the robustness of traditional computer vision techniques and complicate downstream analysis tasks, such as condition assessment or state estimation. This section reviews relevant work in the automated analysis of visual elements, focusing on road markings as a representative case study, geometric image alignment, and self-supervised feature learning, while highlighting the limitations that motivate our approach to address these shared challenges.

2.1. Visual-Element Analysis and Condition/State Assessment

Identifying and localizing visual elements are often necessary precursors for automated analysis tasks in industrial and infrastructure monitoring. In the context of road markings, these involve detecting markings despite challenging conditions experienced by vehicle-mounted cameras [6–8]. Such tasks often necessitate aligning the observed real-world instance to a standardized template or a digital model for consistent measurement, verification against standards, or condition assessment (e.g., quantifying wear or damage) [9,10]. A critical challenge here is that appearance changes due to genuine degradation or state change must be disentangled from those caused by variations in viewpoint, scale, rotation, or illumination. This highlights the fundamental need for robust geometric normalization, typically achieved through aligning the real-world instance with its corresponding template.

However, achieving reliable and accurate template-to-real-world instance alignment remains a significant challenge. Traditional methods often struggle with the large appearance gap between clean templates and degraded, noisy instances. There is currently no widely accepted solid solution for this specific alignment problem in challenging real-world conditions. The ability to robustly align a template to a real-world instance is crucial for reliable downstream analysis. Still, it first requires a method capable of understanding the underlying geometric structure of the template itself in a transformation-robust manner.

2.2. Image Alignment and Registration

Image alignment, also known as registration, aims to find the spatial transformation that maps points or regions between images or a template and an image. This process is crucial for normalizing the view of a visual element's instance (such as a road marking or an industrial label) relative to a canonical template or a digital model, enabling consistent measurement and comparison. Classical feature-based methods, like SIFT [3], SURF [11], and ORB [4], detect local invariant features and use robust estimators like, RANSAC [5], to compute transformations. While effective in many general vision tasks, these methods often struggle significantly when applied to template images of structured elements, such as road markings. Such templates frequently possess simple geometric shapes with limited texture or distinct corner features. Traditional feature detectors designed for complex images often detect only a sparse set of points on these plain structures.

Furthermore, standard SIFT and ORB, while offering some robustness to scale and rotation, are not fully invariant to the general affine transformations commonly encountered in viewpoint changes. This combination of difficulty in detecting a sufficient number of features on simple template structures and limited invariance to affine distortions makes traditional feature-based methods unreliable for robust template-to-transformed-template alignment, let alone the more complex template-to-real-world instance problem. Direct template matching based on correlation is similarly sensitive to geometric variations [12]. Deep learning has also been applied to image alignment; Spatial Transformer Networks (STNs) [13] learn implicit transformations, and more recent deep keypoint correspondence networks learn robust features [14,15]. Our work falls into this broader category but is specifically tailored for the challenge of learning keypoints on structured templates, using a self-supervised approach.

2.3. Deep Learning for Road-Marking Analysis and Alignment

The demand for robust and autonomous navigation systems has accelerated advancements in deep-learning-based road-marking analysis and alignment. Unlike traditional methods, deep-learning models can learn complex patterns directly from data, making them effective in managing the diverse appearances and environmental variations of road markings.

A key application of deep learning in this area is the detection of road markings, using CNNs [16,17] for semantic segmentation, allowing for pixel-level classification of lane lines, arrows, and crosswalks. Many studies have employed encoder–decoder CNN architectures to effectively detect and outline lane markings and road signs in real time, frequently using classical post-processing techniques for precise geometric fitting. These models can accurately identify and localize road markings across a range of lighting and weather conditions.

In addition to detection, deep learning is increasingly used for extracting structured geometric representations that aid in alignment and mapping. Advanced systems, such as the Vectorized-Map-Annotation (VMA) [18] framework, utilize transformer-based architectures to represent road markings as ordered "corner point sequences". This output provides detailed geometric information suitable for dense mapping tasks. Deep models also enhance our understanding of the relationships between road elements; for example, networks, like TopoNet [19], model the connections among lanes, intersections, and traffic signs, supporting the global alignment and interpretation of road layouts.

These developments underscore the crucial role of deep learning in enhancing road-marking analysis, providing effective solutions for traditionally challenging tasks. While many techniques focus on detection, the results they produce often serve as the foundation for subsequent alignment processes. This manuscript presents a novel self-supervised method for learning consistent keypoints on structured, feature-poor templates, thereby distinguishing it from the broader CNN-based detection and segmentation tasks.

2.4. Self-Supervised Keypoint/Landmark/Feature Detection

Learning reliable keypoints, landmarks, or representative features directly from data, without requiring extensive manual annotations, is a promising direction for overcoming labeling costs in various vision tasks, including industrial inspection and infrastructure monitoring. One major category of self-supervised learning focuses on enforcing geometric equivariance or consistency: Models are trained to predict stable features, even when the input image is transformed [20–23]. Another approach involves using reconstruction tasks or bottleneck architectures to force a network to encode an image's structure through a sparse set of points [24,25]. Task-driven methods learn features optimized for a specific downstream task [26]. A common challenge across self-supervised feature-learning methods is ensuring that the learned points or features are well-distributed and consistently located on meaningful parts of the object or indicative of specific states, rather than collapsing to a single point or drifting into the background. This often requires additional regularization.

2.5. Our Approach in Context

As reviewed, achieving robust visual element analysis and condition/state assessment in challenging real-world environments, common to both industrial and infrastructure domains, is significantly hindered by geometric and photometric variations. A critical prerequisite for such analysis is the accurate alignment of the real-world instance with a standard template; however, robust template-to-real-world instance alignment remains a notable challenge, with no widely accepted solution, largely due to the significant appearance gap and complex variations in real-world data.

Traditional alignment techniques often fail to reliably normalize these variations for degraded or noisy instances. Furthermore, as discussed in Section 2.2, these traditional methods also struggle with the simpler task of aligning a template to its geometrically transformed version, primarily because they find insufficient reliable features in the plain structures typical of templates and are limited in their invariance to affine transformations. For such visual perception tasks, CNNs are particularly well-suited due to their inherent ability to learn hierarchical spatial features and capture complex patterns directly from image data, making them the standard choice for image-based analyses.

While self-supervised feature learning (Section 2.4) offers a compelling approach to obtain correspondences or representations without manual labels, existing methods have not been specifically developed and evaluated for the crucial task of learning robust keypoints on structured templates for geometric analysis.

Our proposed GeoTemplateKPNet addresses this gap by presenting a novel self-supervised framework specifically designed to learn robust, geometrically consistent keypoints tailored for structured template images. By training exclusively on synthetic template data and leveraging the advantages of templates, such as the availability of precise masks for the initial localization guidance and the ability to generate vast amounts of heavily augmented training data, our method learns features that are inherently robust to geometric transformations, like affine distortions. This capability is demonstrated through robust template-to-transformed-template alignment, where traditional methods fail. We employ a multi-head architecture to specialize keypoint prediction for different template geometries.

This work serves as a foundational step, demonstrating the potential of our self-supervised approach for learning robust keypoints on templates. While applying these learned keypoints for template-to-real-world instance alignment is the ultimate goal and an area for future work (which may involve strategies like using Generative Adversarial Networks (GANs) [27] to bridge the domain gap between templates and instances), this paper establishes the critical capability of reliably extracting geometrically robust keypoints directly from the template structure itself. Our work distinguishes itself by providing an effective, self-supervised solution for learning keypoints from challenging, feature-poor template data, thereby showcasing its potential applicability in facilitating alignment tasks across various domains.

3. Methodology

This section outlines the proposed GeoTemplateKPNet methodology, detailing the datasets used, network architecture, keypoint representation, coordinate extraction, self-supervised training strategy, self-supervised loss functions, total loss calculation, and evaluation metrics.

3.1. Datasets

We employed a synthetic template dataset exclusively for training and quantitative evaluation in this work. Examples illustrating a base template and an augmented version are shown in Figure 2.

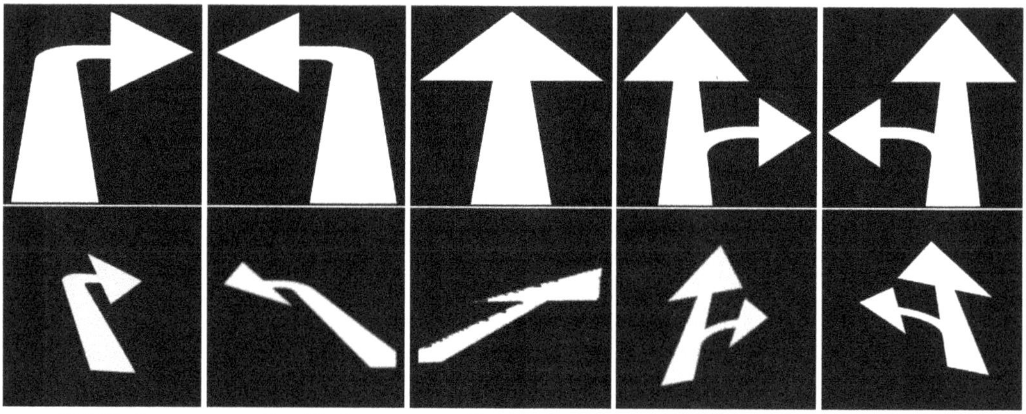

Figure 2. Examples from the synthetic dataset used in this work. The **upper row** shows base synthetic template images, illustrating the clean, ideal forms of different road-marking templates. The **lower row** shows augmented versions of synthetic template images, demonstrating the types of geometric and photometric transformations applied during training (e.g., rotation, scaling, perspective changes, and noise). Each 'Class ID' refers to a specific road-marking sign type (e.g., straight arrow and left-turn arrow), and these IDs are used to select the corresponding class-specific prediction head in the network.

Synthetic Template Dataset

This dataset comprises synthetic template images generated from vector graphics of the five arrow-based road-marking types considered in this work: a straight arrow, a straight arrow with a turn-left arrow, a straight arrow with a turn-right arrow, a turn-left arrow, and a turn-right arrow. These templates are initially simple binary images (black background and white markings), with a consistent resolution of 224 × 224 pixels.

The choice of a synthetic template dataset was primarily driven by its significant advantages for self-supervised keypoint learning. Synthetic data enable the easy and precise generation of ground-truth masks, which are crucial for our Inside Mask Loss (L_{mask}), and allow for rigorous control over geometric transformations, facilitating robust data augmentation. This ensures that the training data consistently contain accurate and well-defined features, essential for training a model in a self-supervised manner without manual keypoint annotations.

For training, we extensively augmented these base templates dynamically during each iteration, using various geometric and photometric transformations from the Albumentations library [28]. The augmentation consisted of several photometric transformations, including brightness, contrast, noise, random posterize, random solarize, random adjust sharpness, and random autocontrast, each applied with a probability of 0.7. Geometric transformations included ElasticTransform, rotation within the range of (−15, 15) degrees, scaling between 0.5 and 1.0, translation within (−0.05, 0.05) of the image height/width, and shear within the range of (−10, 10) degrees. The affine transformation was applied with a probability of 0.8, while the other geometric transformations (ElasticTransform, rotation, scaling, shear, and translation, excluding affine transformations) were each implemented with a probability of 0.7.

We specifically excluded horizontal and vertical flips due to the potential changes in the class identity for certain road markings. This process successfully produced a diverse array of augmented template instances for training, including two thousand augmented instances for each of the five classes, resulting in a total of ten thousand images for Stage 1 pre-training. Additionally, we generated 500 images per class, amounting to 2500 images for Stage 2.

For quantitative evaluation, a separate synthetic test set was created. This test set comprises five hundred affine-transformed images for each of the five template classes, totaling two thousand five hundred images. These transformations were applied to the base templates to simulate geometric variations and evaluate the model's ability to predict consistent keypoints under such changes, forming the basis for template-to-transformed-template alignment experiments.

3.2. Network Architecture

The **GeoTemplateKPNet** (Figure 3) employs a multi-head architecture based on a shared convolutional neural network (CNN) backbone, which we denote as the function ϕ. In our experiments, we explore different pre-trained backbone networks for ϕ, including ResNet-50 [29] or VGG-16 [30]. The backbone (ϕ) takes an input image ($I \in \mathbb{R}^{B\times 3\times H_{in}\times W_{in}}$), where B is the batch size and H_{in}, W_{in} are the input image's height and width, and extracts a feature representation ($F = \phi(I)$). The spatial dimensions of the feature map (F) depend on the specific backbone architecture and the layer from which features are extracted. To achieve a desired final heatmap resolution, features are typically extracted from an intermediate layer of the backbone, where the spatial dimensions are $H_b \times W_b$. For instance, with a 224×224 input image, features might be extracted from a layer yielding a spatial size of 14×14 (corresponding to a total stride of 16 from the input).

To handle the five main road-marking classes used in this work—a straight arrow, a straight arrow with a turn-left arrow, a straight arrow with a turn-right arrow, a turn-left arrow, and a turn-right arrow—the network employs $N_{cls} = 5$ class-specific prediction heads. Each head can be viewed as a function (ψ_c), where $c \in \{0, \ldots, N_{cls} - 1\}$ is the class ID. Given an input image (I) of class c, the corresponding features ($F = \phi(I)$) are routed to the specific head (ψ_c). Each head (ψ_c) is designed to predict K keypoints tailored to its specific class geometry. In this work, we explored different values for the number of keypoints (K) per class, specifically testing $K \in \{3, 4, 5\}$. The architecture described hereafter and detailed in Table 1 corresponds to the configuration for $K = 5$, which was found to yield the best performance within this tested range (See the results in Section 4).

The keypoint predictions for an input image (I) of class c are represented as a set of K heatmaps, denoted as $H_{pred} = \psi_c(\phi(I))$. The spatial resolution of these heatmaps ($H_{out} \times W_{out}$) is determined by the backbone's feature map size ($H_b \times W_b$) and the head's total upsampling factor (U), such that $H_{out} = H_b \times U$ and $W_{out} = W_b \times U$. In our setup with 224×224 input images and features extracted at 14×14, the heads are designed to produce heatmaps with a resolution of 56×56 pixels ($14 \times 4 = 56$), implying a total upsampling factor of $U = 4$.

Each class-specific head (ψ_c) has the architecture detailed in Table 1. The heads primarily consist of transpose convolutional layers for upsampling, standard convolutional layers for feature refinement, and batch normalization and ReLU activations. Dropout layers are incorporated within the heads to provide regularization and enhance the model's generalization capability by mitigating overfitting. A dropout rate of 0.5 was applied. It is important to note that these dropout layers are active exclusively during the training phase to introduce stochasticity and prevent the co-adaptation of neurons. During the testing, the dropout layers are entirely deactivated to ensure deterministic and consistent predictions, which is standard practice in deep learning. These layers are omitted from the main architectural table for the clarity of the core structural components.

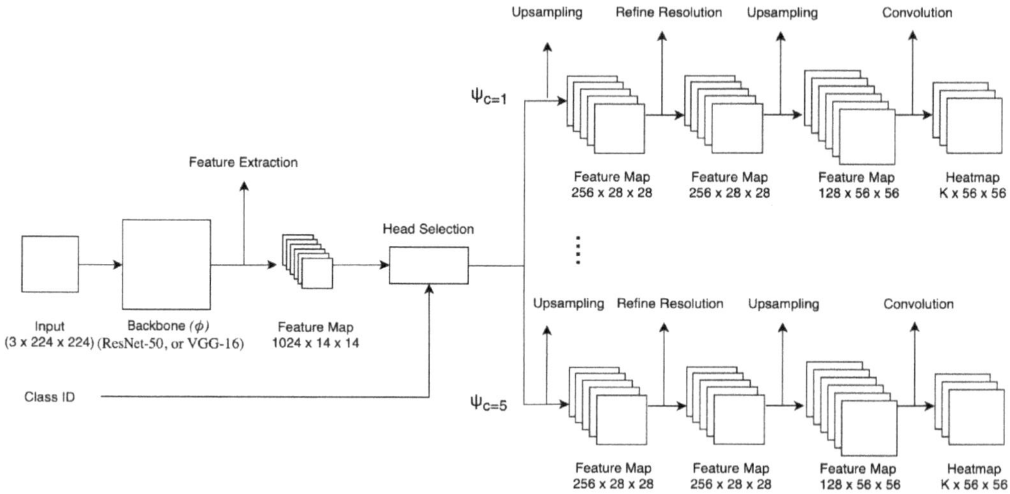

Figure 3. Overview of the **GeoTemplateKPNet** architecture. A shared backbone (ϕ) extracts features (with spatial dimensions of $H_b \times W_b$, e.g., 14×14 for 224×224 inputs, with **either ResNet-50 or VGG-16** as the backbone), which are then passed to class-specific heads (ψ_c) containing transpose convolutions and standard convolutions (as detailed in Table 1) to predict $K \in \{3,4,5\}$ keypoint heatmaps with spatial dimensions of $H_{out} \times W_{out}$ (e.g., 56×56 for 224×224 inputs).

Table 1. Architecture of a single class-specific heatmap prediction head (ψ_c) for $K \in \{3,4,5\}$ keypoints (excluding dropout layers).

Layer Type	Description	Input Channels	Output Channels	Kernel Size	Stride	Padding
ConvTranspose2d	Upsampling	Backbone Features	256	4	2	1
BatchNorm2d		256	256	-	-	-
ReLU	Activation	-	-	-	-	-
Conv2d	Intermediate refinement	256	256	3	1	1
BatchNorm2d		256	256	-	-	-
ReLU	Activation	-	-	-	-	-
ConvTranspose2d	Upsampling	256	128	4	2	1
BatchNorm2d		128	128	-	-	-
ReLU	Activation	-	-	-	-	-
Conv2d	Final prediction	128	$K \in \{3,4,5\}$	1	1	0
Sigmoid	Activation	-	-	-	-	-

3.3. Keypoint Representation and Coordinate Extraction

The network predicts the location of each keypoint (k) as a dense heatmap, which is a part of the tensor $H_{pred} = \psi_c(\phi(I))$ for an input image (I) of class c. Higher values in the heatmap $H_{pred,k}$ indicate a higher probability of the keypoint k being present at that location. To obtain differentiable keypoint coordinates ($P \in \mathbb{R}^{B\times K\times 2}$) from these heatmaps ($H_{pred}$), we employ the spatial softmax operation [31]. Unlike simple non-differentiable peak-finding methods (such as finding the argmax location), the spatial softmax computes a weighted average (center of mass) over the heatmap, providing continuous, sub-pixel-precise, and, crucially, differentiable coordinates. This differentiability is essential for the self-supervised learning framework, as it allows gradients from the downstream losses to flow back through the coordinate prediction process, enabling the model to learn accurate and distinct keypoint locations without manual supervision and preventing keypoint collapse.

The extraction of the coordinates involves the following two steps:

1. **Probability Calculation:** Each keypoint heatmap ($H_{pred,k}$) is normalized to a spatial probability distribution ($p_k(h,w)$), using the softmax function

$$p_k(h,w) = \frac{\exp(H_{pred,k}(h,w))}{\sum_{h'=0}^{H_{out}-1}\sum_{w'=0}^{W_{out}-1}\exp(H_{pred,k}(h',w'))} \tag{1}$$

   where $H_{pred,k}(h,w)$ is the predicted heatmap value for keypoint k at spatial location (h,w), H_{out} and W_{out} are the height and width of the heatmaps;

2. **Expected-Coordinate Calculation:** The continuous coordinate (x_k, y_k) for keypoint k is computed as the expected value (center of mass) over this probability distribution as follows:

$$x_k = \sum_{w=0}^{W_{out}-1}\sum_{h=0}^{H_{out}-1} p_k(h,w)\cdot w \tag{2}$$

$$y_k = \sum_{h=0}^{H_{out}-1}\sum_{w=0}^{W_{out}-1} p_k(h,w)\cdot h \tag{3}$$

   These coordinates are calculated for each keypoint (k) and each image (b) in the batch, resulting in $P_b = \{(x_k, y_k)\}_{k=1}^{K}$. The coordinates lie within the heatmap grid, $x_k \in [0, W_{out}-1]$ and $y_k \in [0, H_{out}-1]$. This coordinate range reflects that in our experimental setup, the visual elements of interest are consistently contained within the boundaries of the input image.

Both the heatmaps (H_{pred}) and the derived coordinates (P) are used in the loss calculations, forming the basis for the self-supervised training signals. The choice of the heatmap resolution factor (e.g., $H_{in}/4 \times W_{in}/4$) in this work was primarily made for experimental simplicity, allowing for the demonstration of the concept, with the potential for exploring other resolutions in future work.

3.4. Self-Supervised Two-Stage Training Strategy

We propose a novel two-stage self-supervised training strategy designed to effectively learn robust keypoints on structured templates without requiring manual annotation. This strategy utilizes the synthetic template dataset exclusively for both training stages. Starting with clean, geometry-based template images in the first stage enables the effective monitoring and adjustment of the learning process, using controllable factors, such as the template mask and known affine transform parameters, thereby providing confidence before attempting more complex scenarios.

Stage 1: Template Pre-training. In this initial stage, the network is trained exclusively in the synthetic dataset of augmented template images described in the section on the synthetic template dataset. These templates are generated from vector graphics of the five road-marking classes considered, with heavy data augmentation applied using the Albumentations library [28]. The augmentation includes various photometric transformations (e.g., brightness, contrast, noise, random posterize, random solarize, random adjust sharpness, and random autocontrast) and geometric transformations (e.g., ElasticTransform, rotation, scale, shear, and translate), with specific probabilities, as detailed in the experimental setup. Horizontal and vertical flips are specifically excluded due to the potential for changes in the class identity for certain road markings.

The primary goal of this stage is to enable the network to learn the fundamental geometric structure of each template class and associate it with the K keypoints. Training is performed for 300 epochs, using the Adam optimizer [32] with a learning rate of 0.0001 and a batch size of 32. The total loss in Stage 1 is a weighted sum of the specific self-supervised loss components (L_{equiv} for rotation and affine transformations, L_{mask}, L_{peak}, and $L_{repulsion}$), as detailed in Sections 3.5 and 3.6.

Stage 2: Template Fine-tuning. After pre-training on templates for 300 epochs, the model weights are used to initialize the network for the second stage. In this stage, the network is fine-tuned using the Adam optimizer [32], with a fixed low learning rate of 0.00001 and a batch size of 32. The training runs until the model converges or the loss stops improving significantly. The training is performed in the synthetic template dataset, using the same augmentation strategy as in Stage 1.

This stage aims to refine the features learned in Stage 1, ensuring robustness to geometric variations present in the augmented templates and optimizing the keypoints for accurate alignment between the templates and their transformed counterparts. Crucially, losses requiring template-specific mask information, such as the inside mask loss (L_{mask}), are not used in this stage, focusing instead on geometric consistency and alignment utility.

3.5. Self-Supervised Loss Functions

The self-supervised training process is guided by a combination of carefully designed loss terms. These losses encourage the network to learn robust, geometrically consistent, and spatially diverse keypoints on the structured templates without requiring manual keypoint annotations. Figure 4 provides a conceptual overview of some key loss components. The specific losses used vary between the two training stages. They are the geometric equivariance loss (L_{equiv}), inside mask loss (L_{mask}), peakiness loss (L_{peak}), repulsion loss ($L_{repulsion}$), and keypoint-driven image reprojection loss (L_{img_reproj}). In the following descriptions, B denotes the batch size, K is the number of predicted keypoints per class, and H_{out}, W_{out} are the height and width of the predicted heatmaps. H_{pred} refers to the predicted heatmaps for the current input image batch (potentially augmented), H_{orig} refers to predictions on the original (untransformed) version of the image batch for the equivariance calculation, P refers to the K keypoint coordinates derived from heatmaps H_{pred} via the spatial softmax (Section 3.3), and M refers to the binary template mask (used only in Stage 1).

3.5.1. Geometric Equivariance Loss (L_{equiv})

This is a primary self-supervisory signal ensuring that keypoint predictions on templates transform consistently with input image transformations applied to those templates. Its objective is to ensure that if an input template image batch (I) is subjected to a geometric transformation (T_θ) (such as a rotation or an affine transformation, specifically excluding horizontal and vertical flips in our setup), resulting in I', the heatmaps predicted from

I' are equivalent to the heatmaps predicted from the original template image batch (I) warped by the inverse transformation ($T_{\theta^{-1}}$). Let H_{trans} be the heatmaps predicted from the transformed image batch (I'). Let $W_{\theta^{-1}}$ be the operation that warps a heatmap grid according to the inverse transformation (θ^{-1}), using bilinear interpolation. The loss ($L_{equiv}(T_\theta)$) for a specific transformation (T_θ) penalizes the L2 norm of the difference between the transformed prediction and the inversely warped original prediction as follows:

$$L_{equiv}(T_\theta) = \frac{1}{B \cdot K \cdot H_{out} \cdot W_{out}} \sum_{b=1}^{B} \sum_{k=1}^{K} \sum_{h=0}^{H_{out}-1} \sum_{w=0}^{W_{out}-1} (H_{trans,b,k,h,w} - W_{\theta^{-1}}(H_{orig})_{b,k,h,w})^2 \quad (4)$$

where b is the batch index, k is the keypoint index, and h, w are the spatial coordinates on the heatmap. In our experiments, this loss is applied for rotation and affine transformations in Stage 1 and for affine transformations only in Stage 2.

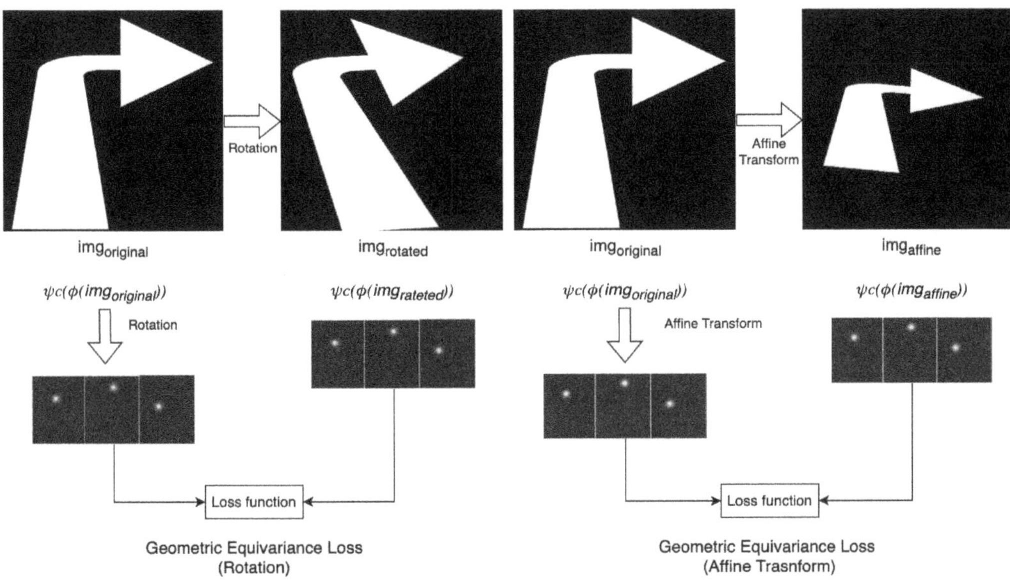

Figure 4. Conceptual overview of some of the self-supervised loss functions, illustrating how the geometric equivariance loss component contributes to learning the desired properties of the predicted keypoints and heatmaps on templates.

3.5.2. Inside Mask Loss (L_{mask})

This loss is used exclusively during Stage 1 (template pre-training), when reliable segmentation masks are available from the synthetic template images. Its objective is to encourage the predicted keypoint heatmap energy to be concentrated within the object boundaries defined by the template's binary mask (M), where $M(p) = 1$ inside and $M(p) = 0$ outside. The mechanism minimizes the heatmap energy located outside the mask by multiplying the predicted heatmaps by the inverse mask $(1 - M)$ and summing the result as follows:

$$L_{mask} = \frac{1}{B \cdot K \cdot H_{out} \cdot W_{out}} \sum_{b=1}^{B} \sum_{k=1}^{K} \sum_{h=0}^{H_{out}-1} \sum_{w=0}^{W_{out}-1} H_{pred,b,k}(h,w) \cdot (1 - M_b(h,w)) \quad (5)$$

where $H_{pred,b,k}(h,w)$ is the predicted heatmap value for batch item b, keypoint k at location (h,w), and $M_b(h,w)$ is the corresponding mask value. Minimizing this sum effectively forces the heatmap values to be close to zero in regions where the template mask is zero, outside the object. This loss is not used in Stage 2, as mask information is not assumed to be available (or relevant) for the fine-tuning objective.

3.5.3. Peakiness Loss (L_{peak})

To encourage sharp, well-localized keypoint heatmaps on the templates with concentrated activations, we utilize the peakiness loss. Its objective is to promote "peaky" heatmaps, where the probability mass is concentrated at a small number of locations, leading to more precise keypoint localization. The mechanism calculates the negative spatial entropy of each heatmap. Minimizing this negative entropy (equivalent to maximizing the peak value and concentrating the distribution) encourages the desired sharpness as follows:

$$L_{peak} = -\frac{1}{B \cdot K} \sum_{b=1}^{B} \sum_{k=1}^{K} \log\left(\max_{h,w}(H_{pred,b,k}(h,w)) + \epsilon \right) \quad (6)$$

where $\max_{h,w}$ denotes the maximum value over the spatial dimensions of the heatmap for batch item b and keypoint k, and ϵ is a low constant (e.g., 10^{-6}) for numerical stability, preventing issues with the logarithm of zero. This loss is used in both Stage 1 and Stage 2.

3.5.4. Repulsion Loss ($L_{repulsion}$)

To prevent different keypoints predicted on the template from collapsing onto the same spatial location and to encourage them to be spatially distinct, we employ the repulsion loss. Its objective is to penalize pairs of keypoints that are predicted to be too close to each other, thus promoting spatial diversity among the learned keypoint locations across the template structure. The mechanism operates on the soft peak locations derived from the predicted heatmaps via the spatial softmax operation (Section 3.3). It calculates an exponential penalty based on the squared pairwise Euclidean distances between the coordinates $P = \{(x_k, y_k)\}_{k=1}^{K}$ for each batch item.

$$L_{repulsion} = \frac{1}{B} \sum_{b=1}^{B} \left(\frac{1}{\binom{K}{2}} \sum_{i=1}^{K} \sum_{j=i+1}^{K} \exp\left(-\frac{||P_{b,i} - P_{b,j}||_2^2}{\sigma^2} \right) \right) \quad (7)$$

where $P_{b,i}$ and $P_{b,j}$ are the predicted 2D coordinates for keypoint i and keypoint j in batch item b, $|| \cdot ||_2^2$ denotes the squared Euclidean distance, $\sigma^2 = 5^2$ is a hyperparameter controlling the repulsion radius (how close points need to be to incur a significant penalty), and $\binom{K}{2}$ normalizes by the number of unique pairs of keypoints. The spatial softmax coordinates ($P_{b,i}$ and $P_{b,j}$) are normalized to the range $[-1, 1]$ based on the heatmap dimensions before calculating the Euclidean distance to make the scale of σ^2 consistent. This loss is used in Stage 1 but not in Stage 2.

3.5.5. Keypoint-Driven Image Reprojection Loss (L_{img_reproj})

This loss is specifically used in Stage 2 to improve the template-to-transformed-template alignment capability of the learned keypoints. Its objective is to encourage the predicted keypoints to be such that an estimated transformation between two template images (a source template and its transformed version), based on these keypoints, accurately warps the source template to match the target-transformed template. The mechanism involves extracting keypoint coordinates from heatmaps predicted for a source template image and a target-transformed template image, assuming a direct kth keypoint correspondence based on the learned class-specific keypoint ordering. An affine transformation (T_{est}) is estimated from the K correspondences ($\{p_{src,k} \leftrightarrow p_{tgt,k}\}_{k=1}^{K}$), using least squares. The source template image (I_{src}) is then warped using this estimated transformation (T_{est}) to produce $I'_{src} = \text{Warp}(I_{src}, T_{est})$. The loss is calculated as the mean-square error between the warped-source template image (I'_{src}) and the target-transformed template image (I_{tgt}) as follows:

$$L_{img\_reproj} = \text{MSE}(I'_{src}, I_{tgt}) = \frac{1}{H_{img} \cdot W_{img}} \sum_{h=0}^{H_{img}-1} \sum_{w=0}^{W_{img}-1} (I'_{src}(h,w) - I_{tgt}(h,w))^2 \quad (8)$$

where H_{img} and W_{img} are the height and width of the images, and the summation is over all the pixel locations ((h,w)). This loss directly pushes the keypoints toward locations that result in accurate image alignment between templates and their transformations. This loss is used in Stage 2 but not in Stage 1.

3.6. The Total Loss

The total loss function used for training is the weighted sum of the applicable loss components. The specific losses included and their weights vary between the two training stages.

For **Stage 1 (Template Pre-training)**, the total loss ($L_{total,S1}$) is a weighted sum of the geometric equivariance loss for rotation (L_{equiv}(rotation)) and affine transformations (L_{equiv}(affine)), the inside mask loss (L_{mask}), the peakiness loss (L_{peak}), and the repulsion loss ($L_{repulsion}$). The weights (λ) control the relative importance of each term and are set as follows: $\lambda_{equiv,rot} = 0.1$, $\lambda_{equiv,aff} = 0.1$, $\lambda_{mask} = 0.3$, $\lambda_{peak} = 0.2$, and $\lambda_{repulsion} = 0.3$.

$$\begin{aligned} L_{total,S1} &= \lambda_{equiv,rot} L_{equiv,rot} + \lambda_{equiv,aff} L_{equiv,aff} \\ &+ \lambda_{mask} L_{mask} + \lambda_{peak} L_{peak} + \lambda_{repulsion} L_{repulsion} \end{aligned} \quad (9)$$

For **Stage 2 (Template Fine-tuning)**, the total loss ($L_{total,S2}$) is the weighted sum of the geometric equivariance loss for affine transformations (L_{equiv}(affine)), the peakiness loss (L_{peak}), and the keypoint-driven image reprojection loss (L_{img_reproj}). The weights (λ') are set as follows: $\lambda'_{equiv,aff} = 0.1$, $\lambda'_{peak} = 0.5$, and $\lambda'_{img\_reproj} = 0.4$.

$$L_{total,S2} = \lambda'_{equiv,aff} L_{equiv,aff} + \lambda'_{peak} L_{peak} + \lambda'_{img\_reproj} L_{img\_reproj} \quad (10)$$

Note that L_{mask} and $L_{repulsion}$ are omitted in Stage 2.

3.7. Evaluation Metrics

Evaluating the performance of a self-supervised keypoint detection method trained and tested on synthetic templates requires metrics that assess the quality of the learned keypoints and their utility for geometric tasks. All the quantitative evaluations in this paper are performed in the designated synthetic template test set described in the section on the synthetic template dataset.

3.7.1. Inside Mask Rate

One metric used to assess the quality and localization of predicted keypoints on templates, particularly in terms of their adherence to the object's structure, is the IMR. This metric is evaluated in the synthetic test set (See the section on the synthetic template dataset). For each image in this set, the calculation is based on the number of predicted keypoints that fall within the ground-truth segmentation mask of the template, divided by the total number of keypoints (K) predicted for that class. The final IMR reported is the average of this ratio across all the images in the synthetic test set.

Let N_{test}^{synth} be the number of images in the synthetic test set, K be the number of predicted keypoints per image, and $p_{i,k}$ be the kth predicted keypoint coordinate for the ith image. Let $M_i(p)$ be an indicator function that is one if point p is inside the ground-truth mask for template image i and zero otherwise. The IMR is calculated as follows:

$$\text{IMR} = \frac{1}{N_{test}^{synth}} \sum_{i=1}^{N_{test}^{synth}} \frac{1}{K} \sum_{k=1}^{K} M_i(p_{i,k}) \tag{11}$$

3.7.2. Keypoint-Matching Comparison

To highlight the advantage of our learned, semantically defined keypoints on templates over traditional feature detectors (like SIFT and ORB) for establishing robust geometric correspondence, we compare their performances in the synthetic template test set. For traditional methods, this involves detecting features on both the source template and its transformed-target version, computing descriptors, matching descriptors (e.g., using nearest neighbor matching with a ratio test for SIFT or the Hamming distance for ORB) and then using RANSAC to estimate an affine transformation from the putative matches and identify inliers. For traditional RANSAC-based methods, M_i is the number of RANSAC inliers found for image pair i. Our method bypasses the matching and RANSAC steps by assuming a direct correspondence between the kth learned keypoint on the source and target templates; however, the number of usable keypoints (M_i) obtained from the model's output can vary per image pair.

The metric used for comparison is the percentage of image pairs with sufficient matches for transformation. For each pair of source and target-transformed template images in the test set, we assess whether the number of successfully localized and usable keypoints (M_i) derived for that pair meets at least the minimum required number (N_{min}) necessary to estimate the geometric transformation (e.g., $N_{min} = 4$ for affine transformations). For a given GeoTemplateKPNet configuration (Backbone, K), M_i is the number of successfully localized and usable keypoints derived from the model's output for pair i.

Let N_{test}^{synth} be the total number of image pairs in the synthetic test set. For each image pair $i \in \{1, \ldots, N_{test}^{synth}\}$, let M_i be the number of sufficient matches (i.e., successfully localized and usable keypoints for GeoTemplateKPNet and RANSAC inliers for traditional methods) found using a given method. Let N_{min} be the minimum required number of matches (e.g., $N_{min} \in \{3, 4, 5\}$). The percentage of image pairs with sufficient matches is calculated as follows:

$$\text{Success Rate} = \frac{1}{N_{test}^{synth}} \sum_{i=1}^{N_{test}^{synth}} S(M_i, N_{min}) \times 100\% \tag{12}$$

where $S(M_i, N_{min})$ is an indicator function defined as

$$S(M_i, N_{min}) = \begin{cases} 1 & \text{if } M_i \geq N_{min} \\ 0 & \text{if } M_i < N_{min} \end{cases}$$

A pair is considered as successful if the number of matches found (M_i) is greater than or equal to the minimum requirement (N_{min}). This metric directly demonstrates the reliability of different approaches in providing the foundational correspondences needed for alignment on template data. For GeoTemplateKPNet configurations (Backbone, K), the single 'rate' value reported in the results corresponds to the success rate where $M_i \geq K$.

3.7.3. Alignment Reconstruction Error

A second key evaluation metric assesses the ability of the learned keypoints to facilitate accurate geometric alignment between a template and its transformed version. We refer to this as the Mean-Square Error (MSE) or ARE. This metric quantifies the pixel-wise difference between a target-transformed template image and a warped-source template image after estimating the affine transformation, using predicted keypoint correspondences. For our GeoTemplateKPNet method, the keypoint correspondences are established by directly assuming that the kth keypoint predicted in the source template image corresponds to the kth keypoint predicted in the target-transformed template image, based on their channel indices and the learned class-specific keypoint ordering. With these K presumed correspondences, an affine transformation is estimated using least squares (e.g., via 'cv2.getAffineTransform' from the OpenCV library [33]). The source template image is then warped using this estimated transform. The ARE is calculated as the mean-square error between the warped-source template image and the target-transformed template image, restricted to the area within the transformed ground-truth mask of the source template. This ensures that the error calculation focuses on the aligned template region. The ground-truth mask of the source template is warped using the estimated affine transformation to define the evaluation area on the target-transformed template image.

Let N_{test}^{synth} be the number of pairs in the synthetic test set. For the ith test pair (source template $I_{i,src}$ and target-transformed template $I_{i,tgt}$), let $P_{i,src}$ and $P_{i,tgt}$ be the K predicted keypoints in the source and target images, respectively. Let $T_{est,i}$ be the estimated affine transformation from $P_{i,src} \leftrightarrow P_{i,tgt}$ correspondences. Let $M_{i,src}$ be the ground-truth mask for the source template and Ω_i be the set of pixel locations within the warped mask area in the target image, $\Omega_i = \{(h,w) \mid \text{Warp}(M_{i,src}, T_{est,i})(h,w) = 1\}$. Let $I'_{i,src}$ be the warped-source template image ($I'_{i,src} = \text{Warp}(I_{i,src}, T_{est,i})$). Then, the ARE is calculated as follows:

$$\text{ARE} = \frac{1}{N_{test}^{synth}} \sum_{i=1}^{N_{test}^{synth}} \frac{1}{|\Omega_i|} \sum_{(h,w)\in\Omega_i} (I'_{i,src}(h,w) - I_{i,tgt}(h,w))^2 \quad (13)$$

where $|\Omega_i|$ denotes the number of pixels in the set Ω_i. This metric directly quantifies the accuracy of the template-to-transformed-template alignment enabled by the learned keypoints.

4. Results

This section presents the experimental results evaluating the performance of the proposed GeoTemplateKPNet framework based on the metrics defined in Section 3.7. We analyze the quantitative results across various evaluations and provide qualitative examples to illustrate the behavior of our method.

4.1. Experimental Setup

The experiments were conducted on a system equipped with an Intel Core i9-12900F processor and an NVIDIA GeForce RTX 3090 graphics card. The implementation was carried out using the following software environment: Python 3.10, PyTorch 2.4.1, torchvision 0.19.1, OpenCV 4.5, and Albumentations 2.0.7. Training utilized the Adam optimizer with the specific hyperparameters detailed in Section 3.4. The model evaluation was performed in the dedicated test sets described in Section 3.1.

4.2. Keypoint-Matching Comparison vs. SIFT/ORB

This evaluation compares the abilities of traditional feature-based methods (SIFT and ORB) and our proposed GeoTemplateKPNet to consistently provide a sufficient number of correspondences required for geometric alignment in the synthetic template test set. The metric used is the percentage of image pairs with sufficient matches for transformation, as defined in Section 3.7.2. Table 2 presents the overall average success rates across all the template classes for different minimum required inlier (N_{min}) thresholds.

Table 2. Overall average percentages of image pairs with sufficient matches for transformation in the synthetic template test set.

Method	Configuration	Success Rate (%)
SIFT + RANSAC	$N_{min} = 3$	81.04
SIFT + RANSAC	$N_{min} = 4$	81.04
SIFT + RANSAC	$N_{min} = 5$	77.48
ORB + RANSAC	$N_{min} = 3$	91.76
ORB + RANSAC	$N_{min} = 4$	91.76
ORB + RANSAC	$N_{min} = 5$	35.64
GeoTemplateKPNet	ResNet-50, K = 3	63.36
GeoTemplateKPNet	ResNet-50, K = 4	21.56
GeoTemplateKPNet	ResNet-50, K = 5	17.28
GeoTemplateKPNet	VGG-16, K = 3	60.00
GeoTemplateKPNet	VGG-16, K = 4	68.24
GeoTemplateKPNet	VGG-16, K = 5	36.84

Table 2 presents the overall average success rates in consistently providing sufficient matches in the synthetic template dataset. For traditional methods, ORB+RANSAC achieves high success rates at lower N_{min} thresholds (3 and 4), while SIFT+RANSAC performs better at $N_{min} = 5$. Our GeoTemplateKPNet method shows varying success rates, depending on the configuration. GeoTemplateKPNet (ResNet-50, K = 3) achieves a 63.36% rate in providing at least three usable keypoints, while GeoTemplateKPNet (VGG-16, K = 4) shows the highest rate (68.24%) among our configurations for providing at least four usable keypoints. VGG-16 with K = 5 has the highest rate (36.84%) for providing at least five usable keypoints.

Comparing GeoTemplateKPNet configurations to those of traditional methods at comparable thresholds, SIFT and ORB generally show higher success rates for $N_{min} = 3$ and 4 than our method does in providing at least that many usable keypoints. However, this metric primarily indicates the model's ability to produce the minimum count of keypoints across the dataset consistently. It does not directly reflect the quality of the resulting alignment or the model's ability to handle various data transformations, which are evaluated using the ARE and qualitative results in subsequent sections. As observed experimentally, ORB+RANSAC often produces visually poor and inaccurate transformations, despite reporting a sufficient number of inliers, suggesting that the matches deemed as inliers are not geometrically accurate, which supports higher ARE values. SIFT+RANSAC, although better than ORB in terms of alignment quality (when successful), still struggles to consistently provide sufficient matches compared to ORB or the number of heatmaps predicted using our model.

4.2.1. Evaluation of the IMR

The IMR metric assesses the quality of the learned keypoint localization by measuring the percentage of the predicted keypoints that fall within the ground-truth segmentation mask of the template in the synthetic test set, as defined in Section 3.7.1. A higher IMR indicates better adherence of the predicted keypoints to the object's shape. Table 3 presents the overall average IMRs across all the template classes for different GeoTemplateKPNet configurations.

Table 3. Overall average IMRs in the synthetic test set for different GeoTemplateKPNet configurations.

Backbone	K	Average IMR (%)
ResNet-50	3	35.49
ResNet-50	4	29.99
ResNet-50	5	30.98
VGG-16	3	30.38
VGG-16	4	28.55
VGG-16	5	36.84

Table 3 shows the overall average IMRs achieved by GeoTemplateKPNet with different backbones and numbers of keypoints (K). For the ResNet-50 backbone, the IMR is 35.49% with K = 3, 29.99% with K = 4, and 30.98% with K = 5. For the VGG-16 backbone, the IMR is 30.38% with K = 3, 28.55% with K = 4, and 36.84% with K = 5. These overall results indicate that the IMR varies with both K and the backbone type, with VGG-16 at K = 5 achieving the highest overall IMR.

To further analyze the performance and understand the reasons behind the overall IMR values, we examine the IMR broken down by individual template classes. Table 4 presents the per-class IMRs for the tested configurations.

Table 4. Per-class IMRs in the synthetic test set for different GeoTemplateKPNet configurations.

Backbone	K	Class 0 (%)	Class 1 (%)	Class 2 (%)	Class 3 (%)	Class 4 (%)
ResNet-50	3	50.33	35.60	7.14	23.19	30.67
ResNet-50	4	28.17	52.50	12.49	32.62	39.77
ResNet-50	5	33.27	32.93	14.02	42.50	41.93
VGG-16	3	53.40	33.07	8.90	22.94	29.40
VGG-16	4	41.73	50.27	28.22	31.90	29.14
VGG-16	5	52.80	43.07	14.81	46.27	33.33

Table 4 highlights the significant variations in the IMR across the different template classes for both backbones and K values. Classes 0 and 1 show relatively high IMR values for most configurations. Class 2 exhibits a consistently low IMR across the configurations, although it improves slightly with K = 4 and K = 5 compared to K = 3. Classes 3 and 4 exhibit varying performances depending on K and the backbone, with some configurations (e.g., ResNet-50 with K = 4/5 and VGG-16 with K = 5) achieving notable improvements in the IMR compared to those with K = 3. This per-class analysis reveals that the model's ability to localize keypoints within the template mask is highly dependent on the specific geometry and the chosen configuration.

4.2.2. Evaluation of the ARE

The ARE, measured as the Mean-Square Error (MSE), quantifies the accuracy of the estimated geometric transformation by comparing a warped-source template image to the target-transformed template image within the object's masked area, as defined in Section 3.7.3. A lower ARE value indicates a more accurate alignment. Table 5 presents the overall average AREs and their standard deviations across all the template classes for different GeoTemplateKPNet configurations, as well as for traditional SIFT+RANSAC and ORB+RANSAC methods, focusing on cases where at least $N_{min} = 3$ matches were found.

Table 5. Overall average AREs in the synthetic test set for different methods.

Method	Backbone	K	Average ARE (%)	Std. Dev. ARE
SIFT + RANSAC ($N_{min} = 3$)	N/A	N/A	0.207	0.193
ORB + RANSAC ($N_{min} = 3$)	N/A	N/A	0.387	0.253
GeoTemplateKPNet	ResNet-50	3	0.139	0.124
GeoTemplateKPNet	ResNet-50	4	0.530	0.239
GeoTemplateKPNet	ResNet-50	5	0.354	0.275
GeoTemplateKPNet	VGG-16	3	0.088	0.058
GeoTemplateKPNet	VGG-16	4	0.298	0.133
GeoTemplateKPNet	VGG-16	5	0.501	0.300

Table 5 presents the overall average AREs and standard deviations for different methods and configurations. Comparing GeoTemplateKPNet with traditional methods in cases where at least $N_{min} = 3$ matches were available for SIFT/ORB, we observe that GeoTemplateKPNet with VGG-16 and K = 3 achieves the lowest average ARE (0.0889), indicating the most accurate overall alignment among tested configurations and traditional methods. GeoTemplateKPNet with ResNet-50 and K = 3 (0.1392) is also competitive with or better than SIFT+RANSAC (0.207) and significantly better than ORB+RANSAC (0.387) at $N_{min} = 3$. For K = 4 and K = 5, the overall average AREs for GeoTemplateKPNet generally increase compared to those for K = 3, with ResNet-50 with K = 4 showing a particularly high ARE of 0.5300. This supports the observation that K = 3 provides the most suitable balance for the overall alignment accuracy. ResNet-50 generally achieves a lower overall average ARE compared to that for VGG-16 with K = 3 but is worse for K = 4 and similar for K = 5. The overall ARE for VGG-16 with K = 5 is 0.501. These overall results suggest that our self-supervised approach can achieve more accurate geometric alignment on template data compared to traditional feature-based methods, particularly with certain configurations, when sufficient matches are available.

Beyond merely establishing correspondences, the ARE serves as a critical indicator of the geometric precision achieved using each method. The consistently lower ARE values exhibited by GeoTemplateKPNet across various backbone and K configurations, particularly the optimal VGG-16 with K = 3, underscore a key strength: Its self-supervised training successfully guides the model to learn keypoints that are not only localizable but also inherently stable and geometrically reliable for estimating accurate transformations. This contrasts sharply with traditional feature-based methods, where even a high count of matches, as observed with ORB+RANSAC, does not consistently translate to accurate geometric alignments, often leading to visually unreliable reconstructions due to imprecise or inconsistent feature localization. This robust geometric understanding by GeoTemplateKPNet is particularly vital for structured, feature-poor templates, where subtle shifts in keypoint prediction can significantly impact the transformation accuracy.

To provide a more detailed understanding of the alignment performance, particularly for template geometries where the model might struggle or excel, we also examine the AREs broken down by individual template classes for each backbone. Table 6 presents the per-class AREs for the ResNet-50 backbone, and Table 7 presents the results for the VGG-16 backbone.

Table 6. Per-class AREs in the synthetic test set for GeoTemplateKPNet with the ResNet-50 backbone.

K	Class 0	Class 1	Class 2	Class 3	Class 4
3	0.094	0.058	NaN	0.150	0.309
4	0.569	NaN	0.215	NaN	NaN
5	NaN	NaN	0.3058	NaN	NaN

Table 7. Per-class AREs in the synthetic test set for GeoTemplateKPNet with the VGG-16 backbone.

K	Class 0	Class 1	Class 2	Class 3	Class 4
3	0.108	0.070	0.112	0.160	0.311
4	0.303	0.270	NaN	0.364	NaN
5	0.267	0.604	NaN	NaN	0.501

Tables 6 and 7 show the per-class average AREs broken down for the ResNet-50 and VGG-16 backbones, respectively. It is important to note that the "NaN" (Not a Number) entries in the ARE tables signify instances where the model failed to predict a sufficient number of geometrically distinct keypoints (typically a minimum of three non-collinear points required for affine transformation estimation) to compute a transformation matrix reliably. This situation is particularly evident for Class 2 (straight arrow) templates, as also reflected in its lower success rates in the keypoint-matching comparison.

Consistent with the overall results, compared to ResNet-50 with K = 3, VGG-16 with K = 3 generally shows lower ARE values across the classes where alignment is possible, particularly for Classes 0, 1, and 2. Classes 0 and 1 consistently exhibit lower AREs for both backbones at K = 3, indicating accurate alignment for these shapes. Class 2 remains challenging, with NaN AREs for ResNet-50 with K = 3 and a calculated ARE of 0.112 for VGG-16 with K = 3, despite a low IMR. This suggests that VGG-16 is sometimes able to find enough points for alignment, even if they are close to or outside the mask. Class 4 consistently shows higher ARE values. For K = 4 and K = 5, the per-class ARE data become much more sparse, with many NaN values, indicating that alignment could not be performed. When calculated, ARE values for K = 4 and K = 5 can be both higher and lower than those for K = 3, depending on the class, supporting the notion that K = 3 likely provides the best balance for the overall accuracy and robustness across the classes. The data for the VGG-16 with K = 5 per-class AREs are missing.

4.2.3. Qualitative Results

This subsection presents selected visual examples to qualitatively illustrate the alignment performance of our proposed GeoTemplateKPNet method (focusing on the K = 3 configuration for both backbones) and to provide a direct visual comparison with traditional feature-based methods (SIFT+RANSAC and ORB+RANSAC) in the synthetic template test set. These examples complement the quantitative metrics by showing the visual accuracy of the resulting geometric alignments and the typical behavior of each method.

Figure 5 presents a visual comparison of the alignment results obtained from GeoTemplateKPNet (ResNet-50, K = 3), GeoTemplateKPNet (VGG-16, K = 3), SIFT+RANSAC, and ORB+RANSAC for several example image pairs from the test set. Each row in the figure corresponds to a single test example, showing the source template, the target-transformed template, and the reconstructed template obtained by warping the source template using the transformation estimated using each method.

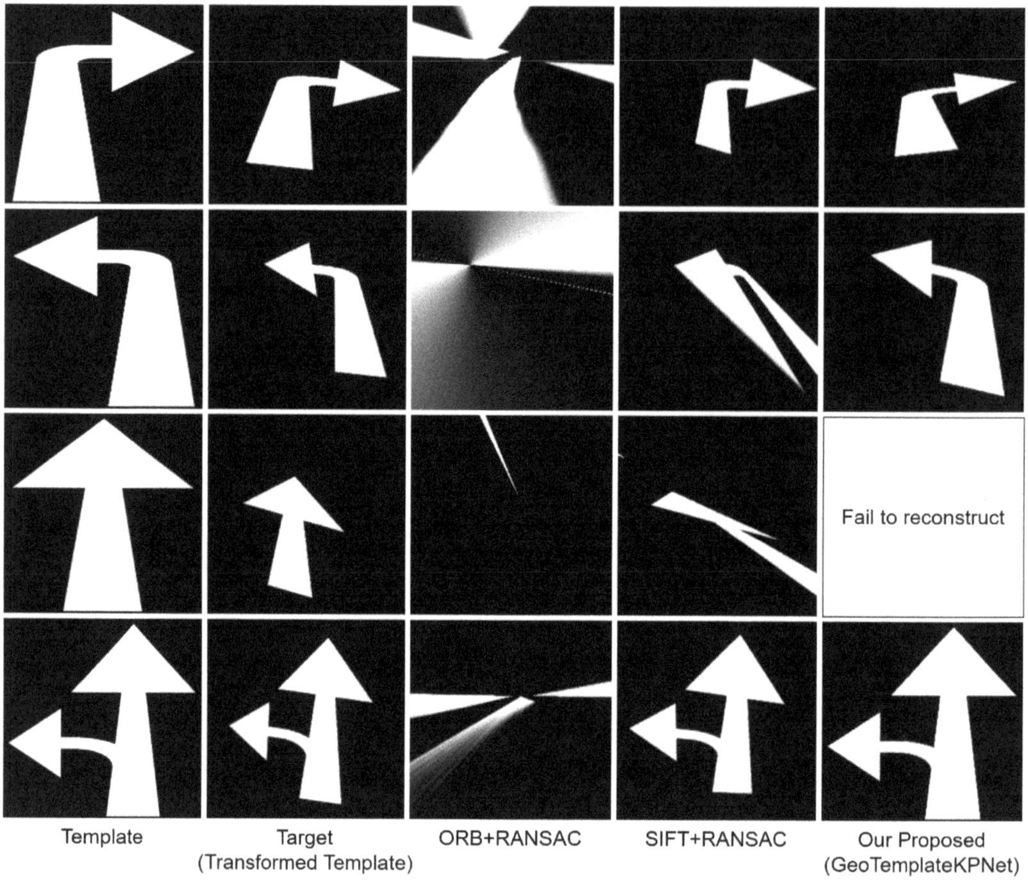

Figure 5. Qualitative comparison of template-to-transformed-template alignment results. Each row shows the source template, the target-transformed template, and the reconstructed template after alignment using ORB+RANSAC, SIFT+RANSAC, and GeoTemplateKPNet (ResNet-50, K = 3), highlighting the differences in the reconstruction accuracies and method reliabilities.

The visual comparisons in Figure 5 highlight the differences in alignment performances. GeoTemplateKPNet, when successfully predicting keypoints (which vary by class and configuration, as discussed in the quantitative results), produces accurately reconstructed templates that closely resemble the original, demonstrating the geometric reliability of the learned keypoints for alignments. While SIFT+RANSAC can also achieve good visual alignment when it finds sufficient reliable matches, it often struggles to consistently provide enough correspondences across the dataset (as shown in Table 2). ORB+RANSAC, despite sometimes reporting a high count of sufficient matches (Table 2), frequently results in visually poor and unrecognizable reconstructed templates, indicating that the matches deemed as inliers by RANSAC are not geometrically accurate for this type of template data (supporting the higher ARE values in Table 5). These visual examples reinforce the quantitative findings, demonstrating that compared to traditional feature-based methods, our self-supervised approach learns keypoints that enable more consistent and accurate alignment on template data.

4.2.4. Ablation Studies

We conducted ablation studies to analyze the impacts of the key hyperparameters and design choices on the overall performance of GeoTemplateKPNet. The effect of the backbone architecture (ResNet-50 vs. VGG-16) is observable by comparing the results presented for these different backbones in Tables 2, 3, and 5. In this subsection, we specifically investigate the effect of varying the number of keypoints (K) predicted per class and discuss class-specific performance trends.

4.2.5. Effect of the Number of Keypoints (K) and Class-Specific Performances

The number of keypoints (K) is a critical hyperparameter that determines the granularity of the geometric representation learned by the model. We evaluated the impact of using different values for K ($K \in \{3,4,5\}$) on the key performance metrics: the IMR and ARE. The overall average results for different K values and backbones are presented in Table 3 (the overall IMR) and Table 5 (the overall ARE).

Table 3 shows that the overall average IMR increases as K increases from 3 to 4, for both the ResNet-50 and VGG-16 backbones, but then drops slightly for K = 5 with ResNet-50 and increases further with VGG-16. This suggests that a higher number of keypoints enables the model to capture the template structure better and localize the keypoints within its mask; however, the optimal K value may depend on the backbone.

Similarly, Table 5 shows the impact of K on the overall average ARE. For both backbones, the average ARE appears to increase significantly as K increases from 3 to 4 and then decreases somewhat for K = 5 (with ResNet-50) or increases further (with VGG-16, data are missing). This supports the observation that while increasing K might improve the structural coverage (IMR), it can negatively impact the overall alignment accuracy (ARE). Compared to higher K values, K = 3 provides the best overall balance for accurate alignment, despite potentially lower IMRs for some classes.

The per-class IMR and ARE tables (Tables 4, 6, and 7) provide a more detailed view, highlighting significant variations in performances across different template classes and configurations. Consistent with the overall trends, increasing K to 4 and 5 appears to benefit the IMR for classes 3 and 4 with both backbones. However, for the ARE, while K = 3 shows consistent performance for most classes where alignment is possible, K = 4 and K = 5 show much sparser data (more NaNs) and higher ARE values (when calculated), indicating decreased reliability in achieving successful alignment with higher K values, despite potential IMR improvements.

The Class 2 (straight arrow) template geometry presents a particular challenge. While the model is often successful in detecting keypoints corresponding to the prominent top and bottom parts of the arrow, capturing sufficient additional distinct keypoints (i.e., the 3rd, 4th, and 5th keypoints) proves to be difficult. If these additional keypoints are predicted too close to the initial two, attempting alignment based on these nearly collinear points can lead to a degenerate transformation, resulting in a messed up and unrecognizable reconstructed template (e.g., three keypoints forming a degenerate rectangle that looks like a straight line), despite the model successfully identifying the basic structure's top and bottom. This inherent geometric challenge contributes to the low IMRs and high/NaN AREs observed for Class 2, particularly with configurations like ResNet-50 with K = 3, where the ARE is NaN. Addressing the specific difficulty of reliably localizing more than two distinct keypoints for simple, elongated structures, such as that in Class 2, is a focus for future work.

5. Discussion

This paper presents GeoTemplateKPNet, a novel self-supervised deep-learning framework that leverages the strengths of CNNs for learning robust, geometrically consistent keypoints specifically tailored for structured template images, as demonstrated on road-marking templates. The experimental evaluation, conducted in a synthetic template test set with applied affine transformations, aimed to demonstrate the potential of this approach to overcome the limitations of traditional methods on feature-poor template data and serve as a foundational step toward template-to-real-world instance alignment.

The quantitative results from the keypoint-matching comparison (Section 4.2), ARE (Section 4.2.2), and IMR (Section 4.2.1), supported by the qualitative results (Section 4.2.3), provide insights into the performance of GeoTemplateKPNet compared to those of traditional feature-based methods and the impacts of different configurations.

The keypoint-matching comparison (Section 4.2) revealed that while traditional methods, like SIFT+RANSAC and ORB+RANSAC, can achieve high success rates in finding the minimum count of matches, particularly ORB at lower N_{min} thresholds, they still fail to consistently provide sufficient correspondences across all the test cases, especially at higher N_{min} values for SIFT. However, a crucial finding highlighted by the ARE analysis (Section 4.2.2) and visually demonstrated in the qualitative results (Section 4.2.3) is that a high match count from traditional methods does not necessarily guarantee geometric accuracy. ORB+RANSAC, despite its relatively high success rate in finding matches, often yields visually inaccurate and unreliable alignments on the template data, as evidenced by its higher ARE values compared to those of SIFT and GeoTemplateKPNet and the poor visual reconstruction quality. SIFT+RANSAC tends to produce better visual alignment when it finds sufficient matches, but its ability to consistently find enough reliable matches is limited compared to those of ORB or the number of heatmaps predicted using our model.

Our proposed GeoTemplateKPNet, by learning to predict a fixed set of keypoints (varying by K), consistently provides a defined number of correspondences for alignment in the template test set when it successfully localizes keypoints. More importantly, the ARE results (Section 4.2.2) demonstrate that when GeoTemplateKPNet successfully predicts keypoints, the resulting template-to-transformed-template alignment is generally more accurate than that achieved using traditional methods. As shown in Table 5, the GeoTemplateKPNet configurations, particularly VGG-16 with K = 3, achieve the lowest overall average AREs, indicating superior alignment accuracy compared to those of both SIFT+RANSAC and ORB+RANSAC. This indicates that the self-supervised learning process effectively guides the model to learn keypoints that are not only localizable but also geometrically reliable for estimating accurate transformations on template structures.

The IMR results (Section 4.2.1) demonstrate that the learned keypoints adhere to the template boundaries, with the adherence generally varying with the K values and backbones. The per-class breakdowns of IMRs and AREs (Tables 4, 6, and 7) highlight significant performance variations across the different template geometries and configurations. Classes with simpler, more prominent features (like Classes 0 and 1) tend to have higher IMRs and lower AREs, indicating more successful keypoint localization and accurate alignment.

The ablation studies (Section 4.2.5) on the effect of K on the performance further demonstrate that the number of keypoints influences the performance. While increasing K might improve the IMR for some classes, such as Classes 3 and 4, which benefit from higher K values, the overall ARE generally increases with higher K values, supporting the observation that K = 3 often provides the most suitable balance for the overall alignment accuracy. However, the studies also underscore a key limitation: the inherent difficulty with certain template geometries, most notably Class 2 (straight arrow). As discussed in

Section 4.2.5, the challenge lies in reliably localizing more than two distinct keypoints for simple elongated structures, which impacts both the IMR (low) and the ability to perform accurate alignment (high/NaN ARE), potentially leading to degenerate transformations.

The failure to reconstruct the straight arrow shown in Figure 5 directly illustrates this challenge. Our model struggled to extract distinct keypoints for this geometrically simple and elongated shape, often resulting in keypoints clustering into two main groups (e.g., one at the center and another near the middle bottom of the arrow). The instability and near-collinearity of these clustered keypoints frequently lead to an unstable or degenerate transformation matrix, causing visually inaccurate alignment or "NaN" ARE values. This specific challenge, particularly with certain template geometries, and the need for improved loss functions or strategies to ensure better keypoint distribution, are important areas for our future research.

While this paper demonstrates the potential of GeoTemplateKPNet to learn robust keypoints and perform accurate geometric analysis on synthetic template data, a significant limitation is that the experimental evaluation is limited to synthetic templates. The domain gap between clean synthetic templates and degraded real-world images, including variations in lighting, wear, and background clutter, presents a substantial challenge for aligning templates with real-world instances. The initial attempts to fine-tune the model directly on real-world data, without the aid of instance masks, proved to be difficult. The learned keypoints struggled to reliably stay within the object's boundaries in the absence of the L_{mask} constraint and in the presence of complex real-world noise.

Future Work

It is important to acknowledge that the current experimental setup does not include direct comparisons with state-of-the-art deep keypoint detection and alignment models. This is primarily because existing general-purpose deep models, often trained on diverse natural images with explicit keypoint annotations, cannot be directly applied to our specific problem. Defining universally consistent and semantically meaningful ground-truth keypoints for all road-marking types is an inherently challenging and often undefined task, which is precisely why our approach leverages self-supervision on synthetic data. Therefore, the focus has been on demonstrating a self-supervised solution that learns geometrically reliable keypoints on feature-poor templates, where traditional methods fail—a unique contribution in itself.

The primary direction for future work is to address the domain gap to achieve robust template-to-real-world instance alignment. This is a critical next step for our self-supervised approach, as the unconstrained nature of real images—including complex backgrounds, varied lighting, shadows, and occlusions—presents significant challenges for our current self-supervision setup. Factors such as background information included in image transformations can destabilize loss functions (e.g., the image reprojection loss), hindering the stable learning of keypoints. Figure 6 illustrates the differences among the template, transformed template, real-world image [34], and transformed real-world image, highlighting the challenge of real-world data, which include the environment, nearby signs/objects, and backgrounds.

To tackle this, future work will involve exploring advanced domain adaptation techniques. These include utilizing GANs [27] to create synthetic templates that more closely resemble real-world degraded instances, thereby generating a synthetic dataset with a distribution closer to that of the target domain for more effective fine-tuning, or using methods such as CycleGAN [35] to translate synthetic templates to resemble real-world conditions or vice versa, potentially enabling more stable self-supervision and mask estimation in the real domain. While crucial, the extensive experimentation and methodical development required for this work fall outside the scope of the present work.

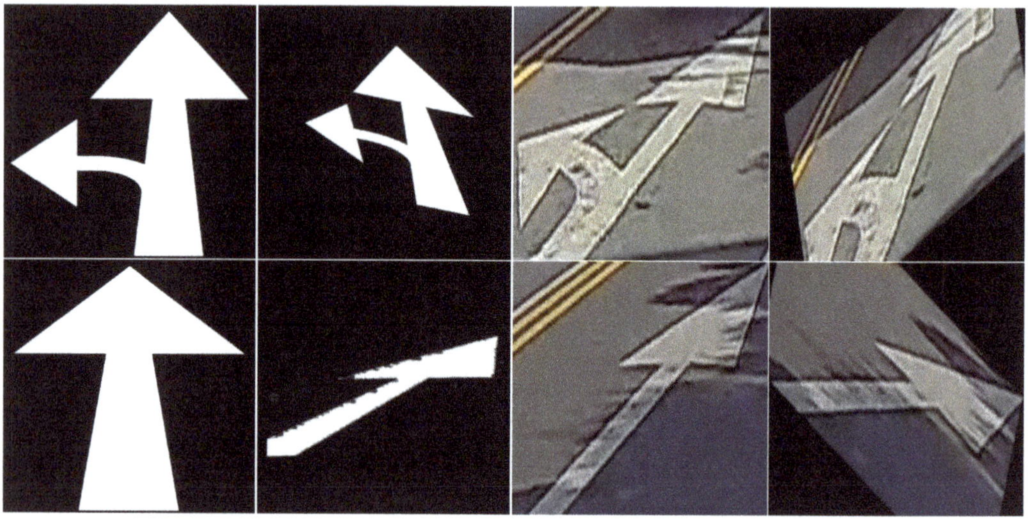

Figure 6. Examples of the (**a**) template, (**b**) transformed template, (**c**) real-world data, and (**d**) transformed real-world data.

Future research directions include extending the framework to encompass a broader range of road-marking types beyond arrow-based templates. This involves investigating its applicability to other common geometric shapes, such as zebra-line crossings, pedestrian crossings, and numerical or textual marking signs. These new shapes present unique challenges, including varying complexities in their geometric structures, different requirements for keypoint distribution, and the need for the robust handling of their canonical forms under diverse transformations. Exploring these additional geometries will further validate the generalizability and robustness of our self-supervised keypoint-learning approach for geometric analysis in real-world intelligent automation and infrastructure-monitoring applications. While not the immediate focus for current offline maintenance processes, evaluating the real-time performance of the proposed method will also be crucial for future real-world deployments, particularly once robust template-to-instance alignment is achieved.

Furthermore, a more in-depth analysis of the individual contribution and optimal weighting of each loss term, including the impacts of hyperparameters, such as σ^2 in $L_{repulsion}$, is warranted. The preliminary findings from our experiments, which involved grid searching for hyperparameter tuning, indicate that each loss function is necessary for the model's convergence; for instance, setting all the λ weights equally leads to non-convergence. Specifically, for the repulsion loss, setting its weight $((\lambda_{repulsion}))$ at lower than 0.3 resulted in keypoints clustering rather than separating effectively, especially for higher K values (e.g., K = 4 and 5), where keypoints tended to converge to two main groups, with subsequent keypoints still appearing close to one of these groups. Therefore, future work will include a comprehensive ablation study to explore these effects further and develop more robust loss functions or strategies for improved keypoint distribution in such challenging scenarios.

6. Conclusions

Geometric shape alignment, while seemingly a straightforward task, presents significant challenges in practice due to factors that hinder reliable feature matching and the absence of standard keypoint definitions for many geometric structures. Achieving robust alignment is crucial for numerous applications, including automated labeling and condition assessment. This paper addresses the foundational aspect of this problem by proposing GeoTemplateKPNet. This novel framework leverages self-supervised learning to automatically learn meaningful keypoints directly from geometric shapes, specifically road-marking templates.

Our work demonstrates that it is indeed possible to train a model to predict geometrically consistent and meaningful keypoints on structured templates, using a carefully designed self-supervised approach. This involved overcoming key challenges, such as preventing the model from finding trivial solutions, like predicting keypoints at the image center, through the use of balanced and targeted loss functions.

The experimental results in a synthetic template test set demonstrate that the learned keypoints enable accurate template-to-transformed-template alignment, outperforming traditional feature-based methods, such as ORB and SIFT, in this task, particularly in achieving lower alignment errors when sufficient correspondences are available. While the proposed method demonstrates the potential of self-supervised keypoint learning for templates, the evaluation also revealed variations in the performance across different template geometries, with the model succeeding in some classes while struggling in others. The multi-head architecture, however, offers the flexibility to combine specialized heads trained for individual classes, thereby optimizing the overall performance in practical applications.

This research establishes a crucial step toward developing robust template-to-real-world instance alignment capabilities. By demonstrating the feasibility of learning reliable keypoints on template structures without manual supervision, our work lays the groundwork for addressing the more complex challenges posed by real-world variations and domain gaps in future research.

Author Contributions: Conceptualization, C.S.-r.-p.; Methodology, C.S.-r.-p. and R.-C.C.; Validation, C.S.-r.-p.; Formal analysis, R.-C.C.; Data curation, C.S.-r.-p.; Writing–original draft, C.S.-r.-p.; Writing–review and editing, R.-C.C.; Supervision, R.-C.C. All authors have read and agreed to the published version of the manuscript.

Funding: This paper is supported by the National Science and Technology Council, Taiwan, Grants No. NSTC-112-2221-E-324-003-MY3 and NSTC-112-2221-E-324 -011-MY2.

Data Availability Statement: Data is contained within the article.

Conflicts of Interest: The authors declare no conflicts of interest.

References

1. Thrun, S.; Burgard, W.; Fox, D. *Probabilistic Robotics*; MIT Press: Cambridge, MA, USA, 2005.
2. Traffic, C. *Manual on Uniform Traffic Control Devices*; US Department of Transportation, Federal Highway Administation: Washington, DC, USA, 2009.
3. Lowe, D.G. Object recognition from local scale-invariant features. In Proceedings of the Seventh IEEE International Conference on Computer Vision, Kerkyra, Greece, 20–27 September 1999; Voluem 2, pp. 1150–1157.
4. Rublee, E.; Rabaud, V.; Konolige, K.; Bradski, G. ORB: An efficient alternative to SIFT or SURF. In Proceedings of the 2011 International Conference on Computer Vision, Barcelona, Spain, 6–13 November 2011; pp. 2564–2571.
5. Derpanis, K.G. Overview of the RANSAC Algorithm. *Image Rochester NY* **2010**, *4*, 2–3.
6. Li, X.; Xie, Z.; Deng, X.; Wu, Y.; Pi, Y. Traffic sign detection based on improved faster R-CNN for autonomous driving. *J. Supercomput.* **2022**, *78*, 7982–8002. [CrossRef]

7. Song, L.; Zhao, F.; Han, J.; Li, S.; Hu, J. Road marking detection from UAV perspective based on improved YOLOv3. In Proceedings of the International Conference on Image, Signal Processing, and Pattern Recognition (ISPP 2024), SPIE, Guangzhou, China, 1–3 March 2024; Volume 13180, pp. 965–974.
8. Chen, R.C.; Dewi, C.; Zhuang, Y.C.; Chen, J.K. Contrast limited adaptive histogram equalization for recognizing road marking at night based on YOLO models. *IEEE Access* **2023**, *11*, 92926–92942. [CrossRef]
9. Xu, S.; Wang, J.; Wu, P.; Shou, W.; Wang, X.; Chen, M. Vision-based pavement marking detection and condition assessment—A case study. *Appl. Sci.* **2021**, *11*, 3152. [CrossRef]
10. Riid, A.; Louk, R.; Pihlak, R.; Tepljakov, A.; Vassiljeva, K. Pavement distress detection with deep learning using the orthoframes acquired by a mobile mapping system. *Appl. Sci.* **2019**, *9*, 4829. [CrossRef]
11. Bay, H.; Ess, A.; Tuytelaars, T.; Van Gool, L. Speeded-up robust features (SURF). *Comput. Vis. Image Underst.* **2008**, *110*, 346–359. [CrossRef]
12. Brunelli, R. *Template Matching Techniques in Computer Vision: Theory and Practice*; John Wiley & Sons: Hoboken, NJ, USA, 2009.
13. Jaderberg, M.; Simonyan, K.; Zisserman, A.; Kavukcuoglu, K. Spatial transformer networks. *Adv. Neural Inf. Process. Syst.* **2015**, *28*, 2017–2025.
14. DeTone, D.; Malisiewicz, T.; Rabinovich, A. Superpoint: Self-supervised interest point detection and description. In Proceedings of the IEEE Conference on Computer Vision and Pattern Recognition Workshops, Salt Lake City, UT, USA, 18–22 June 2018; pp. 224–236.
15. Rocco, I.; Arandjelović, R.; Sivic, J. End-to-end weakly-supervised semantic alignment. In Proceedings of the IEEE Conference on Computer Vision and Pattern Recognition, Salt Lake City, UT, USA, 18–22 June 2018; pp. 6917–6925.
16. Li, Z.; Liu, F.; Yang, W.; Peng, S.; Zhou, J. A Survey of Convolutional Neural Networks: Analysis, Applications, and Prospects. *IEEE Trans. Neural Netw. Learn. Syst.* **2022**, *33*, 6999–7019. [CrossRef] [PubMed]
17. Ronneberger, O.; Fischer, P.; Brox, T. U-net: Convolutional networks for biomedical image segmentation. In Proceedings of the Medical image computing and computer-assisted intervention–MICCAI 2015: 18th International Conference, Munich, Germany, 5–9 October 2015; Springer: Berlin/Heidelberg, Germany, 2015; pp. 234–241.
18. Chen, S.; Zhang, Y.; Liao, B.; Xie, J.; Cheng, T.; Sui, W.; Zhang, Q.; Liu, W.; Huang, C.; Wang, X. VMA: Divide-and-Conquer Vectorized Map Annotation System for Large-Scale Driving Scene. *arXiv* **2023**, arXiv:2304.09807.
19. Wang, H.; Li, T.; Li, Y.; Chen, L.; Sima, C.; Liu, Z.; Wang, B.; Jia, P.; Wang, Y.; Jiang, S.; et al. OpenLane-V2: A Topology Reasoning 959 Benchmark for Unified 3D HD Mapping. In Proceedings of the NeurIPS, New Orleans, LA, USA, 10–16 December 2023; pp. 18873–18884.
20. Gomez, L.; Patel, Y.; Rusinol, M.; Karatzas, D.; Jawahar, C. Self-supervised learning of visual features through embedding images into text topic spaces. In Proceedings of the IEEE Conference on Computer Vision and Pattern Recognition, Honolulu, HI, USA, 21–26 July 2017; pp. 4230–4239.
21. Zhan, X.; Pan, X.; Liu, Z.; Lin, D.; Loy, C.C. Self-supervised learning via conditional motion propagation. In Proceedings of the IEEE/CVF Conference on Computer Vision and Pattern Recognition, Long Beach, CA, USA, 16–20 June 2019; pp. 1881–1889.
22. Gidaris, S.; Singh, P.; Komodakis, N. Unsupervised representation learning by predicting image rotations. *arXiv* **2018**, arXiv:1803.07728.
23. Marcon, M.; Spezialetti, R.; Salti, S.; Silva, L.; Di Stefano, L. Unsupervised learning of local equivariant descriptors for point clouds. *IEEE Trans. Pattern Anal. Mach. Intell.* **2021**, *44*, 9687–9702. [CrossRef] [PubMed]
24. Hu, Y.; Mian, A.S.; Owens, R. Sparse approximated nearest points for image set classification. In Proceedings of the CVPR 2011, Colorado Springs, CO, USA, 20–25 June 2011; pp. 121–128.
25. Kulkarni, T.D.; Gupta, A.; Ionescu, C.; Borgeaud, S.; Reynolds, M.; Zisserman, A.; Mnih, V. Unsupervised learning of object keypoints for perception and control. *Adv. Neural Inf. Process. Syst.* **2019**, *32*, 962.
26. Suwajanakorn, S.; Snavely, N.; Tompson, J.J.; Norouzi, M. Discovery of latent 3d keypoints via end-to-end geometric reasoning. *Adv. Neural Inf. Process. Syst.* **2018**, *31*, 2063–2074.
27. Goodfellow, I.; Pouget-Abadie, J.; Mirza, M.; Xu, B.; Warde-Farley, D.; Ozair, S.; Courville, A.; Bengio, Y. Generative adversarial networks. *Commun. ACM* **2020**, *63*, 139–144. [CrossRef]
28. Buslaev, A.; Iglovikov, V.I.; Khvedchenya, E.; Parinov, A.; Druzhinin, M.; Kalinin, A.A. Albumentations: Fast and flexible image augmentations. *Information* **2020**, *11*, 125. [CrossRef]
29. He, K.; Zhang, X.; Ren, S.; Sun, J. Deep residual learning for image recognition. In Proceedings of the IEEE Conference on Computer Vision and Pattern Recognition, Las Vegas, NV, USA, 26 June–1 July 2016; pp. 770–778.
30. Simonyan, K.; Zisserman, A. Very Deep Convolutional Networks for Large-Scale Image Recognition. In Proceedings of the ICLR 2015, San Diego, CA, USA, 7–9 May 2015; pp. 1–14.
31. Lee, J.; Kim, B.; Cho, M. Self-supervised equivariant learning for oriented keypoint detection. In Proceedings of the IEEE/CVF conference on Computer Vision and Pattern Recognition, New Orleans, LA, USA, 18–24 June 2022; pp. 4847–4857.
32. Kingma, D.P.; Ba, J. Adam: A method for stochastic optimization. *arXiv* **2014**, arXiv:1412.6980.

33. OpenCV. Open Source Computer Vision Library. See OpenCV Documentation. 2015. https://docs.opencv.org/ (accessed on 19 May 2025).
34. Eric Manongga, W.; Chen, R.C. Road Marking Sign Damage Detection and Classification Using Deep Learning and Fuzzy Method. *IEEE Access* **2025**, *13*, 92943–92952. [CrossRef]
35. Zhu, J.Y.; Park, T.; Isola, P.; Efros, A.A. Unpaired Image-to-Image Translation using Cycle-Consistent Adversarial Networkss. In Proceedings of the 2017 IEEE International Conference on Computer Vision (ICCV), Venice, Italy, 22–29 October 2017.

algorithms

MDPI

Article

An Approach to Trustworthy Article Ranking by NLP and Multi-Layered Analysis and Optimization

Chenhao Li, Jiyin Zhang, Weilin Chen and Xiaogang Ma *

Department of Computer Science, University of Idaho, Moscow, ID 83844, USA
* Correspondence: max@uidaho.edu; Tel.: +1-208-885-1547

Abstract: The rapid growth of scientific publications, coupled with rising retraction rates, has intensified the challenge of identifying trustworthy academic articles. To address this issue, we propose a three-layer ranking system that integrates natural language processing and machine learning techniques for relevance and trust assessment. First, we apply BERT-based embeddings to semantically match user queries with article content. Second, a Random Forest classifier is used to eliminate potentially problematic articles, leveraging features such as citation count, Altmetric score, and journal impact factor. Third, a custom ranking function combines relevance and trust indicators to score and sort the remaining articles. Evaluation using 16,052 articles from Retraction Watch and Web of Science datasets shows that our classifier achieves 90% accuracy and 97% recall for retracted articles. Citations emerged as the most influential trust signal (53.26%), followed by Altmetric and impact factors. This multi-layered approach offers a transparent and efficient alternative to conventional ranking algorithms, which can help researchers discover not only relevant but also reliable literature. Our system is adaptable to various domains and represents a promising tool for improving literature search and evaluation in the open science environment.

Keywords: trustworthiness ranking; similarity computation; recommendation system; multi-layered factor analysis; open data

1. Introduction

The scientific research landscape is drowning in papers. A survey showed that the number of new scientific publications per year had already increased to more than seven million in the late 2010s [1], leaving researchers struggling to separate reliable work from questionable studies. This literature flood coincides with a troubling rise in retractions, where flawed or fraudulent research is pulled from the record after publication. Traditional search tools excel at finding relevant papers but fall short in helping scholars assess whether those papers deserve their trust. Several obstacles make this problem particularly hard to solve. The overwhelming publication volume means no researcher can thoroughly evaluate every potentially relevant article. While peer review serves as the primary quality filter, its effectiveness varies wildly across journals and fields [2]. Properly judging an article's trustworthiness demands both time and specialized knowledge. Beyond academia's walls, public confidence in science relies only on researchers citing dependable sources.

To address the challenge of finding trustworthy publications, we proposed an optimized literature search system with three distinct layers that work together. Unlike approaches that focus solely on finding relevant content or just on assessing quality metrics, our system combines both. It uses BERT's language understanding capabilities to match content to queries, then applies a machine learning filter to screen out problematic papers and finally ranks results using both relevance and trustworthiness signals. We have collected abundant datasets to test the proposed approach and achieved positive outputs. A complete pipeline merging semantic search with quality assessment was built and thoroughly tested. Experiments revealed which factors most strongly signal article trustworthiness, with citation behavior proving more indicative than journal reputation. The development of a ranking method successfully balances finding relevant and reliable papers. This approach was validated using a substantial dataset containing both retracted and non-retracted articles across multiple disciplines.

Our research responds to a genuine need in science: helping researchers more efficiently find trustworthy publications relevant to their work. The following sections detail how we gathered our data, built our three-layer approach, and measured its performance, and what our results mean for improving how scientists find and evaluate research literature.

2. Related Work

2.1. Similarity Comparison

Handling the user-input questions and needs is a crucial first step in a search engine ranking algorithm. A similarity comparison process is typically used to find the database's most relevant results based on user input [3]. In this research, a scenario is that we will compare the user-input data with the metadata of the article, which includes the title, abstract, and keywords. Determining the best procedure for our similarity comparison is essential to reducing false positives. Word embedding and similarity computation in natural language processing (NLP) are the two basic steps in establishing a comparison procedure [4]. The most common similarity computation methods include the Euclidean distance [5] and cosine similarity [6]. The Euclidean distance (demonstrated in Equation (1)) measures the distance between two vectors using the formula

$$\mathrm{d}(\mathrm{x},\mathrm{y}) = \sqrt{\sum(\mathrm{xi}-\mathrm{yi})^2} \quad (1)$$

where

$x = (x1, x2,\ldots, xn)$ and $y = (y1, y2,\ldots, yn)$ are the two vectors being compared;

xi and yi are the individual elements at position i in vectors x and y, respectively.

Cosine similarity (demonstrated in Equation (2)) measures the cosine of the angle between two vectors: the smaller the angle, the higher the similarity. The cosine similarity is given by

$$\cos(\theta) = (\mathrm{x}\cdot\mathrm{y})/(||\mathrm{x}|| \times ||\mathrm{y}||) \quad (2)$$

where

$x = (x1, x2,\ldots, xn)$ and $y = (y1, y2,\ldots, yn)$ are the two vectors being compared;

θ is the angle between vectors x and y;

x·y is the dot product: $\sum(xi \times yi)$—the sum of products of corresponding elements;

xi and yi are the individual elements at position i in vectors x and y, respectively;

$||x||$ and $||y||$ are the magnitudes (Euclidean norms): $\sqrt{\sum(xi^2)}$ and $\sqrt{\sum(yi^2)}$.

There are also other methods for similarity computation, such as Jaccard and Hamming, but they are more suitable for binary strings and thus not applicable in our situation [7]. We choose to use cosine similarity because it is scale-invariant—it measures the angle between vectors rather than their absolute differences. This characteristic is particularly important when comparing user-input keywords with article abstracts, as different textual features (such as term frequencies, semantic weights, and metadata elements) often exist at vastly different numerical scales. The Euclidean distance would allow features with larger numerical ranges to disproportionately influence the similarity calculation, potentially masking important relationships in other dimensions [8]. Although there are many new ways to compare document similarity, such as Fuzzy String matching [9] and Graph-based Methods [10], we keep this part standard to focus on other research areas.

For the word embedding process, common NLP methods include TF-IDF, Word2vec, DOC2vec, and Transformers. TF-IDF (term frequency-inverse document frequency) determines a word's importance based on its frequency in the document relative to its frequency across all documents [11]. Word2vec, developed by Google, uses neural networks to capture contextual meanings with methods like Continuous Bag of Words and Skip-gram [12]. DOC2vec extends Word2vec to document-level embeddings [13]. Transformers represent the state-of-the-art methods such as BERT [14], excelling in embedding long sentences.

2.2. *Trustworthiness in Article Discovery*

In article discovery, "trustworthiness" refers to the reliability and validity of information contained in the retrieved scholarly articles. Scientists must have confidence in the papers that they read and use in their research activities. The academic community is aware of the importance of reliability in article discovery. In the past decades, many research studies [15–17] have been conducted to address such concerns. In general, those works have developed their own systems and criteria to determine the trustworthiness of an article. These criteria comprise the standard of the peer review procedure, the credibility of the source, the credentials and work history of the writers, and the number of citations the article has received. Among those metrics, citation is a common way for academics to gauge whether a work is well-liked and influential.

2.3. *Classification Models for Trust Assessment*

Classification models are frequently employed to evaluate a news article's credibility. In those models, attributes such as content correctness, author credentials, and source reputation are used to classify the article's trustworthiness. For example, Castillo et al. [18] pioneered influential work on classification models for credibility assessment, particularly in social media contexts. Their model considered various elements including propagation patterns, external references, and author characteristics to determine content credibility. Pérez-Rosas et al. [19] demonstrated the effectiveness of linguistic feature-based classification models for detecting fake news, in which stylistic elements and content patterns are used to determine credibility. These models provide a static measure of trustworthiness that enables readers to quickly determine the credibility of an article. Their results showed that automated systems could effectively distinguish between credible and non-credible information by analyzing these multi-dimensional features, providing a framework that has influenced subsequent approaches to news trustworthiness classification.

2.4. *Ranking Systems in Academic Article Repositories*

Major article repositories like Google Scholar and Web of Science use various ranking mechanisms to organize search results. Google Scholar combines citations and relevance to match a user's query, where citations serve as a proxy for an article's impact, and relevance ensures the search results pertain to the user's needs [20]. However, Google Scholar operates as a "black box" with a proprietary ranking algorithm that is not disclosed to the public, making it difficult for users to understand the criteria influencing the ranking of search results. In comparison, Web of Science offers single criteria ranking systems such as relevance, citation count, and date posted [21]. While these methods effectively highlight certain aspects of an article, they often overlook other factors contributing to the overall trustworthiness. For instance, a highly cited article may be influential but not necessarily the most current or accurate. Other repositories follow similar approaches. PubMed, for example, primarily ranks articles by relevance and date [22], which can sometimes prioritize newer articles over those that are more impactful or thoroughly reviewed.

While these single-criteria and opaque ranking methods have their merits, they fall short in providing a comprehensive measure of an article's trustworthiness. Users are often left without clear insights into why certain articles are ranked higher than others, which can lead to confusion and potential misjudgment of the quality of the information. To address these limitations, there is a growing need for a transparent, multi-criteria ranking system that integrates various trust indicators. Such a system would consider not only citations and relevance but also factors like the authors' credentials, the reputation of the publication source, the thoroughness of the peer review process, and the article's content quality and recency. We integrated all those considerations into the design of our system, which makes the following contributions:

- Integrated Semantic Relevance and Trust Assessment: Combines BERT-based semantic matching with trustworthiness evaluation to retrieve articles that are both topically relevant and scientifically reliable.
- Robust Problematic Article Filtering: Applies a Random Forest classifier trained on retracted and non-retracted articles to effectively eliminate unreliable publications with 90% overall accuracy.
- Transparent Multi-factor Ranking Strategy: Introduces a scoring model that merges citation, Altmetric, and impact factor data to produce an interpretable and adjustable trustworthiness ranking.
- Validated on Large Cross-domain Dataset: Demonstrates a consistent performance using over 16,000 articles across diverse scientific fields, supporting generalizability and applicability to real-world literature discovery tasks.

The proposed three-layer system will be explained in detail in Section 4. Before illustrating the workflow of that system, we will first introduce the data resources used in this work.

3. Data Retrieval and Pre-Processing

Our study utilized two primary datasets: the Retraction Watch database [23] and a curated collection from Web of Science. The Retraction Watch database, which has garnered significant attention in the scientific community for its insights into publication integrity [24], initially contained 12,195 retracted articles with comprehensive metadata including retraction reasons and citation metrics both pre-retraction and post-retraction. To establish a comparative baseline for non-retracted articles, we also collected 10,000 non-retracted articles from the Web of Science on 3 June 2024. Our sampling strategy employed a systematic approach focusing on five pairs of related research domains, with 1000 articles selected for each domain among the following pairs:

1. Photosynthesis and Cellular Respiration;
2. Quantum Mechanics and Quantum Computing;
3. Ecology and Environmental Science;
4. Virology and Epidemiology;
5. Bacteria and Viruses.

This paired-topic approach ensured a balanced representation across different scientific disciplines while maintaining thematic coherence within each pair. However, the fragmented nature of scholarly metadata across different platforms presented a significant challenge. While repositories such as Google Scholar provide citation metrics and h-indexes, they lack alternative metrics and impact factor data. For the data sources of this study, the Web of Science and Retraction Watch databases also presented limitations in metadata completeness, particularly regarding journal impact factors and alternative metrics. To address these gaps, we implemented a multi-source data enrichment process:

- Altmetric Data Integration: We utilized the Altmetric API to retrieve attention scores for articles using their Digital Object Identifiers (DOIs).
- Impact Factor Collection: Journal impact factors were obtained through the Journal Citation Reports (JCR) database, supplemented by direct extraction from journal websites when necessary.

Following the initial data collection, we conducted a thorough pre-processing phase to address missing values, particularly in impact factor and Altmetric scores. After removing entries with incomplete metadata, our final dataset (Table 1) was reduced to 16,052 articles (11,649 from Retraction Watch and 4403 from Web of Science), providing a robust foundation for our subsequent analysis.

Table 1. Example of the final dataset.

Article Title	Cited	Impact Factor	Altmetric Score	DOI	Retracted	Severity Category
Zika virus: Current concerns in India	29.0	2.7	6.6	10.4103/ijmr.IJMR_1160_17	no	good
Emergence of H3N2pM-like and novel reassortant H3N1 swine viruses possessing segments derived from the A (H1N1)pdm09 influenza virus, Korea	17.0	4.3	8.242	10.1111/irv.12154	no	good
ICTV Virus Taxonomy Profile: Virgaviridae	85.0	3.6	3.0	10.1099/jgv.0.000884	no	good
Taming influenza viruses	13.0	2.5	0.5	10.1016/j.virusres.2011.09.035	no	good
Down-regulation of the long noncoding RNA-HOX transcript antisense intergenic RNA inhibits the occurrence and progression of glioma	3.0	3	1.0	10.1002/jcb.30040	yes	critical
Interleukin-6 promotes the migration and cellular senescence and inhibits apoptosis of human intrahepatic biliary epithelial cells	2.0	3	1.0	10.1002/jcb.30039	yes	critical
MicroRNA-205 acts as a tumor suppressor in osteosarcoma via targeting RUNX2	2.0	3.8	7.33	10.3892/or.2021.8106	yes	critical
MiR-132 inhibits cell proliferation, invasion, and migration of hepatocellular carcinoma by targeting PIK3R3	1.0	4.5	0.25	10.3892/ijo.2021.5238	yes	critical

4. Methodology

Based on the survey of the existing methods and the analysis of data resources, our proposed system consists of a three-layer architecture to provide users with relevant and trustworthy academic article search results. As shown in Figure 1, the system processes user queries through sequential stages of increasing refinement. In layer 1, BERT embeddings are deployed for semantic similarity matching; in layer 2, a Random Forest classifier is applied to eliminate potentially problematic articles; and in layer 3, a novel ranking mechanism is implemented to balance relevance with trustworthiness. Each layer builds on the output of the preceding steps and fulfills a specific function. This multi-layered strategy ensures that the search results uphold the highest criteria of scientific credibility in addition to semantic relevance. The following sections detail each layer of this architecture, from initial query processing to the recommendation result ranking.

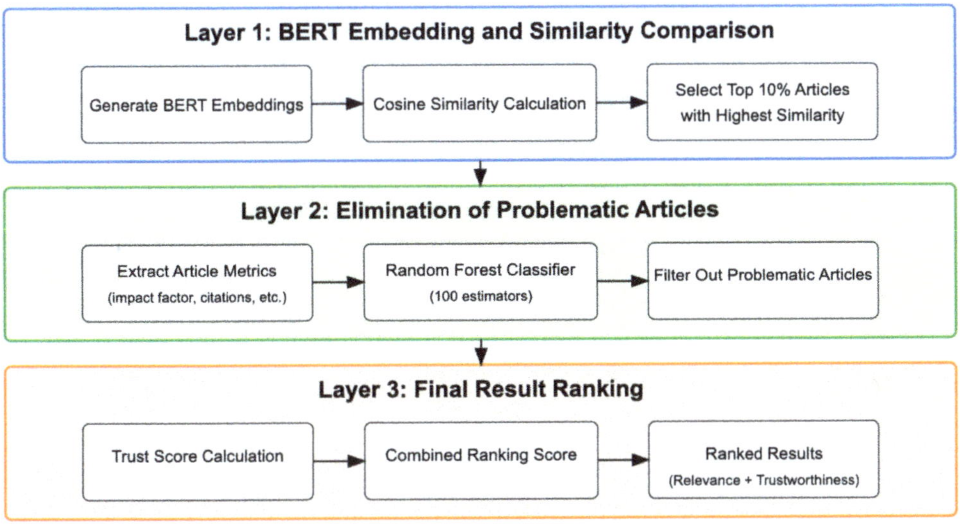

Figure 1. Detailed steps in the three-layer architecture of our proposed system for the trustworthiness ranking and recommendation of academic articles.

4.1. BERT Embedding and Similarity Comparison

In our approach to semantic text analysis, we employ the BERT model, a popular method in NLP, to generate dense vector representations of both user queries and academic articles. The bidirectional nature of BERT allows it to consider the full context of each word, making it particularly effective for understanding complex academic text and technical terminology.

We specifically selected the "BERT-base-uncased" model over other available variants for several reasons. First, we chose BERT-base over BERT-large because the latter's 340 M parameters (compared to BERT-base's 110 M) would significantly increase computational overhead without proportional performance gains for our similarity task. Second, we opted for the uncased version because academic abstracts often contain inconsistent capitalization patterns, and treating terms like "Machine Learning" and "machine learning" as equivalent is more appropriate for semantic similarity matching. Finally, while domain-specific variants like SciBERT exist, BERT-base-uncased provides better generalizability across multiple academic disciplines, which aligns with our cross-domain article retrieval system.

In our work, the selected "BERT-base-uncased" model creates 768-dimensional embeddings that effectively capture the semantic relationships within the text. The initial step involves concatenating each article's title and abstract into a unified text string before generating the embedding. This approach ensures that the full topic and context of the article are captured in the vector representation.

After generating BERT embeddings for both the user queries and the articles, we implement a similarity comparison using cosine similarity measurements. Cosine similarity serves as an effective metric for comparing high-dimensional vectors as it measures the cosine of the angle between two vectors, producing a normalized similarity score ranging from -1 to 1. A score of 1 indicates perfect similarity, while lower scores suggest decreasing degrees of semantic relevance. This normalization makes the metric particularly suitable for comparing texts of different lengths. In our implementation, we select the top 10% of articles with the highest cosine similarity scores for further analysis and refinement. This filtering step ensures that we maintain a manageable set of highly relevant articles while retaining enough diversity for subsequent analysis stages.

4.2. Elimination of Problematic Articles

This stage aims to develop a systematic pipeline to identify and filter out potentially problematic articles. Hence, we design an article elimination process following the similarity comparison to enhance the trustworthiness of our results, based on the observation that not all articles with high similarity scores necessarily represent reliable scientific contributions. We deploy a Random Forest classifier for this task, because of its ability to handle non-linear relationships and provide easy-to-understand feature importance for future analysis (see Layer 2 in Figure 1). Due to the characteristics of our data, the Random Forest classifier can help us solve the following problems. First, this model is effective at handling multiple features without making assumptions about the feature distributions. Second, this model demonstrates robustness against overfitting and shows the capability to capture complex interactions between different article metrics. Third, it provides feedback on feature importance to help identify the key indicators of article trustworthiness.

In our design, the Random Forest classification model incorporates article metrics such as the journal impact factor, citation count (pre-retraction for retracted articles), and Altmetric scores. We split the dataset into training (80%) and testing (20%) sets, maintaining the class distribution through stratification. All features are then standardized using StandardScaler. We implement the model with 100 estimators and default parameters to establish a baseline, followed by hyperparameter fine-tuning using cross-validation to optimize model performance. To establish a filtering mechanism that could be applied to new articles during the user search interaction, the model is trained to classify articles into two categories: those likely to be problematic and those otherwise. To validate our approach, we conduct preliminary evaluations using standard machine learning metrics, such as precision, recall, F1-score, etc. Detailed performance metrics are provided in Section 5. Overall, this elimination process provides an additional layer of validation beyond the content similarity, creating a more robust and trustworthy result for the user.

4.3. Final Result Ranking

While it is important to classify the articles, for search engine applications, users also need the ability to understand the relative trustworthiness among the article results. Hence, we add an additional layer of trust scoring system to address this gap (see Layer 3 in Figure 1). We first convert our retraction severity scores to a 1–100 scale and divide them into 5 severity levels to create a more detailed ranking framework. Using these scores, we train a LightGBM ranking model with the lambdarank objective to optimize the ranking performance. The features include percentile ranks for impact factors, citation counts, and Altmetric scores, along with metrics showing relationships between these values.

In our initial experiment results, citation rank was the most important feature (254.78), followed by relative citation impact (227.88) and impact factor rank (186.03). While the model achieved reasonably good NDCG scores (NDCG@5 of 0.8141, NDCG@10 of 0.8490), analysis of sample rankings revealed limitations. When comparing actual versus predicted ranks for 10 random papers, only 1 had a perfect rank match, and 4 were within one rank position of their true standing. The Spearman rank correlation of 0.443 showed only a moderate relationship between predicted and actual trustworthiness. Given these limitations, we decided to use the feature importance insights to create a simpler, more transparent trust score function for articles:

$$T(a) = w_1 CR(a) + w_2 RCI(a) + w_3 IFR(a), \tag{3}$$

This function (Equation (3)) incorporates the citation rank CR(a), relative citation impact RCI(a), and impact factor rank IFR(a). The weights w_1 (0.25), w_2 (0.23), and w_3 (0.19) reflect the relative importance of each component based on our empirical analysis of feature importance scores from the LightGBM model. To create our final ranking mechanism, we create a score that merges relevance and trustworthiness:

$$R(a) = \alpha \times S(a) + (1 - \alpha) \times T(a), \tag{4}$$

In Equation (4), S(a) measures the query–article similarity, while α balances relevance against trustworthiness. This approach proves particularly valuable for academic searches where both aspects matter significantly. When α equals 0.5, relevance and trustworthiness contribute equally to the final score. Adjusting α to be higher prioritizes relevance, while a lower value emphasizes trustworthiness. This flexibility helps prevent situations where highly relevant but questionable articles or trustworthy but less relevant papers dominate the results.

5. Expanded Experiments, Results, and Discussion

To validate the effectiveness of the proposed three-layer system, we implemented a list of experiments with the dataset collected in Section 3. In the first layer, to evaluate and determine the model used for the word embedding, we trained and tested both BERT and TF-IDF models with the 10,000 articles collected from Web of Science. In the second layer, we trained and evaluated the Random Forest model with the 16,052 articles collected from both the Retraction Watch dataset and Web of Science. In the third layer, the ranking algorithm in Section 4.3 was applied to the result from the second layer and then the ranking result was generated. In the below, Sections 5.1–5.3 will give details about the experimental results in the first and second layers. The steps in the third layer are the same as Section 4.3 and we will omit the details of the workflow here, but in Section 5.5, we will present an exemplar result and discuss the future work of implementing the three-layer system in real-world applications, especially how to assess the ranking results in the third layer with reference data provided by experts.

5.1. Evaluation of TF-IDF and BERT Model Performance

To evaluate the effectiveness of different word embedding techniques, we conducted a comparative analysis of TF-IDF with default parameters of scikit-learn's tfidfVectorizer and BERT models using cosine similarity across various scientific topics. Three article queries of the topics "coronaviruses", "climate change effects", and "quantum computing advancements" were implemented to the raw data of 10,000 articles described in Section 3. For the results, we examined the distribution of top research fields (Figure 2), result overlap (Figure 3), and similarity score distribution and decay (Figures 4 and 5). The patterns in the results demonstrated BERT's superiority in capturing semantic nuances and contextual relationships. When analyzing similarity scores across the three topics—"coronaviruses", "climate change effects", and "quantum computing advancements"—BERT consistently produced better results. For instance, in the "coronaviruses" query, BERT's similarity scores ranged from 0.55 to 0.80, while TF-IDF's scores rapidly dropped below 0.2 after the top few results (Figure 5). Similarly, for "quantum computing advancements", BERT maintained scores between 0.72 and 0.84, compared to TF-IDF's range of 0.22–0.38. BERT also showed a more gradual decline in similarity scores as the rank increased, indicating better relevance even for lower-ranked results. Both methods demonstrated high result diversity, but BERT's top results differed significantly from TF-IDF's, with only 14–23% overlap across queries (Figure 4). This low overlap suggests BERT's ability to identify relevant but less obviously related fields. For example, for the "coronaviruses" query, while TF-IDF heavily favored "Physics", BERT highlighted a broader range including "Science & Technology—Other Topics" and "Virology". These findings consistently demonstrate BERT's enhanced capability in understanding context and semantic relationships, making it particularly valuable for complex scientific literature search and recommendation systems where nuanced topic analysis is crucial. However, it is important to note that TF-IDF's execution time is significantly faster than BERT's, which could be a crucial factor in applications where the processing speed is a priority.

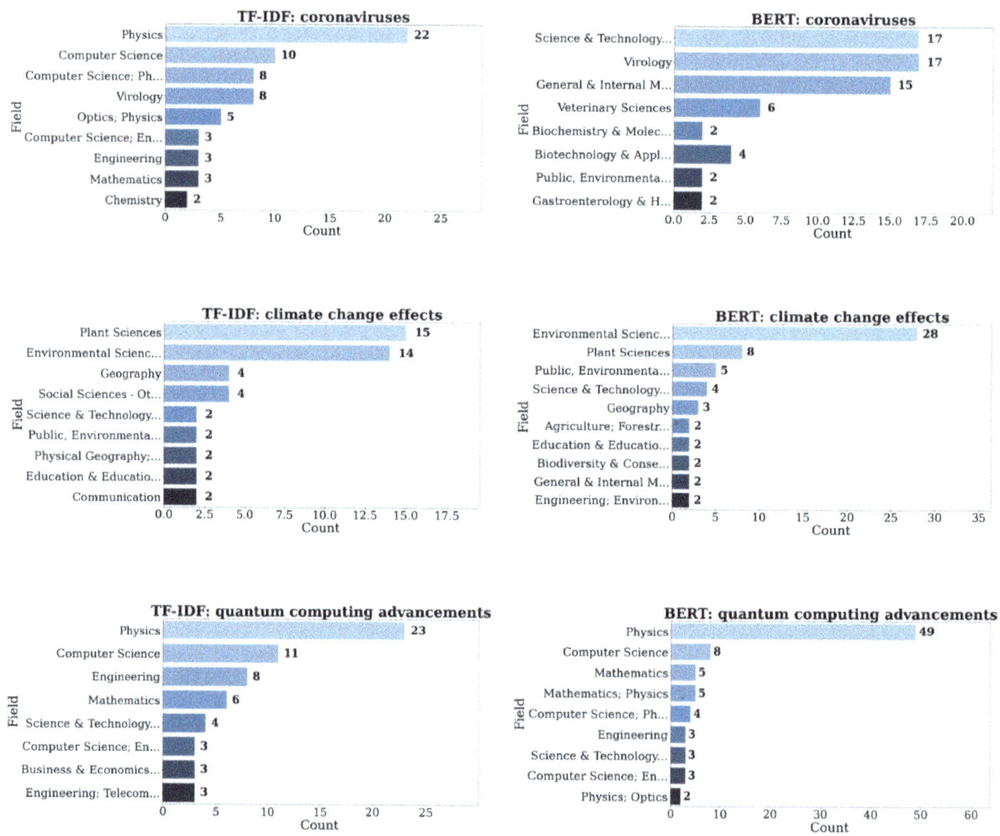

Figure 2. The top fields/topics of three different queries using TF-IDF and BERT methods. The detailed fields/topics in each diagram are from the metadata of the retrieved articles.

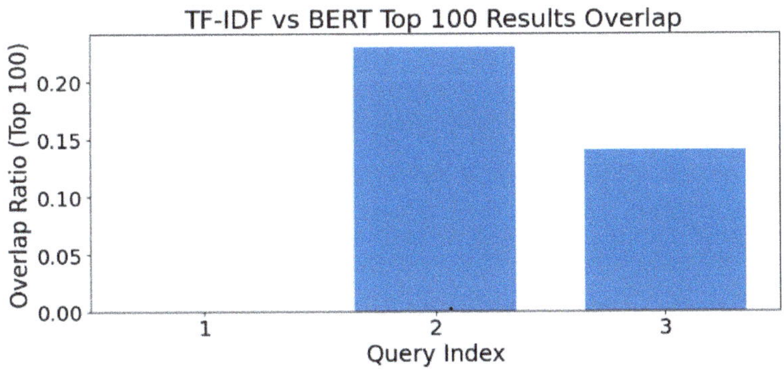

Figure 3. The overlap ratio between TF-IDF and BERT top 100 results for three different queries.

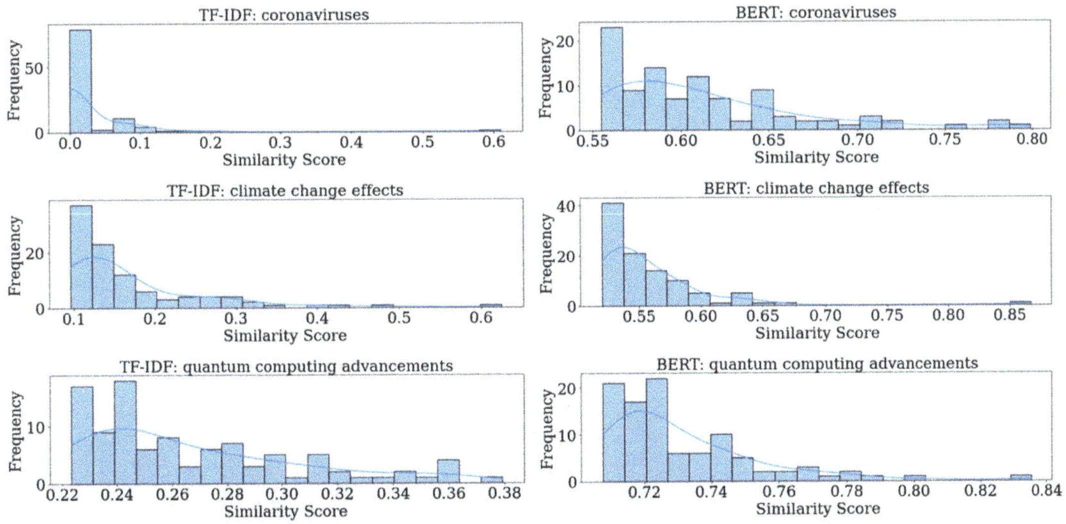

Figure 4. Distribution of similarity scores for query results of three different topics using TF-IDF and BERT.

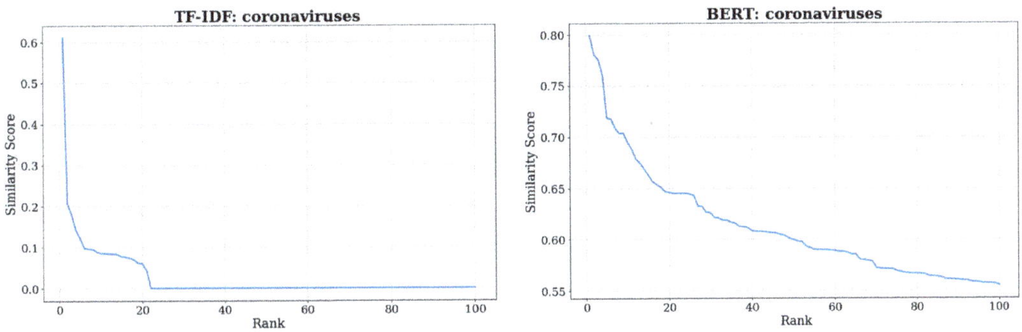

Figure 5. *Cont.*

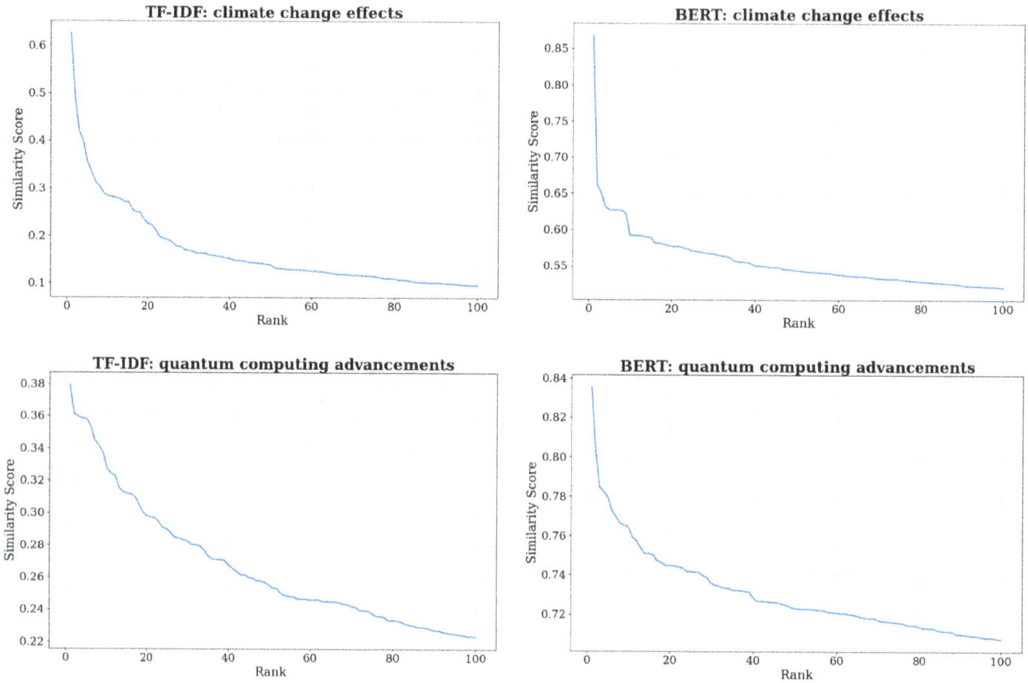

Figure 5. Patterns of cosine similarity decay for query results of three different topics using TF-IDF and BERT.

5.2. Evaluation of Random Forest Model Performance

For the Random Forest classifier, we performed hyperparameter tuning using GridSearchCV with 5-fold cross-validation to optimize model performance. The parameter grid included n_estimators = [50, 100, 200], max_depth = [10, 20, None], min_samples_split = [2, 5, 10], min_samples_leaf = [1, 2, 4], and max_features = ['sqrt', 'log2']. The F1-score was used as the evaluation metric to account for the class imbalance in our dataset. The optimal parameters found were max_depth = None, max_features = 'sqrt', min_samples_leaf = 1, min_samples_split = 10, and n_estimators = 100, achieving a cross-validation F1-score of 0.9275.

Our Random Forest classifier performed well in identifying retracted and non-retracted papers, with an overall accuracy of 90% on the test set of 16,052 articles (for more details for the test dataset, see the end of Section 3). From our experiment results (Table 2), we were able to determine that the model is good at detecting problematic papers. For retracted papers, the model showed a high precision (0.90) and recall (0.97), giving an F1-score of 0.93. For non-retracted papers, the model had good precision (0.89) but lower recall (0.71), with an F1-score of 0.79. The Area Under the ROC Curve (AUC) was 0.93, showing a strong ability to separate the two classes. We will give more details of the AUC in Section 5.2.

Table 2. Performance of Random Forest classification.

Classification Report				
Class	**Precision**	**Recall**	**F1-Score**	**Support**
0	0.89	0.71	0.79	881
1	0.90	0.97	0.93	2330
Accuracy			0.89	3211
Macro Avg.	0.88	0.84	0.86	3211
Weighted Avg.	0.89	0.90	0.89	3211

The confusion matrix (Figure 6A) shows the details of correct and incorrect predictions. The model correctly identified 97% of retracted papers, missing only 3%. For non-retracted papers, 71.0% were correctly classified, while 29.0% were wrongly marked as retracted. This pattern matches our goal of catching most problematic articles, even if some good papers are wrongly flagged.

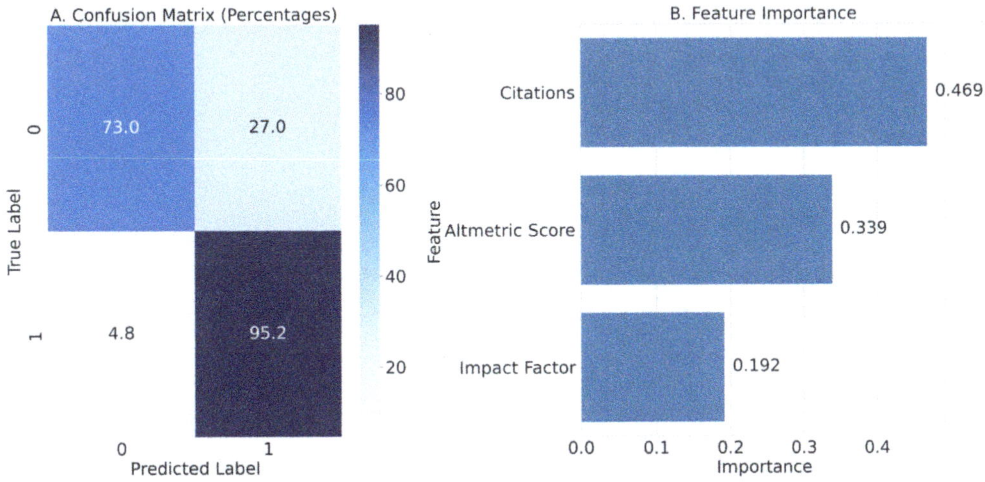

Figure 6. Confusion matrix and feature importance of the Random Forest classification model. The percentage of the model's correct and incorrect predictions is shown in the confusion matrix. The impact of each feature on the model's predictions is shown in the feature importance.

For the feature importance (Figure 6B), we found that the citation count is the most important factor (53.26%), followed by the Altmetric score (30.19%) and impact factor (16.55%). This suggests that the level to which an article is cited and discussed matters more for predicting retraction than the reputation of the journal where the article is published.

5.3. Random Forest Model Validation

We tested the Random Forest model thoroughly to check its stability. The learning curves (Figure 7A) showed some gap between training accuracy (about 0.90) and cross-validation scores (about 0.88). This gap suggests some overfitting, but not enough to harm practical use, as the cross-validation scores remained steady (mean: 0.884, standard deviation: 0.0049). Moreover, the precision–recall curve (Figure 7B) stayed above 0.90 precision until the recall reached about 0.80, with an average precision (AP) of 0.96. This means the model maintains high-quality predictions across different settings. The ROC (Receiver Operating Characteristic) curve (Figure 7C) showed a quick rise and high AUC (0.93), further proving the model's strong performance. The steep initial part of the ROC curve shows that the model can find many retracted papers with few false alarms.

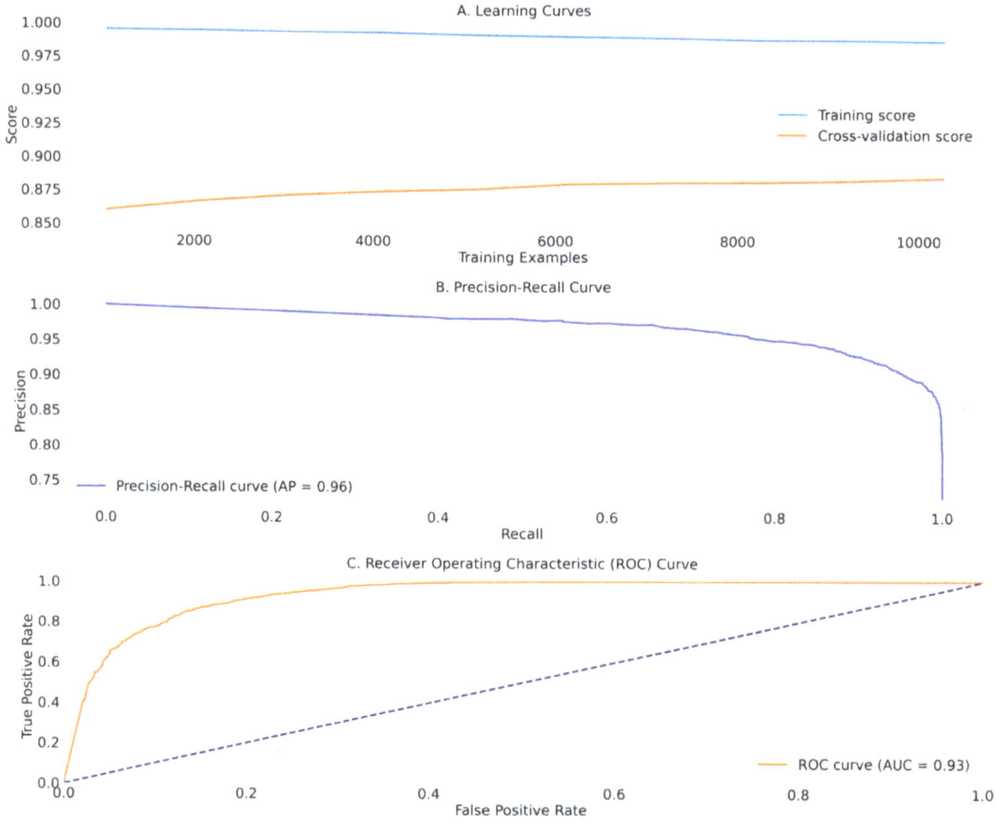

Figure 7. Metrics used to validate the performance of the Random Forest model. The learning curve shows the model's performance with different iterations. The precision–recall curve shows the relationship between precision and recall under different classification thresholds. The ROC curve shows the true positive rate against the false positive rate across different thresholds, the dash line represents the line of no discrimination.

To validate our modeling approach for retraction prediction, we conducted a comprehensive comparison of ten machine learning algorithms (results shown in Table 3): Random Forest, Gradient Boosting, XGBoost, Logistic Regression, Support Vector Machine, Neural Network (MLP), AdaBoost, K-Nearest Neighbors, Decision Tree, and Naive Bayes. All models underwent hyperparameter tuning using 5-fold cross-validation with the F1-score as the evaluation metric to account for the class imbalance in our dataset. Our experimental results show that Gradient Boosting achieved the highest performance with a test F1-score of 0.9336 and AUC of 0.9477, followed closely by XGBoost (F1-score: 0.9333, AUC: 0.9452) and Random Forest (F1-score: 0.9305, AUC: 0.9377). Statistical significance testing using McNemar's test revealed that the differences between these top three models were not statistically significant (Gradient Boosting vs. XGBoost: $p = 1.0000$; Gradient Boosting vs. Random Forest: $p = 0.1980$), indicating comparable predictive capabilities. Despite Gradient Boosting's marginally superior performance (0.31% improvement), we selected Random Forest as our primary classifier due to its superior interpretability through intuitive feature importance rankings, computational efficiency with faster training times and lower hyperparameter tuning requirements, and greater stability with a more consistent cross-validation performance. For scientific retraction detection, the model interpretability and ease of explanation are crucial for gaining trust from the research community, making Random Forest's transparent decision-making process more valuable than the negligible performance difference. The comparison results validate that ensemble methods significantly outperform traditional machine learning approaches, with all three top models achieving F1-scores above 0.93 and demonstrating the effectiveness of tree-based algorithms for this classification task.

Table 3. Performance comparison of machine learning models for retraction prediction.

Model	CV F1-Score	Test F1-Score	AUC	Rank
Gradient Boosting	0.9304	0.9336	0.9477	1
XGBoost	0.9296	0.9333	0.9452	2
Random Forest	0.9275	0.9305	0.9377	3
Decision Tree	0.9185	0.9266	0.8942	4
AdaBoost	0.9061	0.9118	0.8969	5
K-Nearest Neighbors	0.9055	0.9114	0.8931	6
Neural Network	0.9052	0.9092	0.8657	7
SVM	0.8706	0.8685	0.7956	8
Logistic Regression	0.8485	0.8481	0.7476	9
Naive Bayes	0.1227	0.1286	0.5821	10

To validate our feature selection and model design, we conducted an ablation study examining individual feature contributions and model component sensitivity (shown in Table 4). Individual feature analysis revealed that citations achieved the highest standalone performance (F1-score: 0.8690), significantly outperforming the Altmetric score (0.8246) and impact factor (0.8348), confirming citation patterns as the strongest predictor of retraction. Feature combination analysis showed that the optimal two-feature combination of citations + Altmetric score (F1-score: 0.9334) slightly outperformed our full three-feature model (0.9305), with feature removal analysis revealing that removing citations caused the largest performance drop (10.70%) while removing the Altmetric score decreased the performance by 4.58%. Notably, removing the impact factor actually improved the performance by 0.31%, suggesting that it introduces predictive noise; however, we retained the impact factor in our model because it represents an important journal-level quality assessment that complements article-level metrics, provides valuable context for understanding retraction patterns across different journal tiers, enables a comprehensive analysis of institutional factors in research integrity, and maintains consistency with existing retraction studies that consider journal prestige as a relevant factor. Parameter ablation confirmed that the performance stabilized at 100 estimators with minimal variation across different max_features settings, validating our parameter choices and demonstrating model robustness, while the marginal performance cost (0.31%) of including the impact factor was acceptable given its important analytical benefits beyond the pure predictive performance.

Table 4. Ablation study results for feature contributions.

Configuration	Features	Test F1	Performance Drop
Full Model	Citations + Altmetric + Impact	0.9305	-
Best Two-Feature	Citations + Altmetric	0.9334	0.29%
Without Citations	Altmetric + Impact	0.831	−10.70%
Without Altmetric Score	Citations + Impact	0.888	−4.58%
Without Impact Factor	Citations + Altmetric	0.9334	0.31%
Citations Only	Citations	0.869	−6.62%
Altmetric Score Only	Altmetric Score	0.8246	−11.38%
Impact Factor Only	Impact Factor	0.8348	−10.29%

5.4. Class Imbalance Mitigation and Impact Assessment

Our dataset exhibits a natural class imbalance, with retracted papers comprising 72.6% and non-retracted papers 27.4% of the total samples. To evaluate whether this imbalance poses a significant problem, we analyzed its specific performance impacts and found that while the distribution is mathematically imbalanced, it may not be as problematic as initially perceived. The original model achieved a strong overall performance (F1-score: 0.9305), with the primary impact being lower recall for non-retracted papers (70.8% vs. 96.6% for retracted papers), translating to approximately 29% of legitimate papers being incorrectly flagged for editorial review. Overall, this class distribution reflects the current natural retraction patterns in academic publishing data we retrieved, and forcing a perfect balance would artificially distort realistic scenarios.

Rather than employing synthetic data generation techniques that could introduce artificial bias, we implemented cost-sensitive learning (Table 5) with balanced class weights to address this imbalance while preserving authentic data distribution. We evaluated four different weighting strategies, with the balanced weights approach demonstrating the optimal performance by improving minority class recall from 70.8% to 78.1% (10.9% relative improvement) while maintaining a strong overall model performance with only a 0.62% decrease in F1-score. This reduced the false positive rate from 29% to 22%, demonstrating that the imbalance effects are addressable through established techniques without compromising core model functionality.

Table 5. Model cost-sensitive learning results.

Approach	**F1-Score**	**Precision (Non-Retracted)**	**Recall (Non-Retracted)**	**Precision (Retracted)**	**Recall (Retracted)**	**Balanced Accuracy**
No Weights (Original)	0.9305	0.8876	0.7083	0.8975	0.9661	0.8372
Balanced Weights	0.9243	0.8094	0.7809	0.9183	0.9305	0.8557
Custom Weights (Conservative)	0.9203	0.7909	0.7855	0.9191	0.9215	0.8535
Custom Weights (Moderate)	0.9266	0.8344	0.7548	0.9105	0.9433	0.8491

5.5. Exemplar Result and Discussion

In our designed three-layer architecture, the ranking mechanism serves as the final layer, following the BERT-based similarity comparison and article elimination stages as mentioned above in Sections 5.1–5.3. Figure 8 shows an exemplar result in our work after all the steps in the three layers are finished. In this example, "climate change effects" was the input keyword for the literature search. A total of 1605 similar articles were retrieved from the database based on a similarity comparison in the first layer. In the second layer, the filtering algorithm eliminated 646 retracted articles, leaving 959 valid results. Finally in the third layer, based on the proposed ranking method, the top five most relevant articles were presented to the user. This sequential approach ensures that search results are first filtered for relevance, then screened for trustworthiness, and finally, ranked according to our composite scoring system. Overall, the result demonstrates how multi-factor analysis can improve the search result quality beyond simple relevance matching.

Climate Change Effects: Search Analysis

```
Query: 'climate change effects'
Articles found: 1605 → 959 retained (646 eliminated)
Process: BERT embedding → trustworthiness filtering → ranking
```

Top Ranked Results (Final Score | Citations | Impact Factor)

1. The Dynamics of Photosynthesis (0.7869 | 583 | 8.7)
R-Score: 0.6049, T-Score: 0.9690, DOI: 10.1146/annurev.genet.42.110807.091452

2. Time series regression studies in environmental epidemiology (0.7800 | 789 | 6.4)
R-Score: 0.6148, T-Score: 0.9452, DOI: 10.1093/ije/dyt092

3. Environmental Sensor Networks: A revolution in earth system science? (0.7673 | 509 | 10.8)
R-Score: 0.5571, T-Score: 0.9775, DOI: 10.1016/j.earscirev.2006.05.001

4. Environmental sciences, sustainable development and circular economy (0.7410 | 571 | 4.7)
R-Score: 0.5983, T-Score: 0.8836, DOI: 10.1016/j.envdev.2015.09.002

5. Sink regulation of photosynthesis (0.7401 | 976 | 5.6)
R-Score: 0.5526, T-Score: 0.9275, DOI: 10.1093/jexbot/52.360.1383

Examples of Eliminated Articles (Relevance | Problematic Score | Citations | IF)

1. Some health effects of global warming (0.7839 | 1.0000 | 1 | 2.2)

2. Individualistic Sensitivities and Exposure to Climate Change... (0.7828 | 0.9300 | 31 | 11.7)

3. Human and Environmental Dangers Posed by Ongoing Global Tropospheric... (0.7540 | 1.0000 | 1696 | 3.0)

4. A critical assessment of extreme events trends in times of global warming (0.7415 | 0.9900 | 3730 | 2.8)

Note: R-Score = Relevance Score, T-Score = Trustworthiness Score, IF = Impact Factor

Figure 8. An exemplar result following the three-layer architecture of our proposed system. The result shows not only the top recommended articles with additional metadata but also some eliminated articles. It is noteworthy that the eliminated articles shown in this result are all retracted in the real world.

After evaluating the experiment results, we were able to summarize the findings and potential limitations of each layer. In Layer 1, from the experiments we conducted in Section 5.1, we found that using BERT embedding with cosine similarity is the best approach for finding the most relevant articles based on the user-input keywords. In Layer 2, while our Random Forest classification model performed well overall, we found several issues that should be noted. First, our dataset had a significant imbalance, with 72.57% retracted papers and only 27.43% non-retracted papers. This uneven split likely affected how the model learned and may explain why it performed differently in each class. Second, the model was very good at finding retracted papers (97% recall) but less effective at correctly identifying non-retracted papers (71.0% recall). This means that 29.0% of good papers were wrongly flagged as problematic. In real use, this could cause valid research to be unfairly questioned. However, this tendency is suitable for our main goal of filtering out questionable articles from search results. Third, we saw a gap between how well the model performed on training data versus testing data, suggesting some overfitting. Though this did not greatly harm the model's usefulness, it indicates that some patterns the model learned might be specific to our dataset and might not work as well with new data. In Layer 3, our ranking algorithm remains in early experimental stages and requires further validation and refinement with reference data from experts, to determine its effectiveness in real-world applications.

This study holds both theoretical and practical significance for the fields of information retrieval, scholarly communication, and research integrity. Theoretically, it contributes to the advancement of trust-aware search systems by demonstrating how semantic similarity, classification models, and composite ranking functions can be joined in a multi-layer structure to address the challenges of relevance and trustworthiness in academic article discovery. Unlike traditional search systems that rely on single-criterion ranking or opaque algorithms, our method introduces a more interpretable and systematic approach grounded in modern NLP and machine learning. It provides a framework that can be extended to evaluate not only articles but also other scholarly objects such as datasets and software packages. Practically, the system addresses a growing need in the research community for tools that help users confidently identify high-quality literature amid rising publication volumes and concerns about misinformation and retractions. The modular design allows for easy adaptation across disciplines and use cases, while the use of open data sources and transparent scoring functions supports reproducibility and user trust. By placing indicators of scientific reliability alongside topical relevance, this system empowers users to make more informed decisions about what research to read, cite, and build upon. Furthermore, researchers, librarians, and research administrators can use the system to streamline literature reviews, examine citations, and support quality assurance processes in their work.

Based on these findings, we see several ways to improve our work in the future. A fundamental opportunity is to enhance the feature dataset by collecting and developing additional indicators that capture new dimensions of article quality, such as the h-index indicating the impact and productivity of authors, author network analysis, institutional affiliations, and other publication metadata. We will also address the dataset imbalance more fundamentally by expanding our dataset through collaboration with additional journals and academic institutions, with a particular focus on increasing the representation of non-retracted papers. This approach will naturally improve class balance while maintaining data authenticity and ensuring that the model reflects genuine publication patterns rather than artificially modified distributions. For the final ranking (Layer 3), we plan to obtain expert validation through structured surveys to determine the effectiveness of the ranking system across diverse research domains and publication types. The other way to address this problem is to use Large Language Models [25] to determine the effectiveness of the ranking models. To improve accessibility, we will develop an intuitive web interface where researchers can easily find trustworthy articles and understand the process of why those articles are chosen. For example, the trust ranking scores will be shown alongside their search results. Finally, a list of user studies can be conducted with researchers from various disciplines to gather feedback on the system's usability. We hope these enhancements will transform our current research prototype into a practical tool that helps researchers to navigate the ever-expanding scientific literature with greater confidence and discover more trustworthy articles.

6. Conclusions

This study developed a three-layered system to help researchers find trustworthy academic articles. Our system first used BERT embedding to identify relevant articles, then applied a Random Forest classifier to filter out questionable papers and finally ranked results using a custom scoring system that balanced relevance with trustworthiness. The classification model performed well in our experiments, with a 90% overall accuracy, and was especially good at finding retracted papers (97% recall). We found that citation counts were the strongest signs of article trustworthiness (53.26% importance), followed by Altmetric scores (30.19%) and journal impact factors (16.55%). This finding suggests that how the academic community engages with an article may be more important than where it was published when assessing its reliability. While our system performed well in the experiments, it also showed some limitations. The model was more likely to wrongly flag good papers (29.0% false positive rate) than to miss problematic ones. This result matches our goal of filtering out questionable research but also shows that we can improve the method of handling good papers. We hope that this work will be of interest to practitioners in the fields of open data and open science, especially those working on technical systems.

Author Contributions: Conceptualization, X.M. and C.L.; methodology, C.L.; software, C.L.; validation, X.M., J.Z. and W.C.; formal analysis, C.L.; writing—original draft preparation, C.L.; writing—review and editing, X.M., J.Z. and W.C.; funding acquisition, X.M. All authors have read and agreed to the published version of the manuscript.

Funding: This research was funded by National Science Foundation (U.S.) grant numbers 2019609 and 2126315. The APC was waived by MDPI.

Data Availability Statement: The data and code supporting the findings of this study are available in the GitHub repository: https://github.com/Akaoreo/Trust_CF_ranking (accessed on 2 July 2025).

Conflicts of Interest: The authors declare no conflict of interest.

References

1. Fire, M.; Guestrin, C. Over-optimization of academic publishing metrics: Observing Goodhart's Law in action. *GigaScience* **2019**, *8*, giz053. [CrossRef] [PubMed]
2. Kelly, J.; Sadeghieh, T.; Adeli, K. Peer Review in Scientific Publications: Benefits, Critiques, & A Survival Guide. *EJIFCC* **2014**, *25*, 227–243. Available online: https://www.ncbi.nlm.nih.gov/pmc/articles/PMC4975196/ (accessed on 28 March 2025). [PubMed]
3. Pal, S. What is Text Similarity and How to Implement it ? MLSAKIIT. Available online: https://medium.com/msackiit/what-is-text-similarity-and-how-to-implement-it-c74c8b641883 (accessed on 28 March 2025).
4. Intellica.AI. Comparison of Different Word Embeddings on Text Similarity—A Use Case in NLP. Medium. Available online: https://intellica-ai.medium.com/comparison-of-different-word-embeddings-on-text-similarity-a-use-case-in-nlp-e83e08469c1c (accessed on 28 March 2025).
5. Liberti, L.; Lavor, C.; Maculan, N.; Mucherino, A. Euclidean distance geometry and applications. *arXiv* **2012**, arXiv:1205.0349. [CrossRef]
6. Steck, H.; Ekanadham, C.; Kallus, N. Is Cosine-Similarity of Embeddings Really About Similarity? In Proceedings of the Companion ACM Web Conference, Singapore, 13–17 May 2024; pp. 887–890. [CrossRef]
7. Neha. A Simple Guide to Metrics for Calculating String Similarity. Analytics Vidhya. Available online: https://www.analyticsvidhya.com/blog/2021/02/a-simple-guide-to-metrics-for-calculating-string-similarity/ (accessed on 28 March 2025).
8. Qian, G.; Sural, S.; Gu, Y.; Pramanik, S. Similarity Between Euclidean and Cosine Angle Distance for Nearest Neighbor Queries. In Proceedings of the 2004 ACM Symposium on Applied Computing, in SAC '04, Nicosia, Cyprus, 14–17 March 2004; Association for Computing Machinery: New York, NY, USA, 2004; pp. 1232–1237. [CrossRef]
9. Bosker, H.R. Using fuzzy string matching for automated assessment of listener transcripts in speech intelligibility studies. *Behav. Res. Methods* **2021**, *53*, 1945–1953. [CrossRef] [PubMed]
10. Shimomura, L.C.; Oyamada, R.S.; Vieira, M.R.; Kaster, D.S. A survey on graph-based methods for similarity searches in metric spaces. *Inf. Syst.* **2021**, *95*, 101507. [CrossRef]
11. Sammut, C.; Webb, G.I. (Eds.) TF–IDF. In *Encyclopedia of Machine Learning*; Springer: Boston, MA, USA, 2010; pp. 986–987. [CrossRef]
12. Mikolov, T.; Chen, K.; Corrado, G.; Dean, J. Efficient Estimation of Word Representations in Vector Space. *arXiv* **2013**, arXiv:1301.3781. [CrossRef]
13. Le, Q.V.; Mikolov, T. Distributed Representations of Sentences and Documents. *arXiv* **2014**, arXiv:1405.4053. [CrossRef]

14. Devlin, J.; Chang, M.-W.; Lee, K.; Toutanova, K. BERT: Pre-training of Deep Bidirectional Transformers for Language Understanding. *arXiv* **2019**, arXiv:1810.04805. [CrossRef]
15. Bornmann, L.; Daniel, H. What do citation counts measure? A review of studies on citing behavior. *J. Doc.* **2008**, *64*, 45–80. [CrossRef]
16. Ioannidis, J.P.A. Why Most Published Research Findings Are False. *PLoS Med.* **2005**, *2*, e124. [CrossRef] [PubMed]
17. Kousha, K.; Thelwall, M. Are wikipedia citations important evidence of the impact of scholarly articles and books? *J. Assoc. Inf. Sci. Technol.* **2017**, *68*, 762–779. [CrossRef]
18. Castillo, C.; Mendoza, M.; Poblete, B. Information Credibility on Twitter. In Proceedings of the 20th International Conference on World Wide Web, in WWW '11, Hyderabad, India, 28 March–1 April 2011; Association for Computing Machinery: New York, NY, USA, 2011; pp. 675–684. [CrossRef]
19. Pérez-Rosas, V.; Kleinberg, B.; Lefevre, A.; Mihalcea, R. Automatic Detection of Fake News. In *Proceedings of the 27th International Conference on Computational Linguistics*; Bender, E.M., Derczynski, L., Isabelle, P., Eds.; Association for Computational Linguistics: Santa Fe, NM, USA, 2018; pp. 3391–3401. Available online: https://aclanthology.org/C18-1287/ (accessed on 28 March 2025).
20. Beel, J.; Gipp, B. Google Scholar's Ranking Algorithm: The Impact of Citation Counts (An Empirical Study). In Proceedings of the 2009 Third International Conference on Research Challenges in Information Science, Fez, Morocco, 22–24 April 2009; pp. 439–446. [CrossRef]
21. Falagas, M.E.; Pitsouni, E.I.; Malietzis, G.A.; Pappas, G. Comparison of PubMed, Scopus, Web of Science, and Google Scholar: Strengths and weaknesses. *FASEB J. Off. Publ. Fed. Am. Soc. Exp. Biol.* **2008**, *22*, 338–342. [CrossRef] [PubMed]
22. Lu, Z. PubMed and beyond: A survey of web tools for searching biomedical literature. *Database J. Biol. Databases Curation* **2011**, *2011*, baq036. [CrossRef] [PubMed]
23. Retraction Watch. Available online: https://retractionwatch.com/ (accessed on 28 March 2025).
24. Nature Editorial. Why retractions data could be a powerful tool for cleaning up science. *Nature* **2025**, *638*, 581. [CrossRef] [PubMed]
25. Gu, J.; Jiang, X.; Shi, Z.; Tan, H.; Zhai, X.; Xu, C.; Li, W.; Shen, Y.; Ma, S.; Liu, H.; et al. A Survey on LLM-as-a-Judge. *arXiv* **2025**, arXiv:2411.15594. [CrossRef]

algorithms

MDPI

Article

Engine Optimization Model for Accurate Prediction of Friction Model in Marine Dual-Fuel Engine

Mina Tadros [1,2]

[1] Department of Naval Architecture, Ocean and Marine Engineering, Maritime Safety Research Centre (MSRC), University of Strathclyde, Glasgow G4 0LZ, UK; mina.tadros@strath.ac.uk

[2] Department of Naval Architecture and Marine Engineering, Faculty of Engineering, Alexandria University, Alexandria 21544, Egypt

Abstract: This paper presents an innovative engine optimization model integrated with a friction fitting tool to enhance the accuracy of computed performance for a marine dual-fuel engine. The focus is on determining the terms of the Chen–Flynn correlation—an empirical engine friction model—to improve the precision of friction and performance predictions. The developed model employs WAVE, a 1D engine simulation software, coupled with a nonlinear optimizer to identify the optimal configuration of key parameters, including the turbocharger, injection system, combustion behavior, and friction model. The optimization procedure maximizes the air–fuel ratio (AFR) within the engine while adhering to various predefined constraints. The model is applied to four operational points along the propeller curve, with the optimized results subsequently integrated into a friction fitting tool. This tool predicts the terms of the Chen–Flynn correlation through an updated procedure, achieving highly accurate results with a coefficient of determination (R^2) value of 99.88%, eliminating the need for experimental testing. The optimized friction model provides a reliable foundation for future studies and applications, enabling precise friction predictions across various engine types and fuel compositions.

Keywords: FMEP; optimization procedures; 1D engine simulation; Chen–Flynn friction model; marine dual-fuel engine

1. Introduction

The stringent regulations set by the International Maritime Organization (IMO) to reduce the amount of exhaust emissions from marine vessels have led to the rapid development of dual-fuel engines to allow diesel engines to operate with alternative clean fuels [1,2]. These types of diesel engines operate in liquid, such as marine diesel oil (MDO) or heavy fuel oil (HFO), and gas modes, such as hydrogen (H_2) or natural gas (NG), allowing the flexibility of the ship to operate in different types of clean fuel to comply within the limits of energy efficiency indices proposed by the International Convention for the Prevention of Pollution from Ships (MARPOL) [3,4].

Engines contain numerous moving parts, and proper lubrication is essential to keep them functioning smoothly, prolong the component lifespan, and reduce energy losses caused by friction. Inadequate lubrication is a common cause of engine durability and reliability issues, leading to problems such as excessive wear, component seizure, and even catastrophic failures. Maintaining adequate lubrication and minimizing friction is critical for ensuring engine integrity and optimal performance [5–7].

To compute the friction losses in a marine diesel engine, the resistance from the moving components inside the engine must be accounted for. Frictional forces in a marine diesel engine arise from different parts, such as the piston assembly (piston rings and cylinder liner), crankshaft and bearings, valve train (camshafts and rocker arms), and auxiliary components (pumps and turbochargers). In a typical fired engine (diesel or spark-ignition), mechanical friction accounts for approximately 4% to 15% of the total fuel energy [8]. This estimate reflects the average engine performance across a range of operating conditions. However, under extreme conditions, such as idling or very light loads, nearly all the fuel energy may be consumed to overcome friction, resulting in little to no net power output. The thermal efficiency of modern engines generally ranges between 38% and 50%, with 45–50% being a common target in engine development. Mechanical friction typically consumes 10% to 30% of the engine's power output, but under idling conditions, it can approach 100%, highlighting the importance of minimizing friction to improve overall efficiency and performance.

The friction power calculation method is a straightforward approach in which the friction mean effective pressure (FMEP) is determined by subtracting the indicated mean effective pressure (IMEP) and the brake mean effective pressure (BMEP) from each other, as in Equation (1).

$$\mathrm{FMEP} = \mathrm{IMEP} - \mathrm{BMEP} \tag{1}$$

An alternative approach to estimating friction is through the measurement of mechanical efficiency (η_m), as in Equation (2). This equation highlights the direct relationship between friction losses, fuel consumption, and power output; minimizing friction not only decreases fuel consumption but also enhances engine performance by maximizing usable power.

$$h_m = \frac{\mathrm{IMEP} - \mathrm{FMEP}}{\mathrm{IMEP}} \tag{2}$$

Thus, the FMEP is calculated using Equation (3).

$$\mathrm{FMEP} = \mathrm{IMEP}(1 - h_m) \tag{3}$$

Over the years, various technologies have been implemented and refined in diesel engines to enhance performance and reduce friction [9]. For example, the installation of one or more turbochargers has optimized the air–fuel ratio (AFR), indirectly lowering friction by allowing engine downsizing [10,11]. Variable Geometry Turbines (VGTs) have also been introduced to improve the efficiency of turbocharged engines, reducing mechanical stress and internal friction [12]. Optimizing the fuel injection system is critical to maintaining smooth combustion and minimizing unnecessary mechanical loads [13–15]. Additionally, fine-tuning valve timing can decrease pumping losses, which indirectly reduces engine friction [16–18].

Experimental testing is essential for estimating and validating friction forces within engines [19,20], while few experimental studies have been performed. Techniques such as fired engine tests or pressurized motoring tests are commonly used to measure friction. Research has also assessed the lubrication conditions between the piston ring and cylinder liner in different diesel engines, with numerical models validated through experimental data to show how surface roughness affects engine performance [21,22]. In low-speed diesel engines, friction measurements on components such as the piston assembly–cylinder liner, piston rod stuffing box, and crosshead slipper-guide have been conducted to improve tribological performance and reduce fuel consumption [23].

This has led to the exploration of biodiesel blends in lubricating oils, which often exhibit superior lubrication properties compared to conventional diesel [24,25]. For instance, a 10% biodiesel–oil blend can reduce both the friction coefficient and wear scar diameter [26–29]. The addition of nano-lubricants has shown further potential for enhancing the lubrication properties of diesel engines [30–32]. Furthermore, selecting optimal cylinder bore coating materials is vital to minimizing fuel consumption and exhaust emissions while ensuring engine reliability [33,34].

Numerical simulation is pivotal in the development of new engine technologies, enhancing production efficiency and ensuring precision, especially with the increasing complexity of controlling engine subsystems via the engine control unit (ECU). Albrecht et al. [35] emphasized that the 0D/1D models used in this study allow comprehensive control over various engine components while offering faster computational times compared to 3D computational fluid dynamics (CFD) models. While 3D CFD models offer detailed insights into specific phenomena, they are computationally intensive, making 0D/1D models ideal for early-stage development and system-level analysis.

Engine models also serve as valuable tools for simulating performance with different fuels. For example, Wei et al. [36] used AVL's BOOST software [37] to study the impact of Early Intake Valve Closure (EIVC) on engine performance. Their findings revealed that EIVC significantly increases the heat release rate, resulting in higher nitric oxide (NO) emissions and potential misfires under low-load conditions. Mocerino et al. [38] utilized WAVE 2019.1 from Ricardo Wave Software [39] to simulate the behavior of a marine diesel engine, validating the model with experimental data. The model accurately predicted emissions during sea trials, demonstrating its reliability in evaluating engine performance and environmental impact.

Similarly, Shen et al. [40] used GT-Power [41] to explore how turbocharger performance degradation affects overall engine performance in both diesel and gas modes. Their results showed a downward trend in key parameters like the turbocharger speed, boost pressure, peak pressure, and brake thermal efficiency, while the exhaust temperature and emissions increased, highlighting the critical role of turbocharger health in engine efficiency. Stoumpos et al. [42] and Karatuğ et al. [43] investigated the transition of marine engine performance across various operating points using a 1D engine model. This model is developed as a digital twin to reflect real-time engine operation onboard ships, enabling better control and optimization of marine engines under varying conditions.

Thanks to the use of Application Programming Interfaces (APIs), engine models can be seamlessly integrated with third-party software to perform optimization procedures. For instance, Tadros et al. [16] coupled WAVE with a nonlinear optimizer to identify the key parameters of the turbocharger, valve, and injection system of a large marine diesel engine, optimizing performance across the engine's operating range. This model was later adapted to enhance high-speed engine performance, enabling the selection of the optimal operating point with minimal fuel consumption during propeller design [44,45] based on a proper diesel combustion model based on a double-Wiebe function [46]. Zhang et al. [11] applied an artificial neural network (ANN) in combination with the Non-dominated Sorting Genetic Algorithm (NSGA II) to optimize two-stage turbo-assisted and exhaust gas recirculation (TA EGR) in diesel engines. Their approach successfully reduced fuel consumption by 3.5% and cut nitrogen oxide (NO_x) emissions by over 75% across different operating points, demonstrating the effectiveness of advanced optimization techniques in improving engine efficiency and reducing environmental impact. Kolakoti et al. [47] applied Definitive Screening Design (DSD) and ANN modeling to optimize palm oil biodiesel (POBD) production and predict yield outcomes. With 17 experimental runs, a maximum biodiesel yield of 96.06% was achieved. The ANN model demonstrated high prediction accuracy with strong R^2 and low MSE. The produced POBD met ASTM-D675 [48] standards, and engine tests showed significant reductions in NOx (32.46%), HC (40.57%), CO (44.44%), and smoke (39.65%) compared to diesel, along with lower engine cylinder vibration levels.

The empirical friction model is a widely used approach for calculating friction losses in diesel engines. The friction submodules integrated into commercial engine simulation software are typically based on empirical formulas, following the Chen and Flynn correlations [49]. These models rely on standardized coefficient values due to the restricted availability of real data from the engine manufacturer's project guide. While these default values offer a reasonable approximation for many applications, they may limit the model's accuracy in reflecting the specific friction characteristics of an engine, especially in unique or highly customized designs. The developed formula establishes a relationship between the FMEP, engine speed, and pressure. In the WAVE engine, a modified version of the Chen–Flynn correlation is applied to capture friction dynamics accurately. Similar to the original model, the modified equation includes (1) a constant term (A_{cf})—accounts for baseline friction, (2) a load-dependent term (B_{cf})—that varies with peak cylinder pressure, (3) a hydrodynamic friction term (C_{cf})—linearly dependent on mean piston velocity, and (4) a windage loss term (Q_{cf})—quadratic with mean piston velocity. Equation (4) presents the core formula used to calculate the FMEP, reflecting the influence of these parameters on friction losses.

$$\text{FMEP} = A_{cf} + \frac{1}{n_{cyl}} \sum_{i=1}^{ncyl} \left[B_{cf}\,(P_{max})_i + C_{cf}(S)_i + Q_{cf}(S)_i^{\,2} \right] \quad (4)$$

where n_{cyl} is the number of cylinders, P_{max} is the maximum cylinder pressure, and S is the mean piston speed.

Standard values are assigned to each term in accordance with Chen–Flynn's original model, but these parameters can be adjusted to match the performance characteristics of modern engines.

Optimizing these values is a complex process that demands extensive engine testing to accurately determine the BMEP and IMEP and then implement them into numerical models for further comparison [23,50]. Fine-tuning these parameters ensures that the model reflects real-world engine behavior, improving the accuracy of friction loss predictions [51,52].

From the presented literature review, this study fills the gap in the prediction of the friction model by developing an optimization model capable of determining the optimal parameters in the Chen–Flynn correlation for a given engine without requiring experimental tests or real-world friction data. The computed values of the friction correlation will be considered and implemented into a 1D engine simulation to compute the performance of the engine along different operating points in further research.

The developed optimization model integrates WAVE from Realis Simulation [53] with a Matlab 2025a-based optimizer to determine the optimal FMEP values and peak pressure, alongside key engine parameters, at various operating points along the propeller engine curve. The model aims to maximize the AFR while ensuring compliance with predefined constraints. The main results are subsequently incorporated into a friction tool in Excel for a fitting procedure to identify the optimal values of each correlation term through multiple iterations of adjustment.

The model demonstrates high accuracy in predicting the FMEP and can be applied to evaluate the performance of friction models across different engine types. This approach ensures a more precise assessment of engine friction behavior, particularly in cases where manufacturer-specific data is unavailable.

2. Engine Specifications

The engine used in this study to perform the simulation and the optimization procedure is the marine dual-fuel engine MAN D2862 LE448 [54]. It is a dual-fuel engine operating in liquid mode using MDO and in gas mode using hydrogen as a main injection fuel. It is a turbocharged diesel engine with a charge air intercooler and wastegate. The engine itself complies with the limitation of IMO Tier 2 and can be installed on fast workboats and small tugboats. The intake pressure and temperature are set at atmospheric conditions, i.e., 100 kPa and 318 K, respectively. The maximum power of the engine is 749 kW at 2100 rpm. Table 1 shows the main characteristics of the selected engine.

Table 1. Main engine specifications [55].

Parameter	Value
Bore (mm)	128
Stroke (mm)	157
No. of cylinders	12
Displacement (liter)	24.24
Number of valves per cylinder	4
Compression ratio	19:1
BMEP (bar)	17.66
Piston speed (m/s)	10.99
Engine speed (rpm)	2100
Brake-specific fuel consumption (g/kW.h)	208
Power-to-weight ratio (kW/Kg)	0.329

3. Engine Optimization Model

3.1. Overview of the Numerical Engine Model

The optimization model developed in this study integrates WAVE 2024.1 from Realis Simulation [53], as a 1D engine simulation software, with a nonlinear optimizer in Matlab, as shown in Figure 1. The results from the optimization model are subsequently imported into an Excel tool developed by Realis Simulation, which uses the Chen–Flynn model to fit the optimized data and determine the optimal coefficients for the friction equation.

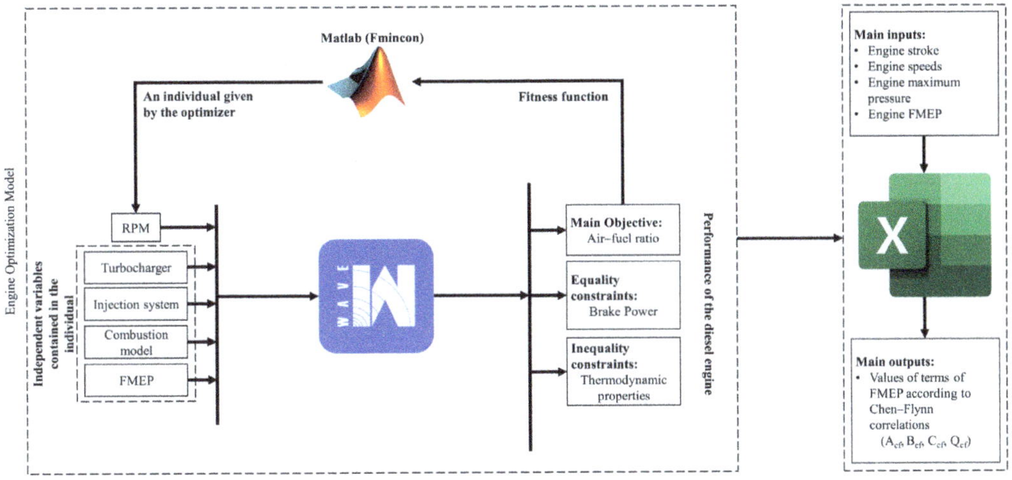

Figure 1. Overview of the developed optimization model for FMEP prediction.

The model has been developed to ensure high accuracy in engine calibration and to find the optimal values of the FMEP along the propeller curve. The engine model optimization finds the combination of the engine parameters, such as the turbocharger, injection system, and FMEP, to achieve a steady state at different operating points.

The model evaluates four specific operating points along the propeller curve to predict both the FMEP and maximum in-cylinder pressure: (1) rated power at 2100 rpm; (2) maximum and minimum speeds (1900 rpm and 1300 rpm) within the maximum torque range; and (3) the minimum engine speed at the propeller curve (600 rpm). The entire FMEP prediction process is conducted in liquid fuel mode, which is then used to compute the engine performance in both dual-fuel engine modes. Once the friction model's coefficients are optimized, they can be applied directly to simulate any operating points along the engine load diagram. This approach enables more accurate friction prediction across varying load conditions and engine modes, providing a robust tool for evaluating engine performance.

3.2. Description of WAVE Model

Firstly, the dual-fuel engine model is constructed in WAVE using the various elements available in the software, which combines flow, mechanical, and control components, as shown in Figure 2. The engine model features two turbochargers, one intercooler, twelve cylinders, and intake and exhaust manifolds. Similar to modern diesel engines, each cylinder is equipped with four valves—two for intake, two for exhaust—along with one injector in the liquid fuel mode, as the main focus of this study. The dimension of each part is collected from the project guide of the manufacturer [55,56].

The compressor and turbine maps for each turbocharger, as shown in Figure 3, are defined and rescaled from existing maps provided by the software to fit the engine's needs for airflow at a given pressure.

The "filling and emptying" method is applied to control turbocharger performance and behavior using the energy and momentum equations recommended by Watson and Janota [57]. This approach treats each manifold or cylinder as a separate thermodynamic control volume, with its dynamics governed by energy and continuity equations as functions of time or crank angle.

Regarding the fuel injection system, the key parameters, including injection timing, profile, pressure, duration, and the injection rate within the cylinder, are considered during the simulation. The rectangular injection rate profile is selected as it is the common rate profile used due to its benefits in achieving a more stable combustion process as well as emissions reduction [58].

Cylinder processes are computed using the first law of thermodynamics [8], incorporating the heat release rate (HRR) during combustion [59,60], and heat transfer based on the empirical formula by Woschni [61].

The total heat added during the combustion process, dQ, as described in Equation (5), is computed for each crank angle. This calculation includes the heat released from fuel combustion, Q_{comb}, and the heat exchange, dQ_w, with the cylinder walls:

$$dQ = Q_{comb} dx_b - dQ_w \tag{5}$$

$$Q_{comb} = m_{fuel} CV \tag{6}$$

$$dQ_w = \frac{hA_w}{\omega}(T_g - T_w)d\theta \tag{7}$$

where m_{fuel} is the amount of injected fuel, CV is the calorific value of the injected fuel, h is the heat transfer coefficient suggested by Woschni, A_w is the area of cylinder walls, ω is the engine speed, T_g is the burn gas temperature, and T_w is the cylinder wall temperature.

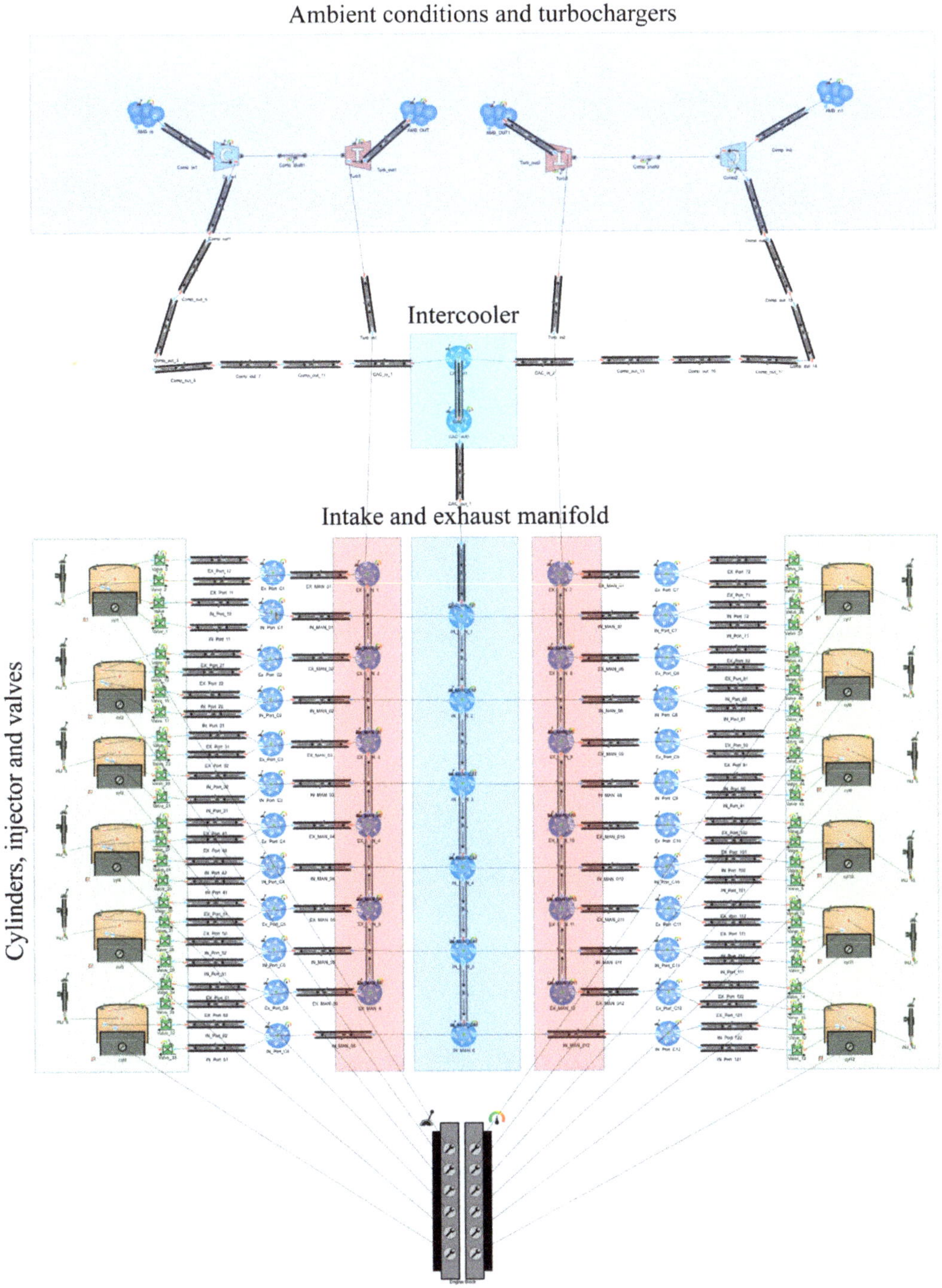

Figure 2. Layout of the 1D engine model implemented in WAVE.

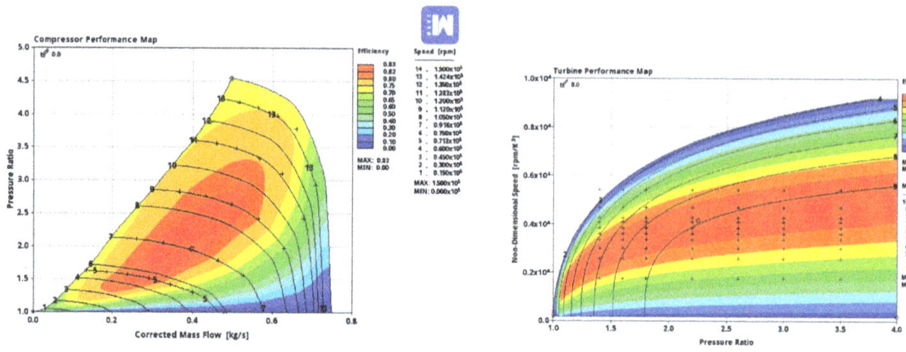

(a) (b)

Figure 3. Maps of (a) compressor and (b) turbine of the installed turbocharger used in the simulation.

The burned mass fraction, x_b, is computed using the equation suggested by Watson et al. [62], as expressed in Equation (8). This formula has been improved by the Realis Simulation team to consider the three phases of combustion. It is well-suited for combustion in the diesel cycle and does not require calibration, except for the reference speed (BRPM), as in Equation (9), to control the burn duration, unlike the single- and multi-Wiebe functions [63]. In some cases, the rated speed can be used as the reference speed [46,64]. The double-Wiebe function is introduced as an alternative to the single-Wiebe function to capture different phases of the combustion process better.

$$x_b = p_f\left\{1-\left[1-(0.75\tau)^2\right]^{5000}\right\}+d_f\left\{1-\left[1-(cd_3\tau)^{1.75}\right]^{5000}\right\}+t_f\left\{1-\left[1-(ct_3\tau)^{2.5}\right]^{5000}\right\} \quad (8)$$

where p_f, d_f, and t_f are the mass fractions of the premix, diffusion, and tail burn curves, respectively. cd_3 and ct_3 are the burn duration coefficients for the diffusion and tail burn curves, respectively, and τ is the burn duration in degrees calculated according to the following expression:

$$\tau = \frac{\theta - \theta_o}{125\left(\frac{RPM}{BRPM}\right)^{0.3}} \quad (9)$$

where θ is the crank angle, θ_o is the start angle of combustion, and RPM is the engine speed.

3.3. Nonlinear Optimizer

To enhance reproducibility and provide clarity on the implemented procedure, a flowchart of the MATLAB-based optimization algorithm is presented in Figure 4. The algorithm begins by defining the initial values and bounds for the key design variables.

These are passed into a nonlinear optimizer, which evaluates a fitness function aimed at maximizing the AFR while satisfying performance and combustion constraints, such as brake power, in-cylinder temperature, maximum pressure, and combustion stability (evaluated using R^2). The nonlinear optimizer used in this study is the local optimizer "fmincon" based on an interior point algorithm [65] and integrated into Matlab. This optimizer has been selected due to its higher accuracy in achieving the optimal solution and lower computational time. The optimizer iteratively adjusts the variables, simulates the engine model in WAVE, and checks convergence until all constraints are met. The final output provides a set of optimized parameters for each operating condition. While it is a local optimizer, the computation can be performed more than once with an updated starting point to achieve the optimal solution and comply with all the constraints. However, the computational time is lower than that of a global optimizer like a genetic algorithm (GA) [66].

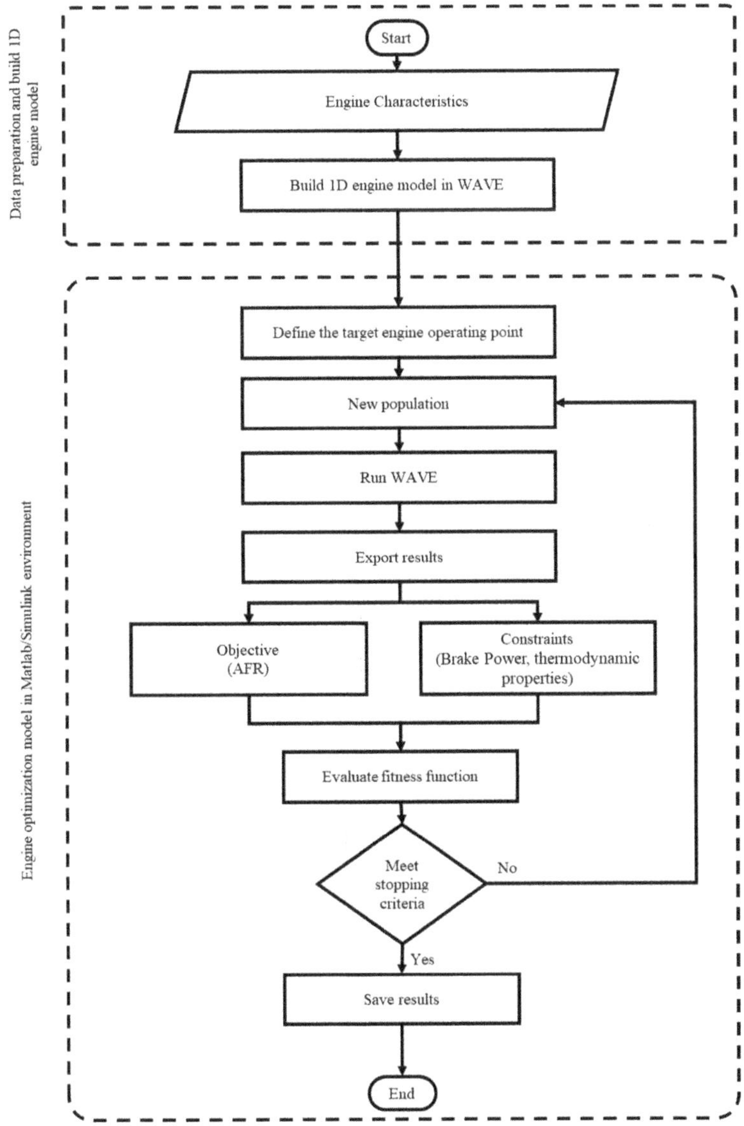

Figure 4. Schematic diagram of the engine optimization model.

The main problem is defined to minimize the objective of the study and specified by the following equation:

$$\min_{x} f(x) \text{ such that} \begin{cases} c(x) \leq 0 \\ c_{eq}(x) = 0 \\ A \cdot x \leq b \\ A_{eq} \cdot x = b_{eq} \\ lb \leq x \leq ub \end{cases} \tag{10}$$

where f(x) is the optimization model objective, c is the inequality constraints, c_{eq} is the equality constraints, A as a matrix and b as a vector are the linear inequality constraints, A_{eq} as a matrix and b_{eq} as a vector are the linear equality constraints, and lb and ub are the lower and upper bounds, respectively.

In this study, the main objective of the optimization problem is to maximize the AFR, unlike previous studies that minimize only the amount of fuel consumption [16,67,68]. Maximizing the AFR helps to not only reduce fuel consumption but also provides a sufficient amount of air, which improves the combustion process, increases the maximum in-cylinder pressure, reduces the maximum in-cylinder temperature, and thus reduces NO_x emissions. The optimization model assists in finding the optimal values of the different parameters along the engine parts with the known amount of the fuel rate (FR) collected from the project guide, such as the turbocharger speed (TS), start of injection (SOI), injection duration (INJ_{Dur}), FMEP, and BRPM. The design variables of the engine optimization model are presented by a five-dimensional vector x = (TS, SOI, INJ_{Dur}, FMEP, BRPM). The last design variable is optimized at the rated operating point and then kept constant while performing the optimization procedures at the partial operating points. The optimization problem is subjected to different equality and inequality constraints.

The main equality constraint of the optimization model is related to the engine brake power, PB, that needs to be achieved, as in Equation (11).

$$P_B\,(x) = P_{B,\,obj} \tag{11}$$

An additional equality constraint is considered only at the rated operating point, which is the known air mass flow rate, $\dot{m}_a$, inside the cylinders.

$$\dot{m}_a\,(x) = \dot{m}_{a,\,obj} \tag{12}$$

However, different inequality constraints are defined using the following expressions:

$$T_{AfterCylinder}(x) \leq 1073\,K \tag{13}$$

$$T_{max}(x) \leq 1950\,K \tag{14}$$

$$P_{max}(x) \leq 180\,bar \tag{15}$$

$$20 \leq AFR(x) \leq 80 \tag{16}$$

$$R^2(x) \geq 0.99 \tag{17}$$

where $T_{AfterCylinder}(x)$ is the exhaust temperature after the cylinder in degree K, $T_{max}(x)$ is the maximum average temperature inside the cylinder, and $P_{max}(x)$ is the maximum in-cylinder pressure in bar.

The square of the coefficient of determination (R^2) is used to evaluate the fuel burn rate along with the combustion duration compared to a polynomial equation from the sixth degree to ensure the smoothness of the curve and, thus, the combustion behavior, avoiding any misfire and unstable combustion. The degree of polynomial equations is selected based on several trials to ensure the best fitting. Due to the different values in the amount of fuel burn rate and the combustion duration, a normalized curve is presented, as shown in

Figure 5. The fuel burn rate curve is rescaled from 0 to 1 to make it easier to identify, and the fitting procedures are performed.

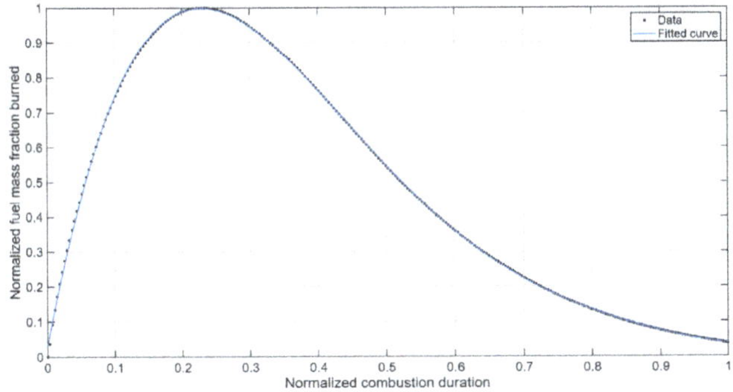

Figure 5. Fitting procedure of the normalized fuel mass fraction burned.

These constraints are implemented into the optimization model by presenting them as a static penalty function, a degree of violation to make the absolute values less than one, as in the following expressions:

$$h_1(x) = \frac{P_B}{P_{B,\ obj}} - 1 \tag{18}$$

$$h_2(x) = \frac{m^{\cdot}_a}{m^{\cdot}_{a,\ obj}} - 1 \tag{19}$$

$$g_1(x) = \frac{T_{AfterCylinder}}{T_{AfterCylinder,\ max}} - 1 \tag{20}$$

$$g_2(x) = \frac{T_{max}}{T_{max,\ max}} - 1 \tag{21}$$

$$g_3(x) = \frac{P_{max}}{P_{max,\ max}} - 1 \tag{22}$$

$$g_4(x) = \frac{AFR}{AFR_{max}} - 1 \tag{23}$$

$$g_5(x) = -\frac{AFR}{AFR_{min}} + 1 \tag{24}$$

$$g_6(x) = -\frac{R^2}{R^2_{min}} + 1 \tag{25}$$

The five optimization variables are subjected to specified ranges, as shown in the following equations:

$$5000 \leq TS \leq 145{,}000 \tag{26}$$

$$-20 \leq SOI \leq 15 \tag{27}$$

$$15 \leq INJ_{Dur} \leq 35 \tag{28}$$

$$0.8 \leq FMEP \leq 3 \tag{29}$$

$$2100 \leq BRPM \leq 3000 \tag{30}$$

where the range of the TS is defined according to the speed range of the compressor map, the ranges of the SOI, INJ_{Dur}, and FMEP are selected based on the common information of the diesel engines [69,70], and the range of the BRPM is defined according to the range suggested by the software.

In order to evaluate the performance of the optimization problem, the objective and both the equality and inequality constraints are implemented into a fitness function to achieve the minimum/maximum value of the objective and comply with all the constraints using the following equation:

$$\text{Fitness function} = \text{AFR}(x) + R\left[\sum_{i=1}^{n} \max(g(x), 0) + \sum_{j=1}^{m} |h(x)|\right] \quad (31)$$

where R is a constant equal to 1000 as previously used by [16,68].

4. Results and Discussions

4.1. Simulation of Marine Diesel Engine

Based on the developed optimization model, the engine's performance is first computed and optimized at its rated power to identify the optimal combination of adjustable parameters such as the TS, SOI, FMEP, and INJ_{Dur} and a constant parameter such as the BRPM. The constant parameter is subsequently fixed while performing optimization at partial load conditions. This initial step serves as a calibration process, where critical factors such as air intake, fuel supply, exhaust temperature, and defined constraints significantly influence the determination of the optimal values for the adjustable variables.

To ensure accuracy and engine stability, each iteration involves simulating 40 cycles. Depending on the number of optimization variables involved, the simulation of each operating point takes approximately 4 to 8 h to reach optimal conditions.

The results, including the values of optimized variables, constraint parameters, and validation parameters, are presented in Table 2. These validation parameters quantify the percentage error between the manufacturer's real-world data and the simulation results, ensuring the model's accuracy and reliability.

Table 2. Computed results from the optimization model and percentage of error between real and simulation data at 100% rated power and 100% engine speed.

	Parameter	**Unit**	**Real Value**	**Simulated Value**	**Percentage of Error [%]**
Optimized variables	TS	[rpm]	-	131,529	-
	SOI	[BTDC]	-	−1.406	-
	INJ_{Dur}	[degree]	-	32.98	-
	FMEP	[bar]	-	2.54	-
	BRPM	[rpm]	-	2957	-
Constraints parameters	$T_{AfterCylinder}$	[K]	-	915	-
	T_{max}	[K]	-	1771	-
	P_{max}	[bar]	-	168.4	-
	AFR	[-]	-	26.2	-
	R^2	[-]	-	0.9999	-
Validation parameters	P_B	[kW]	749	748.74	0.034
	BSFC	[g/kW.h]	208	208	0
	$\dot{m}_a$	[kg/h]	4084	4082.56	0.035
	T_{exh}	[K]	711	733	3.09

Based on the optimized variables, the TS is adjusted at a higher engine speed to enhance airflow, resulting in a compressor efficiency of 78%, as derived from the performance maps. The SOI is optimized to occur a few degrees before the top dead center (TDC), with an injection duration of approximately 33°, ensuring high combustion pressure and a smooth, consistent fuel burn rate.

The FMEP is optimized at 2.54 bar, a value deemed appropriate for this type of diesel engine, balancing efficiency and reliability. The intake and exhaust valve lift ratios are carefully calculated, with the intake valve having a higher lift to maximize fresh air intake and improve the replacement of exhaust gases in the cylinder.

Additionally, the BRPM is set near the midpoint of its operational range, a critical factor in determining combustion duration and ensuring stable engine performance. These optimizations collectively contribute to enhanced engine efficiency and operational stability.

The constraint parameters adhere to the predefined safety limits, ensuring reliable engine operation. The P_{max} remains below 180 bar, while both the $T_{AfterCylinder}$ and T_{max} are kept below their respective limits. This is achieved by maintaining a high air-to-fuel ratio within the cylinders, which not only enhances combustion efficiency but also significantly reduces NO_x emissions, ensuring compliance with IMO Tier II regulations.

Additionally, the R^2 for the fuel burn rate reaches an impressive 99.99%, indicating smooth and consistent combustion behavior throughout the process. This ensures optimal performance while meeting stringent emission standards.

To validate engine performance, key parameters—P_B, brake-specific fuel consumption (BSFC), air mass flow, and T_{exh}—are compared with real engine data. The first three parameters demonstrate excellent accuracy, with deviations of just 0.05%. The T_{exh} in the simulated results is slightly higher than the real data, with a deviation of 2.31%. This difference falls within an acceptable range and is likely attributed to the rescaling of existing performance maps to align with the characteristics of the current engine. These results confirm the reliability of the simulation model for engine performance evaluation.

After validating the engine model at the rated operating point, the optimized constant parameter values are used to simulate performance across three partial operating points. The same optimization methodology is applied to these reduced-variable cases, ensuring consistency and reliability in the approach. The computed results for all operating points are systematically summarized in Table 3. These results show the adaptive behavior of the turbocharger speed, injection timing, and FMEP under varying engine speeds and loads. The increasing AFR at low load highlights the impact of reduced fuel demand, while consistently high R^2 values confirm combustion stability.

Table 3. Optimized engine parameters and corresponding combustion constraint values at three partial load points.

	Parameter	Unit	Case 1	Case 2	Case 3
	Engine speed	[rpm]	1900	1300	600
	Loading ratio	[%]	78.5	30.2	4.5
Optimized variables	TS	[rpm]	120,659	67,592	35,956
	SOI	[BTDC]	−3.69	−2.23	−1.69
	INJ_{Dur}	[degree]	25.68	23.99	17.31
	FMEP	[bar]	2.48	1.86	1.17
Constraints parameters	$T_{AfterCylinder}$	[K]	808	758	494
	T_{max}	[K]	1717	1706	1334
	P_{max}	[bar]	168.5	94.2	73.0
	AFR	[-]	30.19	31.03	68.89
	R^2	[-]	0.9999	0.9998	0.9999

The TS decreases as the load is reduced, achieved by lowering the air supply and boosting pressure. The SOI is adjusted between 0° and −5° BTDC to ensure optimal combustion and achieve maximum in-cylinder pressure. At lower loads, the injection duration is shortened to account for the decreased cylinder combustion temperature and pressure, promoting smooth combustion. The AFR remains stable up to 31:1 for load ratios up to 30%, but it increases significantly at lower loads to enhance combustion efficiency. At 600 rpm, the engine operates at a very low load (4.5%), which results in a significantly reduced fuel injection quantity. However, the air supply remains comparatively high due to the turbocharger configuration and intake system dynamics. This imbalance leads to a high AFR of 68.89. While this value may appear high, such AFRs are typical during idle or low-load conditions in dual-fuel or lean-burn engines, where excess air improves combustion stability and reduces NO_x emissions. This behavior has been observed in similar low-load engine studies and is consistent with expected thermodynamic trends under minimal fueling scenarios.

The R^2 exceeds 0.9996, indicating smooth combustion with no misfires detected, ensuring reliable engine operation. The in-cylinder pressure diagram and fuel burn rate are presented in Figure 6, showing the reliability of the developed model in achieving smooth combustion at four different operating conditions with no misfire under all tested conditions.

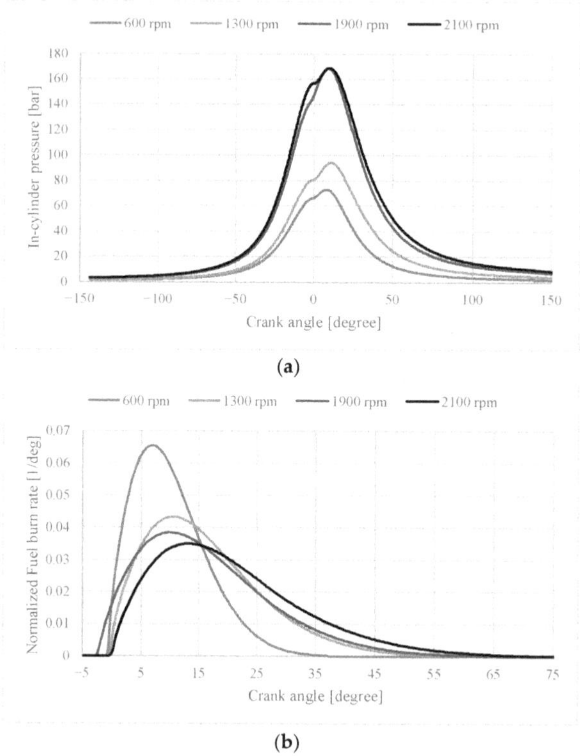

Figure 6. (**a**) In-cylinder pressure diagram and (**b**) fuel burn rate for four different engine operating points.

4.2. Computation of the Terms of the Friction Model

Following the optimization and validation of the engine performance parameters across various load conditions, the next step involves refining the empirical friction model. This is achieved by fitting the optimized simulation results to the Chen–Flynn correlation to ensure accurate and scalable FMEP prediction.

To determine the coefficients of the Chen–Flynn correlation, the FMEP and the P_{max} at each engine speed are incorporated into the friction tool developed by the Realis Simulation team. Using the standard correlation coefficients presented in Table 4 as a baseline, the fitting process is executed with the friction tool to compute the percentage error between the calculated and predicted FMEP values for each engine speed. Initially, the percentage error remains within 7.2% across all speeds. However, to ensure high accuracy for subsequent simulations, it is necessary to minimize these errors further.

Table 4. Comparison between the standard and optimized value of each term in Chen–Flynn correlation.

Term	Standard Value	Optimized Value
A_{cf}	0.5	0.4309
B_{cf}	0.006	0.006
C_{cf}	600	655.3842
Q_{cf}	0.2	0.2

To refine the fitting process, the second and fourth terms of the Chen–Flynn correlation are retained as per the original equation, with fixed values of 0.006 and 0.2, respectively, while the first and third terms are computed based on the data defined in the Excel tool. B_{cf} and Q_{cf} are fixed to the standard literature values (0.006 and 0.2, respectively) due to their relatively low sensitivity to engine-specific variations and the absence of reliable experimental data to refine them. These terms predominantly capture baseline friction behavior associated with pressure and velocity effects that are consistent across engine types. In contrast, A_{cf} and C_{cf} are treated as variable terms and optimized using the friction fitting tool, as they are more influenced by the specific design and operational characteristics of the engine (e.g., surface finish, lubrication, piston speed). This approach strikes a balance between modeling accuracy and practical constraints, ensuring that the refined coefficients accurately reflect the real behavior of the studied engine while maintaining computational efficiency.

Adjustments are made by replacing the computed FMEP values with the predicted ones from the fitting model at engine speeds through multiple iterations. This iterative refinement is repeated across the speed range, starting with the points with a higher percentage of errors, until achieving a stable and improved R^2 between the calculated and predicted FMEP curves. This method ensures enhanced accuracy and reliability of the correlation for future applications.

Figure 7 illustrates the strong correlation between the newly computed values and the predicted FMEP values, demonstrating the effectiveness of the fitting process. The final R^2 value between the two curves is 0.9999, indicating a nearly perfect match. The percentage error across the engine speeds ranges from 0.13% to −0.13%, reflecting a significant reduction in discrepancies and ensuring high accuracy of the model across varying operating conditions. Table 4 shows the new values of each term compared to the standard values.

Comparable studies using empirical fitting techniques and numerical optimization also report R^2 values above 0.98 for friction prediction models [71,72], which supports the validity of our results given the controlled simulation environment and absence of experimental noise.

After incorporating the updated coefficient values into the Chen–Flynn correlation, minor deviations, such as those presented in the computed results in Table 3, are to be expected. These discrepancies arise due to the sensitivity of the correlation to changes in its parameters, especially when applied to complex thermodynamic systems. Nevertheless, the overall trends remain consistent, and the observed variations fall within acceptable error margins for engineering applications. Additionally, the performance of the engine at various operating conditions along the engine load diagram will be calculated.

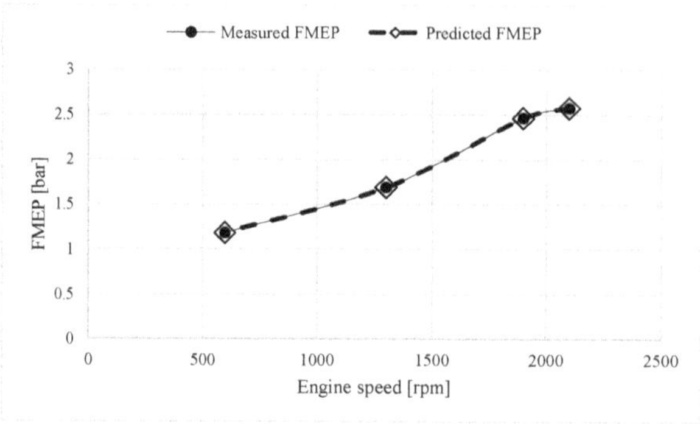

Figure 7. Fitting curve of FMEP.

5. Conclusions and Further Research

This study proposes an optimization method to predict the optimal coefficients of the Chen–Flynn correlation, employing advanced optimization techniques to accurately calculate the FMEP for a given engine, even in the absence of real data.

The approach integrates a 1D engine simulation software with a nonlinear optimization algorithm implemented in MATLAB, creating a robust engine optimization model. This model predicts engine performance while determining the optimal values of critical parameters governing engine behavior across four operating points. Key outputs, including engine speed, FMEP, and P_{max}, are then incorporated into a specialized friction tool for data fitting and validation.

The following has been concluded:

1. The engine model facilitates maximizing the AFR by optimizing the turbocharger performance, injection system parameters, combustion characteristics, and the FMEP. This results in values of up to 68.89 at low-load operation, while maintaining combustion stability ($R^2 \geq 0.9998$).
2. The engine optimization model demonstrates excellent capability in meeting all predefined constraints, ensuring reliability and applicability under varying conditions.
3. The numerical model is computationally efficient and compatible with standard computer systems, offering fast simulation times while maintaining high accuracy in calculated results. It helps to match real engine performance with an error of less than 0.05% in brake power and BSFC, confirming both accuracy and efficiency.
4. The developed approach supports the precise determination of the Chen–Flynn correlation coefficients, enhancing the accuracy of engine performance predictions across the load diagram.

This methodology provides a reliable approach to assessing engine friction behavior, particularly in scenarios where manufacturer-specific data is unavailable. These findings validate the model as a powerful tool for practical engine performance assessment and support its integration into advanced digital twin frameworks for marine propulsion systems.

Future work could explore the performance simulation of dual-fuel engines operating with hydrogen as the primary fuel. Additionally, incorporating a life-cycle assessment (LCA) of emissions can help evaluate the full environmental impact of dual-fuel engines, particularly when transitioning to hydrogen-based fuels. This would provide a more comprehensive comparison between fuel options and support decision-making for sustainable marine propulsion. While this study focuses on steady-state operation, evaluating the model's performance under transient conditions, such as acceleration, deceleration, and load fluctuations, would further enhance its robustness and applicability to real-world marine engine operations. Incorporating transient simulations could also aid in control system development and engine calibration strategies.

Such research aligns with global efforts toward net-zero emissions, positioning hydrogen as a key enabler of sustainable maritime and automotive propulsion systems.

Funding: This research received no external funding.

Data Availability Statement: The data presented in this study is available on request from the corresponding author.

Conflicts of Interest: The authors declare no conflicts of interest.

Abbreviations

0D	Zero-dimensional
1D	One-dimensional
3D	Three-dimensional
A, b	Linear inequality constraints
$A_{cf,}$	Constant term
A_{eq}, b_{eq}	Linear equality constraints
AFR	Air–fuel ratio
API	Application Programming Interfaces
A_w	Area of cylinder walls
B_{cf}	Load-dependent term
BMEP	Brake mean effective pressure
BRPM	Reference speed
BSFC	Brake-specific fuel consumption
c	Inequality constraints
C_{cf}	Hydrodynamic friction term
cd_3	Burn duration coefficients for the diffusion burn curves
c_{eq}	Equality constraints
CFD	Computational fluid dynamics
ct_3	Burn duration coefficients for the tail burn curves
CV	Calorific value
d_f	Mass fractions of the diffusion burn curves
dQ	Total heat added
dQ_w	Heat exchange
ECU	Engine control unit
EGR	Exhaust gas recirculation
EIVC	Early Intake Valve Closure
f(x)	Optimization model objective
FMEP	Friction mean effective pressure
FR	Fuel rate
g, h	Penalty functions
GA	Genetic algorithm
h	Heat transfer coefficient
H_2	Hydrogen
HFO	Heavy fuel oil
HRR	Heat release rate
IMEP	Indicated mean effective pressure
IMO	International Maritime Organization
INJ_{Dur}	Injection duration
lb	Lower bounds

$\dot{m}_a$	Air mass flow rate
LCA	Life-cycle assessment
MARPOL	International Convention for the Prevention of Pollution from Ships
MDO	Marine diesel oil
m_{fuel}	Amount of injected fuel
n_{cyl}	Number of cylinders
NG	Natural gas
NN	Neural network
NO	Nitric oxide
NOx	Nitrogen oxides
NSGA II	Non-dominated Sorting Genetic Algorithm
P_B	Brake power
P_f	Mass fractions of the premix burn curves
P_{max}	Maximum cylinder pressure
Q_{cf}	Windage loss term
Q_{comb}	Heat released from fuel combustion
R	Constant
R^2	Coefficient of determination
RPM	Engine speed
S	Mean piston speed
SOI	Start of injection
TA	Turbo-assisted
$T_{AfterCylinder}$	Exhaust temperature after cylinder
TDC	Top dead center
t_f	Mass fractions of the tail burn curves
T_g	Burn gas temperature
T_{max}	Maximum average temperature inside the cylinder
TS	Turbocharger speed
T_w	Cylinder wall temperature
ub	Upper bounds
VGTs	Variable Geometry Turbines
x	Optimization variables
x_b	Burned mass fraction
η_m	Mechanical efficiency
θ	Crank angle
θ_o	Start angle of combustion
τ	Burn duration
ω	Engine speed

References

1. Tadros, M.; Ventura, M.; Guedes Soares, C. Review of the IMO Initiatives for Ship Energy Efficiency and Their Implications. *J. Mar. Sci. Appl.* **2023**, *22*, 662–680. [CrossRef]
2. Theotokatos, G.; Stoumpos, S.; Bolbot, V.; Boulougouris, E. Simulation-based investigation of a marine dual-fuel engine. *J. Mar. Eng. Technol.* **2020**, *19*, 5–16. [CrossRef]
3. IMO. EEXI and CII-Ship Carbon Intensity and Rating System. Available online: https://www.imo.org/en/MediaCentre/HotTopics/Pages/EEXI-CII-FAQ.aspx (accessed on 10 November 2022).
4. Karatuğ, Ç.; Ejder, E.; Tadros, M.; Arslanoğlu, Y. Environmental and Economic Evaluation of Dual-Fuel Engine Investment of a Container Ship. *J. Mar. Sci. Appl.* **2023**, *22*, 823–836. [CrossRef]
5. Tauzia, X.; Maiboom, A.; Karaky, H.; Chesse, P. Experimental analysis of the influence of coolant and oil temperature on combustion and emissions in an automotive diesel engine. *Int. J. Engine Res.* **2019**, *20*, 247–260. [CrossRef]
6. Jia, B.; Mikalsen, R.; Smallbone, A.; Roskilly, A.P. A study and comparison of frictional losses in free-piston engine and crankshaft engines. *Appl. Therm. Eng.* **2018**, *140*, 217–224. [CrossRef]
7. Karatuğ, Ç.; Ceylan, B.O.; Arslanoğlu, Y. A hybrid predictive maintenance approach for ship machinery systems: A case of main engine bearings. *J. Mar. Eng. Technol.* **2025**, *24*, 12–21. [CrossRef]

8. Heywood, J.B. *Internal Combustion Engine Fundamentals*; McGraw-Hill: New York, NY, USA, 1988.
9. Tadros, M.; Ventura, M.; Guedes Soares, C. Review of current regulations, available technologies, and future trends in the green shipping industry. *Ocean. Eng.* **2023**, *280*, 114670. [CrossRef]
10. Huang, Y.; Surawski, N.C.; Zhuang, Y.; Zhou, J.L.; Hong, G. Dual injection: An effective and efficient technology to use renewable fuels in spark ignition engines. *Renew. Sustain. Energy Rev.* **2021**, *143*, 110921. [CrossRef]
11. Sander, D.E.; Knauder, C.; Allmaier, H.; Damjanović-Le Baleur, S.; Mallet, P. Friction Reduction Tested for a Downsized Diesel Engine with Low-Viscosity Lubricants Including a Novel Polyalkylene Glycol. *Lubricants* **2017**, *5*, 9. [CrossRef]
12. Feneley, A.J.; Pesiridis, A.; Andwari, A.M. Variable Geometry Turbocharger Technologies for Exhaust Energy Recovery and Boosting-A Review. *Renew. Sustain. Energy Rev.* **2017**, *71*, 959–975. [CrossRef]
13. Cong, Y.; Gan, H.; Wang, H. Parameter investigation of the pilot fuel post-injection strategy on performance and emissions characteristics of a large marine two-stroke natural gas-diesel dual-fuel engine. *Fuel* **2022**, *323*, 124404. [CrossRef]
14. Xiang, L.; Theotokatos, G.; Ding, Y. Parametric investigation on the performance-emissions trade-off and knocking occurrence of dual fuel engines using CFD. *Fuel* **2023**, *340*, 127535. [CrossRef]
15. Bejger, A.; Chybowski, L.; Gawdzińska, K. Utilising elastic waves of acoustic emission to assess the condition of spray nozzles in a marine diesel engine. *J. Mar. Eng. Technol.* **2018**, *17*, 153–159. [CrossRef]
16. Tadros, M.; Ventura, M.; Guedes Soares, C. Optimization procedure to minimize fuel consumption of a four-stroke marine turbocharged diesel engine. *Energy* **2019**, *168*, 897–908. [CrossRef]
17. Wei, S.; Wu, C.; Yan, S.; Ding, T.; Chen, J. Miller Cycle with Early Intake Valve Closing in Marine Medium-Speed Diesel Engines. *J. Mar. Sci. Appl.* **2022**, *21*, 151–160. [CrossRef]
18. Kim, J.; Vallinmaki, M.; Tuominen, T.; Mikulski, M. Variable valve actuation for efficient exhaust thermal management in an off-road diesel engine. *Appl. Therm. Eng.* **2024**, *246*, 122940. [CrossRef]
19. Güler, M.; Özkan, M. Energy balance analysis of a DI diesel engine with multiple pilot injections strategy and optimization of brake thermal efficiency. *Appl. Therm. Eng.* **2022**, *204*, 117972. [CrossRef]
20. Singh, D.; Gu, F.; Fieldhouse, J.D.; Singh, N.; Singal, S.K. Prediction and Analysis of Engine Friction Power of a Diesel Engine Influenced by Engine Speed, Load, and Lubricant Viscosity. *Adv. Tribol.* **2014**, *2014*, 928015. [CrossRef]
21. Allmaier, H.; Knauder, C.; Salhofer, S.; Reich, F.; Schalk, E.; Ofner, H.; Wagner, A. An experimental study of the load and heat influence from combustion on engine friction. *Int. J. Engine Res.* **2016**, *17*, 347–353. [CrossRef]
22. Spencer, A.; Avan, E.Y.; Almqvist, A.; Dwyer-Joyce, R.S.; Larsson, R. An experimental and numerical investigation of frictional losses and film thickness for four cylinder liner variants for a heavy duty diesel engine. *Proc. Inst. Mech. Eng. Part J.* **2013**, *227*, 1319–1333. [CrossRef]
23. Li, R.; Wen, C.; Meng, X.; Xie, Y. Measurement of the friction force of sliding friction pairs in low-speed marine diesel engines and comparison with numerical simulation. *Appl. Ocean. Res.* **2022**, *121*, 103089. [CrossRef]
24. Chybowski, L.; Kowalak, P.; Dąbrowski, P. Assessment of the Impact of Lubricating Oil Contamination by Biodiesel on Trunk Piston Engine Reliability. *Energies* **2023**, *16*, 5056. [CrossRef]
25. Mujtaba, M.A.; Masjuki, H.H.; Kalam, M.A.; Noor, F.; Farooq, M.; Ong, H.C.; Gul, M.; Soudagar, M.E.M.; Bashir, S.; Rizwanul Fattah, I.M.; et al. Effect of Additivized Biodiesel Blends on Diesel Engine Performance, Emission, Tribological Characteristics, and Lubricant Tribology. *Energies* **2020**, *13*, 3375. [CrossRef]
26. Mosarof, M.H.; Kalam, M.A.; Masjuki, H.H.; Alabdulkarem, A.; Habibullah, M.; Arslan, A.; Monirul, I.M. Assessment of friction and wear characteristics of Calophyllum inophyllum and palm biodiesel. *Ind. Crops Prod.* **2016**, *83*, 470–483. [CrossRef]
27. Tiruvenkadam, N.; Thyla, P.R.; Senthilkumar, M.; Bharathiraja, M. Development of optimum friction new nano hybrid composite liner for biodiesel fuel engine. *Transp. Res. Part D Transp. Environ.* **2016**, *47*, 22–43. [CrossRef]
28. Thangarasu, V.; Balaji, B.; Ramanathan, A. Experimental investigation of tribo-corrosion and engine characteristics of Aegle Marmelos Correa biodiesel and its diesel blends on direct injection diesel engine. *Energy* **2019**, *171*, 879–892. [CrossRef]
29. Singh, P.; Goel, V.; Chauhan, S.R. Impact of dual biofuel approach on engine oil dilution in CI engines. *Fuel* **2017**, *207*, 680–689. [CrossRef]
30. Mousavi, S.B.; Zeinali Heris, S.; Estellé, P. Viscosity, tribological and physicochemical features of ZnO and MoS_2 diesel oil-based nanofluids: An experimental study. *Fuel* **2021**, *293*, 120481. [CrossRef]
31. Dey, S.; Moni Reang, N.; Deb, M.; Kumar Das, P. Experimental investigation on combustion-performance-emission characteristics of nanoparticles added biodiesel blends and tribological behavior of contaminated lubricant in a diesel engine. *Energy Convers. Manag.* **2021**, *244*, 114508. [CrossRef]
32. Kapłan, M.; Klimek, K.; Maj, G.; Zhuravel, D.; Bondar, A.; Lemeshchenko-Lagoda, V.; Boltianskyi, B.; Boltianska, L.; Syrotyuk, H.; Syrotyuk, S.; et al. Method of Evaluation of Materials Wear of Cylinder-Piston Group of Diesel Engines in the Biodiesel Fuel Environment. *Energies* **2022**, *15*, 3416. [CrossRef]
33. Abril, S.O.; García, C.P.; León, J.P. Numerical and Experimental Analysis of the Potential Fuel Savings and Reduction in CO Emissions by Implementing Cylinder Bore Coating Materials Applied to Diesel Engines. *Lubricants* **2021**, *9*, 19. [CrossRef]

34. Lyu, B.; Meng, X.; Wang, C.; Cui, Y.; Wang, C.e. Piston ring and cylinder liner scuffing analysis in dual-fuel low-speed engines considering liner deformation and tribofilm evolution. *Int. J. Engine Res.* **2024**, *25*, 1776–1798. [CrossRef]
35. Albrecht, A.; Grondin, O.; Le Berr, F.; Le Solliec, G. Towards a Stronger Simulation Support for Engine Control Design: A Methodological Point of View. *Oil Gas Sci. Technol.* **2007**, *62*, 437–456. [CrossRef]
36. Wei, S.; Zhao, X.; Liu, X.; Qu, X.; He, C.; Leng, X. Research on effects of early intake valve closure (EIVC) miller cycle on combustion and emissions of marine diesel engines at medium and low loads. *Energy* **2019**, *173*, 48–58. [CrossRef]
37. AVL. AVL-Development, Testing & Simulation of Powertrain Systems. Available online: https://www.avl.com/ (accessed on 4 October 2017).
38. Mocerino, L.; Guedes Soares, C.; Rizzuto, E.; Balsamo, F.; Quaranta, F. Validation of an Emission Model for a Marine Diesel Engine with Data from Sea Operations. *J. Mar. Sci. Appl.* **2021**, *20*, 534–545. [CrossRef]
39. *Ricardo Wave Software*, WAVE 2019.1 Help System; Ricardo plc: Shoreham-by-Sea, UK, 2019.
40. Shen, H.; Yang, F.; Jiang, D.; Lu, D.; Jia, B.; Liu, Q.; Zhang, X. Parametric Investigation on the Influence of Turbocharger Performance Decay on the Performance and Emission Characteristics of a Marine Large Two-Stroke Dual Fuel Engine. *J. Mar. Sci. Eng.* **2024**, *12*, 1298. [CrossRef]
41. Gamma Technologies LLC. GT-POWER Engine Simulation Software. Available online: https://www.gtisoft.com/gt-suite-applications/propulsion-systems/gt-power-engine-simulation-software/ (accessed on 4 October 2017).
42. Stoumpos, S.; Theotokatos, G.; Mavrelos, C.; Boulougouris, E. Towards Marine Dual Fuel Engines Digital Twins—Integrated Modelling of Thermodynamic Processes and Control System Functions. *J. Mar. Sci. Eng.* **2020**, *8*, 200. [CrossRef]
43. Karatuğ, Ç.; Tadros, M.; Ventura, M.; Guedes Soares, C. Decision support system for ship energy efficiency management based on an optimization model. *Energy* **2024**, *292*, 130318. [CrossRef]
44. Tadros, M.; Ventura, M.; Guedes Soares, C. A nonlinear optimization tool to simulate a marine propulsion system for ship conceptual design. *Ocean. Eng.* **2020**, *210*, 107417. [CrossRef]
45. Tadros, M.; Ventura, M.; Guedes Soares, C. Surrogate models of the performance and exhaust emissions of marine diesel engines for ship conceptual design. In *Maritime Transportation and Harvesting of Sea Resources*; Guedes Soares, C., Teixeira, A.P., Eds.; Taylor & Francis Group: London, UK, 2018; pp. 105–112.
46. Tadros, M.; Ventura, M.; Guedes Soares, C. Data Driven In-Cylinder Pressure Diagram Based Optimization Procedure. *J. Mar. Sci. Eng.* **2020**, *8*, 294. [CrossRef]
47. Kolakoti, A.; Tadros, M.; Ambati, V.K.; Gudlavalleti, V.N.S. Optimization of biodiesel production, engine exhaust emissions, and vibration diagnosis using a combined approach of definitive screening design (DSD) and artificial neural network (ANN). *Environ. Sci. Pollut. Res.* **2023**, *30*, 87260–87273. [CrossRef]
48. *ASTM D6751-24*; Standard Specification for Biodiesel Fuel Blendstock (B100) for Middle Distillate Fuels. ASTM: West Conshohocken, PA, USA, 2024.
49. Chen, S.K.; Flynn, P.F. *Development of Single Cylinder Compression Ignition Research Engine*; SAE Technical Paper; SAE: Warrendale, PA, USA, 1965. [CrossRef]
50. Tormos, B.; Martín, J.; Blanco-Cavero, D.; Jiménez-Reyes, A.J. One-Dimensional Modeling of Mechanical and Friction Losses Distribution in a Four-Stroke Internal Combustion Engine. *J. Tribol.* **2020**, *142*, 011703. [CrossRef]
51. Chen, Y.; Deng, B.; Chen, M.; Hou, K. An approach to estimate CCV (cycle-to-cycle variation) of effective energy output of thermal engine: A case study on a high speed gasoline engine. *Case Stud. Therm. Eng.* **2021**, *28*, 101624. [CrossRef]
52. Özgül, E.; Bedir, H. Fast NOx emission prediction methodology via one-dimensional engine performance tools in heavy-duty engines. *Adv. Mech. Eng.* **2019**, *11*, 1687814019845954. [CrossRef]
53. *Realis Simulation*, WAVE 2024.1 Help System; Realis Simulation: Shoreham-by-Sea, UK, 2024.
54. MAN Diesel & Turbo. Four-Stroke Project Guides. Available online: https://www.man-es.com/marine/products/planning-tools-and-downloads/project-guides/four-stroke (accessed on 22 July 2022).
55. MAN Diesel & Turbo. Technical Data Sheet: Marine Diesel Engine D2862 LE428. Available online: https://www.man.eu/ntg_media/media/content_medien/doc/man_engines_1/produkte/marine_1/Marine_DualFuel_EN.pdf (accessed on 15 April 2023).
56. OEM Off-Highway. MAN Updates Engine Portfolio for Stage IV and Tier 4 Final Construction Machinery. Available online: https://www.oemoffhighway.com/engines/press-release/12163906/man-updates-engine-portfolio-for-stage-iv-and-tier-4-final-construction-machinery (accessed on 15 April 2020).
57. Watson, N.; Janota, M.S. *Turbocharging the Internal Combustion Engine*; Palgrave: London, UK, 1982.
58. Bai, F.; Zhang, Z.; Du, Y.; Zhang, F.; Peng, Z. Effects of Injection Rate Profile on Combustion Process and Emissions in a Diesel Engine. *J. Combust.* **2017**, *2017*, 9702625. [CrossRef]
59. Maroteaux, F.; Saad, C. Diesel engine combustion modeling for hardware in the loop applications: Effects of ignition delay time model. *Energy* **2013**, *57*, 641–652. [CrossRef]

60. Maroteaux, F.; Saad, C.; Aubertin, F. Development and validation of double and single Wiebe function for multi-injection mode Diesel engine combustion modelling for hardware-in-the-loop applications. *Energy Convers. Manag.* **2015**, *105*, 630–641. [CrossRef]
61. Woschni, G. *A Universally Applicable Equation for the Instantaneous Heat Transfer Coefficient in the Internal Combustion Engine*; SAE Technical Paper; SAE: Warrendale, PA, USA, 1967.
62. Watson, N.; Pilley, A.D.; Marzouk, M. *A Combustion Correlation for Diesel Engine Simulation*; SAE: Warrendale, PA, USA, 1980; Volume SAE Paper 800029.
63. Tadros, M.; Ventura, M.; Guedes Soares, C. Assessment of the performance and the exhaust emissions of a marine diesel engine for different start angles of combustion. In *Maritime Technology and Engineering 3*; Guedes Soares, C., Santos, T.A., Eds.; Taylor & Francis Group: London, UK, 2016; pp. 769–775.
64. Tadros, M.; Ventura, M.; Guedes Soares, C. Simulation of the performance of marine Genset based on double-Wiebe function. In *Sustainable Development and Innovations in Marine Technologies*; Georgiev, P., Guedes Soares, C., Eds.; Taylor & Francis Group: London, UK, 2020; pp. 292–299.
65. Byrd, R.H.; Mary, E.H.; Nocedal, J. An Interior Point Algorithm for Large-Scale Nonlinear Programming. *SIAM J. Optim.* **1999**, *9*, 877–900. [CrossRef]
66. The MathWorks Inc. Fmincon. Available online: https://www.mathworks.com/help/optim/ug/fmincon.html (accessed on 2 June 2017).
67. Zhu, Z.; Zhang, F.; Li, C.; Wu, T.; Han, K.; Lv, J.; Li, Y.; Xiao, X. Genetic algorithm optimization applied to the fuel supply parameters of diesel engines working at plateau. *Appl. Energy* **2015**, *157*, 789–797. [CrossRef]
68. Zhao, J.; Xu, M. Fuel economy optimization of an Atkinson cycle engine using genetic algorithm. *Appl. Energy* **2013**, *105*, 335–348. [CrossRef]
69. Challen, B.; Baranescu, R. *Diesel Engine Reference Book*, 2nd ed.; Challen, B., Baranescu, R., Eds.; Butterworth-Heinemann Ltd.: Oxford, UK, 1999.
70. Woodyard, D. *Pounder's Marine Diesel Engines*, 8th ed.; Butterworth-Heinemann: Oxford, UK, 2004.
71. Tormos, B.; Martín, J.; Pla, B.; Jiménez-Reyes, A.J. A methodology to estimate mechanical losses and its distribution during a real driving cycle. *Tribol. Int.* **2020**, *145*, 106208. [CrossRef]
72. Chen, R.; Zhao, B.; He, T.; Tu, L.; Xie, Z.; Zhong, N.; Zou, D. Study on coupling transient mixed lubrication and time-varying wear of main bearing in actual operation of low-speed diesel engine. *Tribol. Int.* **2024**, *191*, 109159. [CrossRef]

algorithms

MDPI

Article

EvoDevo: Bioinspired Generative Design via Evolutionary Graph-Based Development

Farajollah Tahernezhad-Javazm [1,†], Andrew Colligan [2,†], Imelda Friel [2], Simon J. Hickinbotham [1], Paul Goodall [3], Edgar Buchanan [1], Mark Price [2], Trevor Robinson [2] and Andy M. Tyrrell [1,*]

[1] Intelligent Systems & Robotics Research Group, School of Physics, Engineering and Technology, University of York, York YO10 5DD, UK; f.taher@york.ac.uk (F.T.-J.); simon.hickinbotham@york.ac.uk (S.J.H.); edgar.buchanan@york.ac.uk (E.B.)

[2] School of Mechanical and Aerospace Engineering, Queen's University Belfast, Belfast BT7 1NN, UK; a.colligan@qub.ac.uk (A.C.); i.friel@qub.ac.uk (I.F.); m.price@qub.ac.uk (M.P.); t.robinson@qub.ac.uk (T.R.)

[3] School of Mechanical, Electrical and Manufacturing Engineering, Loughborough University, Loughborough LE11 3TT, UK; p.a.goodall@lboro.ac.uk

* Correspondence: andy.tyrrell@york.ac.uk

† These authors contributed equally to this work.

Abstract: Automated generative design is increasingly used across engineering disciplines to accelerate innovation and reduce costs. Generative design offers the prospect of simplifying manual design tasks by exploring the efficacy of solutions automatically. However, existing generative design frameworks rely heavily on expensive optimisation procedures and often produce customised solutions, lacking reusable generative rules that transfer across different problems. This work presents a bioinspired generative design algorithm utilising the concept of evolutionary development (EvoDevo). This evolves a set of developmental rules that can be applied to different engineering problems to rapidly develop designs without the need to run full optimisation procedures. In this approach, an initial design is decomposed into simple entities called *cells,* which independently control their local growth over a development cycle. In biology, the growth of cells is governed by a gene regulatory network (GRN), but there is no single widely accepted model for this in artificial systems. The GRN responds to the state of the cell induced by external stimuli in its environment, which, in this application, is the loading regime on a bridge truss structure (but can be generalised to any engineering structure). Two GRN models are investigated: graph neural network (GNN) and graph-based Cartesian genetic programming (CGP) models. Both GRN models are evolved using a novel genetic search algorithm for parameter search, which can be re-used for other design problems. It is revealed that the CGP-based method produces results similar to those obtained using the GNN-based methods while offering more interpretability. In this work, it is shown that this EvoDevo approach is able to produce near-optimal truss structures via growth mechanisms such as moving vertices or changing edge features. The technique can be set up to provide design automation for a range of engineering design tasks.

Keywords: generative design; evolutionary development; evolutionary algorithm; gene regulatory network; neuroevolution; graph neural network; graph convolutional network; cartesian genetic programming; genetic algorithm; truss optimization

1. Introduction

In traditional design processes, a designer will take a project brief or specification and use their expert knowledge to construct a solution and then test it to see whether it meets the set of requirements. There is normally an iterative process between the design and analysis stages before the part is sent to manufacturing. As a result of time, cost and resource constraints, this approach can lead to design fixation or non-value-adding tasks [1,2]. Generative design (GD) looks to address these issues via automation. Generally, it can be summed up as a series of tools that use advanced algorithms and artificial intelligence to create designs for a given set of criteria. This involves the exploration of a vast number of design options, presenting a range of design solutions to the user for selection [3]. The design solutions that emerge may be different from the general best practice or from what may be possible to discover using manual design processes.

Some GD systems consist of both an expert system and an optimisation system [4]. The expert system emulates the expert's knowledge and ability to generate and critique solutions to a specific design problem. An optimisation system, however, improves designs with respect to some objective criteria. Unlike traditional optimisation, where objectives relate to weight or cost, for example, GD systems also optimise other criteria such as aesthetics or manufacturability. The optimisation task may not be concerned with discovering global optima; instead, a multi-modal optimisation task can be performed to find multiple solutions to a problem.

Commonly, topology optimisation acts as an engine to improve the design of a predefined shape. GD not only deals with topology optimisation but also integrates other techniques such as shape and size optimisation. This integration of different optimisation techniques can often be a limitation to interoperability between the geometric representations required for topology and shape/size optimisation. Generally, topology optimisation utilizes the finite element method (FEM), where the design space is discretised into simple primitives called *elements*. This discretised geometry is discontinuous and can be difficult to map back to the parametric computer-aided design (CAD) model (i.e., boundary representation (B-Rep)) used for shape optimisation [4]. There can also be a high computational cost associated with generating and analysing the large number of designs required for a GD system. For small-to-medium-sized businesses with no access to high-performance computing, this could represent a barrier to adoption.

Bioinspired GD systems apply features of biological systems to the design creation process [5]. In this paper, inspiration is taken from the biological concept of evolutionary development (EvoDevo) to evolve development rules that can be used to generate design solutions for different engineering problems using evolutionary algorithms [6]. This can be thought of as "evolving the designer, not the design". By encoding the development rules in the genome of the evolutionary algorithm instead of in the design itself, a richer exploration of the design space is possible. In this paper, this is applied to the automated design of truss bridge structures, a popular benchmark in structural optimisation [7,8]. In EvoDevo, an initial design is divided into basic units called *cells*, each containing an identical copy of an artificial gene regulatory network (GRN) model. This GRN model governs the growth of the structure through a set of developmental rules applied to each cell. The GRN model itself is encoded in a genome, which is optimised using an evolutionary algorithm.

Learning from graph-structured data using graph neural networks (GNNs) offers a promising approach, as GRN models reason over graphs, with trusses being naturally representable in this format. However, the "black-box" nature of neural network outputs can make interpretation difficult. To address this, a novel configuration of a Cartesian genetic programming (CGP)-based GRN model has been developed within the GNN paradigm, offering more interpretable "white box" outputs. This paper explores both approaches. These GRNs are developed utilising an evolutionary search algorithm to regulate local development mechanisms, including the movement of vertices or the alteration of link features. The objective is to demonstrate that this EvoDevo framework can generate near-optimal truss structures. Once the development rules are established, they may be repurposed to address analogous engineering challenges, hence decreasing the computational expense of the GD system for the end user and facilitating design automation.

The remainder of this paper proceeds as follows: Section 2 reviews prior work in GD, focusing particularly on optimisation paradigms and geometric representations. The proposed EvoDevo framework is proposed in Section 3 in detail. Section 4 describes the experimental setup parameter settings and evaluation metrics. Section 5 demonstrates the experimental results and compares the two proposed GRN controllers. Finally, Section 6 summarises the main findings, outlines the practical results and highlights directions for future work.

2. Related Work

There are two areas of research to consider when applying GD to real-world engineering problems. The first is the *learning algorithm*, which is the means by which appropriate GD is discovered. The second is the *design representation*, which is the means by which the specific design problem is represented to the learning algorithm.

2.1. Gradient- vs. Non-Gradient-Based Methods

Gradient-based methods utilise sensitivities (i.e., gradient information) to explore the design space for optimal solutions. Many such methods can efficiently solve high-resolution problems requiring millions of design parameters using a small number of function evaluations [9]. Common gradient-based methods include density-based (e.g., Solid Isotropic Material with Penalisation (SIMP)) [10] and level-set [11] methods.

For applications in GD, there are several limitations that make gradient-based approaches less attractive. GD systems require optimisation over a wide range of criteria such as manufacturability or multi-physics performance criteria. Therefore, the calculation of gradients may be infeasible due to numerical noise or a large number of variables [12], or, simply, the required objective function may not be differentiable. Gradient-based approaches are also not robust to the noisy or discontinuous search spaces that can result from the non-linearities of GD problems, and they are sensitive to the initial solution [12].

Non-gradient-based or black-box methods often utilise evolutionary algorithms to obtain near-optimal solutions. Compared to gradient-based methods, non-gradient-based methods tend to have higher computational costs due to the need to analyse large populations of designs, therefore needing many simulations. Non-gradient-based approaches tend to be more robust to the limitations mentioned previously for gradient-based approaches. The use of non-gradient-based approaches allows for greater flexibility in terms of application for GD [12,13]. The use of evolutionary algorithms for GD is desirable for the multi-modal optimisation requirements of a GD system. Due to the population-based approach, these methods are able to maintain populations of possible solutions that contain diversity and meet the set objectives.

2.2. Representation of the Design

Within topology optimisation and GD, there have been many attempts to represent the design domain (the structure of the design). Due to the computational cost of non-gradient-based algorithms, the representation chosen for this is paramount, as it defines the search space dimensionality. The chosen structural representation also constrains the possible solutions and the ability to find optimal solutions [12]. For evolutionary algorithms, this representation is synonymous with the genotype. In the literature, the different representations have been grouped into grid, geometric and indirect representations [13].

2.2.1. Grid Representation

In this representation, the design space is discretised by a grid. For evolutionary algorithms, the genotype encodes properties for different locations on the grid. This representation is commonly used in density-based topology optimisation [10]. The resolution of the grid is often high; therefore, the number of grid elements can be controlled within the millions to represent a specific geometry. For evolutionary methods, increasing this grid increases not only the cost of computing a fitness value but also the size of the chromosomes. This large number of grid elements generates an intractable search space, which consequentially requires large computational resources to converge to the global optima [14].

2.2.2. Geometric Representation

In geometric representations, the structure is represented by a set of shape primitives/components, which can either be fixed or free to move. It is the parameters of these primitives that are encoded in the genotype for evolutionary algorithms. The properties of these shape primitives can be the position, thickness or shape of a structure or substructure. The complexity of the solution depends on the number of primitives; hence, the dimensionality of the search space can be greatly reduced compared to that of grid representations [12].

The genotype of Voronoi representations encodes the coordinates and material properties of Voronoi cells. These representations allow for the subdivision of the design domain into arbitrarily shaped polyhedra [15,16]. For level-set methods, the shape boundary is defined by a level-set function. This representation has become widespread for gradient-based optimisation, where it has the advantage of producing smooth, watertight geometry compared to density-based approaches. There have been several approaches that have utilised evolutionary algorithms with a level-set representation. Some of these approaches have used beam-shaped components to construct the level-set boundary [17].

Other approaches have represented the structure as a graph. Encoded in the genotype are the coordinates of the nodes and the properties of the edges (e.g., thickness). The edges can be characterised as Bézier curves, allowing for a larger exploration of shape [18–20] or beam elements, parameterising their shape and thickness [21,22]. This maintains a direct link with the analysis model, similar to grid representations, thereby reducing interoperability issues.

Constructive solid geometry (CSG) involves the use of simple primitives and Boolean operations to create a more complex geometry. Several authors have proposed defining nodes via boundary conditions and using a Delaunay triangulation to produce the edges of the graphs [23,24]. Optimisation involves the parameterisation of these entities. Recently, Wang et al. [14] showed how a CSG representation can be combined with additive manufacturing constraints in a GD system. Watson et al. [4] split the GD process into a topology optimisation step on a grid representation, followed by a shape optimisation step on a graph representation, where the graph was extracted from the grid representation using image processing algorithms.

2.2.3. Indirect Representation

Compared to grid and geometric representations, where the structure is directly parameterised by the optimisation model, indirect representations instead look to implicitly optimise these parameters via a generative model or development rules [12]. Their benefit over grid and geometric representations is that they allow for the formation and re-deployment of problem-specific design patterns [12]. Although this could mean a high computational cost initially in the formation of the generative model, once formed, the ability to redeploy could alleviate the computational cost for the end-user.

Deep learning methods have recently been used in GD and topology optimisation. Within the field of deep learning, there are several different types of generative models, many of which have been used in the application of GD. Previous works have applied variational autoencoders (VAEs) within topology optimisation to allow the network to reconstruct optimal designs for given boundary conditions [25]. Others have used reinforcement learning via a proximal policy optimisation (PPO) model for wheel design [26]. The issue with deep learning methods is that they are not sample-efficient and require large amounts of data that do not exist in the field of engineering. Many of these approaches have utilised grid-based representations, which becomes computationally prohibitive when moving to 3D voxels due to the cubic scaling factor [27]. Conversely, bioinspired algorithms do not require large amounts of initial training data, and they are less dependent on the extensive predefined structure or specific parametric assumptions found in many deep learning algorithms.

The following approaches all take inspiration from different concepts and mechanisms in biology to produce and control the developmental rules used to generate a design. Price et al. [28] created heuristic growth rules for development in a bioinspired GD system. Through cellular division and other plant growth analogies, a design with additive manufacturing constraints was grown from a single cell "seed" to a mature organism by reacting to external stimuli.

EvoDevo has been applied via Lindenmayer system (L-system) representations. Tiago et al. [29] utilised L-systems to model the cellular division of truss structures for topology optimisation. Artificial GRNs have also been used for EvoDevo in structural optimisation. GRNs are the controllers in cells that switch genes on and off due to the state induced by stimuli in the environment, allowing the cells to grow in a certain manner. This allows for the development of an organism from a single cell to a fully developed organism. The use of GRNs for the design of complex structures was first proposed by Steiner et al. [30]. The proposed GRN model included cellular division, cell specialisation into material and void cells and the physical interactions of cells. Later, Steiner et al. [31] added chemotaxis (the movement of cells relative to the concentration gradient of chemicals), cell adherence and repellence.

Neuroevolution is the field of using evolutionary algorithms to optimise the parameters of neural network models [32]. Aulig et al. [33] used a state-based representation, where a neuroevolutionary approach evolved the weights of feedforward neural networks that mapped local sensory information to an update signal for the topology optimisation of a grid-based structure. Others have used forms of the neuroevolution algorithm NeuroEvolution of Augmenting Topologies (NEAT) [34] that can also evolve the topologies of neural networks, as well as the weights and biases. Cheney et al. [35] used HyperNEAT [36] for vibration design using a grid representation. Prior work by Hickinbotham et al. [37] showed the ability to use a GRN evolved using NEAT to move node positions in a Warren truss to produce solutions that are more optimal in minimising objective functions such as the total strain energy and total volume. This combined the GRN approach with state-based approaches and operated on a geometric representation of the design.

Furthermore, Cartesian genetic programming (CGP) [38,39] is a graph-based evolutionary algorithm that allows for the efficient evolution of GRN structures. In general, CGP employs fixed-size grids of nodes (including columns or rows), in which node inputs are mostly from nodes in earlier columns. Also, the genomes in CGP comprise connection genes and primitive functions that are optimised through an evolution process with a mutation operator [40]. CGP offers two practical advantages over other GRN models: computational efficiency and interpretability. During optimisation, only the active sub-graph, often a small fraction of the full genotype, is executed, so evaluation times decrease significantly. In addition, CGP exposes clear routes between inputs and outputs, making the resulting network easier to interpret than GRNs based on GNNs or other neural network models [40,41].

This section highlights how gradient-based, non-gradient and indirect representations each address different aspects of GD. In the next section, we translate these insights into a new framework, detailing our cellular representation, growth mechanisms and the dual GNN/CGP gene regulatory networks that drive development.

3. Proposed Method

3.1. Overview

Akin to Price et al. [28], the approach adopted here is to develop generative models that encompass the development of an organism from a single cell to a fully developed organism (Figure 1). The process starts with a minimal seed that meets the baseline requirements. In each development step, each cell senses its local state via message passing and aggregating information from neighbouring cells. This information is passed through GRNs, which generate growth commands. These commands are necessary for changing the global geometry and the cell states for the next steps. Through a loop of sensing, decision and execution, the cells grow and end up with the optimised structure based on the predefined fitness criteria.

Figure 1. Concept of a design growing from a seed. Growth is regulated through the continuous interaction between external stimuli and the outputs of the GRN.

3.2. Cellular Representation

As discussed in Section 2.2, there are many different ways to represent the geometry for GD. When the geometry is encoded directly into the genome of an evolutionary algorithm, there are not many constraints on what geometries can be represented; however, scaling to complex problems becomes a real and often insurmountable issue. Here, an indirect representation is used, where the genome encodes a GRN represented by a neural network. A key consideration for such a neural network-based GRN is its interaction with geometric data. Traditional neural networks, due to their fixed input vector size, typically require shapes to be described in regular, grid-like formats (e.g., pixels or voxels). Most 3D shape representations such as meshes or B-Reps do not have consistent or predefined arrangements. To enable our GRN to operate directly on such irregular, graph-structured cellular designs, this work leverages GNNs, which have been shown to be able to deal with these kinds of irregular shape representations [42–46]. A geometric representation is therefore constructed with these key limitations and advantages in mind.

As with [28,37], the design is divided into simple primitive entities called *cells*. As in biology, these are the basic building blocks that together can be used to construct more complex systems. Each of these cells is an independent entity that contains a local controller via a GRN for growth but interacts with the global structure through its shared topology. In this paper, cells are considered to only have structural properties and function. A graph is constructed from these cellular entities and their shared topology. In this paper, these cells also represent the finite elements used for the design's analysis, which helps to reduce interoperability issues, in a similar manner to some previous beam element approaches [21,22].

For this initial study, truss structures are explored as the benchmark problems. To represent a truss structure, a heterogeneous graph of multiple node and edge types can be used. Each node represents a distinct cell type, and the edge types represent different adjacency information between the same and different cell types. This graph can have a hierarchy, capturing features from local to global scales, as illustrated in Figure 2. In this paper, two cell types are used, representing the vertices/nodes and edges/members of the truss structure. These edge cells can be characterised as truss elements in a finite element analysis (FEA) when solving statically indeterminate structures. All graph edges are assumed to be undirected, although direction can also be encoded.

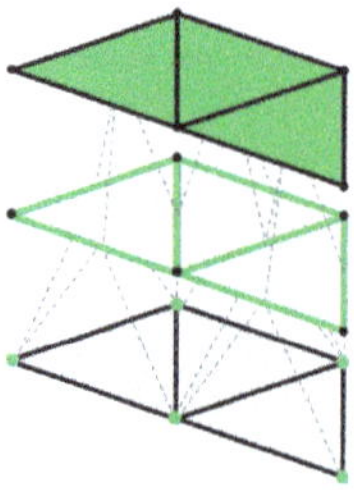

Figure 2. A heterogeneous graph representing a shape, unfurled into a hierarchy of cell types and topologies. Cells can be represented as faces, edges or vertices; however, this paper focuses on the edge and vertex representations.

3.3. *Evolutionary Development*

The EvoDevo algorithm consists of an evolution (evo) process and a development (devo) process. The evo process optimises the GRN model in the shape of genomes. The devo process can be thought of as the life-cycle of the design/organism. It is where the cells of the design will change in terms of shape, size and topology as a sequence of rules in order to adapt to the environment in which they are placed. Once the devo process is complete, the organism, or, more specifically, the shared GRN of the cells, will be given a reward based on its performance. The rewards of the organisms are then used in the selection process in the evo process, which decides which organisms and their genetic material are allowed to pass to the next generation.

3.4. *Development*

The development of a design/organism can be cast as a reinforcement learning problem, where the agent/GRN in each cell interacts with an environment and must produce a sequence of actions (here, devo steps) that yields a trajectory in the objective space to maximise some cumulative reward. The problem is underpinned by assuming the Markov property that the history of all previous states is encapsulated in the current state (e.g., the x and y coordinates of joints and the strain energy and material volume of members). This means that, at any given devo step, a cell's growth decision is only based on its current and potential future states. It is also assumed that the environment is deterministic and that no uncertainty exists between transitions from one state to another. The action space is continuous, where the GRN needs to determine the appropriate values for a set of continuous control parameters corresponding to a given growth mechanism.

3.4.1. Environment

In the proposed framework, the *environment* is the collection of problem-specific properties and constraints that influence the development of the designs. The actions update the cell states at every development step and therefore change and define the search space. The organism and its cells interact with stimuli in the environment, updating the cell states in the process. The environment sets up the problem search space in which solutions can be found. Therefore, knowledge of the problem is required to effectively define the environment to ensure that the desired solutions are output from the system. The search space is defined through the construction of different environmental elements. These relate to the engineering discipline of interest, e.g., structural, thermal or manufacturing. Within an environmental element, different variables can be added, such as stimuli, objectives and constraints. In this paper, the focus is on the structural environmental element that can be used to generate feedback for different structural analysis problems, with other environmental elements being explored in future work.

In this paper, potential designs for statically determinate and indeterminate pin-jointed truss structures are considered. The tension coefficient method and FEA with truss elements are used to calculate the forces on these statically determinate and indeterminate truss structures, respectively. An analytical method via the tension coefficient method is used to speed up analysis where possible. The main objectives explored in this paper are to minimise the total strain energy and the total volume of the designs, with the aim of generating organisms with optimal stiffness-to-weight properties. A lower strain energy value for a given load indicates a higher overall structural stiffness. The total strain energy is the energy stored in a link as a result of its elastic deformation.

3.4.2. Growth Mechanisms

Each cell uses its GRN to make an independent decision on its local growth. Evolutionary selection is used to maximise the design's performance globally (by minimising an objective function). The action space of this growth is parameterised by the growth mechanisms available to the cell: different growth mechanisms allow for different explorations of the design space in terms of shape, topology and size. These growth mechanisms can also be linked to certain engineering disciplines and engineering knowledge. For performance, it is important that there is a direct mapping between the cell and the growth mechanism that acts upon it. This decreases the noise in the search space and allows for more generalizable GRNs. In this contribution, the vertex/node cell type has the ability to change its Cartesian coordinate position, and the edge cell type can alter its cross-sectional area. These parameters can be altered in a continuous range of $[-1, 1]$ at each devo step.

3.5. Gene Regulatory Network

In a single biological organism, the cells all share the same genome but have different gene expression levels as a reaction to the local state of the cell. The GRN is the controller in the cell that switches genes on and off due to stimuli in the environment, allowing for the cell to grow in a certain manner in response. The development of an organism from a single cell to a fully developed organism occurs due to local responses on a cellular level and independently of a global controller. In this work, inspiration is taken from gene regulatory networks and their ability to dictate development without the influence of a global controller using state-based information.

There are many different proxies for gene regulatory networks in the literature. These can be classified into logical, continuous and single-molecule-level models. The different classifications can be placed on a spectrum of ranging model complexities or speed of analysis. Logical models tend to have a lower model complexity but suffer in terms of the speed of analysis. Single-molecule-level models instead have a higher model complexity leading to a lower speed of analysis. Continuous models, which include ordinary differential equations (ODEs), genetic programming and neural networks, lie somewhere in the middle between the other two classifications. As with Hickinbotham et al. [37], the GRN in the system is represented by a neural network. This supports a certain level of model complexity, but, as multiple simulations would also need to be run, faster analysis speeds would also be required.

One major difference from [37] is that a GNN is used instead of a simple feedforward neural network for the GRN. There are several advantages of using a GNN for learning from these kinds of data representations and shapes in general. As discussed previously, shapes can be represented in graphical representations with topological relationships between entities. GNNs are designed to process and learn from this graph-structured data, making them a natural fit to the problem at hand. GNNs are also able to capture both the local and global contexts within a graph. In the context of shape representations, this means that GNNs can effectively capture the local geometric relationships between neighbouring entities while also incorporating global shape information. GNNs can also learn from hierarchical representations by propagating information across the graph, capturing and aggregating features from local to global scales. This propagation of information or message passing is very important, as it enables cell-to-cell communication. This communication is not constrained to cells of the same type, meaning that cells are able to have different types in the representation used here, e.g., both vertex and edge types, as shown in Figure 2, enabling more flexibility and generalisation to the approach.

In the proposed neural architecture, graph convolutional layers are used to filter and aggregate state information from cells and their neighbouring cells. The graph neural network operator [47] used is shown in Equation (1):

$$\mathbf{x}_i' = W_{\text{self}}\mathbf{x}_i + W_{\text{nbr}} \sum_{j \in \mathcal{N}(i)} e_{j,i}\, \mathbf{x}_j. \tag{1}$$

where $\mathbf{x}_i$ denotes the current feature vector of node i, and $\mathbf{x}_i'$ is its updated feature vector after one graph convolution operation. The set $\mathcal{N}(i)$ contains all nodes that share an edge with node i in the graph. The learnable weight matrix W_{self} filters the target node's own features, while W_{nbr} filters the aggregated features received from the neighbouring nodes. The scalar $e_{j,i}$ is the edge weight from node j to node i; it is set to 1 in the present study.

As previously stated, information can be propagated between different cell types. Thus, vertex cells exchange messages not only with other vertices but also with edge cells. Therefore, we decompose the neighbourhood into *intra-type* and *inter-type* sets:

$$\mathbf{x}_i' = W_{\text{self}}\mathbf{x}_i + W_{\text{intra}} \sum_{j \in \mathcal{N}_{\text{intra}}(i)} e_{j,i}\, \mathbf{x}_j + W_{\text{inter}} \sum_{k \in \mathcal{N}_{\text{inter}}(i)} e_{k,i}\, \mathbf{x}_k. \tag{2}$$

Here, $\mathcal{N}_{\text{intra}}(i)$ contains neighbours of the same cell type as node i, whereas $\mathcal{N}_{\text{inter}}(i)$ contains neighbours of a different type. The weight matrices W_{intra} and W_{inter} can therefore learn distinct linear transformations between possibly different feature dimensions, so cell-type X_k is not required to share the same feature size as X_i ($W_{\text{nbr}} = W_{\text{intra}} + W_{\text{inter}}$).

For both types of neural network operators, a leaky Relu activation function [48] and bias operator are used. The GRN also has a fully connected layer after the graph convolutional layer. This uses a hyperbolic tangent or tanh function to give a continuous output for the growth mechanism in the range $[-1, 1]$. The tanh function serves as a stabilising mechanism that maintains equilibrium during development while permitting both positive and negative modifications. The absence of the tanh function results in significant output oscillations, causing simulation failures. For instance, Figure 3 shows the architecture used to optimize the structure by changing the vertex positions and edge cross-sectional areas simultaneously. This is constructed by two GRNs, one for the vertex cells and one for the edge cells. The edge cells hold state information in terms of their strain energy and volume. The vertex cells hold state information in terms of their Cartesian coordinates. The edge cells are able to communicate their state information to adjacent vertex cells. Therefore, the vertex cells make growth decisions based on their own state and the state of adjacent vertex and edge cells. It is decided that the vertex cells should not communicate their state to the edge cells, as it is assumed that the vertex position is not necessary for the mapping of the edge state and its growth mechanism.

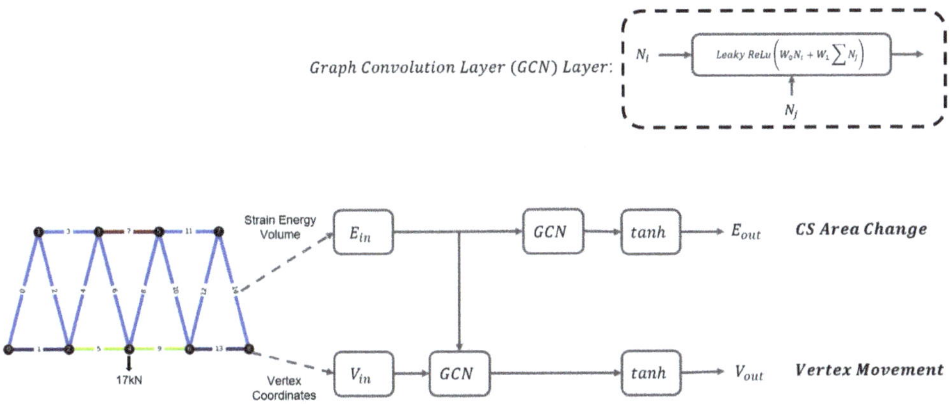

Figure 3. Hybrid control structure: two gene regulatory networks for vertex and edge cells with neighbour message exchange. A vertex GRN updates node positions $(\Delta x, \Delta y)$, while an edge GRN adjusts member areas ΔA.

3.6. *GRN Implemented as Cartesian Genetic Programming (CGP)*

Alongside the GNN, an alternative implementation of a GRN based on CGP is designed. Compared to the GNN, CGP offers a human-readable way to encode a GRN with a grid of nodes and logical operators in a linear chromosome. Each chromosome is simply a vector of numbers that is interpreted to build a directed grid-based graph. The two-dimensional grid consists of R rows and C columns, and each grid intersection hosts a single computational node. The type of computation is determined by an operator chosen from the primitive set such as addition, subtraction, multiplication and division. Every node has exactly k inputs (generally $k = 2$) and one output. In CGP, there is a level-back parameter L, which guarantees acyclicity. Node (r, c) can only read from primary inputs or from nodes situated in columns $c + 1, \ldots, c + L$. In CGP, genomes evolve under a $(\mu + \lambda)$ mutation operator. Indeed, exploration and exploitation rely on point mutation; only with probability ε is a field in the chromosome replaced (primitive or connection) or perturbed, and crossover is omitted.

To implement the CGP-based GRN, several CGP structures are instantiated that differ in the number of inputs, the number of outputs and the way that neighbourhood statistics are aggregated (similar to a GNN). Table 1 lists the exact settings used in these experiments; all genomes share the same grid size, level-back and primitive set.

Table 1. Summary of CGP methods.

CGP Structure	Inputs	Outputs	Purpose
edge	2	1	strain energy & volume $\rightarrow \Delta A$
node	2	2	$(x, y) \rightarrow (\Delta x, \Delta y)$
node–edge (hybrid)	2/2	2/1	two cgp controllers update hierarchically

The edge controller (row 1 of Table 1) is the minimal CGP structure. Each truss cell receives only its own strain energy (SE) and volume (V) and returns a single increment ΔA for the cross-sectional area. Also, the node controller maps the current vertices/node coordinates (x, y) to a displacement vector $(\Delta x, \Delta y)$. Ultimately, two hybrid node–edge controllers co-evolve a pair of CGP controllers. node-cgp controls the node positions, and edge-cgp adjusts the members' cross-sectional areas.

3.7. Evolution and Selection

After each development step, the total normalised strain energy and volume (each is normalised by its initial value) is recorded and summed to give the fitness $F = \text{SE}_n + V_n$. In addition, the incremental reward $\Delta F = F_t - F_{t-1}$ is computed through all development steps, resulting in overall progress rather than single-step jumps. This reward, which is the summation of all ΔF over 10 development steps, is considered the criterion for ranking the performance of each CGP controller and selecting the promising ones for the next evolutionary generation. The selection of 10 steps is determined empirically as a balance between performance enhancement and computational expense [49,50].

3.8. GRN Implemented as Neuroevolution (GNN)

To learn the growth rules that underpin development in different environments, an evolutionary parameter search of the graph neural network GRNs is performed. Neuroevolution has been shown to be a powerful and flexible technique that can be used in a wide range of reinforcement learning problems, especially those with complex and continuous state and action spaces. Therefore, a novel neuroevolutionary genetic search algorithm is proposed to implement this parameter search of the graph neural networks. The genome of each organism in the population encodes the weights and biases of each layer of its graph neural network (GRN). This genetic search algorithm evolves the GRN through the process of mutation and selection. This genetic search algorithm can be seen in Figure 4. The initial populations of the GRNs are parameterised by random weights and biases. Each of these GRNs is placed in their own development loop, where they grow each cell in an organism until a final design is produced. This final design has an associated cumulative reward based on its performance in the environment relative to the predefined objectives. A selection process is then undertaken, where the best performing GRN in terms of this reward metric is passed to the next generation, and offspring are produced via the mutation of the weights and bias parameters of the two parent GRNs.

The mutation rate ε dictates the probability of changing the weights and biases in the GRN. It is randomly sampled from a Gaussian distribution with a mean of zero and a standard deviation equal to the mutation rate. There is a dilemma between the exploration and exploitation of the solution space. The process should not get stuck in local optima or commit to certain GRN parameterisation too early in the generations. An adaptive mutation rate strategy is employed to allow for a wider exploration in the initial generations with a larger probability of mutation occurring, with the mutation rate decreasing in the later generations allowing for more fine-tuning of the better performing GRN. The mutation rate ε can be computed as

$$\epsilon = \frac{\varepsilon_0}{1 + \varepsilon_{\text{taper}}\ \text{generation}_{\text{id}}} \tag{3}$$

where ε_0 is a hyperparameter denoting the initial mutation rate, $\varepsilon_{\text{taper}}$ controls the amount in which the mutation rate is decreased each generation, and $\text{generation}_{\text{id}}$ is the identity of the current generation.

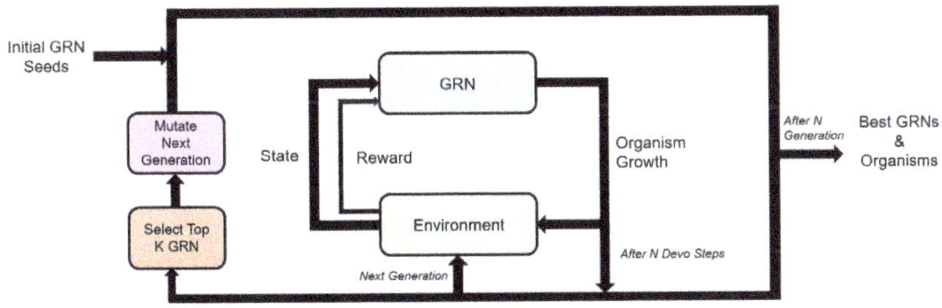

Figure 4. Genetic search algorithm for evolving GRN.

In evolutionary algorithms, letting every GRN reproduce in every generation would be wasteful. Instead, we adopt the elitist selection scheme used in Augmented Random Search [51]. After each generation, individuals are ranked by their reward, and the top k elites (a user-defined hyperparameter) are copied unchanged into the next generation. The remaining population slots are filled by offspring generated through the mutation of these k elites, ensuring an efficient exploitation of high-performing regions while still permitting directed exploration.

3.9. Normalising Inputs

To be able to create a GRN that is able to generalise to new environments, the inputs to the GRN (i.e., cell states) must be normalised. This also helps to ensure that one feature type does not have dominance over another. Normalising the data is difficult, as it is hard to define the minimum and maximum that will be achieved by each cell state feature. A Z-normalisation scheme is applied across the features of each cell's state to set the mean μ to zero and the standard deviation σ to one for the organism at each development step.

$$X' = \frac{X - \mu}{\sigma} \tag{4}$$

The moving average of μ and σ is computed at each development step and is used to help normalise the cost features over the course of development. At each devo step $n \in \{1, 2, \ldots, N\}$, each objective $f_i(x)$ where $i \in \{1, 2, \ldots, k\}$ is normalised by the objective at the initial devo step $f_i^0(x)$.

$$f_i^n(x) = \frac{f_i^n(x)}{f_i^0(x)} \tag{5}$$

The normalised objectives at each devo step $f_i^n(x)$ are then combined into a single objective $F_i^n(x)$.

$$F^n(x) = \sum_{i=1}^{k} f_i^n(x) \tag{6}$$

The reward metric is used to evaluate the organisms in the population. The reward is defined as

$$R = -\sum_{n=1}^{N} \left(F^n(x) - F^{n-1}(x) \right) \tag{7}$$

This essentially defines a comparison of the single objective at devo step n against the initial objective at devo step 0 for N devo steps. The minus sign inverts the sign of the metric for maximisation. Algorithms 1 and 2 represent the neuroevolution procedure described above. The algorithm consists of a two-level nested process: the inner process is the devo stage, where the GRN (either the GNN or CGP) applies the developmental rules, while the outer process (evo) involves the application of the mutation operator.

Algorithm 1 EvoDevoAlgorithm—outer loop

Require: *GRNType* $\in \{\text{CGP}, \text{GNN}\}$ ▷ choose the GRN model
EliteSize (number of top individuals to keep)
OffspringCount (new individuals per generation)
NumGenerations G
MaxDevSteps T
initialise *Population* ← CreateInitialPopulation(*EliteSize*, *GRNType*)
for $g = 1$ **to** G **do**
    for *organism* **in** *Population* **do**
        organism.Fitness ← DevelopOrganism(*organism*, *T*, *GRNType*)
    end for
    EliteGroup ← SelectTop(*Population*, *EliteSize*)
    OffspringGroup ← ∅
    while size of *OffspringGroup* < *OffspringCount* **do**
        Parent ← RandomChoice(*EliteGroup*)
        Child ← MutateGenome(*Parent*, *GRNType*)
        add *Child* to *OffspringGroup*
    end while
    Population ← *EliteGroup* ∪ *OffspringGroup*
end for

Algorithm 2 Development loop—inner loop

Require: *Genome*, *MaxDevSteps T*, *GRNType*
build initial *SeedlingStructure*
CumulativeFitness ← 0
for $t = 1$ **to** T **do**
    gather and normalise current cell states → **InputStates**
    if *GRNType* is CGP **then**
        Actions ← CGP(*Genome*, **InputStates**)
    else
        Actions ← GNN(*Genome*, **InputStates**)
    end if
    apply **Actions** to update geometry and
    recompute physics; update *CumulativeFitness*
end for
return *CumulativeFitness*

3.10. Seedling

The seedling describes the starting point from which the development of the organism begins. This seedling can be thought of as the minimal viable structure required to start interacting with the environment and defining load paths. The seedling is identical across all organisms in every generation. This allows for a fair, objective comparison in the evolutionary selection process. The initial structure of the seedling can be given to the GD system if further optimisation on a sub-optimal design is required. The geometries of this seedling are not constrained, but, in this paper, as in [37], a Warren truss bridge is selected as the seedling.

The proposed framework combines a heterogeneous graph representation with GNN and CGP-based GRNs, with the parameters adjusted using neuroevolutionary search. By combining cellular-level sensing, decision making and actuation within the EvoDevo loop, the system can generate optimum truss architectures from a little seedling. The following section exhibits the use of these approaches to benchmark problems. Table 2 encapsulates the fundamental components of the EvoDevo algorithm and connects each with its biological equivalent. This provides additional insights into the translation of concepts between different domains for the remainder of this paper.

Table 2. Key EvoDevo concepts and their biological counterparts.

This Work	Biological Analogue	Purpose
Seedling truss	Embryo	Minimal viable structure that initiates growth.
Node/edge cells	Somatic cells	Local agents that sense state and apply growth rules.
GRN	GRN	Maps sensed state to growth commands for each cell.
GNN/CGP weights	Genome	Heritable code evolved by the genetic algorithm.
Development step	Cell cycle	One round of sensing, decision and growth.
Growth mechanism	Cell growth	(i) Move a node, (ii) resize an edge.
Fitness	Fitness	Global signal guiding evolution towards better performance.
Genetic algorithm	Darwinian evolution	Selects and mutates GRNs each generation.

4. Experiments

Two GRN varieties (a GNN and CGP) are implemented for the three experimental treatments described here. Each experiment investigates the development of truss bridges, although the approach is not limited to these types of problems. Every evolutionary experiment, unless stated otherwise, uses the parameters in Table 3.

Table 3. Default evolutionary experiment parameters.

Development steps = 10	Generations = 150	Population size = 512
Top $k = 32$	Obj [a] 1: strain energy (se)	Initial mutation rate (ε_0) = 1.0
Mutation rate taper (ε_{tap}) = 0.4	Obj 2: volume (v)	

[a] Objectives.

The number of best individuals that move forward each generation is fixed at $k = 32$ (6.25% of the population). Based on these work experiments, it is proven that smaller values ($k < 16$) lead to premature convergence, while larger values ($k > 64$) slow progress [52,53]. In addition, Figure 5 illustrates how the mutation rate balances exploration and exploitation over the evolutionary generation.

As stated in Section 3.2, two different cell types are used in the experiments: vertex cells (nodes) and edge cells. Also, we apply a combination of node and edge cells as the ultimate design scenario. The node cells are equivalent to the nodes in the truss, and the edge cells are equivalent to the members. Each cell type has different growth mechanisms available to them to globally change the structure. To test whether the GRN of each cell type can learn growth mechanisms to minimise the objectives, the total strain energy and total volume, a Warren truss with seven triangles and edges with equal cross-sectional areas is used as the seedling. The environment consists of a 17 kN load placed on centre vertex 4, with a pinned support at vertex 0 and a roller support at vertex 8. The bottom line of the vertices (0, 2, 4, 6 and 8) are constrained to prevent any movement. This seedling is shown in Figure 6, where the colour of the edges represents the strain energy induced.

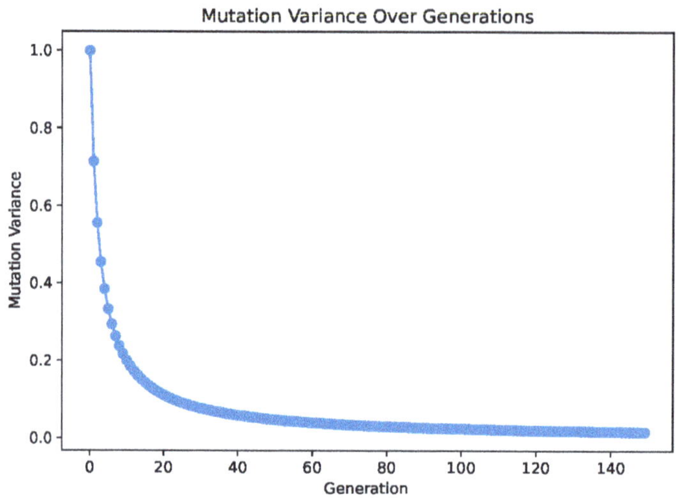

Figure 5. Influence of initial mutation rate $\varepsilon_0 = 0$ and taper coefficient $\varepsilon_{\text{tap}} = 0.4$ on overall mutation rate over evolutionary generations.

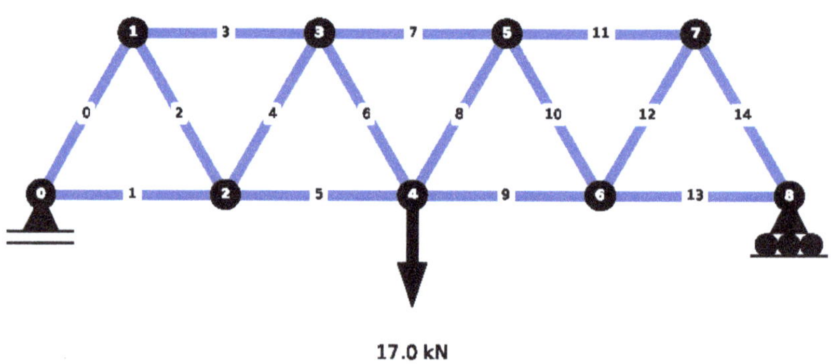

Figure 6. Seedling in single-load (17.0 kN) case environment with 9 nodes and 15 edges.

In the implementation of the GNN structure, the truss is represented as a graph including n vertices and m edges, utilising three binary adjacency matrices in each method (Table 4). All three matrices are static during the development steps and provide the neighbourhood information needed for aggregation.

Table 4. Adjacency and incidence matrices used by the GNN controllers.

$A_N \in \{0,1\}^{n \times n}$	node–node adjacency: $A_N[i,j] = 1$ if vertices i and j share a member
$A_E \in \{0,1\}^{m \times m}$	edge–edge adjacency: $A_E[p,q] = 1$ if members p and q share a vertex
$A_{NE} \in \{0,1\}^{n \times m}$	node–edge incidence: $A_{NE}[i,p] = 1$ if vertex i is an endpoint of member p

As shown in Figure 7, the node-only GNN method converts each vertex's position (x_i, y_i) and the state of its neighbourhood into the final vertex translation $(\Delta x_i, \Delta y_i)$. Each vertex begins with the vector of $\mathbf{n}_i = [x_i, y_i]^\top$. Neighbour information comes from two sums: (i) the *Edge-neigh sum* ($A_{NE}E$), which adds the strain energy and volume of all edges connected to the vertex, and (ii) the *Node-neigh sum* $A_N N$, which adds the x, y coordinates of the neighbouring vertices. Then, these two vectors are concatenated. The vertex and the neighbour features are linearly projected by $W_0 \in \mathbb{R}^{2\times 2}$ and $W_1 \in \mathbb{R}^{4\times 2}$, respectively. Then, these two results are added with bias b_0.

$$\mathbf{h}_i = \mathrm{LReLU}\big(W_0\,\mathbf{n}_i + W_1\big[A_{NE}E \parallel A_N N\big]_i + b_0\big) \tag{8}$$

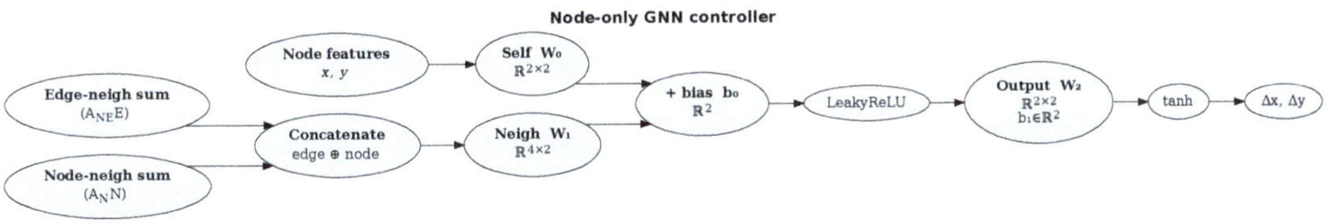

Figure 7. The node-only GNN: This combines coordinates and aggregated neighbour/edge features and then uses linear projections, a leaky ReLU and a final linear tanh function to output $(\Delta x_i, \Delta y_i)$. The weight matrices form the evolvable genome.

The matrices W_0, W_1 and W_2 with the biases b_0 and b_1 are considered the learnable parameters, evolved by the GA during the optimisation process. The output with weights $W_2 \in \mathbb{R}^{2\times 2}$ and bias b_1, followed by a tanh function, produces the vertex movements $(\Delta x_i, \Delta y_i)$.

$$(\Delta x_i, \Delta y_i) = \tanh\big(W_2\,\mathbf{h}_i + b_1\big) \tag{9}$$

The *edge-only* GNN (Figure 8) calculates the cross-sectional update (ΔA_j) for each edge of the truss. Each member starts with the feature vector $\mathbf{e}_j = [\mathrm{SE}_j, V_j]^\top$, including the strain energy and volume. The raw edge features are mapped by $W_0 \in \mathbb{R}^{2\times 2}$, and the summed features of adjacent members, $(A_E E)_j$, are transformed by $W_1 \in \mathbb{R}^{2\times 2}$. These two results are added together; a bias b_0 is also included, and the whole output goes through a leaky ReLU function:

$$\mathbf{h}_j = \mathrm{LReLU}\big(W_0\,\mathbf{e}_j + W_1\,(A_E E)_j + b_0\big). \tag{10}$$

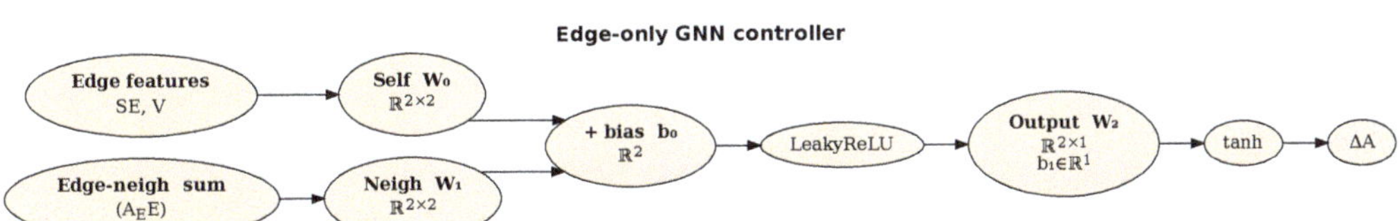

Figure 8. The edge-only GNN: This combines strain energy, volume and neighbour features and then uses linear projections, a leaky ReLU and a final tanh function to output the cross-sectional area update (ΔA_i). The weight matrices form the evolvable genome.

The final linear layer with weights $W_2 \in \mathbb{R}^{2\times 1}$ and bias $b_1 \in \mathbb{R}$, followed by a tanh activation function, calculates the cross-sectional area for each edge member (j):

$$\Delta A_j = \tanh\big(W_2\,\mathbf{h}_j + b_1\big). \tag{11}$$

Finally, Figure 9 shows two parallel GNN controllers for the node–edge method. It consists of two node-only and edge-only methods that update the edge cross-sectional area ΔA_j and joints $(\Delta x_i, \Delta y_i)$ in parallel.

$$\begin{aligned} \mathbf{h}_j^E &= \mathrm{LReLU}(W_0\,\mathbf{e}_j + W_1(A_E E)_j + b_0), \\ \Delta A_j &= 10\,\tanh(W_4\,\mathbf{h}_j^E + b_4) \\ \mathbf{h}_i^N &= \mathrm{LReLU}(W_2\,\mathbf{n}_i + W_3\left[A_{NE}E \,\|\, A_N N\right]_i + b_2), \\ (\Delta x_i, \Delta y_i) &= 10\,\tanh(W_5\,\mathbf{h}_i^N + b_5) \end{aligned} \tag{12}$$

where $\mathbf{e}_j = [\mathrm{SE}_j, V_j]^\top$ and $\mathbf{n}_i = [x_i, y_i]^\top$. In addition, the dashed grey arrow in Figure 9 defines the one-way path $(A_{NE}E)$ from edges to nodes; concluding the edge branch itself does not depend on node data during the process. All six weight matrices and four biases are learnable parameters that the GA tunes during the optimisation process.

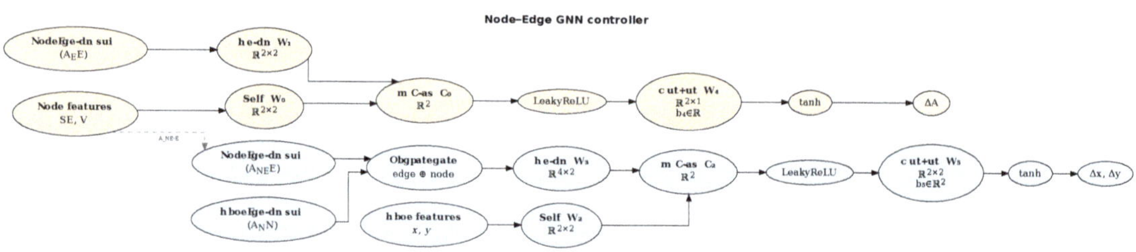

Figure 9. Hybrid node–edge GNN: The blue path maps edge features and their neighbours to the cross-sectional update (ΔA_i), and the red path maps vertex coordinates plus node/edge neighbours to $(\Delta x_i, \Delta y_i)$. The weight matrices form the evolvable genome.

In the CGP implementation, three methods are employed: node, edge, and node–edge methods. The initial two methods employ a single CGP controller, whereas the final method (node–edge) utilizes two interconnected CGP controllers, with each responsible for node position and cross-sectional changes. The structures of the CGP controllers are outlined in Table 5.

Table 5. Cartesian genetic programming parameters used for each method.

Methods	n_{in}	n_{out}	n_{col}	n_{row}	L_{back}	Primitive Set †
CGP_edge	2	1	8	2	3	{Add, Sub, Mul, Const}
CGP_node	2	2	8	2	3	{Add, Sub, Mul, Const}
CGP_node–edge (edge)	2	1	8	2	3	{Add, Sub, Mul, Const}
CGP_node–edge (node)	2	2	8	2	3	

† Primitive set abbreviations: $Add(x, y) = x + y$, $Sub(x, y) = x - y$, $Mul(x, y) = x \cdot y$, $Const$ = constant float.

n_{in} and n_{out} denote the numbers of inputs and outputs, respectively. In addition, n_{row} and n_{col} specify the CGP grid dimensions (rows and columns). Finally, L_{back} (levels-back) defines the maximum number of previous columns that a node can take as input.

4.1. Edge-Only EvoDevo

The first experiment investigated how the edge cells (GNN and CGP) could grow to minimise the objectives. The reward metric combined the total strain energy and volume objectives with equal weighting. The strain energy and volume of the edge cell were given as the input to the GRN, and the output was a delta change in the edge's cross-sectional area, where the cross-sectional area of an edge could not decrease by more than 1% of its original value. For each GNN- and CGP-based method, 15 independent runs were applied.

4.2. Node-Only EvoDevo

The second experiment investigated the node (vertex) cell interactions. Although the control variables were changed to the coordinates, the same reward metric was applied. Each cell's GRN took its current x and y positions (as input) and generated Δx and Δy, which moved the nodes. Similar to the edge experiments, 15 independent runs were carried out for both the GNN- and CGP-based controllers.

4.3. Node-Edge EvoDevo

The third and final experiment employed the node–edge method, in which the node positions and member areas were updated simultaneously at every development step. In the CGP version, two coupled controllers were used: one adjusted the cross-sectional areas, and the other moved the vertices. Therefore, the configuration evolved in a single cycle (single development step). The GNN-based method performed both tasks within a single network.

5. Results and Discussion

5.1. Edge-Only Results

Figure 10 shows the final structure that achieved the highest reward in the edge method among the 15 runs. According to the findings in Figure 10, despite the similar structure of these two optimal controllers, the GNN yields slightly lighter components, resulting in a lower volume. Nonetheless, the developmental steps exhibit significant variation. CGP shows a fast reduction in energy and volume, while the GNN represents a gradual decline in all criteria. The CGP controller update rule for each edge is

$$\Delta A = \mathrm{se}^2\left(5\,\mathrm{se} - v\right)\left(5\,\mathrm{se}^2 - \mathrm{se}\,v - v\right)^2 \tag{13}$$

where se is the strain energy in the structure, and v is the volume. The linear term $5\,se - v$ shows the direction of changes (negative or positive). For instance, if a member stores a lot of strain energy $(5\,se > v)$, the term is positive, and the cross-section grows, whereas if the member carries little energy relative to its volume $(5\,se < v)$, it becomes negative, and the member is thinned. The factors se^2 and $\left(5\,se^2 - se\,v - v\right)^2$ set how big the area change should be. They make the change large when a member is highly stressed and thin and small when the member already has a good balance between strain energy and volume.

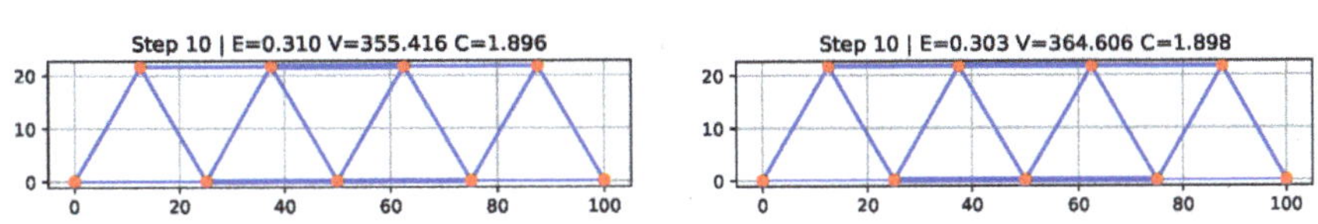

Figure 10. *Cont.*

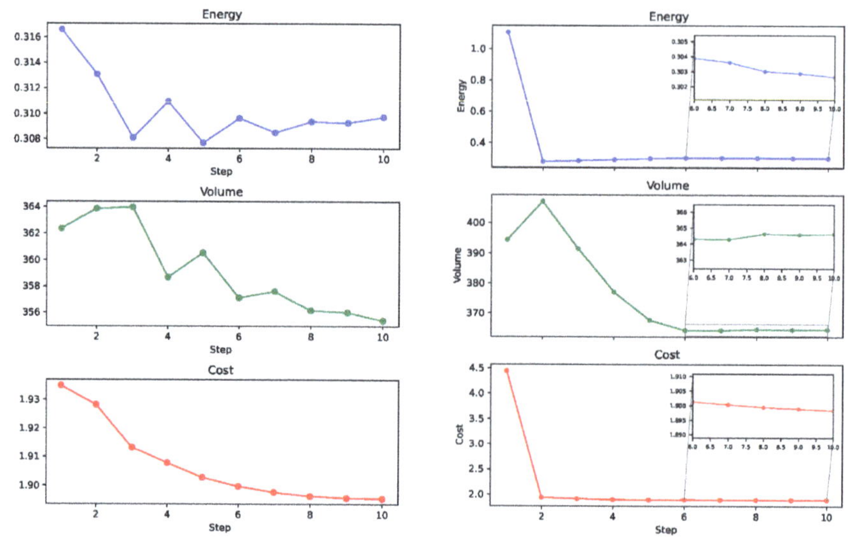

Figure 10. Metrics related to the highest reward structures obtained by the edge-only method after 10 development steps. (**Left**): GNN controller. (**Right**): CGP controller. (**Top row**): best performing structure. (**Second row**): change in strain energy E through devo. (**Third row**): change in volume V through devo. (**Fourth row**): change in cost $C = E + V$ through devo.

5.2. Node-Only Results

Figure 11 shows the structure that achieved the highest reward across the runs for both the GNN and CGP controllers. As shown, both the GNN and CGP controllers followed almost the same trajectories. The total volume increased as a result of the node's relocation, which resulted in the extension of some edges. Conversely, strain energy exhibited a distinct trend and decreased throughout the developmental steps. The results indicate that the controller incorporated a minimal amount of material while achieving greater stiffness, demonstrating an effective trade-off. The CGP controller update rule for each node (x and y position) is

$$\begin{aligned} \Delta x &= x\left(2x - y(2x+y) + y\right)\left(3x - y(2x+y) + y\right) \\ \Delta y &= \left(y^2 - x^2\right)\left(y+1\right) \end{aligned} \tag{14}$$

The controller preserves truss symmetry, as shown by the variable x in the Δx equation, resulting in zero horizontal displacement for any node on the vertical axis ($x = 0$). However, on the vertical axis, because $y + 1 > 0$ is positive for all vertices, the sign of the update is controlled by $y^2 - x^2$. Nodes with $y^2 > x^2$ (located near the centre, where x is small) move upward, whereas nodes with $y^2 < x^2$ (near the supports, where x is large) move downward. Consequently, the initially flat top chord arches after 10 development steps (Figure 11), with the centre nodes elevated and the outer nodes dropped.

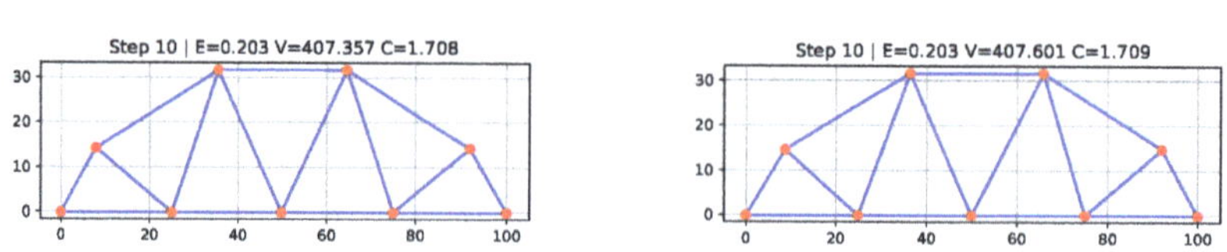

Figure 11. *Cont.*

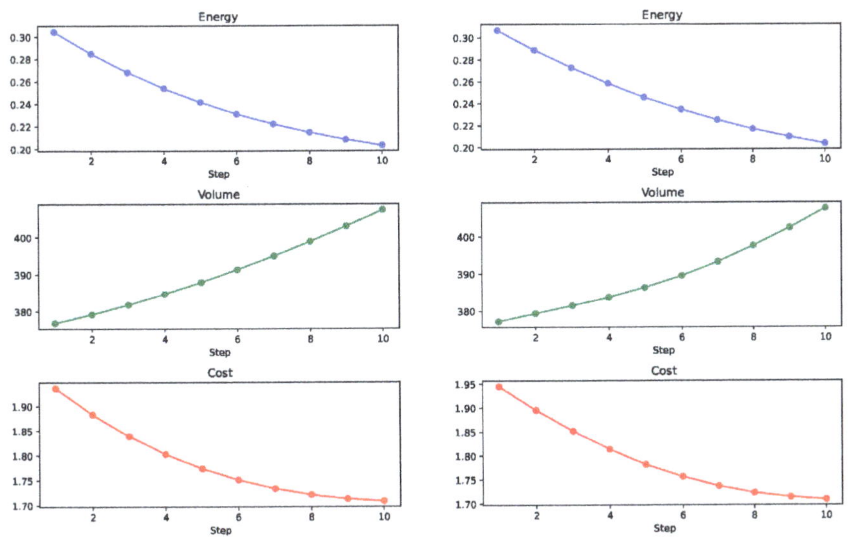

Figure 11. Metrics related to the highest reward structures obtained by the node-only method after 10 development steps. (**Left**): GNN controller. (**Right**): CGP controller. Rows as described in Figure 10.

5.3. Node–Edge Results

Figure 12 illustrates the way in which the node–edge controllers modify the truss structure. The CGP implements a considerable first adjustment, reducing both the strain energy and volume; however, it subsequently shows minimal improvements. The GNN controller, by comparison, decreases the energy and volume more gradually while maintaining this trend across all development steps, ultimately resulting in a lower overall cost. Therefore, Figure 12 demonstrates a potential trade-off: CGP is beneficial when only a limited number of development steps is feasible, whereas the GNN provides superior performance with long runs (development steps).

In addition, based on Equation (15), the coupled CGP controllers applied one rule to each edge (regarding one output) and two rules to each node in each development step, as in the following equation:

$$\begin{aligned} \Delta A &= 2\,\mathrm{se}^2(3\,\mathrm{se} - v) \\ \Delta x &= x\,y \qquad \Delta y = y^2 - x^2 \end{aligned} \tag{15}$$

Regarding the edge update ΔA, the term $2\,se^2$ enhances the updates for highly stressed members, while the linear term $3\,se - v$ determines the sign (positive or negative). The edges whose strain energy is higher than one-third of their volume become thicker, while the rest become thinner. This is the same "energy-to-volume balance" logic that was seen in the edge-only rule (Equation (13)), where $5\,se - v$ played the same role with a different coefficient. Regarding the vertex rules, they were the same as in the node-only experiment, with $\Delta y = y^2 - x^2$ raising the centre nodes and lowering the outer ones, making an arch shape.

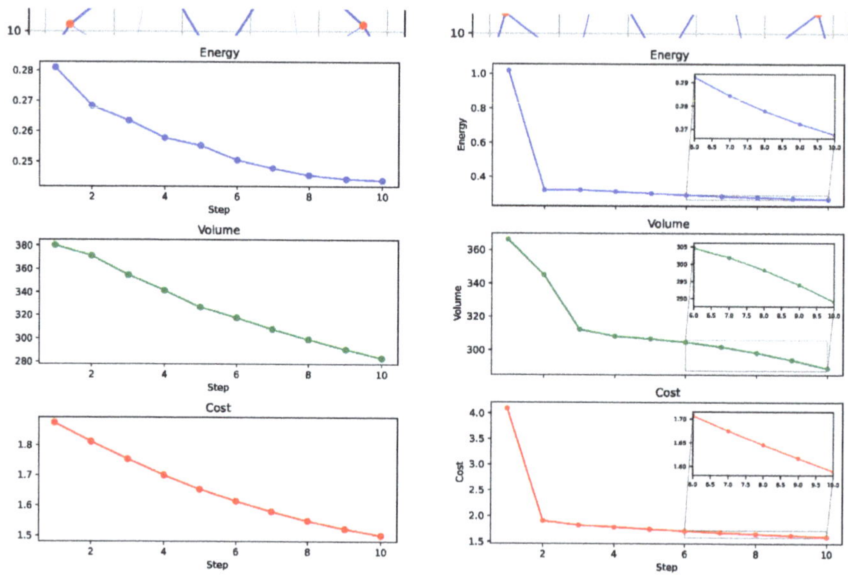

Figure 12. Metrics related to the highest reward structures obtained by the node–edge method after 10 development steps. (**Left**): GNN controller. (**Right**): CGP controller. Rows as described in Figure 10.

5.4. Comparison Between GNN and CGP

Table 6 and Figure 13 depict the best reward obtained from 15 independent runs for each CGP and GNN controller. A clear trend is evident: expanding the control space from the edge method to the node method and ultimately to the combined node–edge method consistently increases the mean reward for both the CGP (0.10 $\rightarrowtail$ 0.39) and GNN (0.10 $\rightarrowtail$ 0.43) controllers. The GNN-based node–edge method has the highest reward score (0.50), but it also has the widest variance, revealing irregular stagnation in the local minimum. In contrast, the GNN-based node–edge variations and all three CGP methods have less variance, producing highly reproducible results. Overall, it is shown that a trade-off exists between performance (reward) and consistency in the GNN and CGP controllers. Furthermore, the CGP-based approaches are integrated as a white box, allowing the expert to interpret modifications based on the acquired equations. The full development trajectories from the 15 runs of the best CGP and GNN controllers (for each method) are presented in Appendix A and Appendix B, respectively. These figures illustrate the evolution of the truss during all 10 developmental stages for the edge-only, node-only and combined node–edge methodologies, demonstrating how each strategy incrementally transforms the truss structure.

Table 6. Summary statistics of best rewards achieved over 15 runs per method.

Method	Num_Runs	Mean	Std	Min	Max
cgp_edge	15	0.098	0.003	0.094	0.102
cgp_node	15	0.282	0.005	0.277	0.291
cgp_node_edge	15	0.389	0.021	0.364	0.447

Table 6. *Cont.*

Method	Num_Runs	Mean	Std	Min	Max
gnn_edge	15	0.103	0.002	0.095	0.104
gnn_node	15	0.291	0.001	0.289	0.292
gnn_node_edge	15	0.425	0.075	0.291	0.500

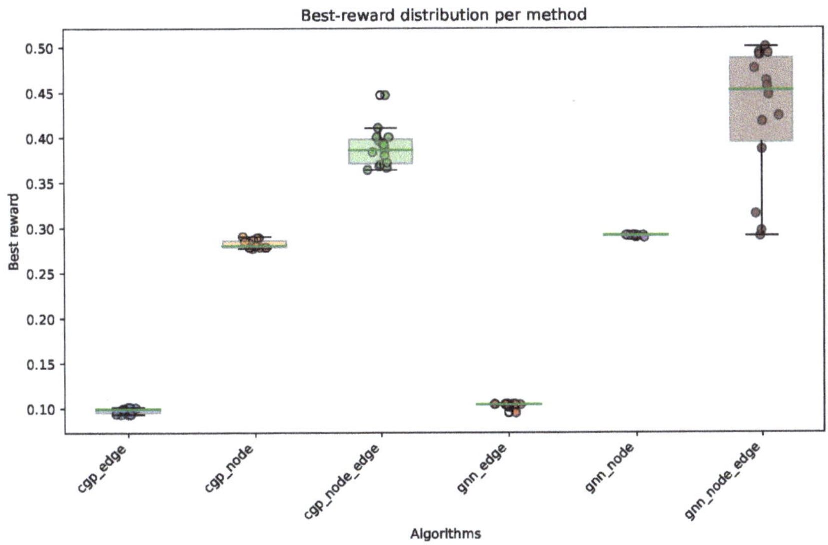

Figure 13. Distribution of the best reward obtained by each algorithm over 15 independent runs. The box shows the inter-quartile range, the horizontal line is the median, and the individual circles represent single runs. The circle's colour varies for each method.

5.5. Generalisation to a New Environment

One of the most important aspects of an indirect representation for generative design systems is the ability of the development rules to generalize to new problems that differ from the one on which they were evolved. To investigate this capability, two additional "seedling" truss benchmarks are created (Figure 14). All the load cases are applied simultaneously to the structure. The first environment is a multi-load, 9 × 15 truss (Figure 14a) in which three point loads of 10 kN, 17 kN and 17 kN are applied to the original 9-vertex, 15-edge Warren seedling introduced in Section 4. The second environment is a single-load 17 × 30 truss (Figure 14b) in which a single 17 kN point load is applied in the middle of the 17-vertex, 30-edge Warren seedling. For each of the two new seedling environments, both GRN controllers (GNN and CGP) are trained and compared with the best node–edge controllers previously evolved on the original single-load 9 × 15 truss. The controller structures and all Evo/Devo parameters are set as described in Section 4 wherever possible.

Table 7 shows the differences in the performance of the trained and frozen (untrained) GNN/CGP controllers on the two new seedling benchmarks. In Environment #1, the 9 × 15 truss with three point loads, both the trained GNN and CGP controllers perform better than the untrained controllers. The trained GNN lowers the cost mainly by decreasing the volume, while the trained CGP achieves the best cost by largely reducing the strain energy. In addition, the gap between the trained and untrained GNNs is smaller than that between the CGPs, showing that the untrained GNN works better. In Environment #2, the larger 17 × 30 truss with a single mid-span load, the outputs of the trained and untrained controllers are more similar. Although the untrained GNN outperforms the untrained CGP, after training, the CGP again delivers the lowest cost, just as in Environment #1. These results illustrate that the generalisation characteristics of both the CGP and GNN controllers vary when changing the structure and parameters of the environments. Figures 15–18 show the final truss geometries and the evolution of energy, volume and cost over the ten developmental steps.

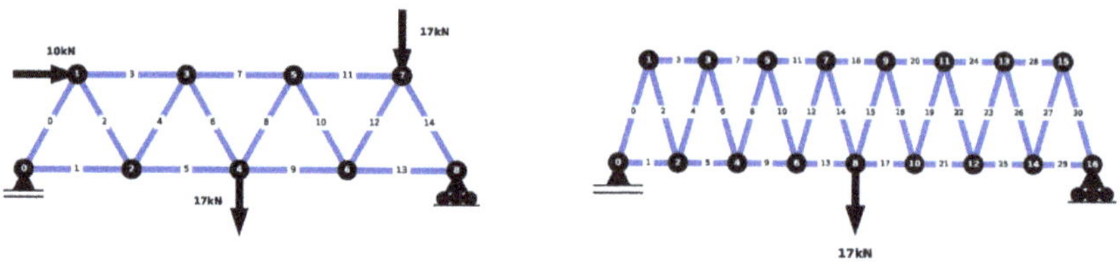

(a) (b)

Figure 14. Seedling truss used for generalisation experiments: (**a**) three point loads with 9 vertices and 15 edges; (**b**) single central load with 17 vertices and 30 edges. Numbers inside the circles denote node indices, while numbers along the edge members denote edge indices.

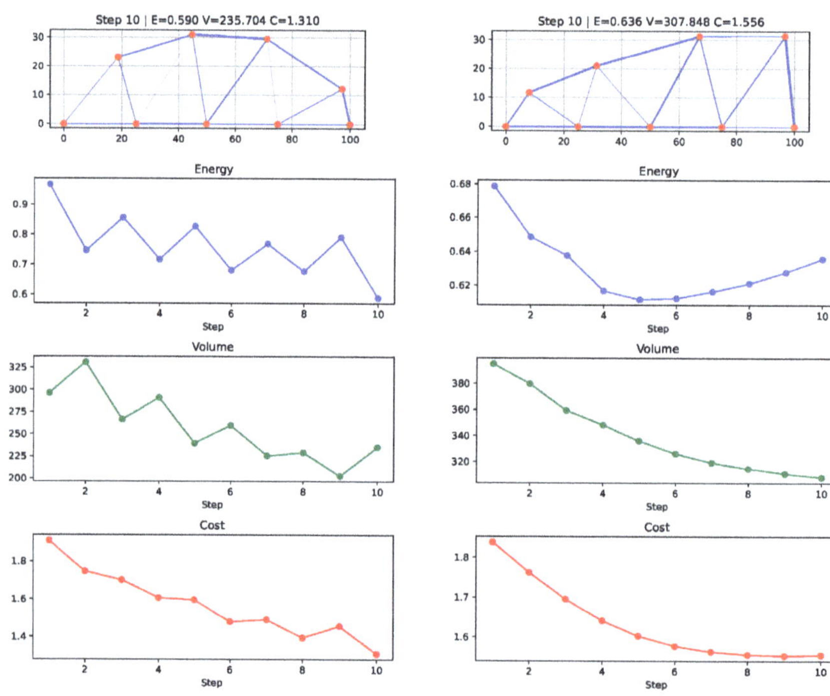

Figure 15. GNN behaviour in Environment #1 (three loads and 9 × 15 truss). (**Left**): trained controller; (**right**): untrained controller. (**Top plots**) show the final geometry after ten devo steps with strain energy E, volume V and cost. (**Lower plots**) trace E, V and cost over the ten devo steps.

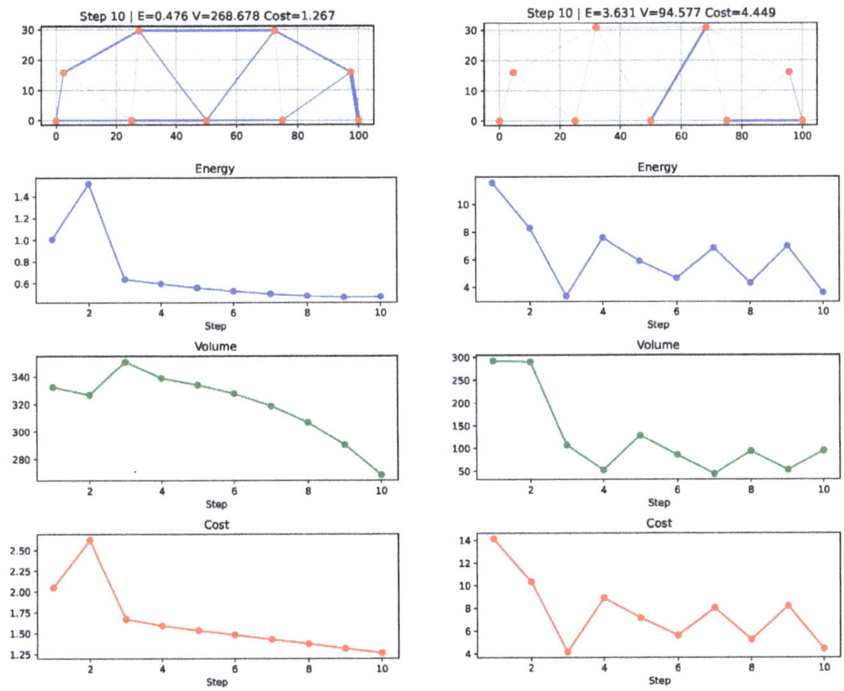

Figure 16. CGP behaviour in Environment #1 (three loads and 9 × 15 truss). (**Left**): trained controller; (**right**): untrained controller. (**Top plots**) show the final geometry after ten devo steps with strain energy *E*, volume *V* and cost. (**Lower plots**) trace *E*, *V* and cost over the ten devo steps.

Table 7. Performance of GNN and CGP controllers on the two new seedling benchmarks for the generalisation test.

Seedling	GRN	Criteria	Trained Controller	Untrained Controller
Environment #1	GNN	Energy	0.590	0.6358
		Volume	235.704	307.848
		Cost	1.310	1.556
	CGP	Energy	0.476	3.631
		Volume	268.678	94.577
		Cost	1.267	4.449
Environment #2	GNN	Energy	1.381	1.732
		Volume	529.189	642.085
		Cost	1.469	1.816
	CGP	Energy	1.201	1.459
		Volume	585.465	518.154
		Cost	1.440	1.500

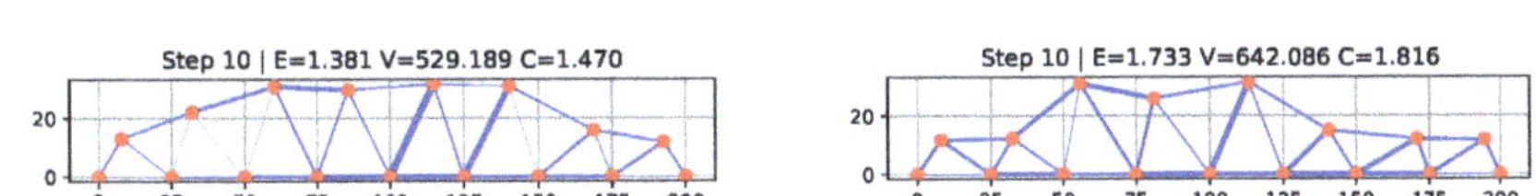

Figure 17. *Cont.*

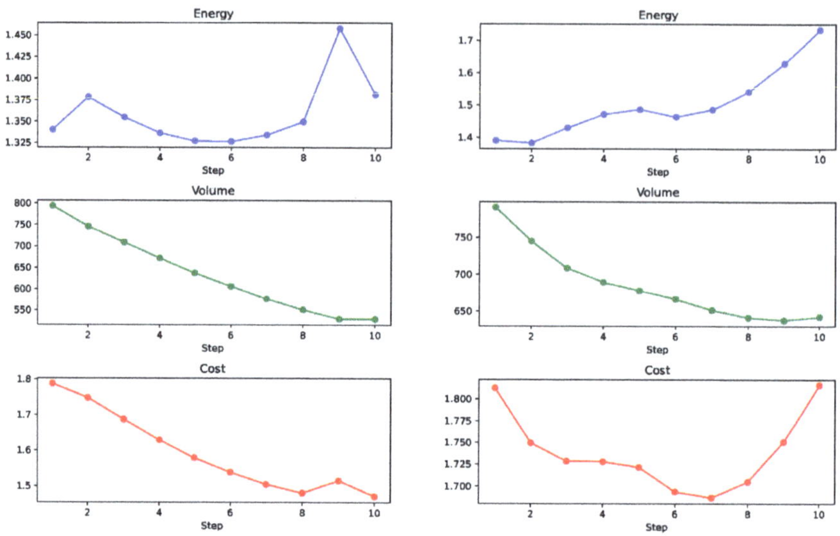

Figure 17. GNN behaviour in Environment #2 (one load and 17 × 30 truss). (**Left**): trained controller; (**right**): untrained controller. (**Top plots**) show the final geometry after ten devo steps with strain energy E, volume V and cost. (**Lower plots**) trace E, V and cost over the ten devo steps.

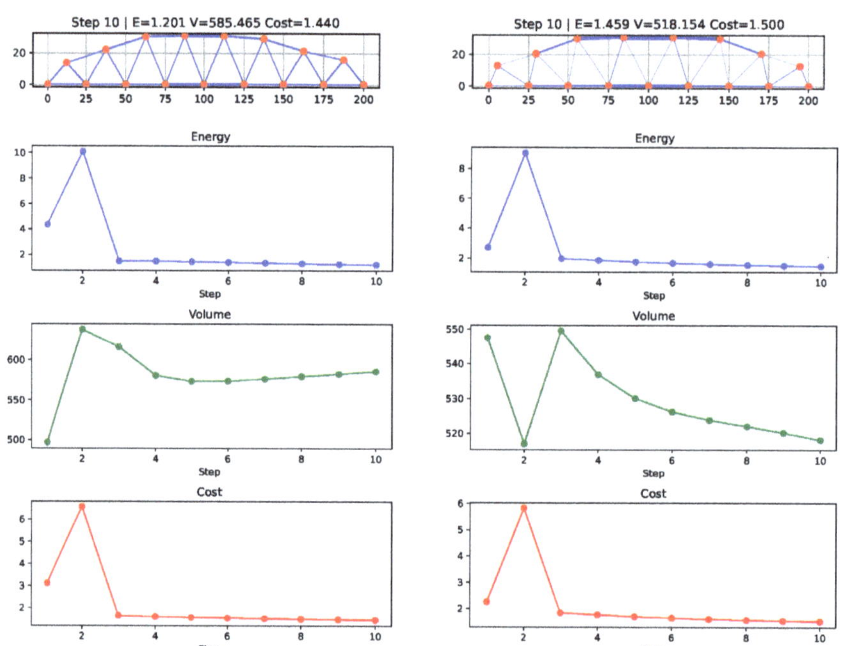

Figure 18. CGP behaviour in Environment #2 (one load and 17 × 30 truss). (**Left**): trained controller; (**right**): untrained controller. (**Top plots**) show the final geometry after ten devo steps with strain energy E, volume V and cost. (**Lower plots**) trace E, V and cost over the ten devo steps.

5.6. Comparison with Other Topology Optimisation Methods

To benchmark the GNN-based truss against established continuum methods, the topology optimisation study in [54] is referred to. This work utilises SolidWorks, ANSYS Mechanical and ABAQUS software (https://www.3ds.com/products/simulia/abaqus (accessed on 11 June 2025)) to optimise three structures, including a small bridge with dimensions of 2555 × 500 × 600 mm that carries a 800 kN distributed bottom load. The weight of the GNN-based truss is estimated and compared to the weight results derived by Solidworks, ANSYS and ABAQUS using the seedling parameters in Table 8 extracted from [54]. Table 9 shows the weights of the small bridge after optimisation compared to those of the GNN-based truss. For the GNN-based truss, the initial cross-sectional area of 75 mm is used. The resulting weight of the GNN-based truss is marginally comparable to the weights of the three methods reported in [54].

Table 8. Seedling and material parameters used in the GNN truss run.

Parameters	Value
Span	2500.0 mm
Height	500.0 mm
Young's modulus	210.0 GPa
Density ρ	7700.0 kg/m^3
Poisson ratio ν	0.28

As shown in Figure 19, after ten development steps, the GNN-based truss has a total volume of $V = 538,357.169$ mm^3. Substitution into Equation (16) with $\rho = 7700$ kg/m^3 and $g = 9.81$ m/s^2 gives a final self-weight of $W = 40.66$ N.

$$\begin{aligned} &V = 538,357.169\ \text{mm}^3, \quad \rho = 7700\ \text{kg/m}^3, \quad g = 9.81\ \text{m/s}^2, \\ &m = V\rho \times 10^{-9} = 4.14535\ \text{kg}, \\ &W = mg = 40.66\ \text{N}. \end{aligned} \tag{16}$$

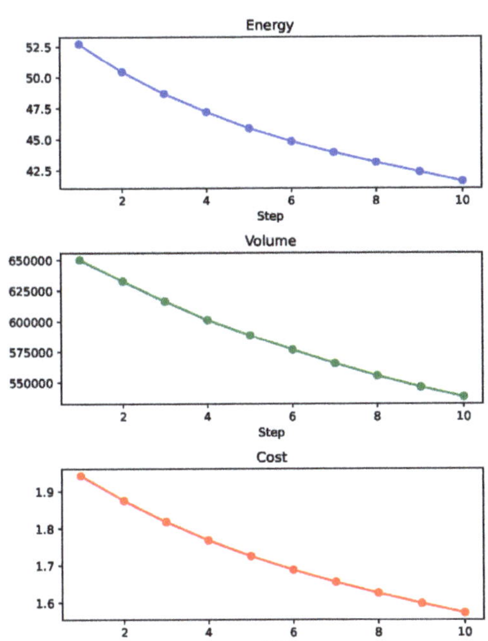

Figure 19. GNN-based truss outputs for energy, volume and cost after ten development steps based on the parameters in [54].

Table 9. Optimised weights of the small bridge and GNN-based truss.

Solver/Method	Final Weight
SolidWorks	49.7
ANSYS	55.5
ABAQUS	43.26
GNN-based truss	40.666

6. Conclusions and Future Works

A new bioinspired generative design system was proposed that utilizes the concepts of previous indirect representation approaches such as cellular representations, evolutionary development, gene regulatory networks and state-based models. The approach involves representing the design as a heterogeneous graph, where the nodes represent different cell types. These cells make growth decisions via a stateful GRN to minimize some global objectives. The novelty lies in the genetic search algorithm established to evolve graph neural networks and the Cartesian genetic programming that can learn re-deployable developmental rules for engineering problems. These approaches were tested on truss structures and were shown to be able to optimise designs in terms of shape and size by changing the vertex positions and edge cross-sectional areas of the truss structures. These growth mechanisms were able to be used individually or in unison to provide better performance. The results revealed that, although GNN exhibited superior performance in terms of accumulated reward compared to CGP, the outcomes were nearly identical. However, CGP provided the opportunity to interpret the evolution and identify the pathway that correlated inputs with outputs in truss structures via their output equations.

The growth mechanisms investigated in this paper affected the shape and size of the design structure. A future avenue of work would be to investigate methods for exploring the design space via a topology change. One way of doing this would be by using a cellular division growth mechanism, or the topology of the initial seedling could also be altered. As only truss structures were used, the proposed system should be applied to other engineering problems and structures to highlight that it is not limited to these structures. In the experiments undertaken in Section 5, a fixed number of devo steps was used. This number was selected empirically after preliminary trials showed a reasonable balance between additional performance gains and computational cost. In the future, more systematic research is required to deterministically define an appropriate value for this parameter. Research could also look into organism behaviour in detail to develop a criterion for when it should stop growing, similar to how the end of a sentence can be predicted in natural language processing (NLP). To achieve a more thorough benchmark, the suggested generative design framework must be assessed in conjunction with proven topology optimisation methods, thus clarifying its performance relative to that of standard engineering software. More work is also needed to improve the generalisability of the pre-trained seeds so that a user would only need to run a development loop for a new environment. Performance could possibly be improved by training the GRN on a larger dataset of different environments. Future work could also look into using multi/many-objective evolutionary algorithms to generate a diverse range of solutions from a pre-trained seed. This cellular representation is agnostic and could be used to represent other entities in a supply chain or manufacturing process, for example.

Author Contributions: Conceptualization, A.M.T. and M.P.; Methodology, A.C., I.F., S.J.H., E.B. and P.G.; Software, A.C., I.F., S.J.H., E.B., P.G. and F.T.-J.; Formal analysis, F.T.-J.; Visualization, F.T.-J.; Validation, F.T.-J.; Writing—original draft preparation, A.C. and F.T.-J.; Writing—review and editing, S.J.H., E.B., P.G., A.M.T., M.P., T.R. and F.T.-J.; Supervision, A.M.T. and M.P.; Funding acquisition, A.M.T.; Project administration, A.M.T. All authors have read and agreed to the published version of the manuscript.

Funding: This research was funded by EPSRC programme Grant Ref EP/V007335/1, "RIED: Re-Imagining Engineering Design".

Data Availability Statement: The software and data can be found at the GitLab repository https://gitlab.com/riedproject (accessed on 11 June 2025).

Conflicts of Interest: The authors declare no conflicts of interest.

Appendix A

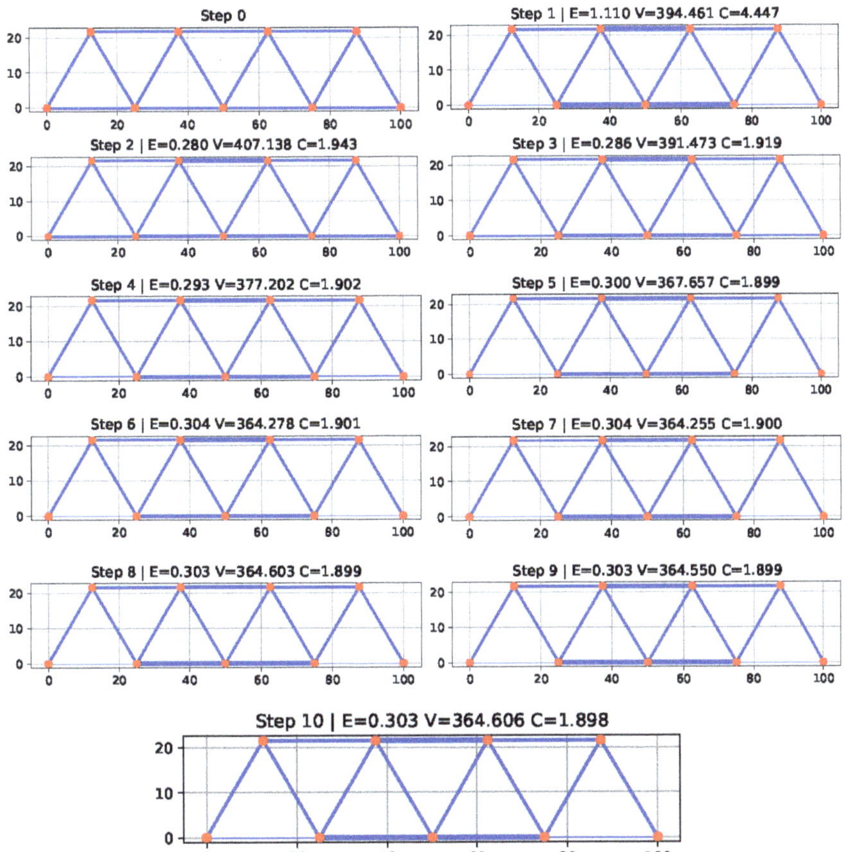

Figure A1. Development sequence over 10 development steps for the best edge-based CGP controller.

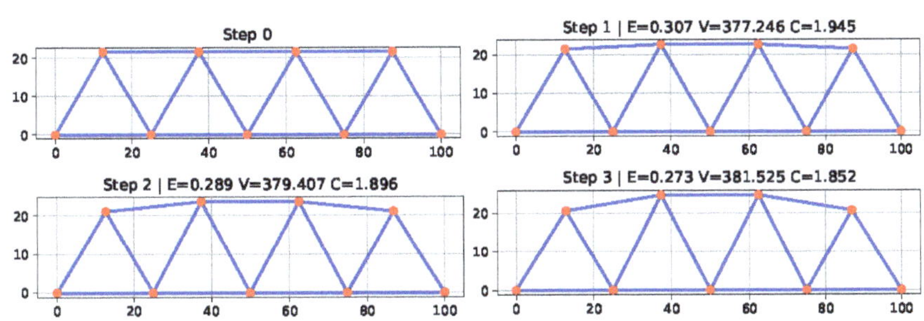

Figure A2. *Cont.*

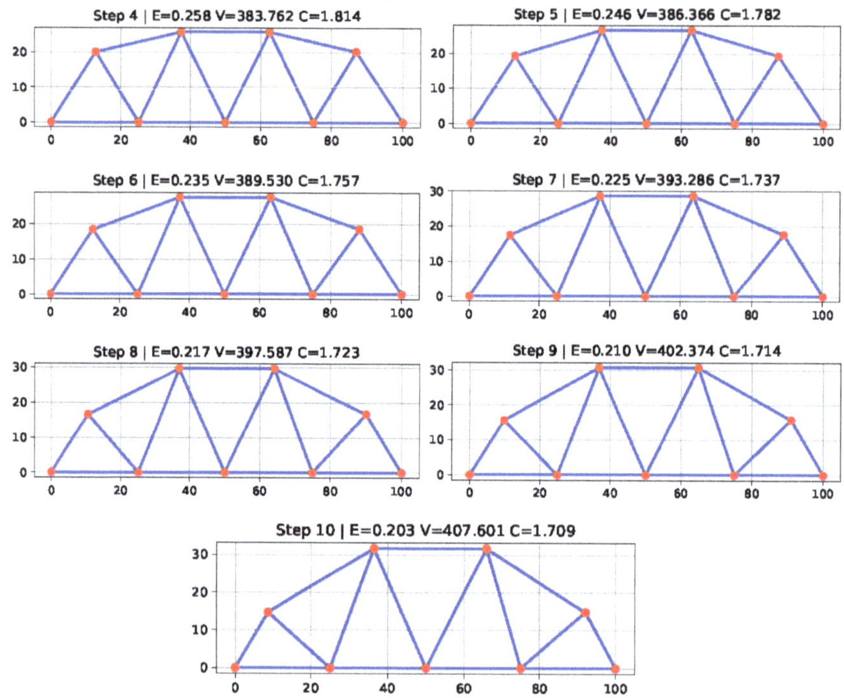

Figure A2. Development sequence over 10 development steps for the best node-based CGP controller.

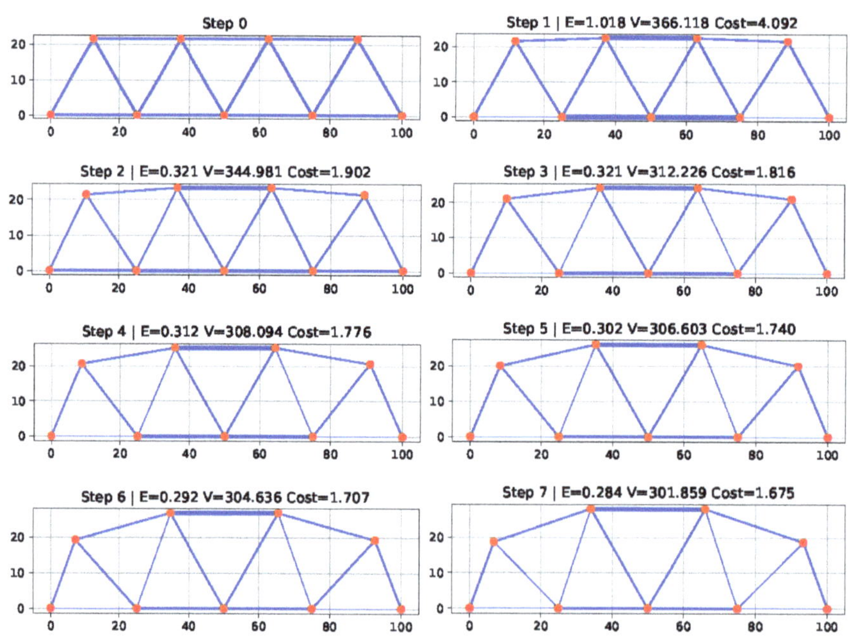

Figure A3. *Cont.*

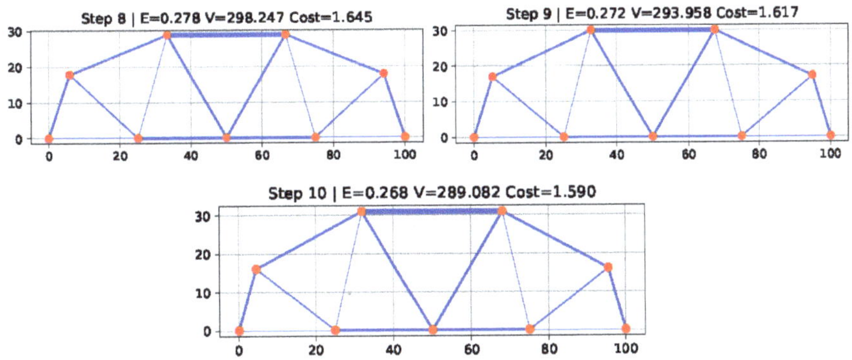

Figure A3. Development sequence over 10 development steps for the best the node–edge-based CGP controller.

Appendix B

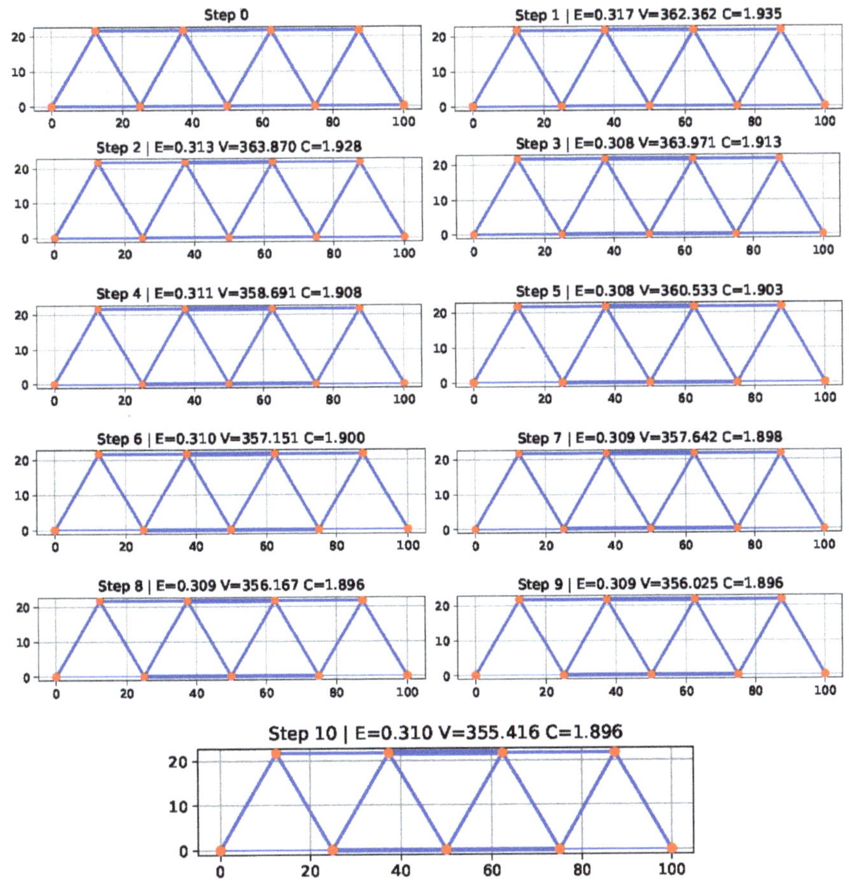

Figure A4. Development sequence over 10 development steps for the best edge-based GNN controller.

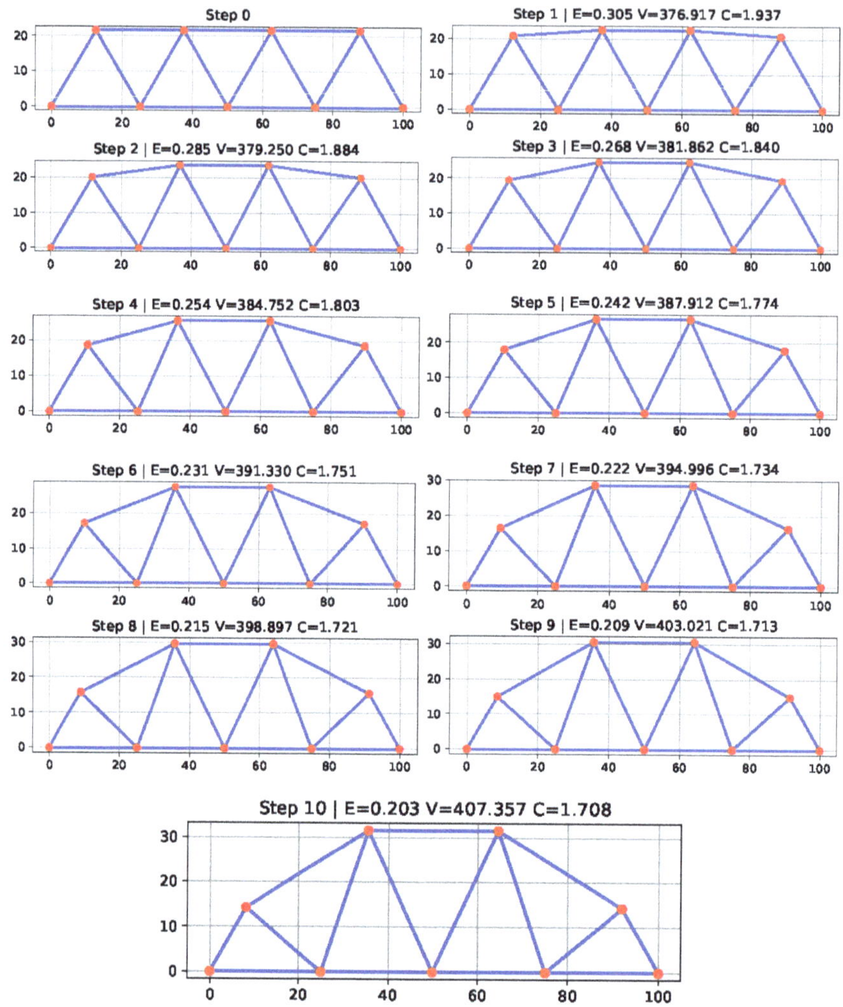

Figure A5. Development sequence over 10 development steps for the best node-based GNN controller.

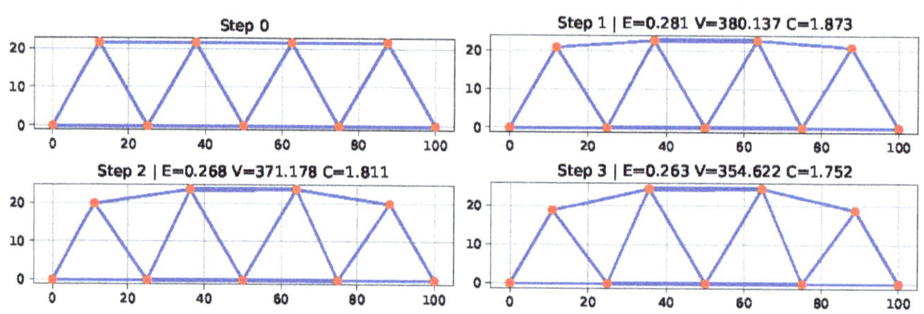

Figure A6. *Cont.*

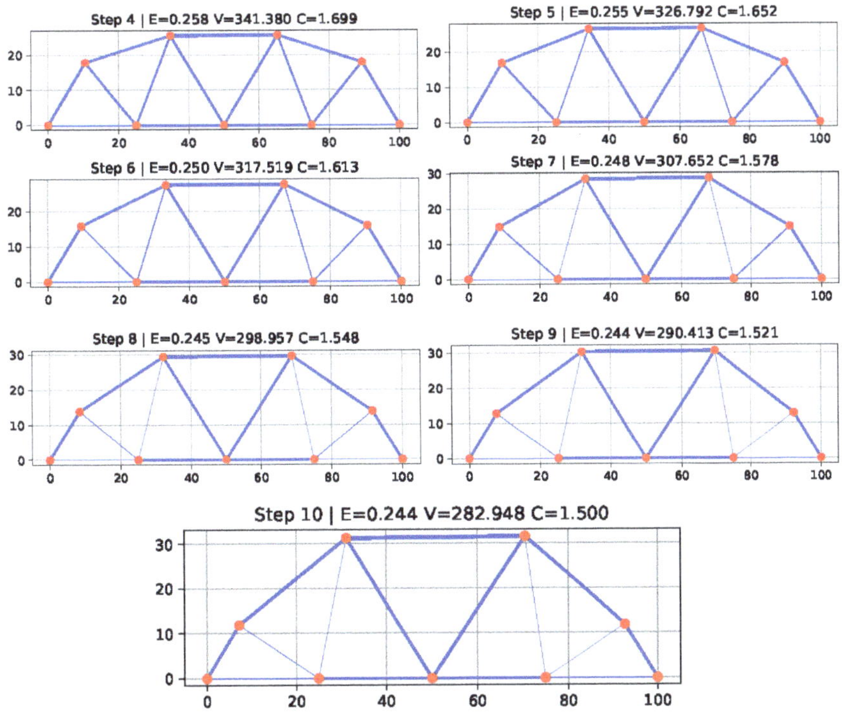

Figure A6. Development sequence over 10 development steps for the best the node–edge-based GNN controller.

References

1. Traversari, R.; Goedhart, R.; Schraagen, J.M. Process simulation during the design process makes the difference: Process simulations applied to a traditional design. *HERD Health Environ. Res. Des. J.* **2013**, *6*, 58–76. [CrossRef]
2. Han, S.; Lee, S.; Fard, M.G.; Pena-Mora, F. Modeling and representation of non-value adding activities due to errors and changes in design and construction projects. In Proceedings of the Winter Simulation Conference, Washington, DC, USA, 9–12 December 2007; pp. 2082–2089.
3. McKnight, M. Generative Design: What it is? How is it being used? Why it's a game changer. *KnE Eng.* **2017**, *2*, 176–181. [CrossRef]
4. Watson, M.; Leary, M.; Brandt, M. Generative design of truss systems by the integration of topology and shape optimisation. *Int. J. Adv. Manuf. Technol.* **2022**, *118*, 1165–1182. [CrossRef]
5. Zhang, W.; Huang, F. An introductory overview to bio-inspired generative design. *J. Mech. Sci. Technol.* **2023**, *37*, 1–5. [CrossRef]
6. Steiner, T. Artificial Evolutionary Development. 2010. Available online: https://scispace.com/pdf/artificial-evolutionary-development-4wgppb4net.pdf (accessed on 24 July 2025).
7. Lingyun, W.; Mei, Z.; Guangming, W.; Guang, M. Truss optimization on shape and sizing with frequency constraints based on genetic algorithm. *Comput. Mech.* **2005**, *35*, 361–368. [CrossRef]
8. Hajela, P.; Lee, E. Genetic algorithms in truss topological optimization. *Int. J. Solids Struct.* **1995**, *32*, 3341–3357. [CrossRef]
9. Sigmund, O. On the usefulness of non-gradient approaches in topology optimization. *Struct. Multidiscip. Optim.* **2011**, *43*, 589–596. [CrossRef]
10. Bendsøe, M.P.; Sigmund, O. Material interpolation schemes in topology optimization. *Arch. Appl. Mech.* **1999**, *69*, 635–654. [CrossRef]
11. Wang, M.Y.; Wang, X.; Guo, D. A level set method for structural topology optimization. *Comput. Methods Appl. Mech. Eng.* **2003**, *192*, 227–246. [CrossRef]
12. Aulig, N.; Olhofer, M. Evolutionary computation for topology optimization of mechanical structures: An overview of representations. In Proceedings of the IEEE Congress on Evolutionary Computation (CEC), Vancouver, BC, Canada, 24–29 July 2016; pp. 1948–1955.

13. Guirguis, D.; Aulig, N.; Picelli, R.; Zhu, B.; Zhou, Y.; Vicente, W.; Iorio, F.; Olhofer, M.; Matusik, W.; Coello, C.A.C.; et al. Evolutionary black-box topology optimization: Challenges and promises. *IEEE Trans. Evol. Comput.* **2019**, *24*, 613–633. [CrossRef]
14. Wang, Z.; Zhang, Y.; Bernard, A. A constructive solid geometry-based generative design method for additive manufacturing. *Addit. Manuf.* **2021**, *41*, 101952. [CrossRef]
15. Schoenauer, M. Shape representations and evolution schemes. In Proceedings of the Fifth Annual Conference on Evolutionary Programming, San Diego, CA, USA, 29 February–3 March 1996.
16. Feng, F.; Xiong, S.; Liu, Z.; Xian, Z.; Zhou, Y.; Kobayashi, H.; Kawamoto, A.; Nomura, T.; Zhu, B. Cellular topology optimization on differentiable Voronoi diagrams. *Int. J. Numer. Methods Eng.* **2023**, *124*, 282–304. [CrossRef]
17. Bujny, M.; Aulig, N.; Olhofer, M.; Duddeck, F. Hybrid evolutionary approach for level set topology optimization. In Proceedings of the IEEE Congress on Evolutionary Computation (CEC), Vancouver, BC, Canada, 24–29 July 2016; pp. 5092–5099.
18. Wang, S.; Tai, K. Graph representation for structural topology optimization using genetic algorithms. *Comput. Struct.* **2004**, *82*, 1609–1622. [CrossRef]
19. Tai, K.; Akhtar, S. Structural topology optimization using a genetic algorithm with a morphological geometric representation scheme. *Struct. Multidiscip. Optim.* **2005**, *30*, 113–127. [CrossRef]
20. Wang, N.; Tai, K. Target matching problems and an adaptive constraint strategy for multiobjective design optimization using genetic algorithms. *Comput. Struct.* **2010**, *88*, 1064–1076. [CrossRef]
21. Wang, S.; Tai, K. Bar-system representation for topology optimization using genetic algorithms. *Eng. Comput.* **2005**, *22*, 206–231. [CrossRef]
22. Sauter, M.; Kress, G.; Giger, M.; Ermanni, P. Complex-shaped beam element and graph-based optimization of compliant mechanisms. *Struct. Multidiscip. Optim.* **2008**, *36*, 429–442. [CrossRef]
23. Ahmed, F.; Bhattacharya, B.; Deb, K. Constructive solid geometry based topology optimization using evolutionary algorithm. In *Proceedings of Seventh International Conference on Bio-Inspired Computing: Theories and Applications (BIC-TA 2012)*; Springer: Berlin/Heidelberg, Germany, 2013; Volume 1, pp. 227–238.
24. Pandey, A.; Datta, R.; Bhattacharya, B. Topology optimization of compliant structures and mechanisms using constructive solid geometry for 2-d and 3-d applications. *Soft Comput.* **2017**, *21*, 1157–1179. [CrossRef]
25. Guo, T.; Lohan, D.J.; Cang, R.; Ren, M.Y.; Allison, J.T. An indirect design representation for topology optimization using variational autoencoder and style transfer. In Proceedings of the AIAA/ASCE/AHS/ASC Structures, Structural Dynamics, and Materials Conference, Kissimmee, FL, USA, 8–12 January 2018; p. 0804.
26. Jang, S.; Yoo, S.; Kang, N. Generative design by reinforcement learning: Enhancing the diversity of topology optimization designs. *Comput.-Aided Des.* **2022**, *146*, 103225. [CrossRef]
27. Riegler, G.; Osman Ulusoy, A.; Geiger, A. Octnet: Learning deep 3d representations at high resolutions. In Proceedings of the IEEE Conference on Computer Vision and Pattern Recognition, Honolulu, HI, USA, 21–26 July 2017; pp. 3577–3586.
28. Price, M.; Zhang, W.; Friel, I.; Robinson, T.; McConnell, R.; Nolan, D.; Kilpatrick, P.; Barbhuiya, S.; Kyle, S. Generative design for additive manufacturing using a biological development analogy. *J. Comput. Des. Eng.* **2022**, *9*, 463–479. [CrossRef]
29. Pedro, H.T.C.; Kobayashi, M.H. On a cellular division method for topology optimization. *Int. J. Numer. Methods Eng.* **2011**, *88*, 1175–1197. [CrossRef]
30. Steiner, T.; Jin, Y.; Sendhoff, B. A cellular model for the evolutionary development of lightweight material with an inner structure. In Proceedings of the 10th Annual Conference on Genetic and Evolutionary Computation, Atlanta, GA, USA, 12–16 July 2008; pp. 851–858.
31. Steiner, T.; Trommler, J.; Brenn, M.; Jin, Y.; Sendhoff, B. Global shape with morphogen gradients and motile polarized cells. In Proceedings of the IEEE Congress on Evolutionary Computation, Trondheim, Norway, 18–21 May 2009; pp. 2225–2232.
32. Stanley, K.O.; Clune, J.; Lehman, J.; Miikkulainen, R. Designing neural networks through neuroevolution. *Nat. Mach. Intell.* **2019**, *1*, 24–35. [CrossRef]
33. Aulig, N.; Olhofer, M. Evolutionary generation of neural network update signals for the topology optimization of structures. In Proceedings of the 15th Annual Conference Companion on Genetic and Evolutionary Computation, Amsterdam, The Netherlands, 6–10 July 2013; pp. 213–214.
34. Stanley, K.O.; Miikkulainen, R. Evolving neural networks through augmenting topologies. *Evol. Comput.* **2002**, *10*, 99–127. [CrossRef]
35. Cheney, N.; Ritz, E.; Lipson, H. Automated vibrational design and natural frequency tuning of multi-material structures. In Proceedings of the Annual Conference on Genetic and Evolutionary Computation, Vancouver, Canada, 12–16 July 2014; pp. 1079–1086.
36. Stanley, K.O.; D'Ambrosio, D.B.; Gauci, J. A hypercube-based encoding for evolving large-scale neural networks. *Artif. Life* **2009**, *15*, 185–212. [CrossRef]
37. Hickinbotham, S.; Dubey, R.; Friel, I.; Colligan, A.; Price, M.; Tyrrell, A. Evolving design modifiers. In Proceedings of the IEEE Symposium Series on Computational Intelligence (SSCI), Singapore, 4–7 December 2022; pp. 1052–1058.

38. Miller, J.; Turner, A. Cartesian genetic programming. In Proceedings of the Companion Publication of the 2015 Annual Conference on Genetic and Evolutionary Computation, Madrid, Spain, 11–15 July 2015; pp. 179–198.
39. Miller, J.F.; Job, D.; Vassilev, V.K. Principles in the evolutionary design of digital circuits—Part I. *Genet. Program. Evolvable Mach.* **2000**, *1*, 7–35. [CrossRef]
40. Miller, J.F. Cartesian genetic programming: Its status and future. *Genet. Program. Evolvable Mach.* **2020**, *21*, 129–168. [CrossRef]
41. Harding, S.; Miller, J.F. Evolution of robot controller using cartesian genetic programming. In *Genetic Programming, Proceedings of the 8th European Conference, Lausanne, Switzerland, 30 March–1 April 2005*; Springer: Berlin/Heidelberg, Germany, 2005; pp. 62–73.
42. Cao, W.; Robinson, T.; Hua, Y.; Boussuge, F.; Colligan, A.R.; Pan, W. Graph representation of 3D CAD models for machining feature recognition with deep learning. In Proceedings of the International Design Engineering Technical Conferences and Computers and Information in Engineering Conference, Online, 17–19 August 2020; Volume 84003, p. V11AT11A003.
43. Colligan, A.R.; Robinson, T.T.; Nolan, D.C.; Hua, Y.; Cao, W. Hierarchical cadnet: Learning from b-reps for machining feature recognition. *Comput.-Aided Des.* **2022**, *147*, 103226. [CrossRef]
44. Jayaraman, P.K.; Sanghi, A.; Lambourne, J.G.; Willis, K.D.; Davies, T.; Shayani, H.; Morris, N. Uv-net: Learning from boundary representations. In Proceedings of the IEEE/CVF Conference on Computer Vision and Pattern Recognition, Nashville, TN, USA, 20–25 June 2021; pp. 11703–11712.
45. Lambourne, J.G.; Willis, K.D.; Jayaraman, P.K.; Sanghi, A.; Meltzer, P.; Shayani, H. Brepnet: A topological message passing system for solid models. In Proceedings of the IEEE/CVF Conference on Computer Vision and Pattern Recognition, Nashville, TN, USA, 20–25 June 2021; pp. 12773–12782.
46. Jones, B.; Hildreth, D.; Chen, D.; Baran, I.; Kim, V.G.; Schulz, A. Automate: A dataset and learning approach for automatic mating of cad assemblies. *ACM Trans. Graph.* **2021**, *40*, 1–18. [CrossRef]
47. Morris, C.; Ritzert, M.; Fey, M.; Hamilton, W.L.; Lenssen, J.E.; Rattan, G.; Grohe, M. Weisfeiler and leman go neural: Higher-order graph neural networks. In Proceedings of the AAAI conference on artificial intelligence, Honolulu, HI, USA, 27 January–1 February 2019; Volume 33, pp. 4602–4609.
48. Maas, A.L.; Hannun, A.Y.; Ng, A.Y. Rectifier nonlinearities improve neural network acoustic models. In Proceedings of the 30th International Conference on Machine Learning, Atlanta, Georgia, 16–21 June 2013; Volume 30, p. 3.
49. Buchanan Berumen, E.; Hickinbotham, S.J.; Dubey, R.; Friel, I.; Colligan, A.; Price, M.; Tyrrell, A. A quality diversity study in EvoDevo processes for engineering design. In Proceedings of the IEEE World Congress on Computational Intelligence, Yokohama, Japan, 30 June–5 July 2024.
50. Dubey, R.; Hickinbotham, S.; Colligan, A.; Friel, I.; Buchanan, E.; Price, M.; Tyrrell, A.M. Evolving novel gene regulatory networks for structural engineering designs. *Artif. Life* **2024**, *30*, 466–485. [CrossRef]
51. Mania, H.; Guy, A.; Recht, B. Simple random search of static linear policies is competitive for reinforcement learning. *Adv. Neural Inf. Process. Syst.* **2018**, *31*, 1805–1814.
52. Črepinšek, M.; Liu, S.H.; Mernik, M. Exploration and exploitation in evolutionary algorithms: A survey. *ACM Comput. Surv.* **2013**, *45*, 1–33. [CrossRef]
53. Hussain, A.; Muhammad, Y.S. Trade-off between exploration and exploitation with genetic algorithm using a novel selection operator. *Complex Intell. Syst.* **2020**, *6*, 1–14. [CrossRef]
54. Tyflopoulos, E.; Steinert, M. A comparative study of the application of different commercial software for topology optimization. *Appl. Sci.* **2022**, *12*, 611. [CrossRef]

MDPI AG
Grosspeteranlage 5
4052 Basel
Switzerland
Tel.: +41 61 683 77 34

Algorithms Editorial Office
E-mail: algorithms@mdpi.com
www.mdpi.com/journal/algorithms

www.ingramcontent.com/pod-product-compliance
Lightning Source LLC
Chambersburg PA
CBHW041944260926
51850CB00018B/793
9783725849116